Labour Economics
in Canada

Labour Economics in Canada

Second Edition

SYLVIA OSTRY
MAHMOOD A. ZAIDI

Volume II of
**Labour Policy
and Labour Economics in Canada**

Second Edition by
H. D. Woods
Sylvia Ostry
Mahmood A. Zaidi

Macmillan of Canada
Toronto

ISBN 0-7705 – 0862 – 6

Library of Congress
Catalogue Card No. 72-79011

Reprinted 1975

Printed in Canada for
The Macmillan Company of Canada
70 Bond Street, Toronto

Table of Contents

List of Tables

List of Charts

Preface

The preparation of this revised edition was motivated by much the same considerations as stimulated the original work – a recognition of the continuing need for a text which concentrates on institutional and quantitative aspects of the Canadian scene and not on review of received theory. In the ten years since the first edition was published the extent and quality of Canadian research in this field has improved significantly and this is one of many welcome signs of growing maturity in this country's social science research effort.

We hope that the readers will judge this present work as a useful contribution to an expanding but not yet overcrowded field. Even though this volume was prepared in very close collaboration, each author has contributed approximately one-half of the material. Chapters I to VI were prepared by Dr. Ostry while Chapters VII to XII were written by Dr. Zaidi. The brief concluding chapter was written jointly by the two authors.

It is a pleasure for us to acknowledge the assistance and advice of the many people who so kindly and generously helped us during the preparation of this book. We are especially grateful to those in Statistics Canada who so patiently responded to our seemingly endless requests for data. Our debt of gratitude is heavy, too, to staff members of the Economic Council of Canada and of the Department of Manpower and Immigration, and to faculty and graduate research assistants at the University of Minnesota, especially Professor M. F. Bognanno and Mr. Sudhin K. Mukhopadhyay. It hardly seems necessary to add that errors and deficiencies in the research and writing are entirely our own responsibility.

SYLVIA OSTRY   OTTAWA
MAHMOOD A. ZAIDI   MINNEAPOLIS

change and inflation, income distribution and the problem of poverty, and wage structures. It seems scarcely necessary to note that the treatment of these various topics will be somewhat less than comprehensive but, wherever possible, bibliographic references will be provided to supplement the material presented. The emphasis throughout is, of course, on *empirical* analysis of the Canadian labour market, for that is the *raison d'être* of this book.

> If, in the Social Sciences, we cannot yet run or fly, we ought to be content to walk, or creep on all fours as infants. . . . For economic and political theorising not based on facts and not controlled by facts assuredly does lead nowhere.
>
> Extract from Lord Beveridge's farewell address as Director of the London School of Economics, 24th June, 1937. Published in *Politica*, September 1937.

I

The Growth of Labour Supply

Labour economics deals essentially with manpower use and reward. Labour-force data are crucial to the understanding of these phenomena in Canada, as in any other country. The labour-force measure is a proxy for labour supply – a 'proxy' because statistics measure what is measurable, and only approximate what is theoretically ideal. Thus a gap yawns between theoretical *concept* and operationally feasible *definition*. This gap can be narrowed as our empirical analysis, guided by theoretical insight, is used to improve our statistical measures. It can be narrowed, but rarely closed. It is useful to spell out, therefore, concept and definition in the case of the labour force, because so much of our analysis will deal with these pivotally important data.

Concepts of Labour Supply

To the economist, the supply of labour at any given time is a *schedule* or *function* relating the quantity of man-hours (of standard efficiency) offered in response to varying levels of wage-rates per hour. The most familiar text-book curve is depicted as sloping upward and to the right on a diagram in which the horizontal axis is labelled 'man-hours' and the vertical, 'dollars per hour'. In explaining the derivation of this curve or function the economist employs the two central concepts of his science: scarcity and choice. The scarcity aspect stems from the fact that there are only twenty-four hours in each day; the choice confronting the worker is that between leisure and remunerative work.

The simplest way of illustrating the concepts of scarcity and choice and the worker's decision-making process is by means of a diagram such as Figure 1.[1] The worker has available to him twenty-four hours

[1]Adapted from Richard G. Lipsey and Peter O. Steiner, *Economics* (New York, 1966), Chapter 33. Any standard economics text may be consulted for further elaboration.

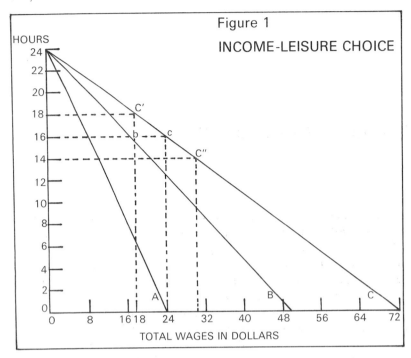

Figure 1
INCOME-LEISURE CHOICE

each day plus the information about the going wage-rate per hour if he sells his labour services in the market. The heavy lines shown in Figure 1 depict three different hourly wage-rates of (moving from left to right) $1, $2, and $3 per hour respectively. The worker may select any combination of hours (of leisure) and total wages along that particular line that is relevant to the labour market in which he is offering his services. Thus, if the going wage-rate is $2 per hour, the individual may, for example, choose 16 hours of leisure and 8 hours of work, yielding him $16 (point b). Now, if the wage-rate rises to $3 per hour, the worker can choose any point (combination of leisure and money from work) on line C. If he continues to divide his day as before, working 8 hours and keeping 16 hours for leisure, he would move to point c and his total earnings would rise from $16 per day to $24. But the change in wages offers him entirely new avenues of improvement over his former position. He can, if he chooses, enjoy both more leisure and more income, i.e. he can increase his consumption of all goods, including leisure. This would be the case if he moved to point C′ on the diagram. Or, since leisure has, in a sense, become more expensive (in terms of earnings forgone, each hour of leisure now involves 'giving up' $3 instead of $2) he might decide to 'substitute' work for leisure and thus very substantially increase his earnings by moving to point C″. The choice he makes will depend on his preferences and cannot be determined *a priori*.

Introduction

This volume follows the original edition in concentrating on the two topics of major interest to labour economists: labour supply and wages. However, in line with the growing emphasis on aggregative economic goals, and on the relationships, both complementary and conflicting, among these, a greater portion of this revised edition is devoted to discussion of important issues in contemporary policy questions – manpower and incomes policy – than to the more traditional areas of unemployment insurance and labour standards. Indeed there is a strong case to be made for extending the discussion even further into the issue of anti-poverty policy, since the problems of mitigating or eliminating poverty are so intimately connected with manpower problems. However, there is a 'trade-off' involved in selecting topics for inclusion in books, once the constraints of size and time are defined, and the authors' preferences (and capacities) have dictated, as in the first edition, the particular 'mix' presented in what follows.

In Chapter I we will examine various aspects of labour supply in Canada, beginning with a brief discussion of concepts and measures as background to an examination of the major determinants of secular growth (population, immigration, and trends in activity), and proceeding to an analysis of long-run changes in composition in Chapter II. This review will conclude, in Chapter III, with a discussion of two other key aspects of supply, *viz.* hours of work and mobility. Chapter IV is devoted to secular changes in labour demand, embedded in the context of the long-run growth of the Canadian economy and focusing, as in the case of supply, on changing composition. A separate chapter (V) is devoted to the analysis of unemployment, a matter of serious economic and social dimensions in this country. Some issues in manpower policy are explored in Chapter VI, and the remaining sections of the volume deal with wages and income aspects of the labour market, including a discussion of real- and money-wage levels, wage

If he substitutes work for leisure (leisure now being more expensive), the rise in wages per hour will have brought forth an *increase* in the supply of labour service offered, and the economists term this the 'substitution effect'. If, on the other hand, he decides to use this higher (potential) income to increase his consumption of leisure as well as other commodities, the increase in wages will have resulted in a *decrease* in the supply of labour (via what is termed the 'income effect'). It is the relative strength of these two effects – entirely dependent on individual preferences – that will determine the shape of the individual's supply of labour at any given time. Moving from the supply of labour of an individual to a *market* supply-schedule and to the notion of a *total* supply, will, of course, involve consideration of other factors (such as the size of the population; the proportion of the population that is economically active; the mobility of the working population; etc.), but *au fond* the concept of labour supply, at least as it applies in the short run, rests on the income-leisure dichotomy and the substitution and income effects that are exposed in the process of individual choice within a framework of scarcity.

As has been mentioned, the economist cannot *a priori* predict the shape of the supply schedule: this is a matter for empirical observation. Unfortunately, the 'pure' concept as described above is largely unsuitable for statistical estimating. About all that can be mustered are a few small-scale studies of the responses of groups of workers to overtime pay or changes in marginal tax-rates. Further, the assumption that workers are free to choose their hours of work according to their leisure-income preferences is clearly inappropriate for the vast majority of industrial wage-earners who work a standard day or week established by statute, custom, or collective agreement. What little flexibility exists, in the form of overtime hours, 'moonlighting', or voluntary part-time, is clearly not of major significance at any given time in the short run.[2] There has, however, been a very substantial long-run reduction in working hours (coincident with a rise in real income) in most advanced countries over the past century or more (see Chapter III). But many factors other than the income-leisure paradigm govern the long-run supply of labour.

The notion of income-leisure choice does, none the less, provide valuable insight into the concept of labour supply. As will be seen, it can be reformulated in terms of family rather than individual decisions

---

[2] Workers can also vary their *annual* hours of labour by choosing to work in casual or seasonal jobs. What proportion of the work force of such occupations and industries select these jobs as a matter of preference rather than necessity because no more steady work is available is not known. There is evidence that many workers in seasonal industries work or seek work in other industries during the off season. Further, the availability of seasonal-unemployment benefits would have to be taken into account in assessing the worker's income-leisure choice: 'leisure' may, in fact, be almost as remunerative as work under certain circumstances.

and in terms of labour-force participation (i.e. working or seeking work – see below for a full definition) rather than hours of work, and this reformulation has provided the basis for models that are adaptable to empirical investigation.[3]

Definition and Measurement

Since our purpose is to study the supply of labour in Canada we must move from the theoretical constructs of the text-book model to the realm of quantitative economics. This does not mean, of course, abandoning the tools of economic analysis; it does mean, however, that the theoretical *concepts* must be adapted to *operationally feasible definitions*, capable of being translated into consistent and reliable measures. Thus, labour supply in Canada is defined in terms of the *labour force*, which, as we shall see, is a definition far from ideal either conceptually or operationally, but which provides the most acceptable and meaningful approximation to the economic phenomenon we seek to study.

The current labour-force measure *approximates* a single point on a total labour-supply curve. Thus, assuming given income-leisure preferences, the supply of labour at a given point in time consists of the total available man-hours (of standard or known efficiency) forthcoming at the current wage-rate. The unit of labour-force measure, however, is persons, not man-hours. The labour force is a count of the numbers of employed and unemployed, i.e. persons assumed to be available for work at going wages, at a given, precisely specified time. This is a not unreasonable approximation to the point on the labour-supply schedule described above, especially since the survey from which the labour-force count is derived also provides additional information on hours of work and characteristics of workers relevant to the notion of 'quality' or 'efficiency'. (See below, pp. 11-12.)

The great merit of the labour-force measure, which is not the only, nor even, in international terms, the most common, measure of labour supply,[4] is its focus on *current activity* as a central criterion of def-

[3]For an exposition of such a model, with extensive empirical testing, see William G. Bowen and T. Aldrich Finegan, *The Economics of Labor Force Participation* (Princeton, 1969).

[4]Few European or Asian countries maintain a current household sample survey for the purpose of measuring employment and unemployment. Most current measures of unemployment are based on administrative statistics, and of employment, on establishment surveys or administrative data. In Canada, prior to 1945 when the Labour Force Survey was initiated, the most comprehensive source of information on labour supply was derived from the decennial censuses of population. The 1951 census was the first to incorporate the labour-force definition. Earlier censuses used the 'gainfully occupied' concept to measure labour supply, a concept based on 'usual occupation'. For a full

inition and classification. Thus, in order to distinguish, at any given time, the economically active from the total (adult)[5] population, the labour-force questions are designed to ascertain an individual's activity with respect to the labour market during a specific reference period, namely the week preceding the week of enumeration. The advantages of such a criterion are both conceptual and operational. Conceptually, one wants to measure a point on the supply schedule: therefore a precisely defined and reasonably short reference period is desirable. A reference period of a day might produce too many random disturbances in the measure because of the effects of holidays, sickness, natural disasters, etc., and because of difficulties of recalling precise activity for a given day. A week appears to be a feasible and appropriate period. In respect to operational considerations, one may assume it is possible to record, in an objective, consistent, and accurate fashion, the response to a question (or series of questions) about an individual's activities at any given time.

The main object of the labour-force enumeration is to classify the adult population[6] into three groups officially defined (in the regular, monthly Labour Force Survey) as follows:

1. The *employed*: all persons who, during the reference week
   (a) did any work for pay or profit, or unpaid work that contributed to the running of a family farm or business; or
   (b) had a job but were not at work because of bad weather, illness, industrial dispute, or vacation, or because they were taking time off for other reasons.

2. The *unemployed*: all persons who, during the reference week
   (a) did no work and were looking for work; or
   (b) did no work and would have been looking for work except that they were temporarily ill, were on indefinite or prolonged lay-off, or believed no suitable work was available in the community; or
   (c) were temporarily laid off for the *full* week, i.e. were waiting to be called back to a job from which they had been laid off for less than thirty days.

discussion of the criteria by which the economically active population is defined, see Frank T. Denton and Sylvia Ostry, *Historical Estimates of the Canadian Labour Force*, 1961 Census Monograph Programme, Dominion Bureau of Statistics (Ottawa, 1967).

[5] Historically, 'adult' has been defined in different ways, reflecting institutional changes such as in school-leaving age, child-labour laws, etc. Prior to 1941, the censuses included persons ten years of age and over. In 1961, the age for inclusion was raised to fifteen years. It is (at time of writing) still fourteen years in the current survey.

[6] In practice, the monthly Labour Force Survey, based on a sample of approximately thirty-five thousand households, covers only the civilian, non-institutional population living anywhere in Canada but in the Yukon and the Northwest Territories. The census coverage is somewhat different. Cf. Denton and Ostry, *op. cit.,* and *1961 Census of Canada, General Review*, The Canadian Labour Force, Bulletin 7.1-12.

3. The *non-labour force*: (civilian) persons fourteen years of age and over (exclusive of the institutional population) who are not classified as employed or unemployed.[7]

It should be noted that the labour force itself is defined as the sum of the employed and the unemployed; the remainder of the adult population is not in the labour force. Thus, the economically active are distinguished within the total population, and the chief distinguishing criterion is current activity, specifically defined.

Although current activity is the focus of the labour-force definition, it is not the only classification criterion used. The labour-force definition and measurement techniques were first developed in the United States within a framework of a national policy directed toward providing work relief for the mass unemployment of the Great Depression. A count of the jobs required for the employable unemployed was the chief requirement of the labour-force measure. *Job attachment* was, therefore, another and important criterion for classifying the adult population. In cases where job attachment (or lack of it) and activity clearly coincide, there are no serious problems of definition or measurement. Thus, persons who worked during the week (activity) obviously had jobs and are counted as employed. Persons who did no work (had no job) but looked for work – by answering or placing advertisements, registering at an employment office or plant, etc. – were engaged in the activity of job-seeking and counted as unemployed. A third group is also not too difficult to classify: those who didn't work (no activity) because they were ill, on vacation or paid leave, etc. They are presumed to have a firm job attachment and are classified as employed. If the labour force included only these three categories, the definition would be precise and unequivocal. There remains, however, a marginal group of persons in the adult population who engage in no activity and whose job attachment is tenuous or non-existent. They may or may not be included among the unemployed – and therefore the labour force – depending on the circumstances of the enumeration.

---

[7]Those not in the labour force are also classified into various categories: going to school; keeping house; too old or otherwise unable to work; voluntarily idle or retired. It is possible for a person to engage in several activities (or status categories) during the reference week. Thus a chain of *priorities* was established so that mutually exclusive groups might be delineated. (In the monthly surveys, questions on the individual's primary and secondary activity during the reference week are asked.) The chain is: with job and at work; seeking work; with job but not at work; non-labour force. Thus, a high-school student who worked on week-ends would be classified as employed, or a housewife who looked for work would be classified as unemployed. A person who worked one day, was laid off, and spent the rest of the week looking for a job would be classified as employed, etc.

The inclusion of this group in the labour-force definition can create serious problems of measurement.[8]

The marginal group referred to above is often termed the 'inactive seekers' (or, somewhat irreverently, the 'believers'), i.e. those persons who didn't work or look for work because they were temporarily ill, on indefinite or prolonged lay-off,[9] or believed no suitable work was available in their community. If such a person *volunteers* the information that he would have sought work except for certain conditions, he is classed as unemployed and in the labour force. If he does not volunteer that information he is classed as 'voluntarily idle' and therefore outside the labour force. Inclusion or exclusion of the inactive seeker thus rests on volunteered and essentially subjective information. At certain times of the year and in certain parts of the country – for example, in the winter season in communities dominated by primary industry – the inactive seekers are an important group. It is of interest to note that in January 1967 the United States adopted a revised labour-force definition that in effect (and among other things) got rid of the inactive-seeker group.[10]

In summary, then, while the labour-force definition does not provide a completely satisfactory means of clearly and unequivocally distinguishing the economically active from the remainder of the adult population, it is preferable to other possible definitions and measures in providing a count of the economically active (labour supply) that is reasonably consistent over time and space. This present section will conclude with a brief résumé of the main sources of labour-force data in Canada.

[8]The labour-force measure is extraordinarily sensitive to minor differences in the wording and ordering of questions, and the quality of enumeration (interviewing). Thus, for example, the very large difference between the 1961 census unemployment count and that of the monthly Labour Force Surveys closest to the census date – the census rate was 3.9 per cent while the May-June average estimate of the Survey was 6.2 per cent – amply illustrates this point. See Sylvia Ostry, *Unemployment in Canada*, 1961 Census Monograph Programme, Dominion Bureau of Statistics (Ottawa, 1968), Appendix A.

[9]In the original labour-force definition, developed in the United States for use in the 1940 census and adopted in the recurring sample surveys beginning March 1940 in the United States and November 1945 in Canada, persons on temporary lay-off (subject to thirty-day recall) were classed as *employed*, presumably because they were considered to have a firm job attachment. In 1956, after review by a group of experts commissioned by the International Labour Office, it was recommended that temporary lay-offs be classified as unemployed. The recommendation was adopted by the United States in February 1957 and by Canada in September 1960. This revision illustrates the point that job attachment is a less precise criterion than is activity, and is therefore a less desirable focus for an operationally feasible definition.

[10]Under the revised U.S. definition, if a person is to be counted as unemployed he must have engaged in some specific job-seeking activity within the four weeks preceding the reference date. Thus, the activity criterion is sharpened up, but the reference period (in this instance) is lengthened. See Denton and Ostry, *op. cit.*, Appendix B.

Data Sources

The most comprehensive source of detailed information on the characteristics of the economically active population in Canada is provided
by the censuses of population, which have been conducted every decade
since 1871. The amount of detail available has of course increased
enormously over the century. In early censuses only a few demographic characteristics were tabulated in addition to a rudimentary
economic classification. By 1931, however, cross-classifications combining demographic with economic data, in which occupation as well
as industry was noted, were available, and each census since that time
has provided an increasingly detailed body of cross-classified data.
Further, in 1921 and in 1931 (and of course, in subsequent censuses)
the unemployed were separately identified. A convenient historical
summary of census material up to the 1951 census may be found in the
Historical Catalogue of D. B. S. Publications, 1918-1960,[11] and further information on both published and unpublished census material
is detailed in the D. B. S. *Catalogue* of 1968 (the most recent) and in
the *Guide to Federal Government Labour Statistics*, 1969. In 1961 a
number of historical tables were published in a separate bulletin (Vol.
III, Part 1, Bulletin 3.1-1). The *General Review* volume of the 1961
census (Volume VII) summarizes many of the more important developments in labour-force growth and change over recent decades
(Bulletin 7.1-12). The *Review* also outlines the main changes in concept
and coverage and thus provides a most useful guide to users.[12]

Current labour-force data are provided by the Labour Force Survey,
a household sample survey initiated by the Dominion Bureau of Statistics in November 1945, first on a quarterly basis and then, in November 1952, on a monthly basis. While sample size limits the amount
of detail that can be provided, the Survey yields a reliable and accurate
count of the level and major compositional aspects of the labour force
and its components. These data are widely used as economic indicators
for the analysis of seasonal and cyclical changes in economic activity.
Each month a bulletin titled *The Labour Force* is published (preceded
by a joint press release issued by the Dominion Bureau of Statistics

[11]Ottawa, 1967, pp. 182-94. See also *Historical Statistics of Canada*, M. C. Urquhart
and K. A. H. Buckley (eds.) (Toronto, 1965), Section C: 'The Labour Force'.

[12]Cf. also Denton and Ostry, *op. cit.*, Appendix C, for a review of concepts and coverage and a reproduction of census questions (relating to economic activity) since
1871.

and the Department of Manpower and Immigration[13]), giving the main current data on the adult population, the labour force, the employed, and the unemployed, as well as some comparative data for the previous month and recent years. In addition a series of Special Tables is available on request, covering more detailed information for Canada, the regions, and (since January 1966) individual provinces. A range of seasonally adjusted series, which are periodically updated, was first issued in April 1967. From time to time the Survey is used as a vehicle for collecting additional information on selected economic, demographic, and social characteristics of the adult population. Some of these data are released in analytical studies – *Special Labour Force Studies*[14] – or included in the bulletin or special statistical reports. A detailed listing of labour-force-survey publications may be found in the *Historical Catalogue*, the 1968 *Catalogue*, and the *Guide to Federal Government Labour Statistics*, to which reference has been made above.[15]

Prior to September 1960, Canada had no official measure of unemployment, but rather two unofficial measures – one based on the Labour Force Survey, the other derived from the operational statistics of the (then) National Employment Service of the Unemployment Insurance Commission. These series were rarely close and sometimes diverged in trend. The deficiencies in the operational measure were thoroughly reviewed by an interdepartmental committee,[16] which recommended the adoption of the Survey measure. From that date the operational statistics were no longer released simultaneously with the labour-force measure, but some information, relevant to unemployment, derived from the operation of the employment service (since January 1966, the Canada Manpower Division of the Department of

---

[13]Before the formation of the Manpower Department in January 1966, the Department of Labour participated with the Bureau in the release. The press release summarizes developments for Canada and the five major regions over the preceding month in respect to labour force, employment, and unemployment. It provides, as well, comparable data for the same month the previous year and, for unemployment, for the twelve preceding months, an actual and a seasonally adjusted rate.

[14]Prepared in the Special Manpower Studies Division of the Dominion Bureau of Statistics. These studies also include analyses of census data as well as reports on methodological aspects of manpower analysis.

[15]A complete sample redesign was commenced in March 1964 and completed in January 1966. Full technical details may be found in the D. B. S. reference paper *Methodology: Canadian Labour Force Survey* (Ottawa, 1965). This reference is found in the 1968 *Catalogue*, which also contains a listing of all Special Tables available on request.

[16]See *Report of the Committee on Unemployment Statistics*, Ottawa, August 1960. Cf. also Sylvia Ostry, 'The Definition and Measurement of Unemployment', Senate of Canada, *Proceedings of the Special Committee on Manpower and Employment*, Vol. VI.

Manpower and Immigration) and the Unemployment Insurance Commission, is still published in a variety of reports[17] and in the *Labour Gazette*, a monthly publication of the federal Department of Labour. A useful review of the data available in this area may be found in the *Directory of Canadian Labour Statistics* by Allan A. Porter,[18] and in the *Guide to Federal Government Labour Statistics*.

Finally, a variety of employment statistics, derived from surveys of *establishments* rather than *households*, are published by the D. B. S. Some series are monthly, some annual: all provide some industry and geographic detail. In some cases other labour-market or related information is also provided: weekly or hourly earnings, hours of work, value of factory shipments, etc. A full review of available statistics may be found in the *Guide*, cited above.

Growth of Population

While the supply of labour in the economist's sense rests *au fond* on the income-leisure choice and is expressed in units of hours of effort forthcoming at given levels of remuneration, labour supply is measured in Canada by the labour force (or some reasonably comparable measure) in units of persons, employed or unemployed as of a given time. In the short run the size of the total supply of labour can vary only as the proportion of the population that participates in the labour market varies. But over the longer run, of course, the population itself will change, either because of variations in the vital processes of growth – births and deaths – or because of changing flows of persons into and out of the country – immigration and emigration. The remainder of this chapter describes the main aspects of the long-run changes in the level of labour supply in Canada derived from these three sources: natural increase in population, net immigration, and trends in labour-force participation.

A century ago Canada's population was approximately three and a half million people; today there are more than twenty-one million. But as may be seen from Table 1, the rate of growth has been very uneven. The modest increases of the decades following Confederation gave way to a surging flood of growth which carried Canada into the

[17]Dominion Bureau of Statistics, *Statistical Report on the Operation of the Unemployment Insurance Act* and *Annual Report on Benefit Periods Established and Terminated under the Unemployment Insurance Act.*
[18]National Industrial Conference Board, Canadian Studies, No. 6, Montreal, 1963.

TABLE 1

Population and Changes in Population, 1861-1970

Year	Population	Numerical increase	Percentage increase
1861	3,229,633	793,336	
1871	3,689,257	459,624	14.2
1881	4,324,810	635,553	17.2
1891	4,833,239	508,429	11.8
1901	5,371,315	538,076	11.1
1911	7,206,643	1,835,328	34.2
1921	8,787,949	1,581,306	21.9
1931	10,376,786	1,588,837	18.1
1941	11,506,655	1,129,869	10.9
1951[a]	13,648,013	2,141,358	18.6
1961[a]	17,780,394	4,132,381	30.3
1951[b]	14,009,429	—	—
1961[b]	18,238,247	4,228,818	30.2
1970[b]	21,377,000	3,138,753	17.2

[a] Excludes Newfoundland.
[b] Includes Newfoundland

Source: *Census of Canada*, 1951 and 1961; D.B.S., *Estimated Population of Canada, by Province* (1970).

twentieth century. This buoyant swell was not sustained, however, but ebbed away to a sluggish course during the decade of the depression. The flow has quickened since the Second World War, as unprecedented numbers have been added to the Canadian population. This record of growth reflects the historical development and interplay of natural factors and net immigration from abroad.

NATURAL INCREASE

Underlying the contribution of natural increase to the growth of the Canadian population are the secular trends in birth- and death-rates. The long-term steady decline in crude mortality-rates over the past century (in Canada from an estimated twenty-two per thousand during the 1860s to just over seven per thousand today: see Table 2) has occurred in all advanced industrialized countries as a consequence of improvements in nutrition, housing, and public-health and sanitation facilities. The most dramatic reduction of mortality has been among children, especially babies. For adults, however, the decline has not been spectacular, although it is somewhat greater for women than for

TABLE 2

Crude Birth-, Death-, and Natural-Increase Rates, 1851-1969
(annual rates per thousand population)

Period	Crude birth rate	Crude death rate	Crude rate of natural increase	Period	Crude birth rate	Crude death rate	Crude rate of natural increase
			Decennial series				
1861-1871	39.6	22.0	17.6	1911-1921	29.2	13.3	15.9
1871-1881	36.9	20.0	16.9	1921-1931	27.3	11.0	16.2
1881-1891	33.6	19.2	14.4	1931-1941	22.0	9.8	12.2
1891-1901	30.3	17.2	13.1	1941-1951[a]	25.8	9.7	16.1
1901-1911	30.7	14.4	16.3	1951-1961[b]	27.7	8.2	19.5
			Annual series				
1921	32.2	11.6	20.6	1944	24.2	9.7	14.5
1922	31.0	11.5	19.5	1945	24.4	9.4	15.0
1923	29.1	11.7	17.4	1946	26.9	9.4	17.5
1924	29.0	10.8	18.2	1947	28.6	9.4	19.2
1925	28.3	10.7	17.6	1948	27.0	9.3	17.7
1926	26.6	11.4	15.2	1949	27.3	9.3	18.0
1927	26.2	10.9	15.3	1950	27.1	9.1	18.0
1928	25.8	11.1	14.7	1951	27.2	9.0	18.2
1929	25.1	11.3	13.8	1952	27.9	8.7	19.2
1930	25.5	10.7	14.8	1953	28.1	8.6	19.5
1931	24.7	10.1	14.6	1954	28.5	8.2	20.3
1932	23.7	9.9	13.8	1955	28.2	8.2	20.0
1933	22.2	9.6	12.6	1956	28.0	8.2	19.8
1934	21.7	9.5	12.2	1957	28.2	8.2	20.0
1935	21.5	9.7	11.8	1958	27.5	7.9	19.6
1936	21.0	9.8	11.2	1959	27.4	8.0	19.4
1937	20.8	10.3	10.5	1960	26.8	7.8	19.0
1938	21.4	9.6	11.8	1961	26.1	7.7	18.4
1939	21.1	9.7	11.4	1962	25.3	7.7	17.6
1940	22.2	9.8	12.4	1963	24.6	7.8	16.8
1941	22.9	10.0	12.9	1964	23.5	7.6	15.9
1942	24.0	9.7	14.3	1965	21.3	7.6	13.7
1943	24.6	10.1	14.5	1966	19.4	7.5	11.9
				1967	18.2	7.4	10.8
				1968	17.6	7.4	10.2
				1969	17.6	7.3	10.3

[a] Excludes Newfoundland.
[b] Includes Newfoundland.

Source: For detailed compilation for years up to and including 1966, see Frank T. Denton, *The Growth of Manpower in Canada*, 1961 Census Monograph Programme (Ottawa, 1970), Table 4; D.B.S., *Vital Statistics*, (1967-9). Reproduced with the permission of Information Canada.

men – no doubt largely as a consequence of the reduced risk of child-bearing. So far as the labour force is concerned, the decline in death-rates has had its chief effect on working-life expectancy (see below) rather than in fluctuations in numbers. The birth-rate has been a far more important factor in the latter respect.

Trends in the birth-rate are not difficult to describe but are extremely difficult to explain and especially to forecast: they are, indeed, the rock on which so many long-term population projections founder. The fertility of any population is influenced by such a wide range of socio-psychological and economic variables that this is hardly surprising. Still, demographers have suggested that there are certain predictable associations, based on their observations of a number of countries over differing periods of time. Thus, the shift of population from rural-farm areas to large urban centres is usually followed by sharply de-clining birth-rates. Further, it appears that economic conditions – particularly if extreme and sustained in character – also influence decisions to marry and to have children. Thus, if the economy is depressed and unemployment is persistently high, marriages are postponed and married couples seek means of limiting family size. The opposite con-ditions will prevail in a highly buoyant, expanding economy.

In Canada, as may be seen in Table 2, the birth-rate declined, with only minor variations, in every decade between 1861 and 1931. During the depression years of the thirties the decline was accelerated, but toward the end of the decade the rate began to rise; it rose most mark-edly after the Second World War, remaining at a high level during most of the 1950s. In part, the high fertility levels of the fifties were a consequence of a 'catching-up' process – more closely spaced births – by young couples whose family plans had been disrupted by the war.[19] By the end of the 1950s fertility trends exhibited another turning-point – one that was certainly not anticipated by most Canadian demo-graphers and economists. Thus, the final report of the 'Gordon Com-mission', The Royal Commission on Canada's Economic Prospects, published in 1957, in discussing the assumptions underlying the com-mission's population projections, states (p.102): 'the birth rate will de-cline, but only moderately, moving down from where it stood in 1955 at 28.4 and varying between 24.2 and 25.6 over the period from 1960 to 1980.' Alas for the hazards of projecting fertility: by 1969 the crude birth-rate had fallen to 17.6, the lowest Canadian rate on record. The high unemployment and stagnation of the late fifties and early sixties

---

[19]See Jean-Noel Biraben and Jacques Legaré, 'Nouvelles données sur la natalité et la fécondité au Canada', *Population* (March-April 1967), cited in J. F. Kantner, J. D. Allingham, R. T. Balakrishnan, 'Oral Contraception and Fertility Decline in Canada', *Demography* (forthcoming).

gave way to a sustained period of growth and prosperity but the renewed economic buoyancy had no effect in braking the steady fall in the birth-rate. The decline in fertility has occurred in every region of the country and the trend shows no sign of abatement, but rather appears, in the past few years, to have gained momentum. There is, of course, widespread speculation about the role of oral contraception in these recent developments and especially in future patterns of fertility.[20]

As will be seen below, in our discussion of the changing composition of labour supply, the 'echo effects' of these fertility trends may clearly be observed in the changing level and composition of the labour force several decades later and also in subsequent generations of the population. But Canada's population of today has also been shaped by the flow of people across its borders over the past century. The following section will therefore be devoted to an examination of the role of immigration in determining the supply of labour in this country.

IMMIGRATION

In one sense, since the native peoples of this country were and are pitifully few in number, Canada is a country of immigrants and the children of immigrants. Yet the contribution of *net* immigration to Canadian population growth of the last hundred years has not been impressive. A reasonably reliable estimate would place it at between 10 and 15 per cent of the total increase over the 1861-1961 century. The reason for this modest showing is that while the immigrant inflow was substantial in almost every decade of the century, so, too often, was the emigrant outflow, mainly to the United States.[21] Canada was, in the striking phrase of one observer, a 'parking-place country'. As

---

[20]For an account of the only (at the time of writing) Canadian study in this area, see Kantner *et al., ibid.*

[21]All available estimates of immigration – and, even more so, of emigration – for the whole of the nineteenth and first two decades of the twentieth century in Canada are open to serious question. For recent decades this remains true for emigration, for which there are no direct measures even today. For a discussion of the major problems and the various available estimates, see Nathan Keyfitz, 'The Growth of Canadian Population', *Population Studies* (June 1950); Norman B. Ryder, 'Components of Canadian Population Growth', *Population Index* (April 1954); Duncan M. McDougall, 'Immigration into Canada, 1851-1920', *Canadian Journal of Economics and Political Science* (May 1961); Pierre Camu, E. P. Weeks, and Z. W. Sametz, *Economic Geography of Canada* (Toronto, 1964); James Pickett, 'An Evaluation of Estimates of Immigration into Canada in the Late Nineteenth Century', *Canadian Journal of Economics and Political Science* (November 1965); K. V. Pankhurst, 'Migration between Canada and the United States', *The Annals of the American Academy of Political and Social Science* (September 1966); Warren E. Kalbach, *The Impact of Immigration on Canada's Population*, 1961 Census Monograph Programme, Dominion Bureau of Statistics (Ottawa, 1970).

Canadian immigration policy during this century has always been selective; the major change in recent years is that the selectivity criteria have changed from an ethnic and racial to a skill and employment orientation. After the special circumstances of the late forties, when the government accepted as immigrants a number of displaced persons and refugees largely without regard to occupational (or ethnic) considerations, the application of the Immigration Act (which allowed for broad ministerial discretion) became increasingly directed to specific labour-supply criteria. A further step was taken in 1962, when new regulations to the act for the first time singled out education, training, and occupational skills as desirable selection criteria. The most recent developments in this direction are imbued in the 1967 revision of the act, which spells out, in much more explicit detail, the intention to regulate immigration in accordance with Canada's manpower requirements.[28] Thus, a point system has been developed which, in assessing the admissibility of an applicant, allocates specific weight to some nine factors: education, occupational demand, occupational skill, employment arrangements, age, knowledge of English and/or French, area of destination, relatives, and personal qualities. Clearly, at least the first seven of these are manpower considerations.[29] In Table 4, below, the effects of the 1962 change in policy toward ever-increasing manpower selectivity may be seen in the changing composition of the inflow. The average proportion of professionals, for example, almost doubled in the period following the 1962 regulations and, as may be seen in the last column, the effect of the 1967 revisions is in the same direction.

While the changing pattern of gross inflow is clear enough, the net contribution of immigration to particular occupation groups is impossible to estimate with any reasonable degree of precision because of the lack of data on emigration and on return flows of both immigrants and emigrants. Various efforts to cut through the statistical jungle created by fragmentary information from Canadian and foreign (mainly U. S.) sources have produced widely varying estimates of net migration.[30] What is indisputable, however, is that Canada has relied heavily on international sources of supply in particular occupations of

[28]See *Canadian Immigration Policy*, White Paper on Immigration, Department of Manpower and Immigration (Ottawa, 1966). See also, for a discussion of immigration policy, Kalbach, *op. cit.*, and Lawrence H. Officer, 'Immigration and Emigration', in *Canada's Economic Problems and Policies* (Toronto, 1970).

[29]In addition, the new regulations provide for admission of sponsored dependants and nominated relatives.

[30]See especially Pankhurst, *op. cit.*

TABLE 4

Immigration into Canada: Labour Force by Occupation Division, 1946-69

Destined to labour force by intended occupation category	1946-55	1956-62	1963-7	1969
	per cent			
White collar	19.1	29.3	42.8	49.9
Managerial	0.7	1.4	2.4	3.0
Professional and technical	7.0	12.9	23.5	31.8
Other white collar	11.4	15.0	16.9	15.1
Blue collar	40.8	43.4	40.9	30.2
Skilled and semi-skilled	31.6	30.0	32.6	27.8
Unskilled labourers	9.2	13.4	8.3	2.4
Primary	25.3	9.1	3.9	3.3
Agriculture	21.7	7.8	3.4	2.7
Other primary	3.6	1.3	0.5	0.6
Others [a]	14.8	18.2	12.4	16.6
Total labour force	100.0	100.0	100.0	100.0

[a] Includes transportation, communication, service.

Source: Department of Manpower and Immigration, Immigration Division.

professionals and in many skilled trades: in some instances the immigrant contribution has exceeded that of domestic sources.[31] While emigration to the U. S. has continued in the post-war period, and has been heavily weighted by high-level occupations, Canada has enjoyed a substantial net addition on balance from all international sources. Canada has been a beneficiary, in other words, of the 'brain drain', from Britain and western Europe in particular. Further, in some occupations – university teachers, for example – there is growing evidence of net movement even from the United States.[32] Over all, it has been estimated that in terms of *human capital*, the net gain to Canada from

[31]This was true, for the period 1950-63, for engineers and architects. See Louis Parai, *Immigration and Emigration of Professional and Skilled Manpower During the Post-War Period*, Special Study No. 1, Economic Council of Canada (Ottawa, 1965), for detailed exposition of this period.

[32]Herbert B. Grubel and Anthony Scott, 'The International Flow of Human Capital', *American Economic Review* (May 1966), and Pankhurst, *op. cit*. This aspect of the 'brain drain' is not universally regarded as an unmixed blessing. For an assessment in the case of the social sciences, see Anthony Scott, 'The Recruitment and Migration of Canadian Social Scientists', *The Canadian Journal of Economics* (November 1967).

migration over the 1951-61 decade was in the order of $12 billion – more than double the value of net capital inflow over the same period.[33] These are, of course, very approximate estimates and suffer from the crudity and paucity of data mentioned above as well as other conceptual and statistical problems. But they do unequivocally confirm the view that the Canadian economy has greatly benefited from the massive international manpower flows of the post-war period.

Finally, it is worth viewing the Canadian situation in the context of a world-wide phenomenon of international flows of highly trained manpower. A recent review of this 'international circulation of human capital'[34] points out the striking differences between the post-war immigration and the migration of the century that ended with the Great Depression. The earlier migration involved almost entirely the movement of unskilled labour, whereas during the recent period unqualified workers have been relatively immobile. It is highly skilled and highly trained manpower that is internationally mobile today, and for most of these migrants the United States is by far the destination of first choice. Canada is, in Professor Thomas's schema, an 'intermediate' country, i.e. a country with very large two-way traffic which may serve as a temporary stopping-place for migrants intending ultimately to move to their preferred destination. 'On a worldwide scale, individual migrants of varying degrees of skill move by stages out of low-income countries via intermediate to more advanced ones, forming currents of migration determined by the magnetic influence of the richest destination.'[35] Thus, over the period 1950-63, Canada had to import almost eight thousand professionals annually in order to keep just under twenty-five hundred.[36] The magetism of the United States stems from both salary differentials and enhanced career opportunities, as well as from non-economic factors, although, as noted above, there are tentative indications that Canada's 'holding-power' may perhaps be increasing in respect to specific occupational groups. For some immigrants Canada is no longer regarded as a 'parking-place' or intermediate country, but a preferred destination in its own right. Given a strengthening of these developments and the larger population base of the country, it is unlikely that immigration will play the same highly volatile role in shaping Canada's labour supply in the future as it did in the past.

[33]Bruce W. Wilkinson, *Studies in the Economics of Education*, Department of Labour, Ottawa, 1965. For another type of estimate (of education costs only, for professionals), see Parai, *op. cit.*

[34]Brinley Thomas, 'The International Circulation of Human Capital', *Minerva* (Summer, 1967).

[35]*Ibid.*, p. 481.

[36]These estimates are from Parai, *op. cit.*, and are questioned by Pankhurst, *op. cit.*, as perhaps overestimating emigration to the United States.

Trends in Participation

We have outlined the growth of Canadian population over the past century and noted the varying impact of domestic supply and immigration on growth. But, of course, total population is not labour supply. While the population at the present time numbers approximately 21 million, a substantial proportion of that total is made up of children (in 1970, 30 per cent were under fifteen years of age) or persons too old to work (in the same year, 5 per cent were seventy years old or more). Even among those who might be considered to make up the potential labour supply, not all will be active in the labour market at any given time. In translating population growth to the growth of labour supply, then, it is essential to focus on the *proportion* of the population that is economically active at any given date. This proportion, expressed as a percentage, is termed the *participation* or *activity rate*. It is usually expressed as a ratio of the labour force to the *adult* population (currently defined in Canada as persons fourteen years of age and over[37]) except for international comparisons where the base most commonly used is the total population. What effect have trends in participation had on the growth of labour supply in Canada?

It is perhaps surprising to observe that – as is evident from Table 5 – changes in over-all labour-force participation have had remarkably little impact on the historical growth of labour supply in Canada. Despite the profound economic and social changes that have occurred since the beginning of this century (the only period for which these data are available[38]), the over-all participation rate has exhibited no long-term trend. Apart from a sharp rise between 1901 and 1911, a consequence of the massive immigration of the period which was heavily weighted by young and prime-age males, the rate has varied by just over one percentage point from its highest to its lowest level.

But, as may also be seen from Table 5, the stability of the over-all rate conceals marked – and markedly divergent – trends in participation for men and women and among certain age groups of each sex. For this reason, while changes in participation have not markedly affected the long-term *growth* of labour supply, they have had a profound effect

[37]The 1961 census defined the labour-force population as persons fifteen years of age and over. The monthly Labour Force Survey, as of the date of writing, has not yet adopted the new minimum age. Clearly, there is some need for upward revision to fifteen or sixteen.

[38]The data in Table 5 are decennial census data adjusted to take into account changes in census coverage and concept. See Denton and Ostry, *Historical Estimates*, for a description of the revision procedures.

TABLE 5

Labour Force Participation Rates, by Age and Sex, 1901-70

Year	Both sexes, 14 years of age and over %	Male						Female					
		All ages 14 and over %	14-19 %	20-24 %	25-34 %	35-64 %	65 and over %	All ages 14 and over %	14-19 %	20-24 %	25-34 %	35-64 %	65 and over %
1901	53.0	87.8	—	—	—	—	—	16.1	—	—	—	—	—
1911	57.4	90.6	—	—	—	—	—	18.6	—	—	—	—	—
1921	56.2	89.8	68.4	94.3	98.0	96.9	59.6	19.9	29.6	39.8	19.5	12.0	6.6
1931	55.9	87.2	57.4	93.9	98.6	96.7	56.5	21.8	26.5	47.4	24.4	13.2	6.2
1941	55.2	85.6	54.6	92.6	98.7	96.1	47.9	22.9	26.8	46.9	27.9	15.2	5.8
1951[a]	54.5	84.4	53.7	94.2	98.2	95.0	39.5	24.4	33.7	48.8	25.4	19.8	4.5
1961[a]	55.3	81.1	40.6	94.4	98.4	95.3	30.6	29.3	31.7	50.7	29.2	29.9	6.1
1951[b]	54.3	84.1	53.5	94.0	98.1	94.8	39.1	24.2	33.4	48.5	25.1	19.6	4.4
1961[b]	55.1	80.8	40.5	94.2	98.0	95.0	30.4	29.1	31.7	50.4	28.9	29.5	6.0
1970[c]	57.2	78.2	42.7	90.0	96.7	93.6	23.2	36.5	32.3	60.8	38.8	38.6	5.6

[a] Excludes Newfoundland.
[b] Includes Newfoundland.
[c] *Labour Force Survey* May-June averages.

Source: Denton and Ostry, *Historical Estimates*, and Labour Force Survey. No age-specific rates are available prior to 1921.

on the *composition* of supply. A fuller understanding of the compositional changes, to be discussed in the following chapter, requires some examination of these changing patterns of labour-force activity. The most important developments have been a decline in the participation of younger and older males and a great and sustained increase in the activity of women, which has almost completely offset this decline. These two compensating phenomena, which may not be unrelated,[39] account for the stability of the over-all rate. Underlying these trends in participation were fundamental changes in the Canadian economic and social structure to which only cursory reference can be made in the broad and general discussion that follows.

MALE PARTICIPATION TRENDS

The total male participation rate declined from close to 90 per cent at the beginning of the century to just over 80 per cent in 1961 and is currently in the neighbourhood of 78 per cent. This substantial fall in the over-all rate is largely attributable to the much more marked decline in activity of both teen-agers and older men (sixty-five and over). There has also been some fall – though far less steep and much more recent – in the participation of young men in their early twenties. On the other hand, the rates of 'prime-age' males (twenty-five to sixty-four), which are the highest activity rates of any population sub-group, have been much more stable than these other rates over the nearly half century for which the data are available.

The dramatic decline in activity of teen-age males is a result of two closely related structural changes in Canada, viz. the increasing urbanization of the country and the extension of high-school and, much more recently, of university education to larger proportions of the population. Teen-age (and younger) boys provided unpaid labour on family farms in the much more rural Canada of sixty years ago, and hence many were counted among the 'gainfully occupied'. The shift in economic activity from farming to secondary and service industries (which will be more fully discussed in subsequent chapters in conjunction with other major structural changes in the economy) would, of

[39]Cf. Clarence Long, *The Labour Force under Changing Income and Employment* (Princeton, 1958), Chapter 8, which suggests that older males have been 'pushed out' of some sectors of industry by younger, better-educated women. It has also been hypothesized that married women may work to keep their sons at school longer. The Canadian data on occupational and industrial trends do not support Long's thesis. The second hypothesis mentioned has not been systematically tested because of lack of appropriate data. But the linkage between the long-run trends in male and female rates and perhaps hours of work as well are likely to be very complex indeed and will require careful theoretical exploration before empirical investigation can proceed.

itself, have had important labour-force effects, not only on boys, but on older males (see below). The rapid urbanization that accompanied and sustained the economic and social transformation of the country, however, buttressed and intensified these effects, especially through the rise in family income and the extension of the public-education system. The requirements of, and opportunities provided by, an industrialized urban Canada, in other words, are the major forces underlying the decline in teen-age labour-force activity. It is of interest to note that the (relative) fall in teen-age participation over the 1951-61 decade alone was greater than in the entire three decades preceding 1951: the rate of decline, that is, very much accelerated after the Second World War.

A number of pervasive economic and social developments have also combined to produce the decline in the participation of the older worker[40] in Canada, and these may be outlined briefly. As with teenagers, some portion of the fall is attributable to the contraction of employment in agriculture: farmers continue working far later in life than do industrial workers. This fact is illustrated by a comparison of the participation rate of males sixty-five years old or more, living in rural-farm areas, and that of urban dwellers of this age: in 1961, the former was more than double the latter. The relatively larger proportion of the self-employed in the older labour force – and the higher proportion of older workers among the self-employed – are also factors of some importance. Thus, in an earlier period of Canadian development, when agriculture was the dominant activity and the small businessman or independent craftsman occupied a central place in the economy, the extension of a man's working-life well beyond his sixties was a much more common phenomenon.

In addition to these underlying structural changes in the economy, a number of institutional factors have played a significant role in reducing older-worker participation, especially in recent years. Thus, the extension of private and public pensions and old-age assistance, and the implementation of compulsory retirement by many companies, have been responsible for the labour-force withdrawal of many older men. The coverage of private pension plans in Canada has expanded rapidly

---

[40]The term 'older worker' is an imprecise one. In the present context (a discussion of long-run trends in participation), we are referring to men sixty-five years of age or more, in large part because more detailed age information is not available. But a market definition of 'older worker' will be very different for different occupations (cf. airline stewardesses and brain surgeons) and will also change as economic conditions change (employers have fewer age barriers in recruiting in tight as compared with loose labour markets). For a discussion of these and related problems, see Sylvia Ostry and Jenny Podoluk, *The Economic Status of the Aging*, Dominion Bureau of Statistics (1966).

in the past two decades, extending now to about 40 per cent of the paid work force.[41] On January 1, 1966, the Canada Pension Plan commenced operation and covered almost all members of the labour force.[42] The Quebec Pension Plan, comparable in most respects, came into operation at the same time. By 1970, retirement pensions under these plans were payable to contributors at age sixty-five who had withdrawn from regular employment, or at age seventy regardless of whether they were working or not. It is too soon, of course, to discern the effects of these developments on labour-force activity, but they can certainly be expected to reinforce the already marked trend to declining participation of older workers.[43]

WORKING-LIFE ESTIMATES

It might be anticipated that the decline in participation of males at both ends of the age distribution would have an important effect on working-life expectancy, i.e. the average number of years, at any given age, during which a man may expect to be economically active. Working-life expectancy reflects the combined effects of the community's underlying mortality conditions, its educational and training arrangements, and its retirement patterns: thus, working-life estimates provide a valuable indicator of social and economic development. They have been widely used in this way in many countries at differing periods of time,[44] but were not until very recently available for Canada. Table 6 presents a set of Canadian estimates prepared in conjunction with the 1961 Census Monograph Programme.[45]

[41]See Dominion Bureau of Statistics, *Survey of Pension Plan Coverage, 1965* (Ottawa, December 1967).

[42]A useful and brief review of old-age security arrangements may be found in Dominion Bureau of Statistics, *Canada Year Book, 1968*, Chapter VI, Part II, 'Public Welfare and Social Security'.

[43]An examination of census data reveals that the high unemployment of the late 1950s and early 1960s may have 'pushed' some older males out of the labour force. Participation rates of males aged sixty-five to sixty-nine and seventy and over were regressed against the over-all unemployment rate and two 'structural' variables (the proportions of the total labour force in primary and in blue-collar occupations) for 235 and 237 counties and census divisions in 1951 and 1961 respectively. In both years the regression coefficient for unemployment was significant and negative. In 1961, when the over-all level of unemployment in Canada was much higher than it had been a decade earlier, the negative relationship was much stronger. See Ostry and Podoluk, *op. cit.*, Appendix E-1.

[44]For a review of some of the findings, see Seymour L. Wolfbein and Ernest W. Burgess, 'Employment and Retirement', in *Aging in Western Societies*, Ernest W. Burgess (ed.) (Chicago, 1961).

[45]Frank T. Denton and Sylvia Ostry, *Working Life Tables for Canadian Males*, 1961 Census Monograph Programme, Dominion Bureau of Statistics (Ottawa, 1969). This monograph describes in detail the methodology of estimation and the data sources.

TABLE 6

Working Life Tables for Males in the Labour Force: Canada, 1921-61.

Age and year	Life (1)	Labour force activity (2)	Retirement (3)
		Average number of years remaining in:	
1921			
20	48.4	43.4	5.0
45	27.7	22.2	5.5
60	16.2	10.5	5.7
65	12.9	7.7	5.2
1931			
20	49.0	43.5	5.5
45	27.8	21.8	6.0
60	16.3	10.2	6.1
65	13.0	7.4	5.6
1941			
20	49.6	43.5	6.1
45	27.6	21.2	6.4
60	16.1	9.4	6.7
65	12.8	6.9	5.9
1951			
20	50.8	43.2	7.6
45	28.0	20.3	7.7
60	16.5	8.7	7.8
65	13.3	6.5	6.8
1961			
20	51.5	43.2	8.3
45	28.5	20.0	8.5
60	16.7	8.2	8.5
65	13.5	5.7	7.8

Source: Denton and Ostry, *Working Life Tables for Canadian Males.*

As may be seen from Table 6, a man who reached the age of twenty in Canada in 1961 could expect to live another fifty-two years, of which about forty-three years would be spent working and just over eight years in retirement. By the age of forty-five he could still expect twenty more economically active years, but for those who survived to age sixty-five, working life was almost over. The changes that have taken place, since 1921, in both life and working-life expectancy are exhibited in Table 6. While the estimates are interesting from many vantage points, perhaps the most noteworthy feature of the table in the present context is that despite the very dramatic decline in participation of younger and older males that has taken place since 1921 (see Table 5) there has in fact been very little shortening of average working life: the estimates of years remaining in the labour force (column [2]) are not much smaller in 1961 than in 1921. The trend to delayed entry and hastened exit from the labour market which has just been described has not had the effect of dramatically reducing the span of economic activity of the male worker in Canada over the past four decades because it has been almost fully counterbalanced by the improvements in life expectancy (due mainly, as we noted earlier, to a decline in infant mortality) over the same period. What has expanded, of course, is the number of years of retirement: from just over five, at age sixty-five in 1921, to almost eight at the same age today. The trend to further extension of the retirement period is likely to continue as reductions in mortality, albeit moderate in extent, are accompanied by the more widespread adoption of present institutional practices encouraging early labour-force withdrawal.

FEMALE PARTICIPATION TRENDS

As may be seen from Table 5, there are marked contrasts between the age-specific participation trends of men and women. The proportions of the youngest (fourteen to nineteen) and oldest (sixty-five and over) women in the labour market have changed remarkably little over the past four or more decades, while it was precisely these age groups for men that demonstrated the most change (decline) over the same period. In the age group twenty to twenty-four, the female rate has been rising in recent years, in contrast with that for males, which has been drifting downward as a consequence of the extension of schooling into university and other post-secondary education. Women are still, on average, better educated than men, but their educational advantage has diminished in recent years as a greater proportion of boys have completed secondary schooling and continued into university and vocational schools. These differential trends in education plus the marked rise in demand for female workers in certain occupation and industry sectors are the chief factors affecting the contrasting participation patterns in the younger age groups.

While, as we have seen, the participation rates for prime-age males have been virtually stable over many decades, the most remarkable increase in activity rates has occurred among females aged twenty-five to sixty-four, particularly those in the age groups thirty-five to forty-four and forty-five to fifty-four (see Table 7). A majority of women in these age groups are, of course, married, and only a small minority are childless.[46] The development that is of greatest analytical interest, therefore, is the marked and continuing tendency to increasing labour-force activity among middle-aged married women, most of them in 'normal' families, i.e. with husbands present and with children. The same phenomenon has characterized all industrialized countries over the past few decades, with minor variations in degree, pattern, and timing, and represents a socio-economic change of fundamental and pervasive implications. It is worth spending some time exploring its dimensions in Canada.

THE LABOUR-FORCE ACTIVITY OF MARRIED WOMEN

While no precise evidence is available, it seems fairly clear that prior to the Second World War fewer than 3 or 4 per cent of all married women in Canada worked outside their homes. Even in 1951, only just over 10 per cent had entered the labour market. Yet today the rate has climbed to over 30 per cent and married women make up over half the female labour force.

It was during the decade of the 1950s that this radical transformation of Canada's work force took place, and the trends have continued, although more slowly, since then (see Table 8). But perhaps the most dramatic development of the fifties – at least in a statistical sense – was the emergence, observable by 1961, of the so-called 'two-peaked' participation profile of women. Thus, whereas in 1951 (and, undoubtedly, in earlier years, although no data are available) participation rates were highest immediately following labour-force entry (age twenty to twenty-four) as young women, having completed their schooling, worked until marriage, by 1961 the peak participation for women in their early twenties was followed by a 'second phase' of working life manifested in the form of a second, though somewhat lower, participation peak for women in their early forties. The emergence of the two-phased working-life cycle (almost exactly a decade later than in

[46]For details, see Sylvia Ostry, *The Female Worker in Canada*, and Jacques Henripin, *Tendances et facteurs de la fécondité au Canada*, both from the 1961 Census Monograph Programme, Dominion Bureau of Statistics (Ottawa, 1968).

TABLE 7

Female Participation Rates by Age: Canada, 1921-70

					Age				
Year	14-19	20-24	25-34	35-44	45-54	55-64	35-64	65 and over	14 and over
1921	29.6	39.8	19.5	12.2[a]	n.a.	n.a.	12.0	6.6	19.9
1931	26.5	47.4	24.4	14.3	12.9	11.3	13.2	6.2	21.8
1941	26.8	46.9	27.9	18.1	14.5	11.1	15.2	5.8	22.9
1951	33.7	48.8	25.4	22.3	21.1	13.5	19.8	4.5	24.4
1961	31.7[b]	50.7	29.2	31.2	32.8	23.1	29.9	6.1	29.3
1970[c]	32.3	60.8	38.8	42.2	41.2	30.1	38.6	5.6	36.5

[a] Women 35-49.
[b] Women 15-19.
[c] *Labour Force Survey*, May-June averages.

Source: Denton and Ostry, *Historical Estimates*, and Labour Force Survey.

TABLE 8

Female Participation Rates, by Marital Status: Canada, 1959-70

Year	Single	Married	Other	Total
1959	50.8	18.0	26.1	26.6
1960	51.9	19.0	27.7	27.9
1961	51.4	21.1	27.8	29.2
1962	50.7	22.0	26.8	29.4
1963	48.1	22.6	27.4	29.4
1964	48.8	24.4	27.5	31.8
1965	48.7	25.8	26.4	31.7
1966	50.1	26.6	27.9	32.9
1967	50.6	28.4	29.1	34.2
1968	49.1	29.6	27.7	34.5
1969	50.8	31.1	28.1	35.9
1970	49.8	32.5	28.5	36.5

Source: Labour Force Survey, May-June averages.

the United States, see Figure 2) was entirely due to the re-entry (or entry) into the labour market of large numbers of middle-aged married women.[47] Today the typical Canadian woman marries earlier than before, works for some time after marriage until she starts a family, and then drops out of the labour market to care for her children until they enter school. Then some of these women – a growing proportion since the 1950s – go back to work in middle age, finding jobs in the expanding white-collar, sales, and service sectors of the economy. It was this 'second flow' of women into the labour force that was a new phenomenon in Canada: at the end of the Second World War it was not yet apparent.

What has accounted for the remarkable influx of women, and especially married women, into the world of work? This transformation in the working-life pattern of women, as is the case with all changes of so fundamental a nature, stems from a multiplicity of pervasive demographic and socio-economic developments. We can do little more here than briefly summarize the major factors influencing these trends, concentrating on the more marked post-war developments.

A factor of overriding importance has operated on the demand side of the market, i.e. the very considerable expansion in recent decades of jobs that are considered especially 'suitable' for female employment (see Chapter IV). It has been argued,[48] and plausibly in our view, that cheapness combined with quality has made female labour particularly attractive to employers in filling the lower and middle-level white-collar jobs, which have been expanding at a well-above-average rate since the end of the Second World War.

Not only is female labour cheaper (although the precise extent of the sex differential is difficult to estimate),[49] but a much larger proportion of women than men complete secondary education[50] and are, therefore, especially suited to those particular kinds of jobs that require high-school graduation and perhaps some, but not extended,

[47]For fuller documentation see Ostry, *The Female Worker*, and *Changing Patterns in Women's Employment*, Department of Labour (Ottawa, 1966).

[48]See Valerie Oppenheimer, 'The Sex-Labelling of Jobs', *Industrial Relations* (May 1968).

[49]Cf. Ostry, *The Female Worker*, for an estimate based on 1961 census data on annual earnings. After adjustments of various kinds (to account for differences between males and females in employment patterns, levels of education and experience, etc.), the ratio of female to male annual earnings was 78-85 per cent, leaving an 'unexplained' gap of 15 to 22 per cent. See also, for a discussion of academic salaries, *C.A.U.T. Bulletins* for April 1967 and February 1969, which estimate a differential of about 20 per cent.

[50]See Michel D. Lagacé, *Educational Attainment in Canada: Some Regional and Social Aspects*, Special Labour Force Studies, No. 7, Dominion Bureau of Statistics (Ottawa, 1968). The relevant proportions in 1966 were 19.0 and 13.1.

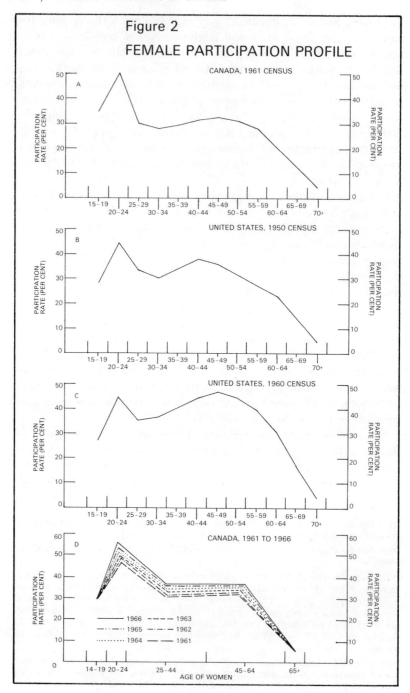

Figure 2

FEMALE PARTICIPATION PROFILE

post-secondary training. Once-powerful social barriers to the employment of married women have largely yielded under the force of these economic pressures.

While expanding job opportunities have no doubt played a major role in stimulating increased labour-force activity among women, changes in supply have also been important. Radical improvements in 'household technology' and the widespread development of commercial substitutes for most household products have, at least potentially, released female labour for the market. At the same time, the long-term reduction of the work week and the more recent very rapid growth in part-time employment[51] have created the possibility of more women combining household tasks and work outside the home. (Shorter working hours have probably also allowed husbands – willing or otherwise – the time to help out in housework and child care.)[52] Finally, in this list of supply changes, long-term improvements in education have not only made female labour more marketable, but have probably also shifted women's preferences in favour of work outside the home. It deserves emphasis that education is a factor of very great importance in explaining female participation, since it affects both the demand and supply conditions in the market.

A number of demographic developments have also favoured the increased participation of women. Of these, one of the most important has been urbanization, already referred to in connection with male participation trends as a factor strongly influencing the *decline* in activity. For women, the urban environment has been especially conducive to market participation. The expansion of female job opportunities has occurred largely in urban-based industries, and social attitudes in the cities have been far more tolerant of working wives than those in the more conservative rural areas.

Changing marital and fertility patterns have also exerted a significant influence on activity trends (as well, no doubt, as having been influenced by them). Over the long run there has been a decline in average family size, with at least some concomitant decline in the burden of child-care responsibilities. But there is certainly no clear-cut or consistent relationship between trends in fertility and female labour-

[51]For an analysis of part-time employment in retail trade, see Canada Department of Labour, Women's Bureau, *Part-Time Employment in Retail Trade* (1969).

[52]A recent survey of child-care arrangements of working mothers carried out by the Dominion Bureau of Statistics in conjunction with the April 1967 Labour Force Survey on behalf of the Women's Bureau of the Department of Labour, showed that a majority (almost 65 per cent) of the children of working mothers in Canada are cared for in their own homes. In these cases it was the father who was most likely to be the person responsible for the children during the absence of the mother.

force participation in Canada or most other countries. Of far more significance were the developments with respect to earlier marriage and earlier family completion – a post-Second World War phenomenon which coincided with the emergence of the two-phase working-life cycle of married women. Finally, in this brief list of important demographic developments, the low birth-rates of the 1930s were reflected by a reduced flow of new labour-force entrants in the post-war years of economic expansion when labour demand was at unprecedented levels. This favourable conjuncture of supply and demand forces was especially conducive to the entry of married women because of a decline in the proportion of single women in the working-age population[53] and declining over-all rates of male participation.

In summary, then, the broad-brush picture just presented suggests that a number of fundamental structural changes in the economy created a particularly favourable demand situation for women in post-war Canada and coincided with developments on the supply side that increased, both absolutely and relative to competing sources, the availability of a cheap, relatively high-quality source of labour supply – the middle-aged married woman. But this capsule history leaves a number of the more important and more interesting questions unanswered. In particular, the student of economics would like to know what effect the secular rise of incomes – of husbands and, at least potentially, of wives – has had on the propensity of wives to work outside the home. In other words, can we say anything about the shape of the long-term supply curve of labour? Some recent statistical studies based on 1961 census of Canada data provide further insight into this highly complex area of socio-economic analysis. The interested reader will want to consult these and similar American works,[54] since the remainder of this discussion will serve only to highlight a few of the major findings so far revealed.

---

[53]See John D. Allingham, *The Demographic Background to Change in the Number and Composition of Female Wage Earners in Canada*, Special Labour Force Studies Series B, No. 1, Dominion Bureau of Statistics (Ottawa, 1967).

[54]A most useful summary of American research in this area will be found in Glen G. Cain, *Married Women in the Labor Force* (Chicago, 1966), with bibliography cited therein. The Canadian research includes Ostry, *The Female Worker*, Appendix, and D. B. S. Special Labour Force Studies Series B, No.'s 2, 3, and 4 (not yet published) as well as ongoing research in the Special Manpower Research Staff of the D.B.S. in this area. The Special Labour Force Series B published as of the time of writing are: No. 1, Allingham, *supra*; No. 2, *Women Who Work: Part 2* (with Byron Spencer); and No. 3, N. H. W. Davis, *Some Methods of Analysing Cross-Classified Census Data: The Case of Labour Force Participation Rates.* Series B, No. 4, is *Married Female Labour Force Participation: A Micro Study* by Byron Spencer and Dennis Featherstone.

CENSUS CROSS-SECTION STUDIES

The labour-force participation of adult males is, in our society, pretty well an autonomous phenomenon: at a certain age men enter the labour market and stay in it, employed or unemployed, until they retire. To a large extent the same is true of single women. For married women, however, the element of choice is present, although from time to time the freedom to choose may be closely circumscribed by economic, social, or familial pressures. The element of choice is what complicates the analysis of the labour-force activity of married women – particularly since the decision-making unit by which the choice is exercised is likely to be the family and not the individual woman. Thus, any study of wives' labour-force activity should take into account not only the wife's characteristics, but those of her husband and family.

Most of the early research in this area focused on the effect of the husband's income and yielded the consistent results that the higher the husband's income the less likely the wife was to enter the labour force. These findings were most puzzling, since they suggested a backward-sloping long-term female supply curve of labour, i.e. declining participation of women with rising male income. But, as we have seen, female activity rates have been rising steadily over the course of several decades as real-income levels have improved. Other influences (some of which have been mentioned above) were obviously sufficiently powerful to counteract the negative 'income effect'. But until the recent studies referred to above, mainly because of lack of appropriate data, little progress was made in quantifying the separate and simultaneous impacts of a number of different factors influencing the labour-force decisions of married women.

The statistical methodology employed in these studies[55] allows us to estimate the impact of influences that are themselves not quantifiable in any simple fashion, e.g. region, rural-urban residence, number and age of children in family, level of education of husband or wife, age of wife, etc., as well as those, such as income, that are so-called 'continuous' or quantifiable variables. The chief findings thus far are suggestive, rather than conclusive, and point the direction for further research. Thus, the following results deserve mention:
1. The presence or absence of pre-school children was, over all, by far the most important factor affecting wives' labour-force activity. It

[55]A similar approach – multiple regression analysis with 'dummy' variables – has been used in the Canadian census studies and some of the American research. This technique permits quantitative estimates of the effects (separate and combined) of both quantitative and qualitative factors.

tended to be a stronger deterrent in larger cities than in rural areas, suggesting that informal or familial child-care arrangements – the most typical type of child-care arrangement in Canada[56] – are probably more accessible in small towns and farming areas than in urban centres. The dearth of day-care centres or similar institutions in Canadian cities has undoubtedly inhibited the labour-force participation of mothers of younger children. On the other hand, the studies revealed that the deterrent effect on participation exercised by the presence of older children in the home is rather weak. Further, when both older and younger children are present, the older children do not mitigate the deterrent effect of the younger, i.e. they evidently do not serve as sub-stitutes for the child-care role of the mother. These findings are com-patible with the historical trends, which demonstrate the most marked rise in participation among older women, few of whom would have pre-schoolers at home.

2. The effect of husbands' income on wives' participation was consist-ently negative, but the strength of the influence varied with the level of income, being much more powerful after a certain 'threshold' level (in the case of these data, $5,000-7,000) was reached. The effect of family income (exclusive of wives' contributions) is also negative and non-linear.

3. The effect of wives' earning power[57] was consistently positive and *very much stronger* than the negative effect of husbands' income. In terms of the income-leisure model, discussed at the outset of this chap-ter, these empirical findings suggest that the price or substitution effect has clearly outweighed the income effect over time.

4. The independent effect of region (the five main regions of Canada – the Atlantic provinces, Quebec, Ontario, the Prairies, and British Columbia – were used in the analysis) on wives' labour-market activity was not very strong, although a discernible influence was revealed in that, *ceteris paribus*, the participation rates were lower in Quebec[58] and the Atlantic region than elsewhere in Canada.

[56]As mentioned in f.n. 52, the April 1967 Child Care Survey reveals that the majority of children of working mothers are cared for in the home by the father, or some other relative or household member. This is true for all children of fourteen years or less and also of pre-school children under six. Only 2 per cent of the pre-schoolers were cared for in a day nursery or nursery school, a finding that underlines the scarcity of such community facilities in Canadian cities at that time.

[57]The education of wives was used as a proxy for earning power in several of the studies.

[58]This 'regional' influence was still significant when the influence of Catholicism (con-sistently and strongly negative) was taken into account.

5. It appears that the net wealth of a family as well as the income flows affects the wife's tendency to enter the labour market. Thus, again *ceteris paribus*, the larger the family's stock of assets, the less likely the wife is to participate, but the greater the amount of its debt, the more likely she is to enter the market.

This research has made a start in answering the important but difficult question, 'Why do more and more wives work?' More research along these lines will be helpful not only in explaining past trends but in more effectively projecting the future. It is already clear from the research presently available, however, that the simplistic view of labour supply suggested by the text-book approach outlined at the beginning of this discussion has only limited relevance to empirical investigation. It is more helpful to shift our attention to family, rather than individual, decisions and to try to uncover the links between the trends of male activity, which exhibit a long-term shift from work to leisure or school, and those of female activity, which demonstrate a reallocation of time from work inside the home, or from leisure, to work outside the home. Another important trend which is related to these developments (although the precise nature of the linkage remains to be explored) is the decline in weekly and annual hours of work (see Chapter III).

II

The Changing Composition
of Labour Supply

All the major demographic and participation trends outlined in the previous chapter have left an imprint in the changing age-sex structure of the population and the labour force. In addition, there have been marked regional shifts over the course of this century as population has moved in response to the broad underlying patterns of industrial change.[1] These regional developments, stemming from the fundamental and pervasive forces shaping technology and consumer demand, have been accompanied by a steady and rapid pace of urbanization, the most visible social manifestation of Canada's industrialization. This chapter will first trace these long-run structural changes, and then, briefly, conclude with a discussion of short-run seasonal and cyclical fluctuations in supply.

Long-run Changes

AGE AND SEX

By far the most important factor affecting the age-sex composition of the labour supply in Canada has been the change in participation described above. The effects of demographic trends, however, are dis-

---

[1]The broad regional pattern in population distribution in Canada has been very little influenced by 'natural' growth, i.e. by variation in vital rates. Of far greater importance have been population flows across provincial boundaries (internal migration) and, to a lesser degree, the distribution of foreign immigrants. Both migrant and immigrant flows have been strongly responsive to economic influences.

cernible in the underlying population. Thus, the persistent decline in mortality rates is observed in the gradually rising share of older population, while the long-run decline in the birth-rate until the end of the 1930s is reflected in the shrinking proportion of children under five years in all census records until 1941 and in the rising median age of the population from just over twenty years in 1881 to almost twenty-eight years in 1951. The increase in the birth-rate during and after the Second World War 'shifted' population into the younger age groups, so that between 1951 and 1961 the median age declined by more than a full year.

While it is sometimes difficult to disentangle the structural impact of immigration from the underlying birth- and death-rate trends, the effects of a very heavy immigrant inflow are easily discerned in disproportionate increases in the young and middle-aged population, and in the sex ratio because of its high male content. These effects are much more marked for the working-age population (fifteen to sixty-four) than for the population as a whole. As has been mentioned previously, during the decade of the 1950s the large inflow of immigrants (in the age range from twenty to forty) helped to fill the gap in working population created by the low birth-rates of the depression years.

Changes in the age-sex structure of the underlying population will, of course, also affect the labour force. But the link between the population and the labour force is the participation rate, and trends in participation have exerted a powerful, independent influence on the structure of labour supply. Thus, for example, while the female share of the working-age *population* rose slightly from 48 per cent to 50 per cent between 1921 and 1970, the comparable share for the *labour force* rose, over the same period, from 17 per cent to almost 33 per cent – a consequence of the long-run decline in male participation and the sharp rise in female rates described in the previous chapter.

Similarly, the age distribution of the labour force has been affected far more by participation than by demographic trends. Thus, for example, while males under twenty accounted for about 8 per cent of the working-age population in 1921 and rose to roughly 10 per cent in 1970, the comparable labour-force shares shrank by nearly half: from just over 10 to around 6 per cent. The steep rise in participation among middle-aged and older married women (thirty-five to sixty-four) was reflected in a near *quadrupling* of their labour-force share, from about 4 per cent in 1921 to nearly 15 per cent in 1970, although the underlying changes in population structure were negligible in comparison. The median age of the female work force rose by over five years between 1951 and 1961,[2] while that of the base population increased by scarcely more than one year. The 1950s, it will be remembered, was the decade in which the 'return flow' of women into the labour force – the second phase of the working-life cycle – first became evident in Canada.

The main outlines of the changing age-sex composition of the Canadian labour supply may be observed in Table 9. The long-run trends, already noted, of 'feminization' and 'aging' are clearly evident over the period for which data are presented, as is the pronounced influence of participational rather than demographic changes in effecting these developments. It is of interest to note that projections[3] of the labour force to 1980 suggest a further rise in the proportion of women (to almost 35 per cent of the total) and a doubling of numbers of women in the older age group, fifty-five to sixty-four years. But the most marked increase by age category for the labour force as a whole will be found in the young adult group aged twenty to thirty-four. There is expected to be a relative shortfall in the thirty-five to forty-four year age group, from which the recruits are drawn for executive and leadership positions in industry and government.

GEOGRAPHIC

There have been marked regional shifts in the Canadian population and labour force since the outset of this century. During the period of rapid settlement in the West – the beginning of the great 'wheat phase' of Canadian development – which preceded the First World War, population in Saskatchewan and Alberta expanded by over 400 per cent, in British Columbia and Manitoba by 120 and 80 per cent respectively. Between 1901 and 1911 more than 60 per cent of the total increase in Canadian population was absorbed west of the Ontario border.

The western boom, however, was not sustained. Only British Columbia continued to experience rapid growth, tripling its share of the Canadian population, from under 3 per cent in 1901 to better than 9 per cent in 1961. The Prairies were severely hit by the Great Depression (population actually declined in Saskatchewan during the 1930s and 1940s) and have achieved only moderate growth-rates since the Second World War. Today they account for about 16 per cent of

---

[2]See Sylvia Ostry, *The Occupational Composition of the Canadian Labour Force*, 1961 Census Monograph Programme (Ottawa, 1967), for an analysis of the changing age structure of the major occupational divisions of the labour force over the 1931-61 period.

[3]See Wolfgang M. Illing, *Population, Family, Household and Labour Force Growth to 1980*, Staff Study No. 19, Economic Council of Canada (Ottawa, 1967).

TABLE 9

Age Composition of the Working-Age Population and the Labour Force, 1921-70

Population, 15-64 years of age (percentage)

Year	Total, both sexes	Males					Females				
		Total	Under 20	20-24	25-34	35-64	Total	Under 20	20-24	25-34	35-64
1921	100.0	52.2	7.6	6.6	13.0	25.1	47.8	7.5	6.8	12.2	21.4
1931	100.0	52.5	8.1	7.1	11.9	25.4	47.5	7.9	6.9	11.0	21.8
1941	100.0	51.6	7.5	6.9	12.2	25.0	48.4	7.4	6.8	11.8	22.4
1951[a]	100.0	50.4	6.1	6.2	12.3	25.8	49.6	6.1	6.4	12.8	24.4
1961[a]	100.0	50.5	6.8	5.5	11.8	26.3	49.5	6.6	5.6	11.5	25.8
1970[b]	100.0	50.0	9.4	6.8	10.0	23.8	50.0	9.0	6.7	10.1	24.2

Labour force (percentage)

Year	Total, both sexes	Males						Females					
		Total	Under 20	20-24	25-34	35-64	65 and over	Total	Under 20	20-24	25-34	35-64	65 and over
1921	100.0	83.0	10.3	9.9	20.3	38.7	6.7	17.0	4.3	4.3	3.8	4.1	0.4
1931	100.0	81.4	9.0	10.6	18.8	39.0	4.0	18.6	4.1	5.2	4.3	4.6	0.4
1941	100.0	79.8	7.9	10.2	19.3	38.5	3.9	20.2	3.8	5.2	5.3	5.5	0.5
1951[a]	100.0	77.8	6.3	9.3	19.3	39.0	3.9	22.2	3.9	5.0	5.2	7.7	0.4
1961[a]	100.0	73.7	5.4	8.1	18.1	39.1	2.9	26.3	4.1	4.5	5.2	12.0	0.6
1970[b]	100.0	67.8	6.3	9.6	15.1	34.8	2.0	32.2	4.6	6.3	6.1	14.6	0.6

Notes: [a] Includes Newfoundland.
  [b] *Labour Force Survey*, May-June averages.

Source: Population: 1961 *Census of Canada*.
Labour Force: Denton and Ostry, *Historical Estimates*, and Labour Force Survey.

Canada's total population. The exception to the Prairie growth pattern is oil-rich Alberta, which in recent years has become one of Canada's fastest-growing provinces.

The most consistent patterns of population growth over the century are found in the central and eastern regions of the country. Ontario and, to a lesser degree, Quebec have enjoyed persistent and generally substantial increases. Today almost two-thirds of the labour force is located in central Canada (Table 10). At the other extreme the Maritimes (and, with the addition of Newfoundland, the Atlantic region) have suffered relative, and at times actual, decline throughout the twentieth century. In recent years this region has accounted for less than 10 per cent of Canada's working population.

These differential rates of regional growth in population and labour force[4] were, in the main, the product of internal migration and the distribution of immigrants from abroad rather than differing rates of natural increase. We shall be discussing some of the influences shaping the massive migration flows in this country in the following chapter (in the section on mobility) but suffice it to say at this juncture that the basic forces that have shaped the regional configuration of this country's work force have been largely economic (and technological), a response to broad underlying patterns of industrial change.

It will be observed from Table 10 that there are differences, in general not large, between the geographic distributions of the underlying population and the labour force, or working population. These differences arise in part[5] because of differences in participation rates among provinces or regions. The interprovincial variation in labour-force attachment, at any given time, in part reflects variation in the economic and social environments of the provinces which influence the labour-force behaviour of the population, and is also in part the consequence of differing population compositions (structural differences) among the provinces.

A detailed analysis of provincial variation in labour-force activity rates[6] reveals that after account has been taken of most major com-

---

[4]For a more intensive look at some aspects of the labour-force configuration and changes see Sylvia Ostry, *Geographic Composition of the Canadian Labour Force*, 1961 Census Monograph Programme, Dominion Bureau of Statistics (Ottawa, 1968).

[5]In part, too, they stem from differences in the age composition of the population. Thus, for example, the Atlantic region has a substantially lower proportion of the population in the working ages than any of the other regions.

[6]See Sylvia Ostry, *Provincial Differences in Labour Force Participation*, 1961 Census Monograph Programme, Dominion Bureau of Statistics (Ottawa, 1968).

TABLE 10

Provincial and Regional Composition of the Population and Labour Force, 1911-70

Province and region	Population[a] (percentage)						
	1911	1921	1931	1941[b]	1951[c]	1961	1970
Canada	100.0	100.0	100.0	100.0	100.0	100.0	100.0
Atlantic region	13.0	11.4	9.7	9.8	11.6	10.4	9.2
Newfoundland	—	—	—	—	2.6	2.5	2.3
Prince Edward Island	1.3	1.0	0.9	0.8	0.7	0.6	0.5
Nova Scotia	6.8	6.0	4.9	5.0	4.6	4.0	3.5
New Brunswick	4.9	4.4	3.9	4.0	3.7	3.3	2.9
Quebec	27.9	26.9	27.7	29.0	29.0	28.9	28.6
Ontario	35.2	33.4	33.1	33.0	32.9	34.3	35.9
Prairie region	18.4	22.3	22.8	21.1	18.2	17.5	16.1
Manitoba	6.4	7.0	6.8	6.4	5.6	5.1	4.5
Saskatchewan	6.8	8.6	8.9	7.8	5.9	5.1	4.4
Alberta	5.2	6.7	7.1	6.9	6.7	7.3	7.2
British Columbia	5.5	6.0	6.7	7.1	8.3	8.9	10.2

	Labour force[d] (percentage)						
Canada	100.0	100.0	100.0	100.0	100.0	100.0	100.0
Atlantic region	12.0	11.1	9.0	9.2	10.0	8.7	7.8
Newfoundland	—	—	—	—	2.0	1.7	1.7
Prince Edward Island	1.2	1.0	0.8	0.8	0.6	0.5	0.5
Nova Scotia	6.4	5.9	4.6	4.8	4.2	3.7	3.1
New Brunswick	4.4	4.2	3.6	3.6	3.2	2.8	2.5
Quebec	23.9	24.5	25.9	27.4	27.8	27.4	27.6
Ontario	36.3	35.3	34.4	34.9	35.7	37.1	37.6
Prairie region	20.2	22.1	22.9	20.9	18.1	17.9	16.6
Manitoba	6.5	6.8	6.9	6.5	5.7	5.3	4.5
Saskatchewan	7.7	8.4	8.7	7.5	5.7	5.0	4.3
Alberta	6.0	6.9	7.3	6.9	6.7	7.6	7.8
British Columbia	7.6	7.0	7.8	7.6	8.4	8.9	10.4

[a] Excludes Yukon and Northwest Territories.
[b] Labour force includes armed services except for 1970.
[c] Includes Newfoundland, 1951 and later years.
[d] Gainfully occupied concept prior to 1951. See 1961 *Census of Canada.* Bulletin 3.1-1 Table I.

Sources: All population data and labour-force data for all years from *Census of Canada.* Labour-force data for 1970 based on May-June averages from Labour Force Survey.

positional differences in the population there remains very little variation in the participation rates of prime-age males from province to province. In other words, the *propensity* of males, or at least prime-age males, to participate in the labour market is little affected by the economic and social differences across this country. This is not so for women (or for teen-age and post-retirement males). Even when population differences have been 'standardized', the behaviour of women with respect to the world of work exhibits substantial variation from province to province. Women, of course, are more likely to be marginal or secondary workers and therefore more responsive to a variety of economic, social, and cultural factors that influence their decisions to work or seek work outside the home. There has, however, been some tendency (though by no means appreciable) for the interprovincial differences in female labour-force rates to narrow in recent years. In contrast, a very marked tendency to convergence of geographic differences in labour-force activity has been observed in the United States.[7]

Finally, it is worth observing that provincial differences in the *utilization* of manpower (using that term to include the effects of differences in population composition, labour-force behaviour, and unemployment) are important factors in explaining regional disparities in earned income. Thus, for example, 'roughly half the gap between the Atlantic Region and the national average can be explained in this way'[8], i.e. by differences in manpower utilization. The effort to achieve a more balanced growth for the country as a whole, to reduce if not to eliminate the distressingly high regional disparities in income, has long been an expressed goal and an object of policy of Canadian governments – a goal as yet some distance from achievement. The problem of regional imbalance, as it is manifested in unemployment and underemployment, will be treated in a later section.

URBANIZATION

Changes in the regional distribution of population in Canada have been accompanied by a steady and rapid pace of urbanization, and an attendant shift from agriculture to non-agricultural activity. Urbanization and industrialization are the joint products of fundamental economic, technological, and social forces. We can do little here ex-

[7]See Simon Kuznets, Ann Ratner Miller, and Richard A. Easterlin, *Population Redistribution and Economic Change* (Philadelphia, 1960), Vol. II.
[8]See Frank T. Denton, *An Analysis of Interregional Differences in Manpower Utilization and Earnings*, Staff Study No. 15, Economic Council of Canada (Ottawa, 1966).

TABLE 11

Degree of Urbanization: 1861-1966

| Year | Percentage of population* | | Urban |
	Total	Rural	
	per cent		
1851	100.0	86.9	13.1
1861	100.0	84.2	15.8
1871	100.0	81.7	18.3
1881	100.0	76.7	23.3
1891	100.0	70.2	29.8
1901	100.0	65.1	34.9
1911	100.0	58.2	41.8
1921	100.0	52.6	47.4
1931	100.0	47.5	52.5
1941	100.0	44.3	55.7
1951[a]	100.0	37.1	62.9
1961[a]	100.0	29.8	70.2
1951[b]	100.0	37.6	62.4
1961[b]	100.0	30.3	69.7
1966	100.0	26.4	73.6

* Excluding the Yukon and the Northwest Territories.
[a] Excludes Newfoundland.   [b] Includes Newfoundland.

Source: Leroy O. Stone, *Urban Development in Canada*, D.B.S., 1961 Census Monograph Programme (Ottawa), and 1966 *Census of Canada.*

cept record this development (Table 11) and point out some of its consequences for the growth and structure of labour supply in Canada.[9]

At the time of Confederation, Canada was a predominantly rural country. There were no cities of size (by contemporary standards) and close to 85 per cent of the population lived on farms or in villages. A century later – a century during which the population had increased sixfold – the degree of urbanization had reached 70 per cent. Moreover, 44 per cent of the population was living in large cities (100,000 and over) or larger metropolitan centres. Urbanization has increasingly come to mean concentration in large centres, and these two phenomena have proceeded together. By 1980 it is anticipated that the urban population will have grown to 80 per cent of the total, while

[9]For a full exploration of the subject see L. O. Stone, *Urban Development in Canada*, 1961 Census Monograph Programme, Dominion Bureau of Statistics (Ottawa, 1967).

the concentration in large cities is likely to be even more pronounced: by 1980 some 60 per cent of Canadians will live in about twenty-nine major metropolitan areas.[10]

Nor has the composition of the rural areas of Canada remained unchanged. In the early 1940s, 60 per cent of the rural population lived on farms, but the proportion had fallen well below 40 per cent by 1961 and is continuing to decline. Many persons living in rural non-farm areas commute to work in urban centres.

In labour-force terms, the urbanization process in Canada is most clearly apparent in the marked shift of industrial and occupational activity out of agriculture (see Chapter IV for discussion of industrial and occupational changes). The long-run *relative* decline of the farm labour force was transformed, after the Second World War, into a sharp *absolute* decrease in numbers. The movement of people off the farm (primarily young people, i.e. new labour-force entrants) during the 1950s and early 1960s made a major contribution to manpower supplies during the post-war period. The farm – non-farm shift, together with new immigration and rising female participation, provided an important offset to shortages of labour-force entrants during the rapid economic expansion of the early and mid 1950s. The agricultural share of the industrial work force today has fallen to well under 10 per cent. Despite the projected increase in urbanization the farm sector is not likely to be a significant source of labour supply in coming decades.

There is another important consequence of urbanization that is of direct relevance to this discussion of labour supply, viz. its influence on female participation rates. The labour-force activity rates of women are very much higher in urban than in rural areas and appear also to vary directly, though not uniformly, with city size.[11] In part, this variation is attributable to differences in job opportunities – clerical and other white-collar work, service jobs, etc. are more abundant in urban than in rural areas, in larger rather than in smaller cities. But other factors are also involved: for example, family size, household technology, community attitudes and customs. Whatever the complex of influences, the association between female participation rates and rural-urban residence is distinct and the gaps in rates are substantial. Thus, as has already been noted, the shift of population from rural

[10]Economic Council of Canada, *Fourth Annual Review* (Ottawa, 1967).

[11]Cf. John D. Allingham and Byron Spencer, *Women Who Work: Part 2*, Special Labour Force Studies Series B, Dominion Bureau of Statistics (Ottawa, 1968), and Sylvia Ostry, *The Female Worker in Canada*, 1961 Census Monograph Programme, Dominion Bureau of Statistics (Ottawa, 1968).

to urban areas, particularly the accelerated movement during the 1950s and early 1960s, was itself a factor contributing to the rise of female labour-force participation. The continuing urban growth and the increasing concentration of population in large urban complexes anticipated throughout the 1970s may be expected to have a similar effect.

Urbanization – or the population 'implosion' as it is called – will have many other implications, which deserve careful study, for manpower developments. In particular, the location of jobs versus the location of living space and the manifold problems of travel-to-work patterns and costs will loom large in this decade.

Shorter-run Fluctuations

Our attention thus far has centred on long-run changes in the size and structure of labour supply in Canada, and we have emphasized the importance of fundamental socio-economic and demographic trends in shaping these changes. Economists are also concerned with short-run fluctuations in the labour market and, in particular, with the way in which labour supply responds to seasonal and cyclical changes in the demand for labour.

Before we examine these seasonal and cyclical fluctuations, however, a more general point is worth stressing. There is, even within a very short period of time, from month to month for example, a great amount of flux and change in the labour force that is not revealed by the regular labour-force data. Very large 'gross flows' in and out of the labour market and between the employed and unemployed lie behind the net changes in the employment and unemployment figures we see each month. In effect, it is the change in these flows that underlies the dynamics of the adjustment process in the labour market. To illustrate the size and nature of these gross flows, data for two pairs of months in a recent year are provided in Table 12.[12] It may be observed from this table that, while most persons do not change their labour-force status between two consecutive months, the amount of movement between certain categories is, in fact, substantial. Thus, for example, reading from the last column of the top half of the table

---

[12]These data are based on response to a question on the labour-force survey schedule that asks the respondent to recall the last month's activity with respect to the regular labour-force and non-labour-force categories. The data are, therefore, affected to some extent by memory or recall bias as well as by sampling and non-sampling error. It is also possible to produce gross-flow data by matching the labour-force schedules for the same individual for two (or more) time periods.

TABLE 12

Gross Flows among Labour-Force and Non-Labour-Force Categories, June-July and August-September 1967

Activity in previous month (June)	*Activity in current month (July)*					
	Em- ployed	Unem- ployed	Keeping house	Going to school	Other	Total
	thousands of persons					
Employed	7285	90	117	17	52	7561
Unemployed	94	146	*	*	*	246
Keeping house	74	*	3647	*	12	3737
Going to school	309	39	63	30	662	1103
Other	79	*	12	*	1153	1252
Total	7841	284	3840	50	1884	13899
(August)			*(September)*			
Employed	7138	73	95	356	73	7735
Unemployed	87	123	*	*	*	222
Keeping house	134	*	3598	61	*	3810
Going to school	24	*	*	207	*	239
Other	128	12	23	871	923	1957
Total	7511	219	3718	1504	1011	13963

* Estimates less than 10,000.

Source: Based on unpublished data from Labour Force Survey.

(the June-July comparison), of the 246,000 persons who were – or recalled they were – unemployed in June, 94,000 had moved into employment by July (second column). Conversely, of the 284,000 who were
unemployed in July (second column, last line), 146,000 had been unemployed the previous month, but 90,000 had flowed into the pool of
unemployed from jobs held in June and another 39,000 had left school
in June and were looking for work in July. In effect, although unemployment increased by just under 40,000 persons between June and
July, almost 140,000 persons became unemployed between June and
July, and 100,000 persons who had been unemployed in June found
jobs or left the labour force by July. In other words, gross flows in
both directions were in the order of six times the net change!

An interesting aspect of Table 12 concerns the flows between the
schools and the labour market. Indeed, the pairs of months included
in the table were chosen to illustrate these particular movements
(which are highly relevant to the discussion of seasonality that follows).

Thus, between June and July large numbers of students enter the labour force, either finding jobs or swelling the ranks of the unemployed. Between August and September, the reverse flow occurs: summer jobs are terminated and job search is abandoned as students return to the high schools and universities. In Table 12, 309,000 persons attending school in June were employed by July and another 39,000 were looking for work (top half of table). Conversely, 356,000 persons left jobs to return to school between August and September. Because of offsetting flows between other categories, the net changes in employment and the labour force are very much smaller than the gross flow of students would indicate. Thus, the short-run fluctuations in labour supply, which will be illustrated and discussed below, are the result of changes in the labour-force status of very appreciable numbers of people.[13]

SEASONAL FLUCTUATIONS

In all countries there is some fluctuation in the demand for labour as a consequence of both climatic conditions and social factors such as holidays, vacations, etc. In Canada the seasonal swings in demand are very marked because of our particularly extreme variations in climate. In winter the severe cold reduces the amount of activity in outdoor industries such as agriculture, fishing, mining, construction, tourism; and in the spring, as the weather moderates and activity in these sectors is resumed, the demand for labour revives. Superimposed on climatic change are the effects on demand of the Christmas 'rush' and other cultural and conventional patterns of community activity.

Seasonal fluctuations in labour supply arise in part as a response to changes in demand, but, especially in recent years, also reflect 'autonomous' swings, i.e. changes that are independent of the pattern of demand. If labour supply adjusted fully to seasonal changes in demand, and there were no autonomous factors operating on the supply side, one would expect participation to rise as the demand for labour increased and to fall as demand diminished, with the result that unemployment would exhibit no seasonality. However, as is well known, Canada has always had a serious seasonal unemployment problem mainly because the labour market does not, in fact, readily

[13]The gross-flow data are not published in either Canada or the United States (because of a variety of technical and statistical problems associated with their production), but would clearly make a valuable addition to the present body of labour-market information and would be especially useful in the analysis of short-run fluctuations. See Mary Hutton and A. N. Polianski, 'Gross Movements of the Labour Force', mimeographed, Department of Manpower and Immigration (December 1966).

adjust to these short-term demand fluctuations.[14] We will concentrate, in this necessarily brief discussion, on the seasonal pattern of unemployment rather than on that of labour supply as a whole. However, it will be observed that the labour force does exhibit a seasonal pattern, and therefore supply is, to some extent, sensitive to seasonal changes in demand.

Because of the importance of seasonality in Canada and its pervasive influence in the economy, more and more statistical information is 'deseasonalized', i.e. an effort is made to separate seasonal fluctuations from underlying long-term trends and cyclical or irregular movements in the statistical series. A variety of methods for seasonal adjustment of statistical data have been developed, but basically all use the notion of an 'average' month and express the unadjusted data in relation to that month.[15] The information presented in Table 13 illustrates the phenomenon of seasonality in the Canadian labour force and unemployment by means of a comparison between the unadjusted and the seasonally adjusted series.

It will be observed from Table 13 that the seasonally adjusted series are derived by dividing the raw data each month by the corresponding 'seasonal factor'. The effect of this operation is to increase the estimates in months of below-average seasonal activity and reduce them when activity picks up for climatic or other seasonally related reasons. The very much larger amplitude of seasonal swings in unemployment than in labour force is strikingly apparent from a comparison of the seasonal factors in columns (2) and (5). The labour force 'high' and 'low' differ by only 2 or 3 percentage points from the 'average month', but the winter 'high' and autumn 'low' of unemployment is well over 30 per cent from the basic seasonally adjusted level. As has already been stated, the adjustment of labour supply to seasonal changes in demand offsets only to a limited extent the impact of seasonality on unemployment in this country.

By removing seasonal fluctuations from labour market and other economic statistics, economic analysts are better able to discern underlying trends and particularly cyclical changes in the economy – changes that might otherwise have been obscured for some period of

---

[14]See, for example, Senate of Canada, *Special Committee on Manpower and Employment, Proceedings*, No. 16 (Ottawa, 1961).

[15]For a description of the techniques presently used by the Dominion Bureau of Statistics, see Julius Shiskin, *Electronic Computers and Business Indicators*, Occasional Paper 57, National Bureau of Economic Research.

TABLE 13

Labour-Force and Unemployment Seasonal Factors, 1969

Month	Labour force			Unemployment		
	Unadjusted series (000)	Seasonal factor	Seasonally adjusted series (000)	Unadjusted series (000)	Seasonal factor	Seasonally adjusted series (000)
	(1)	(2)	(3)	(4)	(5)	(6)
January	7891	0.97240	8115	467	1.30705	357
February	7911	0.97209	8138	473	1.32837	356
March	7919	0.97456	8126	448	1.29601	346
April	8061	0.98329	8198	432	1.17167	369
May	8248	1.00138	8237	386	0.98356	392
June	8403	1.02431	8204	383	0.94707	404
July	8550	1.04874	8153	349	0.91216	383
August	8489	1.04273	8141	318	0.79927	398
September	8126	0.99802	8142	279	0.68527	407
October	8142	0.99814	8157	314	0.74717	420
November	8115	0.99451	8160	354	0.85988	412
December	8095	0.98970	8179	383	0.97049	395

Source: D.B.S., *Seasonally Adjusted Labour Force Statistics* (January 1953–December 1969).

time. However, as a number of analysts have now demonstrated,[16] seasonal fluctuations are not completely independent of underlying economic conditions; the issue of how to deal effectively with this problem of statistical interpretation is very complex and highly contentious.

During the decade of the 1960s in Canada an important new feature affecting the seasonality of unemployment appeared in the form of 'autonomous' changes in supply due to the growing influx of students into the labour market at the close of the school year. Although employment rises in the spring and summer (for seasonal reasons), the flow of students does not occur in response to seasonal changes in

[16] *E.g.* David C. Smith, 'Seasonal Unemployment and Economic Conditions', *Employment Policy and the Labour Market*, Arthur M. Ross (ed.) (Berkeley, 1965); Frank T. Denton and Sylvia Ostry, *An Analysis of Post-War Unemployment*, Staff Study No. 3, Economic Council of Canada (Ottawa, 1964), and David Fairbarns, 'On Cyclical Fluctuations in Seasonal Components of Economic Time Series', mimeographed, C.P.S.A. Conference on Statistics (Ottawa, June 1967).

labour demand but arises from a quite unrelated phenomenon, the institutional arrangements of the educational system. Unemployment in June and July which, in the fifties, was 30 to 35 per cent below the seasonally adjusted level is now only 5 to 10 per cent below 'average'. This marked shift in seasonal pattern reflects the supply changes already noted, i.e. the rapid rise in the school-attending population during the sixties as the post-war babies progressed through secondary and post-secondary education. In earlier years the absolute numbers of students were very much smaller and represented only small, marginal additions to the summer labour supply. Indeed, students, along with married women and retired workers, the so-called secondary workers (see below), constituted the main source of flexibility in labour supply, moving in and out of the market in response to seasonal changes in job opportunities.

Apart from this recent change in the pattern of seasonal unemployment due to changed supply conditions, there is some evidence that the over-all amount of seasonality in Canadian unemployment has slightly diminished since the mid fifties.[17] This is probably due to a variety of factors, including special policy measures (the former Winter Works Programme, designed to reduce seasonal fluctuations in construction activity), technological changes (permitting some extension of activity in primary industries and in construction during the winter months), and the marked growth of the secondary and tertiary industries (relative to primary industries), which are less sensitive to climatic conditions.

CYCLICAL FLUCTUATIONS

We have seen in the preceding discussion that labour supply is affected by the short-run changes in the demand for labour that occur, in a regular fashion, within the course of a year as a consequence of climatic and conventional factors. Is labour supply also responsive to the changing climate of economic activity, i.e. does the tightness or looseness of the labour market affect the size of the labour force? This question has been the subject of a good deal of research in both Canada and the United States in recent years and a brief summary of these investigations merits inclusion here, although the interested reader is advised to seek out the literature for a fuller understanding of the nature of this complex issue.[18]

Two alternative hypotheses have been put forward to explain the

---

[17]Denton and Ostry, *op. cit.*

[18]For the most recent, most comprehensive treatment of the subject in the United States (including a review of all the relevant literature), see the monumental volume by

cyclical response of labour supply, the so-called 'discouraged worker' and 'additional worker' effects. The issue was originally posed in connection with the effects on the labour force of the Great Depression of the 1930s.[19] It was argued that during the 1930s, when increasing numbers of male family heads had lost their jobs, wives and other family members were forced into the labour market to look for work in an effort to restore and sustain family income, i.e. 'additional workers', who were usually outside the labour force, swelled the ranks of the unemployed. An opposing, though, *a priori*, an equally plausible hypothesis, suggested that in periods of recession, when jobs are relatively scarce, workers with a marginal attachment to the labour force will become discouraged and leave the labour market, returning to their primary, non-labour-force activity, but will re-enter during the upswing, as conditions improve.

The 'additional' versus 'discouraged' worker hypotheses have been much more fully elaborated in recent analysis, and more sophisticated and conceptually precise models of cyclical responsiveness of labour supply have been formulated. An important issue relevant to stabilization policy is involved in these discussions which, significantly enough, arose in the recession of the late 1950s and early 1960s: if the level of economic activity itself is an important determinant of the size of the labour force, the 'target' level of full employment should not be defined solely in terms of measured or visible unemployment, which may significantly understate or overstate the degree of under-utilization of labour supply. The timing and strategy of aggregate stabilization policies should, if such be the case, take into account the short-run dynamics of labour-market adjustment.

The notion of cyclical responsiveness of labour supply rests on the assumption that there are two types of workers, primary and secondary. The former (usually defined, in rough terms, as prime-age male heads of families) are assumed to have an unvarying attachment

William G. Bowen and T. Aldrich Finegan, *The Economics of Labour Force Participation* (Princeton, 1969). The major Canadian articles are: S. F. Kaliski, 'The Relation Between Labour Force Participation and Unemployment in Canada', mimeographed, C.P.S.A. Conference on Statistics (June 1962); J. T. Montague and J. Vanderkamp, *A Study in Labour Market Adjustment*, Institute of Industrial Relations, University of British Columbia (1966); Lawrence H. Officer and Peter R. Anderson, 'Labour Force Participation in Canada', *Canadian Journal of Economics* (May 1969); Pierre-Paul Proulx, 'La Variabilité cyclique des taux de participation à la main-d'oeuvre au Canada', *ibid*. (see f.n. 4 for bibliography of main United States articles); and N.H.W. Davis, *Cycles and Trends in Labour Force Participation Rates: The Experience of Canada and the Regions*, Special Labour Force Studies Series B, No. 5, Dominion Bureau of Statistics (Ottawa, 1970).

[19]See W. S. Woytinsky, *Additional Workers and the Volume of Unemployment in the Depression*, Social Science Research Council (1940), and C. D. Long, *The Labor Force Under Changing Income and Employment* (Princeton, 1958).

to the labour market, whether employed or unemployed. The latter (married women, younger males and females, and older, quasi-retired workers) have a more tenuous commitment to the labour force for a variety of cultural and institutional as well as economic reasons, and hence their decisions to participate or withdraw from the market will be more variable and more responsive to changing economic opportunities affecting themselves and primary members of their family. It is the secondary workers, as we have already seen in connection with seasonal fluctuations, who provide the element of flexibility in labour supply in the short run. The question at issue in this discussion is whether, on balance, the movement of these workers is pro-cyclical (i.e. they act as 'discouraged' workers) or contra-cyclical (i.e. they respond as 'additional' workers).[20]

The evidence of the more recent United States' studies very strongly supports the dominance of the 'discouraged worker' or pro-cyclical effect.[21] In Canada the evidence is mixed. Several studies suggest that the 'additional worker' or contra-cyclical effect dominates,[22] while others point either to no discernible cyclical influences[23] or to the prevalence of a 'discouraged worker' phenomenon.[24] In this country, unlike the United States, there is certainly no consensus about either the degree or the direction of the cyclical responsiveness of supply to changing demand conditions in the labour market.

One reason for the uncertainty surrounding the nature of the Canadian pattern of supply response is undoubtedly the variation in the methodology, data, time periods, etc., used in the different studies.[25] This explanation is not acceptable, however, with respect to the marked contrast between the near-unanimity of evidence in the United States and the mixed results obtained by similar approaches in Canada. If there are real differences in the extent and nature of cyclical sensitivity

---

[20]Considering the size of the gross flows of the labour force from month to month, it is, of course, quite possible (and likely) that both types of movement take place and, to a considerable extent, simply serve to offset one another. The question then becomes, if the offset is not complete, which effect is dominant, i.e. what is the 'net' effect on the labour supply as a whole?

[21]Cf. the review and summing-up in Jacob Mincer, 'Labor Force Participation and Unemployment: A Review of Recent Evidence', in R. A. Gordon and M. S. Gordon, *Prosperity and Unemployment* (New York, 1966). There is still a good deal of controversy about data and methodology, however, as Mincer notes.

[22]Proulx, *op. cit.*, and Officer and Anderson, *op. cit.*

[23]Hutton and Polianski, *op. cit.*

[24]Montague and Vanderkamp, *op. cit.*, and Davis, *op. cit.*

[25]This is amply demonstrated in Davis, *op. cit.*, with respect to Proulx's analysis and results.

in the Canadian and American labour markets, the explanation will have to be sought in institutional and socio-economic structural and behavioural differences between the two countries. The study by N.H. W. Davis, employing a novel specification and new data which mitigate some of the methodological deficiencies of earlier studies, suggests that the cyclical sensitivity of Canadian labour supply is, on balance, in the same direction as that in the United States, i.e. pro-cyclical, but very much weaker. In Canada, it appears, only the longer-run *cumulative* effect of slack demand produces a significant response among secondary workers. This response, moreover, is much more marked in some regions than in others, with unfortunate consequences for regional income disparities. A fuller exploration of these interregional differences in Canada and of the Canadian – United States' differences is clearly required.

III

Further Aspects of Labour Supply

The last chapter was confined to an exposition of the changing long-run demographic composition of labour supply in Canada, but also highlighted the main features of the short-run flux and movement that continue to shape and change the work force in this country. Many important aspects of supply remain to be explored. Constraints of space and data must limit our selection to two of these: the change in the *time* dimension of work, and the extent and nature of *mobility* in the working population. However, the topics discussed under the heading of labour demand in the chapter that follows – the evolving occupational, industrial, and educational structure of the labour force – will further extend and fill in the broad outline of supply presented thus far. The distinction between labour supply and labour demand is to some degree artificial in expository analysis: the employed portion of the measured labour force reflects the complex and continuing interaction of forces emanating from both sides of the market.

The Time Dimension of Supply

Economists, true children of Jeremy Bentham, distinguish only two uses of time – uses that are mutually exclusive. As we have seen, the theoretical underpinning of the notion of labour supply is the income-leisure dichotomy, which implicitly assumes that work is painful (disutility) and non-work or leisure is pleasurable (utility), and that the choice between work and leisure exhausts all possibilities. But, of course, as we all know, some work can be pleasurable, while involuntary leisure can be most depressing. Activities such as keeping house or studying at university defy the neat dichotomous classification and may be either a joy or a pain in the neck, depending on one's tastes and circumstances. For many people there is no dichotomy but a range; the *process* of choice is, therefore, much more complicated than the income-leisure model suggests. The *outcome* of the choice of the many individual (and family) decisions is reflected in statistics on hours of work, statutory holidays, vacations with pay, etc. We may view the *outcome* – and shall presently do so, in so far as our partial and faulty data permit – but the *process* remains, for the most part, a black box. In fact we know very little about the way in which individuals, particularly the growing number of secondary workers in the labour force, make these choices or 'trade-offs' between gainful work, pleasurable leisure, and the range of non-work, non-leisure activities available to them.[1]

In what follows we shall confine our attention to two aspects of the 'time dimension' of labour supply: the trend in working hours and the issue of utilizing hours-of-work legislation as an instrument of employment policy.

TRENDS IN WORKING HOURS AND PAID NON-WORK

The average Canadian worker today works a shorter day, fewer days a week, and fewer weeks a year than did his nineteenth-century counterpart. A significant portion of the enhanced capacity to produce that has marked the evolution of the Canadian economy over the long run has been 'consumed' in the form of leisure rather than goods and services.

While the preceding statement cannot be challenged, it is unfortunately impossible to trace or analyse, in any detail, the long-term trend of working hours in Canada. This is so not only because the basic data are sparse, but also, more than is the case for most economic statistics, because they are fraught with definitional confusion. Ideally, we should like to distinguish, for analytical purposes, three quite distinct measures of hours: the *standard*, or normal, *hours*, fixed by law, custom, or collective agreement;[2] *hours worked*, i.e. hours actually spent on the job, including overtime hours worked; and *hours*

---

[1]For an amusing and perceptive discussion of the changing patterns of time allocation, see S. B. Linder, *The Harried Leisure Class* (New York, 1970). Professor Linder distinguishes five categories of time: working time; personal working time (maintenance of one's goods and body); consumption time; cultural time; idleness.

[2]Where no statutory regulation or collective agreement prevails, standard or normal hours usually refer to the number of hours per day or per week in excess of which overtime premiums are paid. For an analysis of industrial, regional, and other aspects of standard hours see W. R. Dymond and George Saunders, 'Hours of Work in Canada', in *Hours of Work*, Clyde E. Dankert *et al.* (eds.) (New York, 1965).

TABLE 14

Selected Measures of Working Hours, Selected Industries and Years

| | Standard hours | | | Measure and industry | | | | | Hours paid | | |
| | Major non-ag. industries[a] | | | Hours worked | | | | | | | |
Year	Manufac- turing	Office workers	Non-office workers	Manufac- turing	Construc- tion	Mining	Trade	Employed non-ag. workers[b]	Manufac- turing	Construc- tion	Mining
1870	64.0										
1901	58.6										
1911	56.5										
1921	50.3										
1926	50.2							49.6			
1931	49.6							44.9			
1936	49.2							45.4			
1941	49.0							48.4			
1946	48.7			40.0	40.4	40.4	43.4	42.4	42.7	38.4	42.7
1951	43.6	38.6	43.6	37.9	40.8	40.7	41.3	40.7	41.7	40.3	43.1
1954	42.5			37.0	40.4	41.1	40.9	39.9	40.7	40.3	42.6
1955	42.3			37.3	39.9	40.4	40.8	39.8	41.0	39.9	43.2
1956	42.1			37.5	39.9	39.6	40.8	39.7	41.0	41.1	42.8
1957	41.7	37.9	41.6	37.0	40.2	38.8	40.4	39.5	40.4	42.4	42.3
1958	41.6			37.0	40.0	38.9	40.5	39.3	40.2	41.9	41.4
1959	41.6			37.2	40.1	39.1	40.9	39.4	40.7	41.1	41.3
1960	41.6			37.0	39.7	39.2	40.7	39.1	40.4	41.6	41.6
1961	41.5			36.9	38.8	39.3	40.5	38.9	40.6	40.9	41.8
1962	41.5			36.9	39.6	39.3	40.2	38.8	40.7	40.7	41.7
1963	41.4	37.6	41.3	36.9	39.5	38.3	39.8	38.5	40.8	40.8	42.0
1964	41.2			36.9	39.5	37.2	39.4	38.3	41.0	41.0	42.2
1965	41.1			36.9	39.6	40.1	39.4	38.3	41.1	41.5	42.4
1966				36.8	39.8	40.1	39.2	38.0	40.8	42.2	42.2
1967	40.8	37.6	40.9	36.7	39.4	39.7	39.0	37.9	40.3	41.3	41.9

[a] For coverage, see *Working Conditions ...*, *op. cit.* Roughly, excludes primary industries and construction. 'Office employees' includes clerical, accounting, secretarial, sales, executive, and administrative categories. 'Non-office' includes non-supervisory production and maintenance workers.
[b] 1926-41 – See *Historical Statistics ...*, *op. cit.*, p. 79, for coverage and definitions.
1946-67 – Employed workers, all status, excluding agriculture.

Sources: Standard Hours –
  Manufacturing:
    1870 – O. J. Firestone, *Canada's Economic Development, 1867-1953* (London, 1958).
    1901-51 – Estimates by George Saunders and Syed M. A. Hameed, Economics and Research Branch, Canada Department of Labour.
    1951-65 – Estimates by Economics and Research Branch.
    1967 – Dominion Bureau of Statistics, *Labour Costs in Manufacturing, 1967.*
  Major industries: estimates from *ibid.* by N. Tandan, Dominion Bureau of Statistics. For coverage see 'Technical Notes,' *ibid.*
  Hours Worked –
  Manufacturing, construction, mining, trade:
    Estimates from unpublished data, labour-force survey, prepared by Wolf Illing, Economic Council of Canada in co-operation with John Kuiper, formerly Dominion Bureau of Statistics.
  Employed non-agricultural workers
    1926-41 – *Historical Statistics of Canada*, M. C. Urquhart and K. A. H. Buckley (eds.), Table Series D, pp. 406-11.
    1946-67 – Illing and Kuiper, *op. cit.*
  Hours Paid:
    Dominion Bureau of Statistics, *Review of Man-Hours and Hourly Earnings.*

paid, i.e. hours for which workers are paid whether working or not, including paid holidays, vacations, sick leave, etc. Clearly, it is possible for each of these three measures to exhibit differing trends over time, since each is responsive to a somewhat differing set of determining pressures. However, only fragmentary series, broken in time, scattered by industry or occupation, and varying in definition and coverage, are available. The long-term trend of working hours, pieced together from these fragments, is shown in Table 14.

STANDARD HOURS

The Royal Commission on the Relations of Labour and Capital of 1889 deplored the lack of leisure for the working man, 'leisure in which to acquire the knowledge necessary to fit him to become a more useful tradesman, a more reliable citizen, or a more intelligent being . . . time [for] amusement, recreation and relaxation.' Little wonder the Commissioners took such a view, since the standard work week at that time was probably well over sixty hours. The changes in normal hours that have taken place since the early days of the factory system in Canada may be observed in Table 14. Over the course of the century since Confederation, the standard hours of Canadian factory workers have shrunk from over sixty to roughly forty per week. The dream of increased leisure which so moved the worthy Commissioners has become a reality for most industrial workers in this country. Further, as Table 14 shows, the normal work week of the average office worker today is approximately thirty-seven and a half hours – well below that for most non-office or blue-collar employees.

It will be observed that the most marked decline in weekly norms (in manufacturing) took place in the first two decades of this century and again during the 1940s and 1950s. Between 1901 and 1921, the standard work week declined by over eight hours. During the 1920s and 1930s, however, it shrank by slightly over one hour. From 1941 to 1961 the normal week resumed its rapid descent, falling sharply by seven and a half hours. What little change has occurred since 1961 is due to an increasing number of establishments conforming to the forty-hour or thirty-seven-and-a-half-hour norm rather than to a decline in the standard week itself. It is, however, too early to decide whether the trend to shorter norms has stopped. As we have seen, there have been similar periods of stability in the past followed by rapid reductions in standard hours. Further, as will be noted below, there has been a marked expansion in paid vacations and statutory holidays in recent years which have shortened the work year but are not accounted for in the standard-weekly-hours data.

Some of this long-term decline in standard hours of work is the result of trade-union action. Although many economists are sceptical about the degree of impact of collective bargaining on wages, there is probably wider agreement that unions have had some effect on weekly and annual hours of work, either directly, through negotiated agreements, or indirectly, through political pressure and subsequent labour-standards legislation. Indeed, the chief rallying-point for the early trade unions in this country was the movement for shorter hours. Many of the first city-wide trades and labour councils grew out of the Nine-Hour Leagues of the early 1870s, and the first attempt to form a national federation of unions in Canada stemmed from the famous Toronto Printers' Strike in 1872 – a strike fought over the nine-hour issue.[3] Professor Logan notes that the Trades and Labour Congress 'from its inception took action...consistently for the reduction of hours'.[4] As early as 1887 it advocated an eight-hour day and a five-hour Saturday for workers on all government contracts. 'In the platform of principles, first enunciated in 1898, one of the first planks was a "legal working day of eight hours and six days to the week".'[5] Although unions represented only a very small proportion of the labour force in this country until the late 1930s, the young labour movement, by raising the issue of shorter hours (and, in the case of some of the more powerful craft unions, by striking bargains for shorter hours) created strong expectations and a more receptive environment for the reduction of the work week, which took place during the first two decades of the century.

The effects of government legislation are more difficult to discern. In the latter part of the nineteenth century and the first decades of the twentieth, provincial legislation governing maximum hours of work in mines, factories, and shops was passed, but these laws covered only women and young people. It was not until the twenties and thirties (the decades when, as noted above, standard hours changed very little) that maximum-hours legislation governing the majority of adult male workers was adopted in some Canadian provinces. Federal legislation,

[3]H. A. Logan, *Trade Unions in Canada* (Toronto, 1948), pp. 38-45; Bernard Ostry, 'Conservatives, Liberals and Labour in the 1870's', *The Canadian Historical Review* (June 1960).
[4]Logan, *op. cit.*, p. 64.
[5]*Ibid.*

until very recently (1965), was confined to the regulation of hours of persons employed in the execution of government contracts.

In summary, then, the marked long-term decline in standard working hours in Canada is unmistakable and striking. It has not proceeded at a steady pace and the causal factors that have influenced it are not clear. Unionism and legislative change have probably played some role in transmitting the real choices of workers between leisure and income, as the productive capacity of the Canadian economy expanded over the course of this century.

HOURS WORKED

The hours that individuals in the labour force actually work will be influenced by the norms in the establishment, but also by economic conditions at any given time. In other words, actual hours worked are likely to be more sensitive to cyclical conditions than are standard hours. The effect of cyclical and other short-term changes in demand will, of course, be superimposed on the secular trend to shorter hours, and will therefore be difficult to disentangle in the statistical data. Unfortunately, no information is available in Canada on overtime hours, which are even more sensitive than the actual work week to changing demand conditions. As the market improves, the employer is likely to respond initially by extending hours rather than increasing employment. In the opposite circumstances, expensive overtime will be cut back before workers are laid off. This pattern is clearly observable in the United States, where overtime data are available.[6]

Information on hours worked for four industries and the non-agricultural work force as a whole is displayed in the centre panel of Table 14. As may be seen from these data, hours actually worked have declined over the past twenty years or more, though by varying amounts and at variable rates, for each of the series over the period shown. It would take a keen eye and an active imagination to discern any impact of cyclical conditions on hours of work in any of the four sectors or the economy as a whole. Working hours were evidently not strongly responsive to either the recession of the late 1950s or the long upswing that began in 1961.

It is of interest to note that in the manufacturing sector – the only one for which information on standard as well as actual hours is

[6]See J. Ross Wetzell, 'Current Developments in Factory Overtime', *Monthly Report on the Labour Force* (April 1965), cited in Myron L. Joseph, *Hours of Work Issues*, Reprint No. 293, Institute of Industrial Relations, University of California (Berkeley, 1967).

available – the average hours *actually* worked were consistently below the average *normal* work week throughout the period from 1946 to the present. This does *not* necessarily mean that there was no overtime component in actual working hours during these years. Statistical differences due to the changing weights of different industries, establishments, and occupations in both series would have to be explored before one could determine the reasons for this phenomenon.

Finally, it will be observed that the steepest drop in hours actually worked has occurred in the trade sector: average working hours have declined by well over four per week since the end of the Second World War. To a very considerable degree, this decline in hours represents the effect of the growing proportion of voluntary part-time employment, mainly female, that has characterized this industry and other service-producing industries in the economy. The increasing proportion of the non-agricultural work force in this category of 'voluntary part-time'[7] is thus an important factor in accounting for the over-all reduction in working hours shown in Table 14. Not only have the industries and occupations that tend to employ part-time workers expanded relative to the total number of available jobs, but the supply of workers in the age-sex groups that tend to provide part-time work has also increased relative to the total labour force. These trends will continue as we extend the period of education, encourage earlier retirement, and facilitate the labour-force participation of married women, for it is the younger and older members of the work force and married women who are the principal suppliers of part-time work on a voluntary basis.

HOURS PAID

It will be observed from Table 14 that hours paid are greater than hours worked,[8] and that the gap between the two has grown over the

---

[7]The Labour Force Survey distinguishes between 'economic part-time', which is involuntary and akin to unemployment, and 'usual' part-time, most of which is voluntary. The former is responsive to changing labour-market conditions, while the latter is a secular phenomenon, which has grown markedly since the early 1950s. See Sylvia Ostry, *Unemployment in Canada*, 1961 Census Monograph Programme, Dominion Bureau of Statistics (Ottawa, 1968), pp. 33-5.

[8]The construction data shows hours paid *less* than hours worked for 1946, 1951, and 1954. Conceptually this is impossible. Statistically, anything can happen! Differences in weighting and coverage and a variety of sampling and non-sampling errors can produce stranger results than these in two series drawn from different sources. Multiple-job holding by construction workers, in industries other than construction, *could* raise hours worked above hours paid, but it is doubtful whether this accounted for the very large gap between the two series in 1946.

past two decades. The gap is very much larger for manufacturing workers than for the construction or mining work force, and the latter two industries exhibit very much more variability in both series (and in the gap between the two) than does manufacturing. (The labour-cost implications of these developments are discussed in Chapter VII.)

The growing difference between hours actually worked and hours paid reflects primarily the increase of paid vacations, statutory holidays, and other forms of paid leave in Canadian industry since the end of the Second World War. Before the war, paid leisure was virtually unknown for industrial workers in Canada. By 1968, 96 per cent of non-office workers were in firms providing some paid holidays, and well over 80 per cent of these workers had eight or more holidays during the year.[9] The extension of paid vacations has been equally remarkable. A substantial majority (64 per cent) of non-office workers receive two weeks' paid vacations after one year or less of employment with a firm. Longer-service employees may receive three, four, or even five weeks' vacation: in 1968 two-thirds of industrial workers (excluding those in agriculture) were guaranteed three weeks of paid vacation before completing eleven years of service, and nearly 20 per cent received four weeks after fifteen years.[10] These important fringe benefits, formerly the exclusive privilege of white-collar workers, have become an increasingly important element in the 'total remuneration' of the blue-collar labour force.[11] There has been, in general, a shift from wage to non-wage items in the 'income' of workers, and in particular a shift from money income to leisure. It should be remembered that this leisure has been taken partly in the form of reduced working hours, partly (and increasingly) through holidays and vacations, but also, as was noted in the previous chapter, by means of delayed entry into and hastened exit out of the labour force.

THE EMPLOYMENT POTENTIAL OF
REDUCING WORKING HOURS

Although today a majority of the labour force in Canada is employed in establishments having a standard forty-hour, five-day week, a surprising number of workers still put in very long hours. In 1967 almost

[9]*Working Conditions in Canadian Industry*, 1968, Canada Department of Labour, Economics and Research Branch, Table 1.

[10]*Ibid.*, Table 2.

[11]In 1968, labour costs for paid absence (holidays, vacations, sick leave, personal leave) constituted almost 10 per cent of gross payrolls in manufacturing. See Dominion Bureau of Statistics, *Labour Costs in Manufacturing, 1968*, Table 20.

one-quarter of the non-agricultural labour force worked forty-five hours or more per week and almost 10 per cent worked fifty-five hours or more. These proportions were very much the same as they had been a decade earlier, although the standard work week had declined over the same period. These very long hours of work represent overtime and multiple job holding as well as the habitual work week of persons for whom a norm or standard is purely nominal or non-existent. Because such a substantial number of workers have continued to work such long hours despite changes in standards and economic conditions, the question has often been raised – by the union movement in particular – whether these excess hours can be translated into jobs for unemployed and underemployed workers.

This question, a legitimate and important one, has been much more thoroughly aired in the United States[12] than in Canada, where very little information on the extent and nature of the long work week is available. A special survey, attached to the regular Dominion Bureau of Statistics Labour Force Survey of June 1967, does, however, provide some limited insight into the problem.[13]

That survey revealed that more than one and a half million employees usually worked more than forty hours a week at one job, i.e. that they habitually worked longer than what is today accepted as a standard or normal work week in the Canadian economy (and not because of 'moonlighting'). These workers, nearly 80 per cent of whom were male, tended to be concentrated in particular occupations, industries, and regions. Thus, nearly 40 per cent were in the trade, community, business, and personal-service *industries*; over 40 per cent were in the service and skilled and semi-skilled production *occupations*; 46 per cent were in Quebec and the Atlantic provinces. Finally – and this is perhaps the most surprising fact revealed by the survey – relatively few (only 16 per cent) of these workers reported they were working overtime, and still fewer (just over 6 per cent) had received any overtime pay during the reference week of the survey. In the United States, on the other hand, a similar survey in May 1964 demonstrated that over 30 per cent of workers who usually worked more than forty hours a week received premium pay.

Clearly, what these figures suggest is that the standard work week has not been effectively implemented in a substantial portion of the Canadian economy. Large numbers of workers continue to work very

[12]For an excellent summary, see Joseph, *op. cit.*, and especially the references to the various Subcommittees on Labor, House of Representatives, 88th and 89th Congress of the United States.

[13]The results of this special survey have not yet been published.

long hours for employers who do not thereby incur penalty payments. The poorer regions of the country and, to some extent, the lower-paid industries and occupations carry a disproportionate share of these habitual long-hour workers. The comparison with the United States, cited above, suggests that the legislative or collective-bargaining regulation of hours in this country has had a very limited effect.

Whether or not raising the costs to employers of longer hours would increase job opportunities is difficult to predict. Essentially, what is involved is a comparison of the costs of overtime versus the costs of hiring additional workers, which include search and training costs and fringe benefits. Some overtime may be unavoidable, and hence the alternative may not be new hires but the interruption of production or reduced or poorer-quality service, or even the shrinkage of full-time jobs through a shift to part-time work, which may have happened in retail trade in the United States.[14] Detailed studies of each industry would be required in order to arrive at defensible conclusions in this area.

Another interesting finding of the 1967 special survey was that nearly one-fifth of the long-hour workers regularly worked nights and week ends. This suggests that some sort of rotating-shift arrangement might be effective in translating the extra-long hours into jobs. Again, the key element would be a comparison of alternative costs.

Another group often cited as a potential source of new jobs are the so-called moonlighters – persons holding two or more jobs at the same time. The June 1967 survey showed that there were just over 220,000 of these workers in Canada at that time, or approximately 3 per cent of the employed labour force (up very slightly over the 1960-1 estimate of 2.6 per cent[15] and well under the United States figure of more than 5 per cent).

On average, these moonlighters worked only about fifteen hours a week at their secondary jobs. Most of the unemployed, on the other hand, are looking for full-time jobs. Although conceivably it might be possible, if moonlighting were controlled, to induce employers to convert some of these part-time jobs to full-time jobs (by rearranging work schedules, etc.), it seems highly unlikely that public policy could be effectively implemented in this area. Unions do try to discourage members from dual job-holding in the same industry, since it undercuts wage-rates, but most secondary jobs are in industries other than those

---

[14]Joseph, *op. cit.*, pp. 340-1.

[15]*Multiple Jobholding in Canada, 1960-61*, a joint study by the Dominion Bureau of Statistics and the Department of Labour.

of principal employment. Moonlighting is most common among married males in the twenty-five to forty-four year age group, suggesting it is mainly a consequence of family life-cycle pressures. Its incidence does not appear to be related to the hours of work of the principal job. Indeed, the moonlighting rate was higher among long-hour workers than among those working a standard week or less. Thus, the fear sometimes expressed by policy makers that a reduction in the work week would lead to more dual job-holding, and therefore a reduction in jobs, does not seem realistic. On balance, then, moonlighting does not appear to be a phenomenon closely related to employment levels one way or the other.

The issues involved in this question – the relationship between employment and hours of work – are obviously very complex and, as has been suggested above, too little 'hard' information is available to provide even a tentative answer. Legislative and bargaining pressures can reduce the standard work week, but employers will generally hire additional workers only if that is the least expensive alternative. Further, unless productivity rises as a consequence of the reduction in hours (which, historically, was probably the case as hours were reduced from the very high levels of the early years of this century), real costs will rise and, *ceteris paribus*, output will be reduced. Even if productivity increases do compensate fully for the reduction in hours,[16] this simply means that the same output can be produced with a smaller man-hour input. Effective implementation of hours standards can probably redistribute a given amount of work by transferring real income from the fully employed to the underemployed and unemployed. For social and other reasons, this may be a desirable objective of public policy.[17] But in order to *increase* job opportunities, aggregate demand must be increased. Again, the *distributional* impact of the increment in demand between the presently fully-employed and other workers merits careful investigation.

[16]For a review of the effects of hours reduction on output, see David G. Brown, 'Hours and Output', in Dankert *et al.*, *op. cit.* The burden of evidence, such as it is, suggests that reduction of a work week of between forty and fifty hours will not induce compensatory rises in productivity. See L. G. Reynolds, *Labor Economics and Labor Relations* (New York, 1959). Edward Denison estimates the optimum work week at 48.6 hours (*The Sources of Economic Growth in the United States*, Supplementary Paper No. 13, Committee for Economic Development (1962), p. 40).

[17]However, the economic costs of such a policy should also be considered in an over-all evaluation. See Melvin Reder, 'Hours of Work and the General Welfare', in Dankert *et al.*, *op. cit.* Reder also deals with the equity (distributional) considerations and suggests alternatives to work sharing that are less costly in terms of efficiency.

Mobility in the Labour Market

In a country like Canada the essence of the labour market is change. The economy is characterized by continually shifting patterns of demand for labour, occupationally, industrially, regionally, seasonally, cyclically, and secularly. If the labour market is to function adequately, the supply of labour must be flexible enough to respond to the growth and movement of the economy. In fact, the adjustment process is slow and imperfect, and excess supply and demand for labour exist simultaneously in different markets.

The mobility of labour is not an end in itself, but is desirable in so far as it contributes to basic economic objectives – to allocative efficiency, to a more effective reconciliation of price and employment levels, and to distributional equity. In one sense, however, mobility has value *per se*. If by mobility one means the fundamental freedom to move up the social and economic ladder, or freedom to move (or *not* to move) physically – an 'open' as opposed to a 'stratified' and controlled society – then a basic social value *is* involved. The discussion that follows is very much more restricted than a full treatment of the subject, covering socio-political aspects, would require.[18] Our focus is, quite naturally, on labour-market adjustment, and even within that sphere data deficiencies rule out discussion of a number of important aspects of mobility in Canada.

Most mobility data available for empirical analysis measure selected aspects of an individual's labour-market status – industry, occupation, firm, locality of employment, labour-force attachment – between two points in time. Thus, what is measured is *actual* change or non-change and not the *propensity* to change which would be more meaningful to economists.[19] The distinction between voluntary and involuntary movement which is sometimes made in mobility studies is helpful, but the voluntary type of movement is an inadequate proxy for propensity, since it also reflects many other factors such as opportunities for change, costs of movement, labour-market information, etc.

---

[18]The classic Canadian study of socio-economic aspects of mobility is John Porter, *The Vertical Mosaic* (Toronto, 1965). For some information on intergenerational linkages in educational attainment, see Michel D. Lagacé *Educational Attainment in Canada: Some Regional and Social Aspects*, Special Labour Force Studies No. 7, Dominion Bureau of Statistics (Ottawa, 1968).

[19]See Herbert S. Parnes, 'Labor Force and Labor Markets', in *A Review of Industrial Relations Research*, Woodrow L. Ginsburg *et al.* (eds.) (Madison, 1970), for references to the limited number of studies that have attempted to measure propensity.

In this review we must, of necessity, concentrate entirely on *geographic* mobility because virtually no reliable data have been available on occupational, industrial, or interfirm movement in Canada.[20] Canadian studies of geographic movement have been based on data drawn from four sources: decennial censuses,[21] unemployment-insurance records,[22] family-allowance records,[23] and sample surveys.[24] While a résumé of these studies would be far too lengthy for presentation here – and the references cited are by no means exhaustive, some highlights of the main findings will be presented as they relate to: (a) the correlates of mobility (characteristics of migrants); (b) the extent and nature of mobility; and (c) mobility and the level of economic activity.

THE CORRELATES OF MOBILITY

What are the characteristics of the mobile worker? Some limited answer to this question emerges from the Canadian studies on geographic movement.

Perhaps the clearest finding, common to Canadian and other investigations, is that migrants tend to be younger than the general population. The inverse relationship between mobility rates and age,

[20]A study based on unemployment-insurance records, H. F. Greenway and G. W. Wheatly, 'Movements within the Canadian Insured Population, 1952-6', mimeographed, Dominion Bureau of Statistics (Ottawa, 1960), did provide information on occupational and industrial mobility. Subsequent analysis of the basic records, however, revealed that substantial coding and reporting error, especially of occupations, seriously distorted the mobility rates and rendered much of the information meaningless.

[21]See Leroy O. Stone, *Migration in Canada: Regional Aspects*, 1961 Census Monograph programme, Dominion Bureau of Statistics (Ottawa, 1969). Also another Census Monograph by M. V. George, *Internal Migration in Canada: Demographic Analyses* (Ottawa, 1970). See also John Vanderkamp, 'The Effect of Out-Migration on Regional Employment', *Canadian Journal of Economics* (November 1970).

[22]In addition to the Greenway and Wheatly research cited above, parts of which were published in the *Canadian Statistical Review* (July 1960, November 1961, January 1962, February 1962, and April 1962), forthcoming Special Studies of the Economic Council of Canada will be based on unemployment-insurance data.

[23]See John Vanderkamp, 'Interregional Mobility in Canada: A Study of the Time Pattern of Migration', *Canadian Journal of Economics* (August 1968), and Thomas J. Courchene, 'Interprovincial Migration and Economic Adjustment', *Canadian Journal of Economics* (November 1970).

[24]See May Nickson, *Geographic Mobility in Canada: October 1964 – October 1965*, Special Labour Force Studies No. 4, Dominion Bureau of Statistics (Ottawa, 1967). Two other special surveys, undertaken in conjunction with the Labour Force Survey, dealt with other aspects of mobility, viz. sequential job change (October 1966) and job tenure (October 1967). No published results are yet available.

for the labour-force population of males and females separately, is shown in Table 15, based on sample-survey data. For both sexes mobility rates are highest in the early twenties, although five-year migration rates from 1961 census data[25] display a peak at ages twenty-five to twenty-nine.

The reasons for the inverse association of mobility with age (after twenty) are many. Young workers, who have not yet become committed to a particular job, are more prepared to shop around and shift location in their search for work. The costs of movement, both monetary (especially forgone earnings and loss from sale of homes) and psychic (community and family ties, etc.), are probably lower for younger than for older workers, while the expected benefits, in the form of improved lifetime earnings in a better location, will accrue over a longer time.

In contrast, older workers are more likely to have stronger job attachments, involving accumulated seniority and other rights associated with length of service, as well as stronger family and community ties. The costs of movement, both monetary and psychic, are likely to be higher, while the benefits will not accrue over as long a period.

The youngest group (fourteen to nineteen) includes many who are still attending school full-time and are not yet able to move on their own, although some teen-agers move in order to attend university in another area.

As the data show, the *pattern* of mobility rates by age are similar for males and females, probably because migration involves family moves. The female rates are generally somewhat lower than the male rates (except for teen-agers) but, as the census data showed, the sex differential has narrowed over time.

The survey information further reveals some interesting facts about mobility and household status. One would expect that family heads would be less inclined to move than single persons without family responsibility. This is found to be the case for household heads over thirty-five years of age. For somewhat younger men (twenty-five to

[25]The 1961 census migration data were gathered from a 20 per cent sample of households and based on a response to a question that compared place of residence on June 1, 1956, with that on June 1, 1961. The rates estimated from these data are thus five-year rates and would not take account of moves during that period. All characteristics of individuals relate to 1961, i.e. not to the period at the time of migration. The 1965 survey data (see f.n. 24) were based on response to a similar question concerning residence (October 1964 and October 1965), but also included questions concerning labour-force status at the beginning of the period, i.e. October 1964, as well as an attitudinal question concerning motivation for moving.

TABLE 15

Mobility Rates[1] by Age and Sex for Population 14 and Over: Canada, October 1965

Age	Males	Females
	Percentages	
All ages	6.7	6.2
14-19	5.9	6.8
20-24	15.6	15.1
25-34	11.1	8.9
35-44	5.6	4.8
45-64	3.3	3.2
65 and over	2.5	2.3

[1]Migrants as percentage of total population of group.

Source: Dominion Bureau of Statistics, Special Labour Force Studies, No. 4

thirty-four) there is no difference in mobility rates between heads of households and others, while for the twenty to twenty-four year olds, the most mobile group, the household heads are *more* mobile. Family responsibility evidently tends to decrease mobility for older men but to increase a young family man's efforts to search out better career opportunities. Possibly, too, more of the young single males are still at school and not yet in the labour force full-time.

There appears to be a strong association between mobility and employment status, which has been documented in a number of studies, viz., at any given time the unemployed show higher mobility rates than do the employed. This is not to say that an increase in over-all unemployment will raise over-all mobility, for the opposite is true (see below). But *cross-section* data from surveys or from unemployment-insurance records show strikingly higher mobility rates (both geographic and inter-industry) for the unemployed than for the employed. Further, the mobility rates of those not in the labour force are higher than those of employed persons.

Finally, mobility is strongly associated with certain socio-economic characteristics. Thus, the census five-year migration rates are highest for English-speaking Protestants, while relatively low rates are shown for Jews and French-speaking Roman Catholics. In general, persons with higher levels of education and training are more mobile than the poorly educated and low-skilled.

THE EXTENT AND NATURE OF MOBILITY

There is a great deal of geographic movement in Canada. In international terms, the Canadian population is more mobile than that of most other countries, with the possible exception of the United States.[26]

The 1961 census revealed that 18 per cent of the labour force had changed their municipality of residence between 1956 and 1961. Moreover, these figures understate the actual migration flows over this period since they report only the mobility of surviving movers and ignore multiple and return migration of workers who moved several times or who moved and returned to their original municipality during the five-year period. Evidence from sample-survey data confirms the high over-all mobility rate for Canada. Thus, between October 1964 and October 1965 6.5 per cent of all persons of labour-force age had changed their municipality of residence at least once during the twelve-month period.[27]

Both census and survey data show that most internal migration in Canada takes place within rather than between provinces. Of the five-year migrants in the census 80 per cent had moved within their province of original residence. Similarly, in the period October 1964 to October 1965 over three-quarters of the migrants of labour-force age moved intraprovincially.

It is hardly surprising that most migration is intraprovincial rather than interprovincial in Canada, since, for the most part, although certainly not invariably, the latter moves cover longer distances and are therefore more costly in both monetary and personal terms. The ratio of interprovincial to intraprovincial migration varies from province to province, being considerably higher for provinces in the Atlantic and Prairie regions than for Quebec, Ontario, and British Columbia.[28] For the latter two provinces there is probably less to be gained economically by moving to another region; for Quebec, language and cultural barriers impede movement to other provinces. In the poorer, smaller provinces the spur of economic advantage would tend to encourage movement to other, more prosperous areas.

While the volume of interprovincial flows is dwarfed by comparison with the amount of movement within provinces, it is none the less

[26]International comparisons of mobility rates are hazardous because of differences in classification of areas and time periods. Some estimates of U.S. and Canadian internal migration rates suggest that the former are somewhat higher than ours, while others, based on different data sets, suggest the contrary.

[27]Nickson, *op. cit.*

[28]Economic Council of Canada, *Design for Decision-Making, Eighth Annual Review* (Ottawa, 1971).

substantial, especially in terms of *gross flows*, i.e. the total inflows and outflows across provincial boundaries. This may be seen in Table 16. A large proportion of the inflow to the less prosperous regions – the Atlantic provinces, Quebec, Manitoba, and Saskatchewan – is 'return migration', consisting of movers who were originally from the poorer areas and who, having at some time left the region, decide to return.

The pattern of net interregional migration, shown in Table 16, reflects a long-standing historical situation.[29] The major net flows are into British Columbia in the West and into Ontario in central Canada. Alberta has made net gains since the end of the 1940s. These are the rich and growing areas of the country. The two Prairie provinces experience the largest net outflow followed by Quebec and the Atlantic region. This pattern of net flows suggests that economic motivation – the search for jobs or better jobs – is and has been an important determinant of geographic mobility in Canada.

These data, and a number of studies in Canada and elsewhere, suggest that 'net geographic migration . . . is generally in the direction of greater economic opportunity as measured by differentials in income, in employment opportunities, or both.'[30] Some direct evidence on the motivation underlying migration was provided by the labour-force survey data mentioned earlier. Job-related motives were reported as the main reason for moving by over 60 per cent of the sample of males (seventeen to sixty-four years of age) in 1964-5. A similar survey in the United States reported that job-related reasons accounted for 52 per cent of the migration of this group of males,[31] so it would appear that not only is economic motivation a dominant factor in internal migration in Canada, it is probably a more important factor in this country than in the United States.

The motivation for moving varied with the type of move and with age. Generally, the shorter the move, the more likely it was to be motivated by personal (non-economic) reasons. For longer-distance moves, involving greater cost and risk, economic motivation was dominant.

---

[29]See R. Marvin McInnis, 'Provincial Migration and Differential Economic Opportunity', in Stone, *op. cit.*, Chapter 5. Intercensal net migration rates have been positive for Ontario and British Columbia since the beginning of the century. The Maritimes have consistently had net out-migration over the same period.

[30]Herbert S. Parnes, 'Labor Force Participation and Labor Mobility', *A Review of Industrial Relations Research*, Woodrow L. Ginsburg *et al.* (eds.) (Madison, 1970), Vol. I, p. 59. See for summary of international studies. For Canada, see Courchene, *op. cit.*

[31]See Samuel Saben, 'Geographic Mobility and Employment Status, March 1962-March 1963', *Monthly Labor Review* (Washington, D. C., August 1964).

TABLE 16

Interregional Migration Flows, Male Workers,[1] *1967-8*

Region	Gross flows		Net flows	
	Out-movers	*In-movers*	*Out-movers (negative)*	*In-movers (positive)*
Atlantic	8,940	7,657	1,283	
Quebec	13,912	8,775	5,137	
Ontario	20,453	21,743		1,290
Manitoba/ Saskatchewan	13,808	8,385	5,423	
Alberta	9,000	12,292		3,292
British Columbia	8,887	16,148		7,261

[1]Male income-tax filers.

Source: Economic Council of Canada, *Eighth Annual Review* (1971).

Migration for other than economic reasons was most important for the youngest and oldest men. The young men were often moving with their parents or going away to continue their schooling. The older men included many who were moving on the occasion of retirement from the labour force.

While the desire for economic betterment may stimulate geographic mobility, does moving pay off? Geographic mobility has been analysed as a form of investment in human capital,[32] within a conceptual framework developed for the analysis of education, which will be described in the next chapter. Migration is undertaken at a cost, including not only the actual expense of the move and the non-pecuniary costs but also forgone earnings, and yields a return over the working lifetime of the worker. The decision to migrate should be made, in the light of this analytical framework, only if the present value of anticipated future benefits exceeds the present value of the costs associated with the move. A factor of extreme importance is the role of uncertainty, or lack of information. The worker may have only partial or even misleading information about job opportunities outside his local area.

The evidence concerning the economic return from migration is somewhat mixed. A recent American study concludes that 'the two main migration movements in recent economic history do seem to be

[32]See, for example, Larry A. Sjaastad, 'The Costs and Returns of Human Migration', *Journal of Political Economy* (October 1962), Supplement and references in Parnes, *op. cit.*

associated with higher earnings rates, the movements out of the South and the movement to the urban centers',[33] but other studies are somewhat more guarded in their conclusions.[34]

In Canada, the labour-force survey data showed that migration tended to improve the probability of employment. Thus, of the men who were unemployed in October 1964, a very much higher percentage of those who had migrated than of those who had not migrated had found jobs by October 1965.[35] Other information, derived from income-tax records, showed that the increase in annual income between 1965 and 1968 was greater for workers who moved interprovincially than for those who moved intraprovincially (except for Ontario, where the reverse was true) and that both types of migrants improved their incomes more than did the non-migrants.[36] These are very partial studies, however, and a good deal more analysis is required before we can determine the economic benefits of migration. Moreover, as will be seen in Chapter XII, despite substantial internal migration in this country, much of it in the 'right' economic direction, regional differences in wages have been remarkably persistent over a long period of time.

MOBILITY AND THE LEVEL OF ECONOMIC ACTIVITY

An important question concerns the effect of the over-all level of economic activity on the extent and nature of geographic movement. If, as is suggested above, geographic mobility does play some role in adjusting labour supply to changing patterns of demand – does, in other words, facilitate the adjustment process in the economy – is this role affected by the over-all unemployment rate, and if so, how?

The evidence in this area is both strong and unequivocal.[37] While at any given time the mobility rates of the unemployed are higher than those of the employed (see above), an increase in the over-all level of unemployment tends to: (a) reduce the mobility rate of both the employed and unemployed; (b) reduce the average distance of moves; and (c) lead to more 'return migration' to less prosperous areas.

Thus, the higher the level of unemployment, the less is the amount

[33]John B. Lansing and James N. Morgan, 'The Effects of Geographical Mobility on Income', *The Journal of Human Resources* (Fall, 1967), p. 456.

[34]See Parnes, *op. cit.*, pp. 62-4, for review of findings on this matter.

[35]Nickson, *op. cit.*, p. 12.

[36]Economic Council of Canada, *Eighth Annual Review, op. cit.*

[37]For Canada, see especially Vanderkamp, *op. cit.*, and Courchene, *op. cit.* For review of international studies see Parnes, *op. cit.*

and the poorer is the quality of migration. Unemployment impedes the adjustment processes of the economy and is therefore costly not only in terms of lost output (and human suffering), but also because it creates structural problems by impeding the adaptive processes of the market.

While cyclical fluctuations in economic activity have an adverse effect on geographic mobility, it appears that migration may be 'improving' over time. Courchene presents data to show that distance is less of a deterrent than it used to be (the comparison is for the periods 1952-9 and 1960-7), probably because transportation costs have declined and perhaps information sources have increased and improved.[38] Hence 'for given values of all variables, the migrant will move further than previously . . . migration is becoming more efficient over time.'[39]

In order to explore this finding more thoroughly, one would have to examine the effects on mobility of such factors as pension plans, unionism, occupational licensing, government transfer programs (especially unemployment insurance), labour-standards legislation, and so on. Many of these 'institutional' factors are likely to be mobility-impeding, and as they become more important and widespread one would expect them to affect the secular rate of mobility. A good deal of research remains to be done in this important area of labour-market analysis.

[38]Courchene, *op. cit.*, p. 571.
[39]*Ibid.*

IV

Growth and Change
in Labour Demand

The long-run growth of labour demand depends on the growth of the economy's productive capacity. Our knowledge of the growth process, while still incomplete, has improved considerably over the past few decades,[1] as improved data and methodology have permitted economists to probe more deeply into the subject. Thus, efforts have been made to identify and, where possible, to quantify the contribution of a variety of factors to the growth of productive capacity. The major causes of economic growth appear to be the accumulation of physical capital; technological change (including the growth of new knowledge and its application); the improvement of human resources through better education, training, mobility, and health; and, finally, a range of non-quantifiable but important social and cultural factors which are reflected in changing institutions and in the behaviour of individuals and groups in the society. In a more general way, the sources of growth may be described in terms of changes in the *quantity* of resources (human and non-human); in the *quality* of resources; and in the *efficiency* with which resources are combined in the productive process and in the socio-cultural environment.

The long-run growth in the economy not only determines the overall growth in the demand for labour, it also effects fundamental changes in the pattern of demand. The demand for labour (as for all productive factors) is a derived demand, reflecting the demand for the goods and services that labour helps produce. As the productive capacity of an economy expands, the demand for some commodities grows far more rapidly than others; this, in combination with differential changes in productivity among industries, results in marked

[1] A good deal of the Canadian literature on growth is to be found in the *Annual Reviews* and various Staff and Special Studies of the Economic Council of Canada. See also Thomas A. Wilson and N. Harvey Lithwick, *The Sources of Economic Growth*, Studies of the Royal Commission on Taxation (Ottawa, 1968), No. 24.

shifts in the relative importance of different industries and, through invention and technology, in the creation of entirely new industries and linked groups of industries, e.g. automobiles and all the industries spawned by the car; television, and its constellation of ever-expanding activities; etc. These shifts (which, it should be noted, have themselves been an important source of growth in the past) are clearly apparent in the changing industrial composition of the labour force over time. Further, these changes in industrial activity also affect the occupational structure of the working population because, of course, the kind of work people do (occupation) differs somewhat in different industries, although there are some activities common to all industries. The occupational 'mix' of the work force is also affected by other aspects of economic growth – by changing technology (the *way* people work) and by improvements in and extension of education and training (the *skill* with which people perform given tasks). Nor are these changes independent of each other; for example, an increase in the supply of one type of labour will, via changes in the price of this factor relative to close substitutes, induce substitution of the now-cheaper for more expensive types of labour or even for other, non-labour factors. Thus, in the long run, growth and change are inextricably interwoven, as are, of course, supply and demand. The changes in the composition of the labour force that will be described below are both consequence and cause of growth. Our measures represent the complex interaction of supply and demand over the long sweep of development of the Canadian economy.

In this chapter, we will briefly trace the major long-run shifts in the industrial, occupational, and educational structure of the Canadian labour force. (The industrial and occupational structure of wages are discussed in later chapters.) The great interest in the 'human-capital' approach to education justifies a short digression to describe some Canadian research in this area. Finally, the chapter will conclude with a closer look at some aspects of economic growth during the post-war period, which in terms of historical experience has been one of unusually high activity in Canada. An appendix deals with the problem of measurement of labour demand: we use the labour force as a proxy in lieu of any other presently available alternative.

Long-run Changes in Industrial and Occupational Composition

As has been stated above, the changes that occur in the industrial distribution of the labour force reflect a wide complex of forces shaping the final demand for goods and services (and, hence, the derived demand for labour) as well as the technical relationships of production in, and the productivity of, individual industries. There is, further, a continued interplay between changes in demand and changes in supply; in some periods independent developments on the supply side may, by affecting relative prices and by means of inter- and intra-factor substitution, play an important role in refashioning the pattern of labour-force development. Thus, for example, the massive immigration of unskilled labour at the beginning of the century was reflected in structural changes of the work force. Over the long run the most important element on the side of supply has been the extension of public education, to be discussed shortly. The effect of technology is, of course, pervasive, leaving its imprint in the form of new industries and new occupations.

INDUSTRY

Research into the long-run development of many countries and of the same country at different stages of growth has revealed a common pattern of development. That these principles of growth constitute one of the hardiest generalizations in economics is attested to by the observation of Sir William Petty in 1691 that 'there is much more to be gained by Manufacture than by Husbandry; and by Merchandise than by Manufacture . . .' and the assertion, more than two and a half centuries later, by Colin Clark, that: 'A wide, simple and far-reaching generalization is to the effect that, as time goes on and communities become more economically advanced, the numbers engaged in agriculture tend to decline relative to the numbers in manufacture, which in turn decline relative to the numbers engaged in service.'[2]

Unfortunately, data restrictions preclude any but the briefest outline of these changes in terms of the industrial deployment,[3] but to some extent these same developments are also illustrated by occupational trends for which the information is very much richer.

From Table 17 it is apparent that the major changes in the indus-

[2]Colin Clark, *The Conditions of Economic Progress* (London, 1957), p. 492. Quote from Sir William Petty cited in Clark, *ibid.* See also Simon Kuznets, 'Quantitative Aspects of the Economic Growth of Nations, II: Industrial Distribution of National Product and Labour Force', in *Economic Development and Cultural Change*, Supplement (July 1957), and *Modern Economic Growth* (New Haven, 1966).

[3]A set of historical estimates back to 1911 have been prepared by R. Marvin McInnis, Queen's University. See 'The Industry Structure of the Canadian Work Force: Long-Run National Changes', mimeo., presented to the Annual Meeting of the Canadian Economics Association (Winnipeg, June 3-6, 1970).

TABLE 17

Labour Force Distribution by Major Industry Group, 1931-61

Industry	1931		1941		1951		1961	
	Number 000's	*Per cent*	*Number* 000's	*Per cent*	*Number* 000's	*Per cent*	*Number* 000's	*Per cent*
Total civilian labour force	3,917.6	100.0	4,196.0	100.0	5,214.9	100.0	6,342.3	100.0
Primary	1,293.3	33.0	1,320.6	31.5	1,111.7	21.3	903.3	14.2
Agriculture	1,124.0	28.7	1,082.3	25.8	827.2	15.9	640.4	10.1
Forestry and fishing	97.5	2.5	145.0	3.5	180.6	3.5	143.6	2.3
Mining	71.8	1.8	93.3	2.2	103.9	2.0	119.3	1.9
Secondary	1,093.5	27.9	1,209.9	28.8	1,717.1	32.9	1,963.1	31.0
Manufacturing	800.0	20.4	983.9	23.4	1,364.7	26.2	1,494.7	23.6
Construction	293.5	7.5	226.0	5.4	352.4	6.7	468.4	7.4
Tertiary	1,530.4	39.1	1,657.4	39.5	2,328.8	44.7	3,344.1	52.7
Electricity, gas and water	28.1	0.7	25.9	0.6	62.0	1.2	70.5	1.1
Transportation and communication	317.0	8.1	292.3	7.0	433.5	8.3	500.2	7.9
Trade	395.6	10.1	468.4	11.2	711.3	13.6	931.8	14.7
Finance	93.1	2.4	90.4	2.2	144.2	2.8	229.7	3.6
Community and business service	251.4	6.4	277.7	6.6	431.2	8.3	764.4	12.1
Government service	100.8	2.6	117.2	2.8	203.5	3.9	363.3	5.7
Recreation service	18.8	0.5	17.7	0.4	28.7	0.6	39.8	0.6
Personal service	325.6	8.3	367.9	8.8	314.4	6.0	444.4	7.0
Industry not stated	0.5	0.0	8.0	0.2	57.2	1.1	132.0	2.1

Source: Noah M. Meltz, *Changes in the Occupational Distribution of the Canadian Labour Force, 1931-1961* (Ottawa, 1965), Table A-5. Reproduced with the permission of Information Canada.

trial dimensions of the Canadian work force over the past three inter-censal decades have been the drastic decline in agriculture, especially after 1941, and the impressive rise in the service-producing or tertiary industries: trade, finance, transportation, government, recreation, personal, business, health, and educational services, and so on. (It should be noted that the tertiary group of industries provides the major source of employment for women workers.) The changes in the relative share of the goods-producing or secondary industries have been much more moderate, showing a modest upward drift until 1951. More current data, from the Labour Force Survey, based on a slightly different classification (Table 18), reveal a continuation of these trends: further marked decline in agriculture, a virtual 'plateau-ing' in the secondary sector, and continued expansion in the tertiary or service-producing industries. This same pattern, with minor varia-tions, is characteristic of all advanced countries. In the United States today, six out of every ten workers are employed in the service-pro-ducing industries, and it is expected that by 1980 the number will rise to seven out of ten.[4]

The decline in agricultural employment is a result both of a very marked rise in output per man or man-hour associated with substantial capital investment, increased farm size, and improvements in other 'inputs' such as fertilizers, pest control, seed and livestock strains, etc., and of a slow rate of growth in the per-capita demand for food prod-ucts, particularly in the developed countries of the world. In the econo-mist's terminology, the income elasticity of demand for agricultural output is very low and productivity growth is very rapid. Where the opposite conditions prevail, i.e. where productivity improvements are small[5] while income elasticities of demand are very high, as is likely in many of the service-producing sectors, employment growth will be very rapid. In recent years, increases in demand for government-pro-vided services, especially education, health, and social welfare, which are not subject to the cost-reducing discipline of a competitive market, have contributed significantly to the rapid growth of the tertiary sector.[6] Some of the increase in service employment, moreover, is

[4] See 'The United States Economy in 1980', *Monthly Labor Review*, U. S. Department of Labor, Bureau of Labor Statistics (April 1970).

[5] There are formidable problems of measurement of output and productivity in the service sector. See *Production and Productivity in the Service Industries*, Victor R. Fuchs (ed.) Studies in Income and Wealth, No. 34, National Bureau of Economic Re-search (New York, 1969).

[6] Employment in the 'public' sector (including government proper and government-supported agencies and institutions) grew from 20 per cent to almost 33 per cent of total employment between 1947 and 1965. See Donald Gow, 'Earnings Trends and Wage Determination in the Public Sector', mimeo., Task Force on Labour Relations

TABLE 18

Percentage Distribution of the Experienced Labour Force by Industry,
Annual Averages, 1961-9

Industry	Year								
	1961	1962	1963	1964	1965	1966	1967	1968	1969
All industries	100.0	100.0	100.0	100.0	100.0	100.0	100.0	100.0	100.0
Primary	14.3	13.6	13.1	12.5	12.1	10.8	10.5	10.3	9.7
Agriculture	10.8	10.3	9.9	9.3	8.5	7.5	7.4	7.1	6.7
Forestry	1.9	1.6	1.6	1.5	1.3	1.2	1.2	1.2	1.2
Fishing and trapping	0.3	0.4	0.5	0.4	0.4	0.4	0.4	0.4	0.3
Mines, quarries, oil wells	1.3	1.4	1.2	1.3	1.9	1.7	1.5	1.6	1.5
Secondary	31.3	31.3	31.4	31.7	31.1	31.8	30.9	30.1	30.2
Manufacturing	24.0	24.1	24.3	24.9	23.8	24.4	23.9	23.3	23.5
Construction	7.3	7.2	7.1	6.8	7.3	7.4	7.0	6.8	6.7
Tertiary	54.4	55.1	55.5	55.8	56.8	57.4	58.6	59.6	60.1
Transportation, communication and other utilities	9.4	9.5	9.4	8.9	9.0	8.7	9.0	8.9	8.9
Trade	16.6	16.6	16.4	16.6	16.5	16.4	16.4	16.6	16.5
Finance, insurance and real estate	3.8	3.8	3.8	3.9	4.0	4.1	4.1	4.2	4.4
Community, business and personal service / Public administration and defence	24.6	25.3	25.8	26.4	27.3	28.2	29.1	29.9	30.3

Source: Labour Force Survey: unpublished annual averages.

related to the increase in output of the secondary industries, as workers are required to distribute and service the ever-increasing stream of goods, especially consumer durables, produced by the highly productive manufacturing sector. In more general (and admittedly oversimplified) terms, then, the dramatic changes in the industrial mix of the labour force depicted in Tables 17 and 18 stem from marked divergences between the income elasticities of demand and productivity in the broad industrial sectors of the economy. An analysis of more detailed information, over a longer sweep of time, would of course, bring into play a wider range of explanatory factors to enrich this *simpliste* approach.

OCCUPATION

A different and, for our purposes, in many ways a more revealing[7] classification of the labour force is in terms of occupation rather than industry. In principle, occupational designations are based on the *nature of the work performed.* This means that the chief requirement of an analytically useful classification system, from an economist's point of view,[8] is that occupational categories be technically homogeneous, i.e. the employer regards any worker within a particular category as pretty well substitutable for any other.[9] But occupational classifications should also tell us something about the degree of skill needed to perform the necessary tasks satisfactorily, because a major concern of manpower analysis is with the educational and training requirements of jobs and like characteristics of workers.[10] Unfortu-

---

(Ottawa, 1968). During the decade of the fifties and sixties, expenditure by all levels of government grew from less than one-quarter to nearly one-third of the gross national product. See Economic Council of Canada, *Sixth Annual Review* (Ottawa, 1969), Chapter 3.

[7]Occupational data reflect in a more penetrating fashion both the underlying technological changes in the economy and the characteristics of jobs which, according to economic theory, are of most significance in determining wage rates and therefore the allocative mechanisms of the labour market.

[8]Sociologists are also, of course, very concerned with occupational data but from a different vantage point than that of economists. The focus of much sociological analysis has been with the study of social mobility and the notion of social class. Other matters of great interest to sociologists, which also involve the use of occupational information, deal with the social organization of work and interpersonal relations in work situations.

[9]In technical terms the cross-elasticities of substitution of workers *within* jobs in a particular category should be greater than the cross-elasticities of substitution of workers *between* job categories.

[10]Since occupational data are used to classify jobs and workers, an analytically useful system should be linked to technical considerations (demand) and worker characteristics (supply). The movement of workers among jobs is governed by preferences and by education and training. Tastes and preferences are not directly measurable, but education

nately, the Canadian system of classification has focused entirely (and not entirely successfully) on the criterion of work performed and has ignored the notion of skill requirements. Moreover, in early censuses industrial and occupational designations were blurred and confused, and while the system has improved in more recent decades, the occupational categories are still not free from industrial designations. Finally, the classification has changed for each census since 1861, which makes long-run trend analysis a very difficult and hazardous task indeed! That Canadians are not alone in this dire condition, and that, in some respects, the world changes very little, is best illustrated by a quote from Charles Booth, writing about the British occupational statistics at the end of the nineteenth century:

> ... there is such a want of fixity of principle or method, that even competent authorities have been seriously misled regarding the apparent results. Possibly these changes were to a large extent necessary or unavoidable, but surely attention might have been drawn to them and some explanation given, instead of which there is not so much as a footnote. The seeker after information is left to grope his way in the dark; if by chance he stumbles on the truth, well and good, if not he but adds his quota to the enormous total of false information before the public.[11]

The long-run occupational trends depicted in Table 19 represent a good deal of digging and patching and pasting of historical census data (groping in the dark is perhaps too strong!). But because the major changes in composition were so radical and sweeping, their outline emerges clearly despite the inadequacies of the underlying information.

The growth of the Canadian labour force over this century has been characterized by two massive occupational shifts – obviously related to the industrial shifts described above: a marked shift away from agricultural pursuits and a decisive movement toward white-collar jobs. The effect of long-run distributional changes on the relative shares of blue-collar and manual occupations has been virtually negligible by

---

and training are – although not without difficulty. On the supply side, then, the system should aim for categories for which the cross-elasticities of supply within categories are higher than the cross-elasticities of supply between categories. The skill measure should be directed at the *functional* requirements of the job. The new Canadian Classification and Dictionary of Occupations (C.C.D.O.), first implemented in the 1971 census, makes some provision for identifying general educational and specific vocational-training requirements for each job title identified in the Dictionary. For a very informative discussion of some of these matters see Sidney A. Fine, *Use of the Dictionary of Occupational Titles to Estimate Educational Investment*, Upjohn Institute (Kalamazoo, 1968). Cf. G. Cain *et al.*, 'Occupational Classification: An Economic Approach', *Monthly Labor Review*, (February 1967).

[11]*Journal of the Statistical Society of London* (June 1886).

comparison. The full significance of this transformation of the work force is perhaps best grasped initially by visual means such as the bar diagram in Figure 3. Superimposed on the present distribution is that distribution as it would have been if the labour force had simply grown on the basis of the 1901 occupational configuration. If the 1901 patterns had been frozen for the past seventy years there would have been over three and a quarter million farmers and farm workers in Canada today instead of barely half a million. On the other hand, there would have been only one and a quarter million white-collar workers instead of the over three and a half million at present in the Canadian working population. Clearly, as the work force has expanded since 1901, an enormous shift has taken place – a shift among industries, as we have already seen, but also a shift in the occupational structure of the work force within industries. It is far beyond the scope of this chapter to examine these changes in any detail,[12] but some brief observations on the decade-by-decade patterns are not amiss. It might also be well to note that while our interest lies in outlining the main features of long-run, secular change, the decennial census data also reflect changes arising from fluctuations in the level of business activity. The business cycle not only has a differential impact by industry (and, hence, indirectly by occupation), but, since employers tend to hire or lay off production workers much more readily than they do supervisory, professional, and clerical staff, directly affects the occupational composition of employment within industries.

While the major shifts in the job-content of the Canadian economy are well known and, of course, by no means confined to this country, what is less familiar, perhaps, is that these changes have not evolved in a smooth and steady fashion over the course of the past six decades or more. This is apparent even in the case of the dramatic and persistent shift out of agriculture. Thus, the numbers engaged in farming continued to grow for the first three decades of this century, which included the great 'wheat phase' of Canadian history, although at a pace outstripped from the beginning by those in the population with other occupational attachments. The much steeper fall of the agricultural share after 1941[13] reflects the combined effects of the relative and the absolute decline of agricultural occupations, a con-

[12]See Noah M. Meltz, *Changes in the Occupational Composition of the Canadian Labour Force, 1931-1961* (Ottawa, 1965), and Sylvia Ostry, *Occupational Composition*, 1961 Census Monograph Programme, Dominion Bureau of Statistics (Ottawa, 1967).

[13]During the 1930s, the wheat economy of the west was seriously damaged, not only by the collapse of world wheat markets, but by severe drought, especially in Saskatchewan. However, the non-farm sector was in the throes of the Great Depression, so that movement off the farm was discouraged and, indeed, some 'back flow' probably occurred.

TABLE 19

Percentage Distribution of the Labour Force, 15 Years of Age and Over[a], by Occupation Division, as of 1951, and Sex, for Canada[b]: 1901 to 1961 Censuses

Note.— 'Gainfully occupied' rather than 'labour force' concept used prior to 1951. See 1961 *Census of Canada*, Bulletin 3.1-1, Tables 3, 3A, and Introduction.

Occupation division (as of 1951)	1901 T	1901 M	1901 F	1911 T	1911 M	1911 F	1921 T	1921 M	1921 F
All occupations	100.0	100.0	100.0	100.0	100.0	100.0	100.0	100.0	100.0
White collar occupations	15.3	14.0	23.6	17.0	14.9	30.5	25.3	21.1	48.3
Proprietary and managerial	4.3	4.8	1.2	4.7	5.2	1.6	7.3	8.2	2.0
Professional	4.6	3.1	14.7	3.8	2.4	12.7	5.4	3.0	19.1
Clerical	3.2	2.9	5.3	3.8	3.0	9.4	6.9	4.7	18.7
Commercial	3.1 {	3.2 {	2.4 }	4.4	4.1	6.7	5.1	4.5	8.4
Financial				0.3	0.3	d	0.6	0.7	0.1
Blue collar occupations	27.8	27.5	30.1	30.3	30.9	26.3	25.8	27.2	17.9
Manufacturing and mechanical	15.9	13.8	29.6	13.6	11.7	26.2	11.4	10.3	17.8
Construction	4.7	5.4	d	4.8	5.5	d	4.7	5.5	d
Labourers[e]	7.2	8.2	0.5	11.9	13.7	0.1	9.7	11.4	0.1
Primary occupations	44.3	50.5	3.8	39.5	44.8	4.5	36.2	42.1	3.7
Agricultural	40.3	45.9	3.8	34.4	39.0	4.4	32.6	37.9	3.7
Fishing, hunting and trapping	1.5	1.8	d	1.3	1.5	0.1	0.9	1.1	d
Logging	0.9	1.0	—	1.5	1.8	—	1.2	1.4	—
Mining and quarrying	1.6	1.8	—	2.3	2.6	d	1.5	1.7	d
Transportation and communication	4.4	5.0	0.5	5.6	6.3	1.5	5.5	5.9	3.0
Service	8.2	2.9	42.0	7.6	3.1	37.2	7.0	3.5	26.8
Personal	7.8	2.6	42.0	7.3	2.8	37.1	5.8	2.1	25.8
Not stated occupations	—	—	—	—	—	—	0.2	0.2	0.3

Occupation division (as of 1951)	1931			1941[c]			1951			1961		
	T	M	F	T	M	F	T	M	F	T	M	F
All occupations	100.0	100.0	100.0	100.0	100.0	100.0	100.0	100.0	100.0	100.0	100.0	100.0
White collar occupations	24.5	20.2	45.4	25.3	20.5	44.7	32.0	25.4	55.4	37.9	30.6	57.3
Proprietary and managerial	5.6	6.4	1.6	5.4	6.2	2.0	7.4	8.7	3.0	7.8	9.6	2.9
Professional	6.1	3.7	17.8	6.7	4.5	15.6	7.3	5.3	14.4	9.8	7.7	15.5
Clerical	6.7	4.4	17.7	7.2	4.5	18.3	10.7	5.9	27.5	12.7	6.7	28.6
Commercial	5.4	4.8	8.3	5.4	4.5	8.7	6.0	4.7	10.4	6.8	5.6	10.0
Financial	0.7	0.9	0.1	0.6	0.7	0.1	0.6	0.7	0.1	0.8	1.0	0.2
Blue collar occupations	27.5	30.2	14.5	27.1	29.6	16.8	29.4	33.0	16.5	26.6	32.4	11.1
Manufacturing and mechanical	11.6	11.3	12.7	16.1	16.2	15.4	17.2	17.9	14.6	16.1	18.4	9.9
Construction	4.7	5.7	d	4.7	5.8	d	5.5	7.1	0.1	5.2	7.1	d
Labourers[e]	11.3	13.2	1.7	6.3	7.6	1.4	6.6	8.0	1.8	5.3	6.9	1.2
Primary occupations	32.4	38.2	3.7	30.5	37.5	2.3	19.8	24.6	2.8	12.8	16.1	4.3
Agricultural	28.6	33.7	3.6	25.7	31.5	2.3	15.7	19.3	2.8	10.0	12.2	4.3
Fishing, hunting and trapping	1.2	1.4	0.1	1.2	1.5	d	1.0	1.3	d	0.6	0.8	d
Logging	1.1	1.3	—	1.9	2.3	d	1.9	2.5	d	1.2	1.7	d
Mining and quarrying	1.5	1.8	—	1.7	2.1	d	1.2	1.6	d	1.0	1.4	d
Transportation and communication	6.3	7.1	2.4	6.4	7.5	1.7	7.8	9.2	2.9	7.7	9.7	2.2
Service	9.3	4.2	33.9	10.5	4.6	34.3	9.8	6.5	21.2	12.4	8.5	22.6
Personal	8.2	3.0	33.8	9.3	3.2	34.2	7.2	3.3	21.0	9.1	4.2	22.1
Not stated occupations	d	d	d	0.2	0.3	0.2	1.2	1.3	1.2	2.6	2.7	2.5

[a] 10 years and over in 1901.
[b] Excluding Yukon and Northwest Territories: including Newfoundland in 1951 and 1961.
[c] Excluding persons on active service, June 1941.
[d] Less than 0.05%.
[e] Labourers in all industries except those engaged in agriculture, fishing, logging or mining.

Source: Based on data from *Census of Canada*, 1901 to 1961.

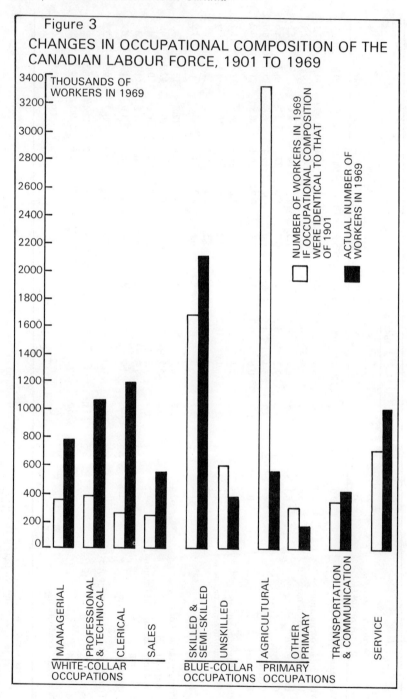

Figure 3

CHANGES IN OCCUPATIONAL COMPOSITION OF THE
CANADIAN LABOUR FORCE, 1901 TO 1969

sequence of expanding off-farm job opportunities, at income levels well above those provided by agriculture, which siphoned off the increasing numbers of the rural population made redundant by the enhanced pace of mechanization and of other improvements in farm production during those years. During the 1960s (Table 20), the agricultural share of occupations continued its steep descent, falling from just over 10 per cent to less than 7 per cent by 1969.

As in the case of agricultural occupations, the growth path of the white-collar group has scarcely been smooth and steady. The pattern was marked by two phases of rapid expansion, one in the second decade of the century, straddling the First World War, and the more recent period, from 1941 to the present, which was initiated by the Second World War. Between 1921 and 1941, however, the white-collar occupations barely kept pace with the growth of the total work force, and hence their labour-force share remained fairly constant throughout the 1920s and 1930s.

It is worth while pointing out that the decade of the 1940s appears in retrospect as a watershed in the transformation of the work force of this country. By 1951, for the first time in our history, the census recorded a smaller number of workers in primary occupations than in manual pursuits: the age of industrialism had arrived! But by 1951 the manual workers were themselves outnumbered by the white-collar work force. Together the professionals, managers, clerks, and salesmen formed the largest single occupational sector of the working population. Since then, the pre-eminence of the white-collar worker has become ever more pronounced. The seed of the post-industrial society was already planted at the time industrial Canada came of age.

Within the major division of white-collar occupations there was a good deal of similarity in the growth patterns of the component groups. The striking advance of the sector as a whole between 1941 and 1961 was in considerable degree attributable to the proliferation of clerical occupations, largely as a consequence of changes in the scale and type of business operations which brought with them the so-called 'paperwork revolution', and to the expansion of governmental activities. It is worth noting that the growth of the clerical group of occupations was accompanied by a radical transformation of the sex composition of the work force: in 1901, 20 per cent of the clerical group was female, but in 1961, 60 per cent was female.

The professional group, which advanced very rapidly during the intercensal decade of the 1950s – indeed, led the list of expanding occupations between 1951 and 1961, had been growing at a much slower pace over most of the earlier part of the century except for a spurt

TABLE 20

Percentage Distribution of the Experienced Labour Force by Occupation, Annual Averages, 1961-9

Occupation	Year								
	1961	1962	1963	1964	1965	1966	1967	1968	1969
All occupations	100.0	100.0	100.0	100.0	100.0	100.0	100.0	100.0	100.0
White collar	38.1	39.1	39.2	39.6	40.2	41.6	41.8	42.8	43.6
Managerial	8.8	8.9	8.9	8.9	9.0	9.1	9.1	9.1	9.3
Professional and technical	9.3	10.1	10.1	10.2	11.1	11.9	12.1	12.5	12.9
Clerical	12.8	12.9	13.1	13.1	13.2	13.9	13.9	14.4	14.6
Sales	7.2	7.1	7.1	7.3	6.9	6.6	6.7	6.8	6.8
Blue collar	30.8	30.7	30.8	30.5	30.9	31.6	31.2	30.5	30.4
Craftsmen, production process, and related workers	24.8	25.1	25.3	25.0	25.5	26.3	26.5	25.8	25.9
Labourers and unskilled workers	6.0	5.6	5.6	5.6	5.4	5.3	4.7	4.7	4.5
Primary	13.4	12.7	12.3	11.6	10.9	9.8	9.6	9.2	8.5
Farmers and farm workers	10.8	10.3	10.0	9.3	8.5	7.6	7.5	7.2	6.7
Loggers and related workers / Fishermen, trappers, and hunters	1.8	1.6	1.6	1.5	1.3	1.3	1.3	1.2	1.1
Miners, quarrymen, and related workers	0.8	0.8	0.7	0.8	1.1	0.9	0.8	0.8	0.7
Transportation and communication	7.0	6.7	6.6	6.6	6.4	5.7	5.6	5.5	5.4
Service and recreation	10.7	10.8	11.1	11.7	11.6	11.3	11.8	12.0	12.1

Source: Labour Force Survey (unpublished data).

forward between 1911 and 1921, mainly as a consequence of the federal government's war-time role. A roughly similar pattern of change is observed for the proprietary and managerial group, but *within* this group there have been conflicting growth trends, with the independent proprietors declining in importance as the managerial occupations have grown with the growth of the modern corporate form of industrial organization and the expansion of government. In neither of these two white-collar groups have women made any significant inroads over the past six or more decades, in marked contrast to the clerical occupations and the commercial and financial occupations, which have shown a fairly steady, though modest, pace of growth over the six decades, and an increasing 'feminization'. The proportion of women in this occupational group rose from about 10 per cent at the turn of the century to almost 50 per cent today.

As Table 20 reveals, while the share of the white-collar sector continued to rise during the 1960s, this is mainly because of a sustained growth in the professional and technical occupations. The slow-down in growth for clerical and especially sales occupations suggests that the strength and direction of the longer-run secular forces, at least as they have been operating since the end of the Second World War, may be undergoing change. Technological developments in the field of computer and other forms of office and communication equipment may have had some effect in limiting employment for certain types of clerical workers, just as changing merchandising techniques may have damped down the growth in the sales work force despite the very substantial expansion in the volume of trade.

As is apparent from Tables 19 and 20, the blue-collar share of the Canadian labour force today is not strikingly different from that at the outset of the century. Within the blue-collar division, however, the component occupation groups have exhibited marked – and markedly divergent – variations in growth-rates over this period. The rapid growth of the unskilled sector in the opening decade of this century (from just over 7 to almost 12 per cent) reflects in very large degree the massive impact of immigration from central and eastern Europe. Too much emphasis should not be placed on the more modest changes in this category recorded by the censuses of 1921 and 1931, since the unskilled tended to be treated as a residual category in census classification. The years of the Great Depression, however, witnessed a precipitate decline in the numbers of unskilled workers, and despite a temporary halting in the shrinkage of their labour-force share, induced by the war-time boom in manufacturing and construction, the decline was resumed during the 1950s and 1960s, largely as a consequence of changing technology which resulted in continuing substitution of machines for unskilled manual labour. The proportion of the unskilled today is less than 5 per cent of the work force; there is only limited scope for further decline.

A somewhat different growth pattern was exhibited by the largest component group in the blue-collar division: the skilled and semi-skilled manual workers (the census classification system, unfortunately, does not permit us to distinguish between the two).[14] A steady shrinkage in their labour-force share until 1931 was sharply reversed by the onset of the Second World War, and in the two decades following 1941 this group of occupations (found primarily in the manufacturing and construction industries) expanded at a slightly quicker pace than did the total labour force. This occupational group is especially sensitive to fluctuations in the level of economic activity, as may be observed by the effects on the growth-rate of the economic slow-down of the late fifties and early sixties (Table 20). The cyclical sensitivity of these occupations makes it more difficult to discern the trends underlying the changes in their labour-force share in recent years. Analysis is further impeded by the inadequacies of the data base. The skilled construction occupations as a group have maintained a fairly stable share of the total labour force over the entire period,[15] although within this group, of course, individual occupations have no doubt experienced wide variation in growth-rates as a consequence of changes in construction methods, materials used, and consumer tastes. The information on skilled trades in manufacturing is too patchy to trace any long-run trend, although it is possible to discern, at least in the 1951-61 decade, an increasing proportion of supervisory workers, inspectors and foremen. In most industries, mechanization, standardization, and mass production have required closer supervision not only of men but of goods and machines. This may, however, be a temporary development *en route* to fully automated processing which includes quality control of output. Finally, more sophisticated technology

---

[14]A different and, in many vital respects, more meaningful classification system of occupations has been developed by J. G. Scoville and applied to data from the 1941, 1951, and 1961 censuses: Dominion Bureau of Statistics, *The Job Content of the Canadian Economy, 1941, 1951, and 1961*, Special Labour Force Studies No. 3 (Ottawa, 1967). Scoville's analysis reveals that the skill and training requirements of occupations – the 'job content level', as he terms it – of the Canadian labour force as a whole rose between 1941 and 1961 as higher-level jobs increased their relative share of employment. See also Ontario Department of Treasury and Economics, *Trends in Job Families and Educational Achievement of the Ontario Labour Force* (Toronto, 1969). This study uses the Scoville approach to analyse and project the job content of the Ontario labour force.

[15]Ostry, *Occupational Composition.* Construction occupations were identified as a separate group until the 1961 census.

has likely eroded semi-skilled employment in manufacturing in the post-war period, but once again the data are too fragile to demonstrate this effect.

Of the remaining two major occupational divisions, the transportation and communications occupations exhibited a small but steady growth in share over the first six decades of the century but have tapered off slightly in recent years. The service group of occupations, as may be seen from Tables 19 and 20, has been increasing its share of the labour force since the 1920s, except for a slight decline in the 1941-51 decade. Within this group as a whole, government, business, and community-service occupations have claimed a growing share relative to personal-service occupations over the entire period, except during the Great Depression when the numbers of service workers (of whom the vast majority were in the personal-service occupations) grew more rapidly than any other occupational group except manufacturing and mechanical occupations. This shift into personal-service activities during the depression has been observed in many countries, and some portion of it may be considered a form of disguised or hidden underemployment. During the war and early post-war years, the numbers in personal service declined, but they more than recovered this loss by 1961 as a consequence of above-average growth during the fifties. (Perhaps some part of the growth in personal-service occupations in the late fifties and early sixties may have been due to lack of higher-paying alternative job opportunities.)

Finally, it is worth commenting on the sex composition of this occupational group. In 1901 more than two-fifths of all female jobs were in service occupations. Even today these occupations account for more than one-fifth of the female work force. Low-paid personal-service occupations are still, to a considerable degree, though less than formerly, a female preserve.[16]

In conclusion, then, the major broad changes that have occurred in the occupational deployment of the Canadian work force over the course of this century have been a drastic shrinkage in farming pursuits and in unskilled manual labour and a dramatic proliferation of white-collar work – professional, technical, clerical, commercial, and managerial. A continuation of these trends, at a more moderate pace, is projected over the seventies.[17] Once we move below the level of broad occupational sectors to an examination of more detailed job

[16]For a more detailed analysis of the changing sex composition of occupations as well as other structural aspects of intra-occupational change see *ibid.*, Chapter 4.

[17]B. Ahamad, *A Projection of Manpower Requirements by Occupation in 1975*, Department of Manpower and Immigration (Ottawa, 1969).

categories, however, it is both more difficult to trace the long-run, changing patterns and to estimate the future requirements. As we have pointed out, the occupational composition of the labour force reflects changes in labour supply as well as demand. As requirements change, the occupational choices of workers are refashioned in accordance with these changing requirements. Since the process of adjustment is highly imperfect, however, and, in any case, never instantaneous, at any given time shortages or surpluses of particular groups of workers will arise and the market will register these disequilibria in a variety of ways – persistent job vacancies, persistent unemployment, changes in relative wages. One path to facilitating more effective adjustment of labour supply to demand is to increase the flexibility of labour through improved general education. Specific manpower policy provides another approach to the problem of improving and supplementing the defective allocative mechanisms of labour markets. We shall turn, now, to an examination of the changing educational structure of the work force and, in a later chapter, will review the major developments in Canadian manpower policy.

Education

Changes in occupational structure are sometimes cited as evidence of the changing quality of the work force. At best they are equivocal in this respect, and no effort has been made here to assess them in these terms. A more direct, though by no means fully satisfactory, mode of evaluating 'quality' changes is through measures of the educational level of the working population, including formal education as well as technical, vocational, and on-job training. Unfortunately, Canada is poorly served by data in this crucially important area, though no more so than most countries, and it must be remembered that there are ten different provincial systems of schooling to consider as well as the problems connected with the often radically differing experiences of the substantial immigrant population.

Little reliable historical data measuring even formal educational attainment on a consistent basis are available.[18] A reasonably effective

[18]For an examination of the census data on the educational level of the major occupation groups from 1931 to 1961, see Ostry, *Occupational Composition*. For an historical analysis using a broader range of data sources, see also Gordon W. Bertram, *The Contribution of Education to Economic Growth*, Staff Study No. 12, Economic Council of Canada (Ottawa, 1965).

alternative to 'piecing together' the historical data is the use of current statistics, using age classifications, to give some notion of changes over time. In Table 21, the Canadian population in selected age categories is distributed according to level of education – years of formal schooling – in a recent year (1969). Each of the six cohorts completed its education and entered the labour force at a different period in this century. Hence, the differences in level of education between successively younger cohorts provide a reasonably good guide to the changing quality of labour supply (or potential supply) over the past half-century or so in Canada. As a rough measure of changes in level of education, we use the percentage difference in the proportion who completed secondary schooling or better.

It may be seen that, while there have been improvements in the quality of Canada's working population over the past six decades or more, the rate of progress in this respect was marked in the earlier part of the century, no doubt because of the low base level from which the calculation is derived. A more marked improvement may be observed for those who completed their education during the Great Depression than during the 1940s, perhaps because in the former decade massive unemployment induced some, at least, to stay on at school rather than venture into the uninviting world of work. The experience of the post-war period has been one of sustained improvement, greater for males than for females, with the 1960s showing the biggest spurt forward since the early years of the century. Perhaps the progress in education in this country over the course of our history is best summarized by some startling comparative statistics: over 40 per cent of Canadians born around 1900 failed to finish primary school, while today 52 per cent of the young Canadians who enter the labour force have completed secondary school or better.

Further progress in education is expected throughout the seventies. Rising enrolment and higher completion rates suggest that nearly all young people will complete secondary school by the end of the decade. Further, by 1980-1 it is expected that one-third of Canada's eighteen-to twenty-four-year-olds will be attending full-time university or college, compared with 5 per cent in 1955-6.[19] This will help to narrow the still-substantial gap in both educational level and university enrolment ratios between Canada and the United States.[20]

---

[19] For a full analysis of these projections see Z. E. Zsigmond and C. J. Wenaas, *Enrolment in Educational Institutions by Province: 1951-52 to 1980-81*, Staff Study No. 25, Economic Council of Canada (Ottawa, 1970).

[20] *Ibid.* It is projected that the Canada–United States disparity will disappear at the elementary and secondary level and continue to narrow at the university level.

TABLE 21

Improvements in Educational Level of Population, by Sex: Canada, Pre-1920 to Present

Age of cohort in 1969	Period in which cohort was born	Period in which cohort probably finished school	Improvement in educational level[a]		
			Both sexes	Male	Female
65 and over	Around beginning of century	Before 1920	—	—	—
55-64	1905-14	During 1920s	46.7	51.0	44.5
45-54	1915-24	During 1930s	19.0	23.8	14.8
35-44	1925-34	During 1940s	10.2	12.9	8.3
25-34	1935-44	During 1950s	23.7	21.4	26.0
20-24	1945-49	During 1960s	29.6	31.4	27.9

[a] Percentage increase in proportion of cohort with completed secondary schooling or better.

Source: Based on data from Dominion Bureau of Statistics, 'Supplement to Labour Force Survey', January 1969 (unpublished).

Viewed in terms of the acquisition of formal education, the quality of Canada's labour supply has clearly improved markedly over the long run. Of course, our measure of quality is grossly inadequate: years of formal schooling are, at best, a plausible but inadequate proxy for this phenomenon. The stock of vocational and occupational training, both formal and informal (i.e. acquired on the job), is also a vitally important (and perhaps even more directly relevant) aspect of labour quality, but virtually no information is available on worker-training in Canada.[21] The quality of the work force is also strongly affected by

[21] A special survey, conducted by the Dominion Bureau of Statistics in November 1966 in conjunction with the monthly Labour Force Survey, yielded some limited data which have, however, never been published. An estimate, derived from this survey, suggests that less than one-quarter of the Canadian labour force had received formal vocational or technical training (defined, in the Survey, as completing a course of at least three-months' duration in normal school, teachers' college, school of nursing, trade or apprenticeship, institute of technology, business school, correspondence course, or armed services). A roughly comparable survey in the United States (for April 1963) showed that nearly 40 per cent of the U. S. labour force had taken formal job training: U. S. Department of Labor, *Formal Occupational Training of Adult Workers* (Washington,

improvements in health, stemming from better medical services, sanitation, etc. In point of fact, and we shall be discussing this shortly, the notion of labour-force 'quality' is closely related to the idea of 'investment' in human resources, which has the effect, among other things, of increasing the productive capacity of the individual worker.

Before turning to the investment aspects of education, it is useful to point out that the changing educational composition of the Canadian labour force, in common with other compositional changes we have treated, is both consequence and cause of economic growth and reflects changing factors of both demand and supply. On the demand side, as the industrial pattern of output changes, thereby affecting occupational requirements, these in turn affect the demand for particular levels of and combinations of education and training. Thus the forces shaping the level and composition of economic output also feed through the system and shape the educational mix. But education itself is a causal factor in the growth process. A growing number of studies in several countries have suggested that education makes a significant contribution to growth-rates and living standards. The seminal work in this area of analysis, Edward Denison's *The Sources of Economic Growth in the United States and the Alternatives before Us,* and his more recent study *Why Growth Rates Differ* documented the proposition for the United States and other countries. Employing Denison's methodology and assumptions, a parallel Canadian study[22] concluded that roughly one-quarter of the increase in real per-capita income over the period 1911 to 1961 was attributable to the increased educational stock in the labour force.

Finally, it remains to note that individual decisions to acquire education, especially high-level education, are essentially long-run decisions (and strongly affected by social as well as economic factors as we have seen), so that supply responds with some lag (and often some considerable cost to the individual) to the changing requirements of industry. These lags and 'temporary' maladjustments provide a major rationale for manpower policy and manpower planning. However, success in this area is difficult to cite. In recent decades, government

---

1964). Further comparison of the Canadian–United States data suggests that the 'gap' in training between the two countries is probably wider than it is in formal education. In both countries the amount of training is positively associated with the level of formal schooling.

[22]Bertram, *op. cit.* For an international comparison of the Canadian post-war experience, see also Dorothy Walters, *Canadian Income Levels and Growth,* Staff Study No. 23, Economic Council of Canada (Ottawa, 1968).

policy, which has poured increasing resources into educational and training activity, has strongly influenced the supply of highly educated manpower. In large part this policy was premised on the view that there would be large and persistent shortages in the supply of these people. More recently, however, increasing concern is being expressed about serious surpluses in high-level manpower, and, at the time of writing, there is some evidence of a tendency to temper the policy of encouraging, through public subsidy, advanced levels of post-secondary training. The requisite data and analytical base for effective manpower planning have yet to be developed, however. The problem is exacerbated in Canada because education is entirely under provincial jurisdiction.

EDUCATION AS INVESTMENT IN HUMAN CAPITAL:
DIGRESSION

As is the case with most 'new' concepts in economic doctrine, the genealogy of the notion of human capital – linked most closely to Theodore Schultz and Gary Becker – can be traced well back in time, usually to Adam Smith, certainly to Alfred Marshall. But the full flowering of the conceptual and empirical exploration of the idea is a recent phenomenon, of the decade of the 1960s, which witnessed an outpouring of literature on education, training, health, mobility, information search, etc., as *investment* phenomena which greatly enhance the capacity of humans as *producers* and are undertaken *for that reason* (if not solely, then significantly).[23]

Because in recent decades so much of the investment in human capital, in contrast with physical capital, has taken place in the public rather than the private sector (education, training, health, labour-market information, mobility have all become increasingly government-financed), a good deal of the analysis of the phenomenon has been concerned with public-policy issues. Indeed, a parallel development of the 1960s, the proliferation of cost-benefit studies in the human-resources area,[24] is closely linked to the analyses of private and public rates of return on investment in education.

[23]A very useful compendium of the 'state of the art' at the beginning of the decade is to be found in *The Journal of Political Economy*, Supplement (October 1962). The articles cover all the major areas: education, health, on-job training, migration, labour-market information, as well as theoretical aspects of the subject. While much more empirical work has been produced since the *J. P. E.* survey, the main boundaries of the subject have not been significantly altered. See, however, Jacob Mincer, 'The Distribution of Labor Incomes: A Survey with Special Reference to the Human Capital Approach', *Journal of Economic Literature* (March 1970).

[24]For an excellent collection of articles on this subject see *Cost-Benefit Analysis of*

The economic aspects of education are twofold: there is a consumption component, consisting not only of present consumption, but, much more importantly, of future consumption (education is like a very durable consumer-durable), and an investment component, consisting of the acquisition of skills and knowledge that can be sold in the market at a price. The consumption aspects of education have received far less attention from economists than have the investment components. Indeed, the durable-consumption component of education – the contribution of a flow of services enhancing lifetime real income – is not measured at all in the economic accounts. Economists have chosen to acknowledge the existence of consumption aspects and then proceeded to focus attention entirely on the investment component. Further, most economic analyses of investment in education merely mention, but do not pursue, the 'external' effects of education,[25] i.e. the effects on persons other than the individual beneficiary, although public support for education is premised – most often implicitly and not as a consequence of specific empirical analysis which, admittedly, would be extremely difficult – on the belief that these externalities are large and benign. Finally, although it is recognized that many factors other than education, i.e. other than investment in human capital, affect earnings, factors such as intelligence, ambition, the home environment, etc., which are themselves closely correlated with educational attainment, many studies have either ignored them or simply introduced arbitrary adjustment procedures, because it is so difficult to secure appropriate data to 'adjust' for the effects of these and other relevant variables.[26]

The purpose of this brief section is simply to review some of the Canadian studies on investment in education, but it is hoped that the reader will be stimulated to read further in the large and growing literature on human-resource questions that is being produced in the

---

Manpower Policies, G. G. Somers and W. D. Wood (eds.), Industrial Relations Centre, Queen's University (Kingston, 1969).

[25]Cf., however, Burton Weisbrod article, in *Journal of Political Economy*, Supplement, *op. cit.*, and his *External Benefits of Public Education* (Princeton, 1964), and 'On the Monetary Value of Education's Intergeneration Effects' (with William J. Swift), *Journal of Political Economy* (December 1965).

[26]Cf. Denison, *op. cit.*, who *assumes* that 60 per cent of the observed earnings differentials among groups classified by education arise *as a result* of differences in educational levels. He himself comments on the largely arbitrary nature of the assumption. It was, in fact, derived from a study of 2,759 high-school graduates from three states who graduated over thirty years ago and were largely selected from high-performing or high-I.Q. groups. For a much more elaborate multivariate study see J. N. Morgan *et al.*, *Income and Welfare in the United States* (New York, 1962). Using fourteen explanatory variables they were able to explain only 35 per cent of the variance in income. However, education was the most powerful explanatory variable.

United States,[27] the United Kingdom,[28] and elsewhere.[29]

A major reason for the small number of Canadian studies on education as investment is the paucity of relevant data. As Miss Jenny Podoluk points out in her own study,[30] the first in this area, the requisite data (by no means ideal) were available for the first time from the 1961 census. Miss Podoluk deals only with *private* rates of return of males.[31] Estimated private costs of secondary schooling consisted of two items: books and the *earnings forgone* by the student, who instead of continuing his education could have been earning an income from employment. The private costs of university consisted of forgone earnings (minus scholarships) plus tuition, books, and transportation. In both instances, of course, forgone earnings – opportunity costs, in economists' terms – are by far the largest element of private cost. It should be noted that the study assumed that all private costs of education were investment costs, i.e. no consumption elements in education were considered. Forgone earnings were estimated from cross-section data on income from employment classified by sex, age, and schooling: for high-school students the income forgone was assumed to be best approximated by the earnings of workers with only elementary education, and for university students the estimates were based on earnings of high-school graduates in the relevant age group, adjusted for summer earnings of university students but not for taxes. These estimates of costs utilized a standard methodology followed, with only minor variation, in all similar studies. The fact that the methodology is standard is dictated less by its theoretical acceptability than by its empirical feasibility, i.e. lack of information usually precludes more refined estimating procedures. We will return to this point below.

The difference between private and social costs (the Podoluk study treated only the former) consists of: public expenditure on education

---

[27]An excellent source of material in the United States may be found in the *Journal of Human Resources*, published by the University of Wisconsin and started in 1965.

[28]Of particular interest are the publications and reprints of the Unit for Economic and Statistical Studies on Higher Education, London School of Economics and Political Science.

[29]For a bibliography of studies in a number of countries see Theodore W. Schultz, *The Economic Value of Education* (New York, 1963), and M. Blaug, 'The Rate of Return on Investment in Education in Great Britain', *Manchester School* (September 1965), who cites studies made in the Soviet Union (in 1924!), Mexico, Chile, Venezuela, and Israel.

[30]J. R. Podoluk, *Earnings and Education*, Dominion Bureau of Statistics (Ottawa, 1965). This was an advance release from her census monograph, *Incomes of Canadians*.

[31]Lifetime earnings (unadjusted and discounted) are also estimated for different occupations and levels of schooling. Despite theoretical (and computational) objections to internal rates of return, they are used for ease of presentation.

with respect to depreciation and interest on capital equipment; salaries of teachers and auxiliary staff; land rent; materials such as stationery, books, and other supplies. The return to public investment will, therefore, not be identical to that for the private individual, whose chief cost is earnings forgone (which is, of course, also a cost to the public in terms of lost output, unless the economy is operating at less than full employment, in which case forgone output may be viewed as forgone potential output). Since higher education is heavily subsidized in most countries – and Canada is no exception – the social return on investment in education is likely to be considerably lower than the private return (over all and especially for certain occupations; see below) unless external (third-party) benefits are large and positive. Unfortunately, the external effects are difficult to quantify; even if quantifiable, difficult or impossible to monetize and often incommensurable.

The cost estimates as described above involve a major assumption, i.e. that earnings forgone by students at a given level of education can be reasonably approximated by estimates based on earnings of employed persons at the immediately preceding level of education.[32] It has been pointed out, with some cogency in the view of this author, that this is a questionable assumption since 'students differ systematically from non-students, characteristically having richer, better connected, more highly educated parents, being of above average intelligence and more highly motivated.'[33] While it is, of course, possible to make some arbitrary adjustment (upward) to forgone-earnings estimates, this skirts the more fundamental issue (one that pervades the entire exercise, and not any single calculation) that social and political, i.e. *value*, considerations are involved in the 'investment in education' approach and not simply more or less sophisticated or ingenious mathematical computations.[34]

As mentioned above, cost estimates follow a standard methodology in most studies. Estimates on the benefit side, however, display more variation. It is beyond the intention of this brief section to explore the differing approaches, but it is worth mentioning that there are three major types: discounted (net) present value of lifetime earnings; bene-

---

[32]Various adjustments can be made for unemployment risk, part-time earnings, tax, etc. But these are of an essentially minor nature.

[33]Stephen Merrett, 'The Rate of Return to Education: A Critique', *Oxford Economic Papers* (November 1966), p. 290. Another common criticism of forgone earnings estimates suggests that if students were working rather than at school, the wage rates of the particular cohort would be lowered. But in advanced countries, at least, only marginal changes are being considered and this criticism is not valid. It may be, however, for 'revolutionary' changes in developing countries.

[34]For a cogent expression of this view see Neil W. Chamberlain, 'Some Further Thoughts on the Concept of Human Capital', in Somers and Wood, *op. cit.*

fit/cost ratios; internal rates of return.[35] We will concentrate only on the latter, i.e. rates of return. The Podoluk study, again employing a standard methodology, uses cross-section estimates of employment income by age, and assumes that the differences between lifetime earnings of cohorts with differing levels of education reflect (result from) differences in schooling. The internal rate of return is the discount rate that yields a present value of zero for the net income stream derived from additional education or, alternatively, equalizes the present value of total benefits and total costs. It is possible to use before-tax or after-tax earnings or income from employment and to make other adjustments (for mortality and participation), but these are essentially minor variations on a theme.

More telling is the assumption made with respect to the importance of factors other than education (ability, drive, home background, motivation, market imperfections, etc.) which might account for the differences in earnings streams between cohorts with differing levels of educational attainment. The Podoluk study attributes 100 per cent of the difference in earnings streams to education and derives an estimate of just over 16 per cent return to secondary schooling and close to 20 per cent return to a university degree. Using the (arbitrary) Denison assumption that 40 per cent of the difference arises from other factors would reduce these estimates very considerably. This will be illustrated below with results from the Stager study.

Apart from the problem alluded to above – that many factors other than education, but closely associated with educational attainment, affect differential earnings streams (see Chapters X, XI, and XII on wage structures in Canada) – there are several other difficulties associated with the standard methodology of human-resource investment analysis. Thus, as Miss Podoluk notes, 'a ... serious limitation of the ... analysis is that it is based on cross-sectional data secured at one point in time. Substantial increases have occurred in earnings in recent decades, whether measured in current dollars or in real terms. Adjustments should (possibly) be made for the probable secular growth in earnings.'[36] Further, as she points out, such adjustments should take

---

[35]For a useful review (in articles containing Canadian material) see Bruce W. Wilkinson, 'Present Values of Lifetime Earnings for Different Occupations', *Journal of Political Economy* (December 1966), and his *Studies in the Economics of Education*, Occasional Paper No. 4, Economics and Research Branch, Department of Labour (Ottawa, 1965); David Stager, 'Monetary Returns to Post-Secondary Education in Ontario, 1960-64', mimeographed, paper presented to the Société Canadienne de Science Economique at the University of Ottawa, October 1968, Department of Political Economy, University of Toronto; Ian Drummond, 'Labour Markets and Educational Planning', in *The Canadian Labour Market*, Arthur Kruger and Noah Meltz (eds.) (Toronto, 1968).
[36]Podoluk, *op. cit.*, p. 65.

into account future changes in occupational or skill differentials. Others have pointed out that on-job training, an important factor leading to higher earnings, is ignored in these estimates of rates of return. If, as some United States evidence suggests, investment in on-job training is positively associated with investment in academic education, some portion of the observed differential in earnings streams should be attributed to this form of investment rather than to formal schooling.[37]

Another Canadian study, by David Stager,[38] provides additional insight into the area of investment in education by extending the estimation of returns (measured in terms of net present values, benefit-cost ratios, and internal rates) from a social as well as a private vantage; before and after taxes; for males and females separately; and for different types of post-secondary education. The estimates relate to the province of Ontario for the period 1960-4. Again, constraints of space dictate a meagre selection of Stager's findings, and the interested reader should consult the original work to appreciate the comprehensiveness of its scope. We shall confine ourselves, as before, to internal-rates-of-return estimates simply to illustrate three points: (a) differences between private and social return; (b) effects of differing assumptions concerning the proportion of earnings differentials resulting from education; and (c) variation in rates of return to different types of post-secondary schooling.[39]

The Stager study shows, among other things, that social returns to post-secondary schooling in Ontario are generally lower than private returns, and both types of estimates are strongly affected by the assumption made with respect to the proportion of differential earnings attributed to education. Thus, in 1961, assuming 100 per cent of the differential stems from schooling, social returns were 12.5 per cent compared with 15.4 per cent return to private individuals. The social rate drops to 9.4 per cent if it is assumed that two-thirds of the differential results from education, and to 8.6 per cent assuming 60 per cent from education. The respective private rates drop to 11.7 per cent and 11.0 per cent. These are all, of course, pretty hefty figures. But, being average or aggregate estimates, they mask considerable variation by

[37]See Jacob Mincer, 'On-the-Job Training: Costs, Returns, and Implications', in *Journal of Political Economy*, Supplement, *op. cit.*

[38]*Op. cit.* See also his 'Some Economic Aspects of Alternative Systems of Post-Secondary Education', mimeographed, paper presented at the Seventh Canadian Conference on Educational Research, Victoria, January 1969, Department of Political Economy, University of Toronto.

[39]Drummond, *op. cit.*, also provides estimates (of cost-benefit ratios) to differing types (degrees or occupations) of post-secondary education, but much of his underlying data is so questionable that the results are not worth reproducing here.

faculty and institution. Thus, the private rates range from over 30 per cent for dentistry to around 10 per cent for education, less than 1 per cent for social work, and zero for theology (for which profession, one hopes, the psychic returns are sufficiently high to compensate). This wide variation in returns (the reasons for which require analysis) points up the danger of generalizing on the basis of aggregate figures with respect to public-policy decision.

Bruce Wilkinson, in a study that also examines interoccupational variations in earnings streams, suggests that 'variations in ability, on- and off-the-job training, knowledge regarding opportunities in the jobs with larger returns, unemployment rates for persons of different skill levels, and perhaps variations in bargaining power or tradition-based wage salary scales' are possible important explanatory factors.[40] Similar variation, and similar explanation, are proffered in the study by Ian Drummond who stresses the importance of combining the cost-benefit approach – or rates of return – with manpower forecasting for 'effective' educational and manpower planning.[41]

This brief summary of some of the Canadian literature on education as an investment is presented to illustrate that such an approach can illuminate aspects of the allocative mechanism of the labour market and of public-policy issues in an important social area. One would hope that this analysis will be extended to cover non-academic and non-formal training to broaden our understanding of the market and of evaluation of the policy-making process. It would be dangerous, however, to claim too much for the methodology. Key problems in the field of education, relevant to public-policy issues, also require attention. Some of these questions concern the fundamental issue of equality of educational opportunity and the issue of fiscal equity (who pays, who benefits),[42] to which is related the question of alternative methods

[40]Wilkinson, *Journal of Political Economy, op. cit.*, p. 569. He also examines intra-occupational variation in earnings streams from diverse amounts of education and finds it to be far smaller.

[41]Drummond, *op. cit.*, pp. 286-9. See also W. G. Harman, *Three Approaches to Educational Resource Allocation*, Institute for the Quantitative Analysis of Social and Economic Policy (University of Toronto, 1968). For a useful review of projection techniques see Ozay Mehmet, *Methods of Forecasting Manpower Requirements*, Ontario Department of Labour (Toronto, 1965).

[42]This issue has been receiving a good deal of attention in the United States recently. In particular, see W. Lee Hansen and Burton Weisbrod, *Benefits, Costs and Finance of Public Higher Education* (Chicago, 1969). For some Canadian data see Richard W. Judy, *On the Income Redistributive Effects of Public Aid to Higher Education in Canada*, Institute for Policy Analysis (University of Toronto, 1969). See also Systems Research Group, *Cost and Benefit Study of Post-Secondary Education in the Province of Ontario, 1968-1969* (Toronto, 1971).

of financing post-secondary education and training;[43] the development of real output measures of different levels of the educational system;[44] the design and evaluation of experimental programs to test the effectiveness of alternative methods of producing educational services.[45] The largely unresolved problems of manpower projections and manpower planning, already mentioned, deserve an important place on this list. Readers seeking research topics in the field of education in Canada will find plenty of uncultivated – and potentially very fertile – terrain!

This concludes our exposition and analysis of the major features of long-run growth and change in Canada as they have left their imprint on the composition of the labour force. We now turn, rather more briefly, to a concluding note on more recent growth patterns.

A Note on Recent Growth

Viewed from a long-run perspective, growth-rates in Canada during recent years have been unusually high. The average annual percentage change in real output, estimated at 3½ per cent over the past century, had reached more than 5 per cent during the long upswing of the 1960s. This was partly attributable to faster growth in employment, at about 2½ per cent per year compared with only about 1½ per cent per year over the preceding three decades. In addition, productivity, measured in terms of output per employed person, rose from about 2 per cent to over 2½ per cent a year. Because population growth has also been rapid, per-capita output has risen somewhat less than total output. None the less, the rise in output per head of population in post-war

---

[43]For an excellent Canadian study in this area see Gail Cook and David Stager, *Student Financial Assistance Programs*, Institute for the Quantitative Analysis of Social and Economic Policy (University of Toronto, 1969). See also Douglas G. Hartle, *Financing Education: the Major Alternatives*, Institute for the Quantitative Analysis of Social and Economic Policy (University of Toronto, 1968).

[44]In the United States a National Assessment of Education is now under way. It will provide some continuing information on the knowledge and basic intellectual skills of a sample of the population. Despite its limitations, it represents a major step in the direction of attempting to measure some portion or aspect of 'real' output. For a discussion of some of the issues involved in measuring output see David Stager, 'Measuring the Output of Educational Institutions', in Kruger and Meltz, *op. cit.*, and D. A. Dawson, *Educational Quality Indices*, Working Paper 70-07, Department of Economics, McMaster University (Hamilton, 1970).

[45]For an excellent presentation of the arguments favouring this approach, see Alice M. Rivlin, *Systematic Thinking and Social Action*, Brookings Institution (Washington, 1971).

Canada has been remarkable and unprecedented in our history. Real G.N.P. per capita is now almost triple the level of the late 1920s.

Over the post-war period as a whole, however, the growth process has been highly uneven. Indeed, variability – both temporally and across industries (and occupations) – is a hallmark of growth. The main outline of the temporal and industrial pattern is easily described, although the underlying detail and causal nexus are, of course, exceedingly complex. Only the briefest of summaries of the record of post-war growth is presented here. The interested reader will find a more comprehensive treatment in the annual reviews and various staff and special studies of the Economic Council of Canada.

The years immediately following the Second World War (1946-53) were characterized by consistently high employment and sustained increases in productivity and total output, a consequence of strong external and domestic demand forces and expansionary monetary and fiscal policies. By the middle and late 1950s, many of these special and highly favourable expansionary forces had lost strength. A factor of great importance was the loss of momentum in the United States' economy. The period 1954-7 was transitional: marked by somewhat higher unemployment, slower gains in productivity and output, and some deterioration in Canada's international position, it was followed by a period of serious stagnation, lasting from 1958 until the early sixties. Along with large-scale unemployment (averaging, at the national level, close to 7 per cent) other strains and weaknesses in the economy were exposed as productivity lagged and Canada's competitive position weakened further. Public debates and concern focused on the source and nature of Canada's high unemployment and on the most effective policies to deal with it.

The early sixties brought another turning-point, ushering in an era of long-term expansion and growth, the longest peace-time expansion in Canadian history. This 'golden age' (which didn't quite survive untarnished to the end of the decade) was characterized by a strong thrust in the growth of aggregate supply, the manpower aspects of which consisted mainly of the flood of new entrants – the children of the 'baby boom' of the 1940s, whose entry had been delayed by more extended schooling – and of middle-aged and older married women, who entered the labour market in increasing numbers. The enlargement of total demand was the corresponding side of the equation, without which the high growth-rates in employment could not have been sustained. Major expansion in consumer incomes and expenditure, in public-sector spending on services and social capital, and in exports provided the necessary conditions for high growth performance. By the end of the decade, however, domestic sources of growth had largely ebbed away (a consequence, in the main, of restrictive monetary and fiscal policy), and the main source of strength was external demand, fed by an undervalued currency. The seventies were ushered in with rising unemployment and moderating, but uncomfortably high, price pressures.

The powerful expansion of aggregate demand over the long upswing of the sixties stimulated impressive gains in total employment: over one and three-quarter million workers between 1961 and 1969. Of course the composition of the increased demand affected the industrial and occupational distribution of the over-all increment (see Table 22).[46] Thus, for example, despite above-average rises in the demand for new machinery and equipment, non-residential construction, and exports, which provided a stimulus to the lagging manufacturing and construction industries, substantial improvements in productivity resulted in a modest slippage in their share of total employment. The sharp advance in government expenditure for goods and services during most of the period was reflected in the rapid growth of employment in community services (43 per cent of the increment of new jobs) and in the expansion of the professional and technical groups (25 per cent of the increment). As may also be seen from Table 22, the female share of additional employment almost matched the male portion and nearly one-quarter of the incremental growth was in voluntary part-time work, largely female.

FACTORS UNDERLYING GROWTH

The main factors underlying Canadian growth from 1950 to 1967[47] are summarized in Table 23. It may be seen that the most important source of growth in each of the three sub-periods (and over the entire seventeen-year span) was the increase in factor inputs, accounting for around 60 per cent of the total growth. The growth of labour resources[48] was

---

[46]The base year chosen for the data in Table 22 is 1961 rather than 1960 because occupation and industry data are not available on a comparable classification basis prior to 1961.

[47]This section is based on Dorothy Walters, *Canadian Growth Revisited: 1950-1967*, Staff Study No. 28, Economic Council of Canada (Ottawa, 1970). (See also her earlier Staff Study No. 23.)

[48]Most of the contribution to growth from labour resources stemmed from growth in employment. Hours of work declined throughout the period and, therefore, exerted a (small) negative effect on output. The effects of age-sex changes were negligible and educational improvements were positive but modest in each of the three sub-periods. For the detailed estimates see Walters, *op. cit.* (1970), Tables 2 and 3.

TABLE 22

Percentage Distribution of Employment Increase, 1961-9

	Distribution of employed, 1961	Percentage of new jobs 1961-69
Total employed	100.0	100.0
Industry		
Primary	14.2	−6.6
Secondary	30.2	27.4
Manufacturing	24.0	21.3
Construction	6.2	6.1
Tertiary		
Transportation, communication, and other utilities	9.3	7.5
Trade	16.9	15.5
Finance, insurance, and real estate	3.9	6.5
Community, business, and personal service	19.5	42.9
Public administration and defence	5.9	6.8
Occupation		
White collar	39.8	61.4
Managerial	9.2	10.9
Professional and technical	9.9	25.5
Clerical	13.3	20.1
Sales	7.4	4.9
Blue collar	29.2	30.8
Craftsmen, production process, and related workers	24.2	29.9
Labourers and unskilled workers	5.0	0.9
Primary	13.5	−8.8
Transportation and communication	6.8	0.4
Service and recreation	10.9	16.2
Sex		
Male	72.4	51.6
Female	27.6	48.4
Labour-force attachment		
Full-time [a]	92.1	75.5
Part-time [b]	7.9	24.5

[a] Usually work 35 hours or more.
[b] Usually work less than 35 hours.

Source: Labour Force Survey.

TABLE 23

Distribution of the Contribution of Factor Inputs and Output Per Unit of Input to Growth of Net National Income: Canada, 1950-67

Source of Growth	1950-5	1955-62	1962-7
	per cent		
Net national income	100	100	100
Factor inputs	59	56	62
Labour	25	37	45
Capital	33	19	17
Output per unit of input	41	44	38
Improved allocation of resources	21	10	8
Economies of scale	12	13	12
Residual sources of growth	9	21	17

Note: May not add due to rounding.

Source: Walters (1970), *op. cit.*

more important in the middle and third period than in the early fifties, when Canada experienced a major investment boom. The relative importance of capital was almost twice as great in the earlier period than in the more recent years.

While expansion of factor inputs was the dominant 'cause' underlying growth in output, as Table 23 demonstrates, enhancement of productivity (output per unit of input) accounted for some 40 per cent of Canadian growth over the post-war period, rather more in the earlier years and less in the upswing of the 1960s. The main reason for the decline in the contribution of productivity as the period progressed was the narrowing scope for improvement stemming from reallocation of resources, i.e. the farm–non-farm shift and the movement out of small non-farm family business.

It is of some interest to place the Canadian experience in an international context. The Canadian growth-rate over this period was somewhat higher than that in the United States, much higher than in the United Kingdom, but well below that in Germany and lagging far behind the rate of that star performer in the international growth league, Japan. Sources of growth showed marked international differences as well. In both Canada and the United States, the major contribution derived from growth in factor inputs. In western Europe, on the other hand, improvements in productivity were more important, accounting for more than 60 per cent of growth.

TECHNOLOGICAL CHANGE

This analysis of growth does not, cannot, isolate the effects of technological change, which is a basic pervasive factor affecting productivity, i.e. the efficiency with which resources are combined in the production of output. The influence of innovation is also masked, to some degree, in the estimates of the contribution of capital and labour, and lurks, unidentified, in the 'residual'. But technological change is of special interest to the manpower analyst. Whatever the over-all contribution to growth and rising living standards, technological change will inevitably produce dislocations in the job market because of its uneven impact on different occupations and communities. Because the market process operates so imperfectly, the adjustment to change can be slow, painful, and costly to the workers and communities involved. A major concern of manpower policy, then, inevitably lies in the area of facilitating (and anticipating) adjustment to technological change.

There are, however, serious problems in planning effective policies in this area. The impact of technological change on employment levels and skill composition cannot be determined *a priori*, nor, if one accepts the view that 'automation' implies, in some sense, a new form of technological change, by reference to the historical record. Theory and an examination of historical evidence can, of course, point the direction to the most fruitful lines of empirical investigation. Unfortunately, the measurement of technological change and its effects is fraught with conceptual and statistical difficulties, so that a number of key issues – the pace of change, its determinants and diffusion; the nature, the source, the form of changing technology; the interaction with other growth variables; etc. – remain essentially unsettled, even in countries, notably the United States, where, in marked contrast to the Canadian situation,[49] a large body of empirical research has been accumulated in recent years.[50] Thus, much of what follows by way of brief comment on Canadian developments must be viewed as extremely tentative.

---

[49]In Canada the situation is particularly serious. Apart from ongoing research at the Department of Manpower and Immigration and the Economic Council, the author is aware of only four published empirical studies in this area: Senate of Canada, *Proceedings of the Special Committee on Man-Power and Employment*, No. 6, Submission by Economics and Research Branch, Department of Labour (Ottawa, 1961); Duncan R. Campbell and Edward B. Power, *Manpower Implications of Prospective Technological Change in the Eastern Canadian Pulpwood Logging Industry* (Ottawa, 1966); J. C. McDonald, *Impact and Implications of Office Automation* (Ottawa, 1964); and Yehuda Kotowitz, 'Technological Progress and Labour Displacement', in Kruger and Meltz, *op. cit.*

[50]For a compendium of the results of recent studies see Technology and the American Economy, Report of the National Commission on Technology, Automation and Economic Progress, *The Employment Impact of Technological Change* (Washington, 1966), Appendix, Vol. II.

Some of the employment effects of technological change in Canada in recent decades are, so to speak, visible to the naked eye. No sophisticated measures or analyses are required to relate the impact of mechanization in primary industries to the major reductions of employment in that sector. Rapid increases in productivity, associated with substantial capital investment, and uncompensated by sufficient expansion of demand, have resulted in a substantial decline in numbers employed over the past two decades. The process of adjustment – the rural-urban shift of the labour force – has not been accomplished without heavy cost to individuals and communities, as witnessed by the still-wide rural-urban gaps in income and in manpower utilization in most advanced countries.

Further, the impact of changing production processes may be observed in the shrinking employment in some traditional occupations – locomotive firemen, pattern-makers, metal polishers, boiler firemen, blacksmiths, weavers, coremakers, filers and grinders, stone-cutters, provide a few such examples – and in the rapid growth of some new occupations: computer programmers, office-appliance operators, a variety of inspection and quality-control occupations in metal work and electronics, etc.

The case of the primary industries or the handful of specific occupations provide *examples*, obvious and easily visible, of the impact of technological change in Canada in recent decades. But they provide little basis for *generalization*, based on insight, as to the employment consequences of technological change and hence insufficient guidance to policy-makers. Much more evidence is required. Thus, for example, the statement that 'in general, an outstanding ... consequence of technological change is to raise educational and skill requirements'[51] has not been documented. Evidence derived from studies in the United States points to no such firm conclusion. Case studies suggest either a decline in skill content or no significant change.[52] As for office automation, while some occupational upgrading is expected, 'what is far from clear ... is the nature, extent and tempo' of this effect.[53] Fundamental and far-reaching decisions about education and training policy must rest on firmer evidence.

What can be said of the pace of change during the post-war period and its effect on employment and unemployment? The most common measure of the pace of technological change is the rate of productivity increase – usually, although not ideally, output per man-hour. The

[51]Economic Council of Canada, *First Annual Review* (1964), p. 155.
[52]*The Employment Impact, op. cit.*, Part 3.
[53]McDonald, *op. cit.*, p. 17.

limited data available in Canada suggest that the rate of productivity improvement over the fifties and sixties was somewhat in excess of the long-run rate, implying an acceleration of technical change. Econometric analysis supports this view and suggests, further, that post-war technological change was, on balance, labour saving, in contrast with the neutral process of the pre-war period.[54] During the late 1950s, the 'structuralists' argued that the high levels of unemployment were due to an increase in structural unemployment arising from automation, i.e. accelerated, labour-saving technological change. This contention was proven incorrect by subsequent events: the unemployment rate receded with the expansion of aggregate demand during the 1960s. (See below for discussion of structural unemployment.)

Finally, what of the underlying sources of technological change in Canada? A knowledge of the main determinants of technological change is essential in understanding its development and anticipating its future course.

Much of Canadian technology is borrowed from other countries and undoubtedly this will continue to be the case for many years. Of particular significance, in this respect, is the role of foreign (United States) direct investment in Canada. It has been widely assumed that the spill-over of technical innovation from the United States, via the subsidiary firm, is a major determinant of the rate of technological change in Canada.[55] Recent investigation would not, however, support such a firm and unequivocal conclusion. Thus, studies prepared for the *Report of the Task Force on Foreign Ownership and the Structure of Canadian Industry* (1968) suggest that 'nationality of ownership is irrelevant to economic performance or that foreign ownership does not produce above-average benefits that can be perceived from data on productivity and size.'[56] Rather, it would appear that 'the nature of the Canadian environment within which firms operate is a more important determinant of their behaviour.'[57] Increased competitiveness, tax change, improvement in the training of *entrepreneurs* are recommended as growth-inducing policies.

Expenditure on research and development (R and D) is another important determinant of the pace of technological change. (Perhaps it

[54]Kotowitz, *op. cit.*, and 'Production Functions in Canadian Manufacturing 1926-39 and 1947-61', mimeographed, paper delivered at the Conference on Statistics, June 1967.
[55]See, for example, J. P. Francis, 'Technological Change, Productivity and Employment in Canada', mimeo., O.E.C.D., North American Joint Conference on the Requirements of Automated Jobs and their Policy Implications (Washington, 1969), p. 6.
[56]*Task Force Report, op. cit.*, p. 80.
[57]*Ibid.*, p. 82.

might be more accurate to say that R and D is an important pre-determinant; if not followed through by application in production, R and D expenditure will have little effect on industrial activity.) In 1965, Canadian expenditures on R and D were about 1.3 per cent of G.N.P., compared with 2.3 per cent for the United Kingdom (1964-5) and 3.4 per cent for the United States (1963-4). By 1968-9 the Canadian figure had risen to nearly 1.5 per cent, but the gap remained large. Canada's ranking in terms of non-defence R and D, while better, is still low. Government expenditure comprised over half – about the same proportion as in Britain and less than in the United States. Foreign-owned firms in Canada do relatively more research than resident-owned firms, but very much less than the parent firms, mainly in the United States.

There are, of course, many links in the chain that begins with science and technology and ends in more rapid economic growth. The Economic Council, in its *Fifth Annual Review*, outlines some of the important elements in a public-policy strategy designed to stimulate productivity through more effective application of scientific and technological knowledge. These include, among others, programs to strengthen management; to 'tap into' the world's supply of science and technology; to support, selectively, R and D work in Canadian industry. It is important to note that rapid technological change will place a special burden of adjustment on the labour force – a matter we shall be discussing in the chapter on manpower policy – and the council stresses the importance of special programs designed to facilitate adjustment and readaptation as essential to improving 'the environment for innovation'.[58]

In conclusion, a full-scale discussion of the determinants of economic growth, an area of abounding literature but still-vast uncharted terrain, is obviously inappropriate here. The Canadian government is exhibiting increasing concern with these questions – manifested in a variety of ways, including its efforts to formulate a national science policy.[59] At the same time, the public image of science, technology, and economic growth itself has become increasingly blemished of late, and fundamental questions – does bigger mean better? does more mean less? – are put with increasing insistence. The anti-growth sentiments stem in large part from growing awareness of the adverse spill-overs

[58] *Fifth Annual Review* (1968), p. 57. See Chapter 3 for a more extended discussion of 'Science, Technology and the Economy'.
[59] Cf. Senate of Canada, *Proceedings of the Special Committee on Science Policy*, (Ottawa, 1968-9).

or negative externalities of the growth process, but, at least in some quarters, also involve a more 'bedrock' questioning of value systems. While we cannot pursue these matters, they are mentioned to caution the reader against assuming that their omission reflects an absolute ordering of priorities. It simply reflects the judgment – which may be questioned – that, given the current state of the art of manpower economics and public-policy making, these issues are largely tangential to the modest scope of the present book. We are quite prepared to admit that a decade hence the preceding sentence may strike the reader as quaint, if not archaic. If so, that will be further evidence of the rapidity of change, not simply economic, but social and political.

Appendix

PROBLEMS OF MEASURING LABOUR DEMAND

It has become a cliché of current discussions about the labour market to say that the existing system of intelligence is lopsidedly focused on *labour supply* and that a gaping void in that system is the lack of statistics on the current *demand* for labour. Clichés, of course, develop through constant repetition of a given statement, and such is the case with this one. Thus, in Canada, in December 1965, the Economic Council noted, in its *Second Annual Review*, that 'nothing is more crucial to the . . . improvement of the functioning of the labour market than job vacancy data.' In the United States, the President's Committee to Appraise Employment and Unemployment Statistics (the Gordon Committee) reported in September 1962 that 'It is doubtful that any suggestion for the improvement of knowledge about the Nation's job markets was more frequently voiced to this Committee than that calling for job vacancy statistics.' In February 1965, Arthur Burns, president of the National Bureau of Economic Research, opened a conference on the Measurement and Interpretation of Job Vacancies with the statement that: 'The absence of [job vacancy] statistics is, I think, the most serious gap in our entire scheme of economic intelligence.' Similar quotes can be marshalled from a variety of sources, but it hardly seems necessary to labour the point.

Despite this chorus of concern decrying the lack of job-vacancy statistics and urging the need for remedying this deficiency, there has been distressingly little 'hard' analysis, within a theoretical framework, either of the concept or the uses of vacancy statistics. Distressing this may be, but it is not surprising. Economic theorists have devoted themselves to the refinement of an elegant theory of demand, rooted in production theory and highly abstract notions of consumer behaviour. Such constructs, uncontaminated by contact with reality, provide no basis on which to build an operationally feasible definition of labour demand. Labour economists have shown less reluctance to dirty their hands by grubbing around with 'facts', but their output to date, promising though some of it is, can hardly be described as a general theory of the dynamics of the labour market. In a perfect world we would move from theory to measurement back to testing and refinement of theory. In this highly imperfect, real world, we grope our way from shaky, partial, *a priori* reasoning to rough first approximations of measurable concepts. Hopefully, the statistics that are thus derived may, when used in conjunction with a variety of other information, permit us to probe labour-market processes and gradually improve both our measures and understanding of these phenomena.

It should be pointed out that there are two types of vacancy data, designated by source. Thus, vacancy statistics are produced as a by-product of administering an employment service. These are often called operational statistics, a term that denotes their source but not necessarily their use: such statistics may be used for operational, i.e. placement, or for analytical purposes. They have, however, serious deficiencies for the latter use. Vacancy statistics can also be produced by means of a survey of establishments. These survey statistics can also be used for operational, i.e. placement, or for analytical purposes. More reliable, analytically meaningful vacancy data can only be produced by means of specially designed surveys. But there are many difficulties inherent in any such effort. A few of these are discussed in what follows.

CONCEPT

At first glance it appears that the concept of job vacancies is easily derived if the analogy with unemployment is kept in view: an unemployed man is one who is seeking a job; a vacant job is one that is seeking a man. But, in fact, a number of problems confront us in developing a definition of job vacancies that is both measurable and of potential analytical significance. Indeed, it is safe to say that there are undoubtedly many more problems than those of which we are presently aware. No doubt, new information on job vacancies will serve, in John Dunlop's phrase, to 'extend the frontiers of ignorance, by raising many more questions than have been answered'. The purpose of this appendix is simply to raise, for consideration, a few of the conceptual issues that have emerged in the recent discussions of job-vacancy measures that have taken place here and in the United States.

A key issue, in this area, concerns the coverage of vacancy statistics. Because of overwhelming response problems, any measure of job vacancies that is conceivable at the present time will have to be confined to vacancies open to the 'external' market, i.e. open to employees outside the establishment. Students of the labour market have long been aware of the distinction between the 'internal' and 'external' market. Clark Kerr[1] has pointed out that there is great variation in the extent to which employers recruit, for various job categories, from within or from outside their organization. Such variation is determined by institutional, technological, and economic factors, and detailed studies of industrial labour markets are required in order to map and explain the characteristics of these internal markets and their links – through ports of entry – with the exterior. It has been argued that job-vacancy statistics that exclude internal vacancies will be of doubtful analytical significance. A less extreme position, and one that is hardly assailable, is that job-vacancy statistics will have to be carefully interpreted in the light of detailed knowledge of the rules of the internal markets of given industries.

Thus, to provide an obvious and well-known example, a comparative analysis of vacancy trends in the construction industry and the manufacturing sector will be meaningless unless informed by the fact that, roughly speaking, what are interestablishment transfers or external vacancies in construction will be intra-establishment or internal vacancies in manufacturing. Again, rules governing recall will vary from establishment to establishment, and, given an institutionalization of such rules through union agreements, from industry to industry. An extension of the duration of recall rights in one company (or industry) will reduce vacancies (if workers on recall are not considered 'new' workers), and this reduction will be misinterpreted unless the change in rules is known. Seniority provisions delineate precise districts and promotion ladders within large firms. A vacancy for a maintenance electrician or carpenter in one firm may, in another firm with differing seniority regulations, appear as a starting-job in common labouring. Finally, to take an extreme example from abroad, the traditional Japanese system for hiring in the large firm sector involved only one port of entry and lifetime tenure. Obviously,

[1]'The Balkanization of Labor Markets', in *Labor Mobility and Economic Opportunity* (Cambridge, 1954).

under such a system, an occupational delineation of job vacancies has no significance whatsoever. Today this system is breaking down under the pressure of economic and social changes, and a complex 'external market' is beginning to emerge.

These examples might be multiplied many times, for there is enormous variability in the arrangements by which companies recruit labour from the external market and deploy it within the internal market. Thus, even the best information on external job vacancies will be partial and will have to be carefully interpreted in the light of additional information about the procedures governing the placement, maintenance, and promotion of labour within the firm. It may well be, however, that the process of providing information on external job vacancies will act as a stimulus to manpower planning in many companies, and hence facilitate the collection of more comprehensive information on labour-market processes. It deserves to be stressed that if the collection of job-vacancy data proves to be one step in the direction of this larger process of rational planning for manpower requirements within firms, then the institution of vacancy surveys will have accomplished far more than the provision of additional market intelligence, important as that may be.

Setting aside the problems raised by the exclusion of internal vacancies from our measure of current labour demand by no means clears the field of knotty conceptual difficulties. One of these concerns the question of the *duration* of vacancies.

A simple count of numbers of vacancies may well be misinterpreted if information on the time dimension is lacking. Thus, a vacancy that can be filled in two or three days will not have the same economic significance as one that lasts two or three months. The first type may be considered 'frictional' – in analogy with frictional unemployment – while the latter, more persistent vacancies may be indicative of structural maladjustments in the market. An over-all equality of numbers of vacancies and numbers of unemployed cannot be interpreted as an indication of balance in the market if there are significant differences in the average duration of the demand and supply stocks.[2] Further, it should not be assumed that there is a simple parallel, in terms of economic significance, between long-term unemployment and long-duration vacancies. The firm has many more degrees of freedom in dealing with long-term vacancies than does the individual faced with an extended period of joblessness. Thus,

[2]Myron L. Joseph, 'Current Surveys on Measuring Job Vacancies', *American Statistical Association Proceedings* (1965), p. 308.

the firm can, and often will, change its hiring specifications or even modify its production function in the face of severe labour shortage. While it is true that a man who has been unemployed for many months and has exhausted his unemployment benefits will be prepared to offer his services at very low wages, he may still be unable to find work because market wage-rates are, for institutional reasons, rather inflexible in a downward direction. So, for these and other reasons, it is clearly desirable to secure, in addition to a count of vacancies, at least enough information on their time dimension to permit us to distinguish long-duration from other vacancies. Ideally, of course, one would like a more detailed break-down on duration than this simple dichotomy, but in this instance, as in most others, there has to be a compromise between the maximum information that is desired and that which it is feasible to collect. The general problem of response in a job-vacancy survey will be dealt with separately, below.

Another conceptual issue of importance concerns the source or origin of job vacancies. It has been argued that current job-vacancy data cannot be interpreted in the absence of parallel labour-turnover information.[3] Thus, for example, a substantial proportion of labour demand, in many industries and occupations, stems from labour turnover, especially voluntary quits. There is clearly a difference in the economic significance of vacancies stemming from voluntary quits and vacancies arising from the creation of new positions – for reasons of either cyclical or longer-run changes in demand. Further, as some studies of the labour market suggest,[4] new vacancies create quits and, of course, quits create vacancies. It is obviously useful to have data that permit one to trace this reinforcing spiral. But some would argue further that information on current job vacancies, even if supplemented with turnover data, presents a very partial picture of labour demand, because firms think of labour requirements in terms of anticipated turnover[5] and we should collect current and also short-term *ex ante* information. An experiment along these lines demonstrated

[3]Charlotte Boschan, 'Job Openings and Help-Wanted Advertising as Measures of Cyclical Fluctuations in Unfilled Demand for Labour', in *The Measurement and Interpretation of Job Vacancies*, National Bureau of Economic Research (1966).

[4]S. Behman, 'Labor Mobility, Increasing Labor Demand, and Money Wage-Rate Increases in United States Manufacturing', *The Review of Economic Studies* (October 1964).

[5]Robert Ferber and Neil Ford, 'The Collection of Job Vacancy Data Within a Labor Turnover Framework', in *Employment Policy and the Labor Market*, Arthur M. Ross (ed.) (Berkeley, 1965).

that current openings are very small – 10 to 15 per cent – relative to openings anticipated one month ahead, and moreover the two series exhibit different time trends.

The argument for collecting short-term *ex ante* data may be persuasive, but, beyond this, neither current nor short-term anticipated data ideally suit some of the more urgent needs of policy-makers in this sphere. What would be most useful, at least for certain types of analysis, is forecast data for varying periods of time from several months to several years. Of course, in gathering any information some compromise must be effected between needs and costs, taking into account the costs of development (including the cost of time) which loom large in any new and difficult survey. We shall return to this question later, but now we must confront a key problem in the job-vacancy field, one that is crucial to any assessment of costs, especially development costs. This is the problem of response.

The fundamental problem of response in a job-vacancy survey is rooted in the characteristic behaviour of establishments with respect to their hiring and deployment of manpower. It is, therefore, a formidable problem, since it is inherent in the very activity we are seeking to measure. Two characteristics, shared in varying degree by all but the very smallest establishments,[6] confront the survey-taker:

1. There is rarely a single locus of responsibility of decision regarding employment;
2. There are rarely complete or even partial statistical records within establishments or firms from which a comprehensive count of job vacancies can be made.

These two characteristics are obviously related. The first would not present serious difficulties without the second; the second would be of less consequence in the absence of the first. We may, therefore, treat this as a general problem. Its implications are quite clear: in order to collect job-vacancy information we must determine who, in the establishment or firm, has the information. This may be (is likely to be) impossible to determine in advance, and hence, at least in the early stages of an ongoing program, response error is likely to be high. Thus,

---

[6]In very small establishments the owner or owner-manager generally makes all decisions, and the absence of records may not present undue difficulties in the collection of job-vacancy information since so few employees are concerned. Experimental surveys have indicated that response rates among such establishments tend to be lower than average, however, and response error tends to be high, although for reasons other than those suggested here.

experience with experimental surveys has shown that even in estab-lishments with a well-developed personnel department, the personnel officers may become aware of vacancies only after they have been filled, because hiring activities are decentralized. Different categories of jobs relate to differing 'hiring-points' in the enterprise. Information must be collected from all hiring-points if it is to be comprehensive but not overlapping.

Specification of All Hiring Points is a Prerequisite of Data Collection.

These twin problems – determining the loci of response in the establish-ment, and the absence of records – place a severe constraint on the kind of job-vacancy data that can be collected with a reasonable ex-pectation of reliability. Thus, for example, we have emphasized the crucial importance of securing some minimal information on the time dimension of vacancies and have suggested that, ideally, one would like at least as detailed a distribution in this sphere as is available for the unemployment measure. But experimental programs have shown that response error is likely to be substantial for vacancies at both ends of the duration spectrum. Easily filled vacancies of short duration may not be reported both because of difficulties of recall and because the responsibility for hiring such workers may be highly decentralized and diffused, and the location of response points may be difficult in a regular survey.

Reporting of long-duration vacancies is subject to a different kind of response error centring on the concept of 'actively seeking'. Essentially this is an analogous problem to that raised by the 'inactive seeker' in the measurement of unemployment. It is important that the definition of job vacancies focus on objective activity; otherwise it is difficult to ensure a stable measure, i.e. one that is consistent from enumerator to enumerator and from enumeration to enumeration. But in a very tight market an employer may be making no attempt to fill vacancies because previous experience has shown that qualified workers are simply not available. Further, an employer may change his hiring specifications for a long-duration vacancy if a worker of a quite dif-ferent occupational background is available and can be trained, or can release another worker, already employed, for the required job. Again, in a full-employment situation, a highly qualified person may be hired even though a formal job-opening does not exist.

Further, job-vacancy information is required in occupational, indus-trial, and area detail if it is to be used to implement an active man-power policy. The collection of occupational information raises certain response problems. There is no standard occupational terminology among employers even within the same industry. This would seem to preclude, at least for the present, the development of a pre-coded list of occupations for survey purposes. The only alternative appears to be coding the employer's own job titles. Experimental studies have suggested that this is feasible, i.e. that job titles can be coded to a detailed level of a given coding system within a reasonable margin of error. But much more work remains to be done before one can say this problem is solved. In particular, a systematic follow-up procedure with employers is required to evaluate the reliability of the occupational coding.

Finally, there are special, additional, response problems involved in the collection of *ex ante* data. Thus, it is likely to increase the number of response points in the establishment or firm. The persons responsible for current hiring are not often likely to be those responsible for company planning. Further, the accuracy of anticipated data cannot be assessed in the same way as that of current information. Essentially, it depends on the ability and willingness of the respondent to forecast. In general, the more extended the forecast period, the greater the possibility of 'error'. It is interesting that the Swedes, who have had the widest and longest experience in conducting demand-forecast surveys, are the most sceptical about their utility. Thus, at the N.B.E.R. Conference in 1965 the Swedish delegate remarked: 'Such factors as the subjective estimates of management, the influence of many exogenous factors, gradual adaptation to the actual state when shortage becomes permanent, make the figures ambiguous and inexact. This must be taken not as resignation but as a conclusion.'[7]

This brief review of some of the important conceptual issues is meant to serve as background to the outline of the Canadian Job Vacancy Survey. The survey itself is fully described elsewhere[8] and the interested reader may consult the reference for details of definition and design.

---

[7]N.B.E.R., *op. cit.*, pp. 285-6.
[8]Sylvia Ostry and Alan Sunter, 'Definitional and Design Aspects of the Canadian Job Vacancy Survey', *Journal of the American Statistical Association* (September 1970).

V

Unemployment

Introduction

We have, thus far, been reviewing trends in labour supply and demand in Canada and have, from time to time, referred to problems of adjustment between the two. Maladjustment in the labour market may take a variety of forms: it may be signalled by persistent shortages of certain types of labour, resulting in rising wages and impaired production flows, or it may be manifested by labour surplus, i.e. unemployment or underemployment in portions of the market. But unemployment is not necessarily a sign of a malfunctioning labour market:[1] as we shall see, there are several sources of unemployment other than that stemming from a mismatching of supply and demand. It is thus useful to begin this chapter with a brief definitional section on sources or types of unemployment. We will then proceed to a descriptive summary of the characteristics of the unemployed in Canada and conclude with an exploration of the notion of full employment as a goal of public policy, and incomes policy as an instrument for achieving this goal.

Sources of Unemployment

The memory of the Great Depression is fast fading in Western society. More than thirty years have passed since the 'hungry thirties' and, as

[1]In neo-classical economics, however, all (except frictional) unemployment is 'voluntary', stemming from the downward rigidity of money (and real) wages. An important aspect of the 'Keynesian revolution' was its contention that a reduction in money wages would not serve as an effective cure for unemployment. For a recent review of the literature and a look at the Canadian data, see Ronald G. Bodkin, 'Real Wages and Cyclical Variations in Employment: A Re-Examination of the Evidence', *Canadian Journal of Economics* (August 1969).

124

Figure 4 clearly shows, the post-war generations have no first-hand experience of what total and massive disruption of the economy can mean. The thirties stand out – in grim contrast – as a unique period, when unemployment reached levels of almost 20 per cent and when a level of 10 per cent marked a 'recovery'. Hopefully, we can regard that time as *sui generis*. Moreover, major changes in the structure of the economy and in public policy, including the provision of an unemployment-insurance system and other income-support measures, have greatly reduced the disastrous economic effects of unemployment on the working population. But the social consequences of unemployment for individuals and families are always deleterious, and the dimming image of the Great Depression should not inure us to this fact.

Economists distinguish two major types or sources of unemployment: demand-deficient and non-demand-deficient. Conceptually, one may usefully make this distinction – and, indeed, extend it to include further subcategories within each major type – because doing so enhances our understanding of the problem and of effective policy-making. But this does not mean, of course, that we can label individuals at any given time and say that Mr. A. is unemployed because of a deficiency of demand while Mr. B. is unemployed because of the installation of a machine that now dispenses with his services in the plant. Mr. B. may have *lost* his job because of a change in production methods in his firm, but he may not be able to *find* another job because the economy as a whole is suffering from a recession. Further, although we can and do attach labels to different types of unemployment as though each were quite separate and distinct, there is some empirical evidence to suggest that, in fact, they are interrelated in a causal sense, in particular that some types of structural unemployment rise in recession while other types increase as the labour market tightens. The dynamics of the labour market – and of the economic system – are, in other words, too complex to be captured in a neat and tidy classification system. This *caveat* should be kept in mind when reading what follows.

DEMAND-DEFICIENT UNEMPLOYMENT

As the name states, this type of unemployment arises when the level of aggregate demand is insufficient to clear the market of total labour supply.[2] It is usually associated with a decline in particular components of aggregate demand, especially private investment or government expenditure, and is sometimes called cyclical unemployment. The

[2]Labour supply itself may be affected by the level of demand – see above, Chapter II.

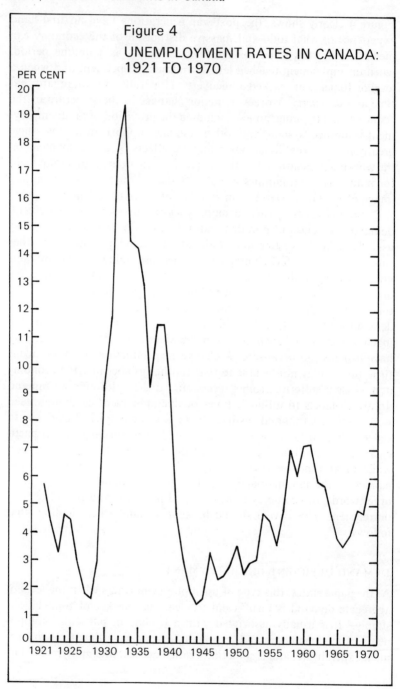

Figure 4

UNEMPLOYMENT RATES IN CANADA: 1921 TO 1970

latter designation implies short-term inadequate demand, but a more persistent deficiency of demand, lasting beyond short-term business fluctuations, may also produce sustained unemployment.

We accept, almost intuitively, the idea that fluctuations in aggregate demand will result in fluctuations in the demand for labour and hence, unless fully offset by movements in supply, in fluctuations in the level of unemployment. Indeed, the empirical record testifies that this association does exist. The unemployment rates shown in Table 24 exhibit a close negative correlation with deviations of per-capita G. N. P. from its long-run growth trend. Thus, when demand for output is above average, unemployment is low; and the opposite is also true.

But while the association between aggregate demand and unemployment is close, it is by no means perfect or unvarying over time and space. Economists are now well aware that we are largely ignorant of the patterns of response that firms adopt when changes in aggregate demand are induced by government monetary and fiscal policies, and hence the *timing* of this response, as well as its magnitude, is extremely difficult to predict. Thus, while one may say that the policy prescription for 'curing' demand-deficient unemployment is straightforward enough – aggregate demand should be raised to its 'appropriate' level by means of expansionist monetary and/or fiscal policy designed to stimulate the private and/or public sector – the real-world situation is much more complicated and difficult to analyse than this would suggest. Part of the difficulty arises because of the problem of differential and varying lagged response already mentioned. This in itself creates serious problems for forecasting, and these are exacerbated in policy-making because strategies directed toward reducing demand-deficient unemployment will also have an important effect on another strategic goal of contemporary societies, the control of inflation. We shall be discussing this matter at greater length in the concluding section of this chapter.

It is important to note that demand-deficient unemployment does *not* affect all industries, occupations, regions, and demographic groups uniformly. It would be very convenient for the economic analyst if it did, since it would provide a means of distinguishing cyclical from structural problems! However, a decline in aggregate demand will affect different industries quite differently (if for no other reason than variation in income elasticities of demand) and hence have a differential effect on industrial and occupational employment. In general, a decline in aggregate output affects the investment and durable-goods industries more strongly than the 'soft' consumer-goods or service sector. Further, employers faced with the necessity of reducing their

TABLE 24

Unemployment Rates by Region, Annual Averages, 1946-70

Year	Region					
	Atlantic	Quebec	Ontario	Prairies	British Columbia	Canada
	(per cent)	(per cent)	(per cent)	(per cent)	(per cent)	(per cent)
1946	7.7	4.3	2.8	2.4	4.2	3.8
1947	6.5	2.7	1.8	1.8	3.1	2.6
1948	6.2	2.5	1.7	1.7	3.5	2.6
1949	6.9	3.6	2.3	2.2	3.9	3.3
1950	8.4	4.6	2.5	2.2	4.4	3.8
1951	4.7	3.2	1.8	1.8	3.7	2.6
1952	4.6	3.9	2.2	1.9	4.1	3.0
1953	5.5	3.8	2.1	1.9	4.0	3.0
1954	6.6	5.9	3.8	2.5	5.2	4.6
1955	6.5	6.2	3.2	3.1	3.8	4.4
1956	6.0	5.0	2.4	2.2	2.8	3.4
1957	8.4	6.0	3.4	2.6	5.0	4.6
1958	12.5	8.8	5.4	4.1	8.6	7.0
1959	10.9	7.9	4.5	3.2	6.5	6.0
1960	10.7	9.1	5.4	4.2	8.5	7.0
1961	11.2	9.2	5.5	4.6	8.5	7.1
1962	10.7	7.5	4.3	3.9	6.6	5.9
1963	9.5	7.5	3.8	3.7	6.4	5.5
1964	7.8	6.4	3.2	3.1	5.3	4.7
1965	7.4	5.4	2.5	2.5	4.2	3.9
1966	6.4	4.7	2.5	2.1	4.5	3.6
1967	6.7	5.3	3.2	2.4	5.2	4.1
1968	7.4	6.6	3.6	2.9	5.9	4.8
1969	7.5	6.9	3.2	2.9	5.0	4.7
1970	7.6	7.9	4.3	4.4	7.6	5.9

Notes: Rates from 1946 to 1952 inclusive have been adjusted for timing of the Labour Force Survey which was conducted quarterly before November 1952. Newfoundland is included in estimates for the Atlantic region.

Rates from 1956 to 1966 are based on estimates revised to take account of 1961 census population counts.

Source: Based on data from Labour Force Surveys.

work force will try to retain more highly skilled and trained workers (who can perform less-skilled work, if necessary), will be more reluctant to lay off office and supervisory staff who perform 'overhead' functions, and may be required to observe union rules with respect to seniority and lay-offs. Thus, the impact of a cut-back in over-all demand will affect the young and the unskilled and semi-skilled blue-collar worker in the durable-goods and construction sectors much more seriously than it will the skilled worker with seniority, white-collar groups, and workers in many service industries. This aspect of unemployment incidence will be brought out below when we discuss the characteristics of the unemployed.

NON-DEMAND-DEFICIENT UNEMPLOYMENT

This type of unemployment stems not from a gap between over-all labour demand and supply, but essentially from a mismatching between demand and supply. In a dynamic economy, firms and workers are constantly adjusting to changes in price and opportunities for employment. Some of these adjustments are accomplished in a short time and the unemployment is of limited duration. Other changes, reflecting more fundamental shifts in the economy – changes in consumer tastes, introduction of new products, major technological innovations, depletion of natural resources, etc. – involve long-run declines in employment opportunities for certain industries, occupations, or localities. Unemployment will rise in such industries, occupations, and localities while the surplus labour is in the process of adjusting to the changed structure of demand. The ease or difficulty of adjustment will vary with the nature of the structural change, the speed of change, and the personal characteristics of the individuals involved. If the economy is growing strongly, i.e. demand is rising, the process of adjustment will be eased.

It is possible, from the foregoing, to distinguish two subcategories of non-demand-deficient unemployment:[3]

1. *Frictional*: short-duration unemployment arising from the movement into the labour force of new entrants and re-entrants and from the movement of workers from one job to another. Since a high level of employment may stimulate more 'job hopping and shopping' and induce a greater flow of secondary workers into the market, frictional unemployment may rise in periods of rapid growth. Its duration, already short, may presumably be further reduced by provision of better labour-market information. But frictional unemployment does not represent a serious economic or social problem and, indeed, may be regarded as a sign of a healthy, growing and changing economy.

---

[3]Seasonal unemployment, which has been referred to above, in Chapter II, may also be classified as a non-demand-deficient subcategory, arising from variations in climate and other seasonal factors affecting production, consumer buying habits, and labour-force entries and exits. In this instance, the 'mismatch' is temporary, extending over the period of a year.

2. *Structural*: long-duration unemployment arising from structural changes in the character of the demand for labour that require some form of transformation of labour supply, i.e. change in occupation, industry, locality, a more or less-time consuming process. In the extreme case, where such transformation is a very lengthy process, structural unemployment will shade into unemployability. Clearly, the economic and social consequences of structural unemployment are extremely serious for the individuals, families, and communities affected.

While structural unemployment (like poverty) has always been with us, the analysis of its nature and incidence received little attention in Canada until the late 1950s. For several years following 1957, however, during the period of prolonged stagnation of the North American economy, a more widespread public concern emerged, and a lively debate about the source of the higher unemployment engaged economists and others outside the profession. This debate focused attention on the subject of unemployment in a fashion and to a degree unknown in this country and the United States since the 1930s (when, however, far less information was available). The major issues and evidence are described at great length and in exhaustive detail in an article by John Winder[4] and need only be briefly summarized here.

The question that perturbed economists and others in the late 1950s was whether the high unemployment (averaging close to 7 per cent between 1958 and 1962 compared with 3½ per cent for the years between 1946 and 1957) was caused by a significant increase in structural unemployment or simply stemmed from inadequate aggregate demand. The structuralist school argued that the economy had been undergoing a fundamental transformation involving a shift from goods-producing to service-producing activity, accompanied by an accelerating pace of technological change in the goods-producing sector. Further, the nature of the technological change was significantly different from that experienced in the first industrial revolution. The new technology, instead of *creating* jobs for the less skilled (by replacing the artisan by a machine that opened up employment opportunities for machine operators, etc.), would *absorb* the jobs of the semi-skilled and the unskilled, and even most of the skilled, and leave only a relatively few openings for men required to maintain and repair the new, automated factories. The effect of these developments, it was claimed, was becoming evident in the rising levels of unemployment of male blue-collar workers who, displaced by these fundamental structural changes

---

[4]'Structural Unemployment', in *The Canadian Labour Market*, Arthur Kruger and Noah Meltz (eds.) (Toronto, 1968). See also bibliographic information cited therein.

in the economy, were, for a variety of reasons – lack of training, inadequate education, inappropriate locality, etc. – unable to fit into the new jobs created in the expanding white-collar, service-type sectors.

It should be noted that the point at issue was *not* whether there was a problem of structural unemployment in North America (there certainly was, and has been, and is) but whether or not the higher over-all levels of unemployment in the late 1950s stemmed primarily from an *increase* in structural unemployment. The structuralist school cited, as evidence that it did, the concentration of unemployment in certain age-sex, educational, industrial, occupational, or regional groups, and data on productivity growth in the goods sector. The remedy for this ailment, they argued, was not an expansion of aggregate demand, which under the circumstances could only serve to stimulate increases in costs and prices, but selective measures designed to reduce unemployment of specific groups and alleviate particular shortages and bottle-necks (evidence of which was usually not cited). Retraining and mobility were required to reshape the square pegs but, so the argument went, there was no shortage of round holes.

The structuralist argument could not be refuted *a priori*, since it presented a quite logical hypothesis concerning the nature, pace, and impact of economic change in the North American setting. The demand-deficient school also turned first to an examination of the incidence of unemployment, but cited evidence that there had been no significant 'independent' changes in concentration, i.e. changes not associated with variations in the over-all unemployment rates.[5] Thus, the observed increased severity of unemployment among particular groups, they argued, appeared to stem largely from the rising gap between actual and potential or desirable aggregate demand. The policy prescription, therefore, was couched in terms of traditional stabilization tools, i.e. easing of monetary and fiscal policy to stimulate demand.

During the long upswing of the 1960s, although the 'structuralist debate' continued among economists, public interest in the issue waned

---

[5]For presentation of the Canadian data in this fashion, see Pierre Paul Proulx, 'The Composition of Unemployment in Canada', *Employment, Unemployment and Manpower*, F. Bairstow (ed.), McGill Industrial Relations Centre (Montreal, 1964); Frank T. Denton and Sylvia Ostry, *An Analysis of Post-War Unemployment*, Economic Council of Canada (Ottawa, 1965). For a review, see S. F. Kaliski, 'Structural Unemployment: A New Stage in the Debate', *The Canadian Banker* (Autumn 1967). For a different approach, see John Vanderkamp, 'An Application of Lipsey's Concept of Structural Unemployment', *Review of Economic Studies* (July 1966); S. F. Kaliski, 'Structural Unemployment in Canada: The Occupational Dimension', *Canadian Journal of Economics*, (May 1969). See also Mahmood A. Zaidi, *The Labour Market and the Intrafactor Allocation Mechanism in Canada*, Economic Council of Canada (Ottawa, 1967).

as the high levels of unemployment receded with the increase in aggregate demand. While it was generally agreed that history had proved the case, i.e. that the structuralists were wrong with respect to the causes of the high unemployment of the late 1950s and early 1960s, it was also argued that both sides were mistaken in searching out the sources of unemployment through an examination of its *incidence*. Recent discussions have tended to focus less on the 'mismatching' definition of structural unemployment, which leads to an examination of incidence, in favour of policy-centred definitions that stress the trade-off between employment and price stability (see, below, in the last section of this chapter). The clear-cut dichotomy between aggregative *or* selective policy has given way to questions of how to achieve an effective blend or mix of both. Cost-benefit analyses of manpower programs and questions of mobility and wage-price flexibility are important elements in this framework.

The Characteristics of the Unemployed

As we have already stressed in our preceding discussion, the incidence of unemployment is always uneven by personal or social characteristics of individuals or by economic or regional characteristics of groups. To some degree, the *incidence* is related to the *level* of unemployment. But it is, in fact, a matter of degree and the main features of the 'profile of unemployment' within a given country do not change radically, except under conditions of profound institutional or economic transformation. What follows is a brief sketch of the unemployment profile in post-war Canada.[6]

AGE AND SEX

Age and sex are major correlates of both the rate and, as will be seen shortly, the duration of unemployment. As Table 25 indicates, the rates for males in Canada are consistently and substantially higher than for females, and the disparity worsens as the general level of unemployment rises. This is a long-standing relationship, since during the Great Depression the rate for males climbed to over 20 per cent while that for females was around 9 per cent.[7]

[6]For more detailed information see Sylvia Ostry, *Unemployment in Canada*, 1961 Census Monograph Programme (Ottawa, 1968), on which this section is based.
[7]Cited above, p. 5, from 1931 Census of Canada Monograph, *Unemployment* (Ottawa, 1942).

TABLE 25

Unemployment Rates, Age and Sex: Canada, 1953-70

Sex and Age	Year		
	1953-6	1958-61	1967-70
	(per cent)	*(per cent)*	*(per cent)*
Both sexes, 14 years and over	3.8	6.8	4.9
Total males, 14 years and over	4.3	7.9	5.6
14-19 years	8.8	15.9	12.7
20-24 years	6.3	14.9	8.0
25-34 years	4.0	7.4	4.4
35-44 years	3.2	5.9	3.9
45-54 years	3.6	6.5	3.9
55-64 years	3.7	7.1	5.0
65 years and over	(3.6)	5.2	(4.8)
Total females, 14 years and over	2.2	3.5	3.6
14-19 years	4.5	7.7	9.1
20-24 years	(2.3)	4.0	4.1
25-34 years	(2.1)	(2.7)	2.1
35-44 years	(0.9)	(2.1)	2.3
45-54 years	(1.2)	(1.9)	2.3
55-64 years	(1.3)	(2.4)	(2.1)
65 years and over	—	—	(2.2)

Note: Rates calculated from unemployed estimates of fewer than 10,000 are shown in brackets.

Source: Dominion Bureau of Statistics, Labour Force Survey.

The lower female rate reflects, in part, the greater concentration of women in jobs that are less susceptible to unemployment – white-collar work, service-producing industries. But female rates are also lower than those for males for any given occupation or industry, so this is not the whole story. Further, the relationship between male and female unemployment rates in Canada is the *reverse* of that in other industrial countries, including the United States, where the pattern of employment is so similar to that in Canada. This puzzling contrast between Canadian and international experience may stem, at least to some degree, from the fact that Canadian women are less firmly committed to labour-force activity than women in these other countries, and hence move in and out of the labour market more frequently, thereby by-passing unemployment.

If sex differences in unemployment are persistent and striking, so are those for different age groups. From Table 25, it is apparent that unemployment rates are generally very much higher among younger persons than among mature workers. More detailed information shows that teen-age rates have been more than double the over-all unemployment rate throughout the entire post-war period. Many factors contribute to this situation. First, some of these young people are still attending school and thus looking for part-time or seasonal work only. As the school population increases, so do the numbers seeking part-time or part-year work. We have already noted the effects of this supply phenomenon on seasonal unemployment. Teen-agers and workers in their early twenties who have left school and are just beginning their working lives suffer above-average unemployment, because they have little or no job seniority to protect them against lay-off. Further, they are, as we have seen, far more mobile than the mature worker with greater family responsibility[8] and tend to 'shop around' in the labour market. Although better educated than the average labour-force member, the younger worker lacks on-job experience and thus may be placed at a disadvantage in competing for some types of production jobs. It is, alas, not possible from the data available to determine the relative importance of these and other causes of the distressingly high unemployment rates of young workers in Canada. In particular, one would be interested in the relative weight of voluntary and involuntary unemployment, and the extent to which the over-all teen-age rate might be reduced by improved information services, especially in the educational institutions which feed directly into the labour market.

As may be seen from Table 25, female rates of unemployment drop precipitately and exhibit little variation after the age of twenty-five. For males, the lowest rates are found in the 'prime ages', thirty-five to forty-four. Males between the ages of forty-five and sixty-four are often referred to as 'older workers'[9], and their somewhat higher unemployment rates may be evidence of market difficulties related to their lack of educational qualifications relative to the younger thirty-five to forty-four cohort. The markedly lower rate of unemployment for males of sixty-five and over reflects both voluntary retirement and, perhaps, some forced labour-force withdrawal in years of high over-all unemployment.

[8]An above-average proportion of workers in the age group fourteen to twenty-five is, of course, single, and there is some reasonably good evidence that single persons are (*ceteris paribus*) more likely to be unemployed than are married or other workers. See Ostry, *Unemployment*, Appendix B, for results of regression analysis displaying this finding.

[9]See Sylvia Ostry and Jenny Podoluk, *The Economic Status of the Aging*, Dominion Bureau of Statistics (1966), for a discussion of the characteristics and problems of the older worker.

EDUCATIONAL ATTAINMENT

The type of work people do is largely governed by the amount of formal schooling and training they have. Unskilled and semi-skilled jobs, sporadic and intermittent work in seasonal industries and occupations, are generally the only non-farm jobs available to persons without high-school education, and these are the jobs that tend to be subject to above-average unemployment and underemployment. Further, in a relatively loose labour market an employer can afford to be more selective in his hiring requirements, and the simplest rule of selectivity (though not always the most relevant) is the level of formal education of the applicant. In white-collar work, the most rapidly expanding sector of the economy, a completed high-school education is a *sine qua non* of employment, and the same condition appears to be developing in the skilled manual job markets as well. For these and, no doubt, many other reasons, there is a close relationship between the education of workers and their unemployment experience.

From Table 26, it may be seen that the unemployment rates of workers who failed to complete primary-school education are more than four times those of workers who completed high school. High-school drop-outs were almost twice as likely to be unemployed as were graduates. The risk of unemployment for those who went beyond high school was less than one-third that of the average worker.

Further, as Table 26 demonstrates, at each age group unemployment rates were higher for those with less education than for the better educated. It is also interesting to observe from these data that the age differentials in unemployment noted above, in particular the high unemployment rates of the younger workers relative to the more mature labour force, are revealed at each educational level. However, a far larger *proportion* of the older than of the younger unemployed have relatively little education, so that the lower educational level of older workers does contribute to their unemployment experience. Thus, whereas almost half of the unemployed over the age of forty-five years had not completed elementary school, the comparable ratio for the young (fourteen to twenty-four) worker was just under 15 per cent.

OCCUPATION AND INDUSTRY

An individual's work, in the sense of the sort of job he does or his *occupation,* is a factor of some importance affecting his risk of unemployment. As has already been noted, much of the supervisory, professional, and clerical staff in industry is regarded almost as 'over-

TABLE 26

Unemployment Rates by Age and Level of Education:
Canada, January 1969

Level of Education		Age			
	Total 14 years and over	14-19 years	20-24 years	25-44 years	45 years and over
	(per cent)	*(per cent)*	*(per cent)*	*(per cent)*	*(per cent)*
Some elementary school or less	12.0	23.7	18.1	11.1	11.0
Completed elementary school	7.4	20.0	13.7	6.4	5.6
Some secondary school	6.0	11.6	9.6	3.9	4.3
Completed secondary school	3.7	10.6	5.0	2.5	2.1
Some university or degree	1.6	*	*	*	*
All levels of schooling	5.9	12.7	7.7	4.4	5.2

*Estimate less than 10,000.

Source: Based on data from Dominion Bureau of Statistics *Supplement to Labour Force Survey* (January 1969) (unpublished).

head' or 'fixed capital', and employers will normally lay off production workers much more readily than they will these white-collar
workers. The *skill* of a worker – broadly defined to encompass education, training, and work experience – also affects his risk of joblessness. An employer, faced with a retrenchment in production, will be
more inclined to discharge an unskilled worker who has little training
'invested' in him. The same rationale will encourage him to retain his
more skilled workers to avoid both the loss of training and the added
burden of recruiting expenses when conditions improve and such
workers are likely to be in relatively short supply. Further, a skilled
worker can, if the alternative is unemployment, do the work of an unskilled or semi-skilled man, whereas substitution in the opposite direction is not usually possible.[10] Moreover, institutionalized protection
devices, especially in collective agreements, are likely to apply more
to skilled than to unskilled workers, although this is less true today
than in earlier years. For these and other reasons, the less skilled are
generally more prone to unemployment, especially demand-deficient

[10]Cf. Walter Y. Oi, 'Labor as a Quasi-Fixed Factor', *Journal of Political Economy*
(December 1962); Melvin Reder, 'Wage Structure and Structural Unemployment', *The
Review of Economic Studies* (October 1964) and 'The Theory of Frictional Unemploy-
ment', *Economica* (February 1969).

unemployment, although a particular structural change – a change in technology, for example – may affect a given occupation or family of occupations that are highly skilled.

The *industry* in which a worker is employed also influences his risk of joblessness. Not all industries are equally responsive to declines in demand, since not all goods and services exhibit identical income elasticities. As we have pointed out, construction, consumer durables, and durable manufacturing generally are much harder hit in a recession than are light manufacturing or service industries. Workers in mining and logging are much more vulnerable than those in agriculture. Further, average annual unemployment rates in some industries may be high because of a high seasonal component: logging and construction are examples. Finally, longer-run structural changes in patterns of consumer demand, in technology, and in resource allocation may raise the unemployment risk in particular industries, although these patterns cannot be established by *a priori* reasoning.

Table 27 shows unemployment rates[11] for major occupation groups for selected years from 1961 to 1969 (no earlier data are available from the labour-force survey). It may be seen that the lowest rates throughout the period are those of the white-collar group.[12] Among manual workers, the unskilled are far more prone to joblessness than are the semi-skilled and skilled who are classified together in the category 'craftsmen, production process and related workers'. As the over-all employment situation improved after 1961, the unskilled rate declined markedly, though still remaining well above average. The blue-collar occupations are drawn from a variety of industries, although they are more heavily represented in manufacturing and construction than in others, and their unemployment rates strongly reflect conditions in those industries. This is true to an even greater degree for the transportation group of occupations, which is heavily concentrated in the transportation industry.

[11]Unemployment rates classified by occupation and industry have to be used with caution as indicators of the 'source' of unemployment. This is partly due to deficiencies of classification, especially by occupation, which have already been described. Also, the occupation or industry designated is that of *lost employment*. Workers displaced in a given industry who find intermittent employment in another will be attributed to the latter. This may mask the extent to which certain industries 'generate' unemployment. Workers are less likely to shift occupational attachments, so that the masking effect – especially at the broad occupational level – is probably small.

[12]More detailed data from the 1961 census shows that within the white-collar sector clerical and sales workers had unemployment rates more than three times as high as managerial and professional workers, but still well below the average for all workers. Ostry, *Unemployment*, Table 9B.

TABLE 27

Unemployment Rates by Occupation and Industry: Canada, Selected Years

OCCUPATION

Year	Total	White collar	Skilled and semi-skilled	Unskilled	Primary	Trans-portation	Service and recreation
	(per cent)	(per cent)	(per cent)	(per cent)	(per cent)	(per cent)	(per cent)
1961	7.1	2.5	9.2	21.7	6.8	10.2	5.6
1963	5.5	2.0	6.7	17.2	5.6	7.8	4.7
1966	3.6	1.3	4.3	11.8	3.9	4.5	3.1
1969	4.7	1.9	5.8	13.1	4.7	5.3	4.3

INDUSTRY

Year	Total	Agriculture	Forestry, fishing and trapping	Mining and quarrying	Manufac-turing	Construction	Transportation and other utilities	Trade	Service and finance
	(per cent)	(per cent)	(per cent)	(per cent)	(per cent)	(per cent)	(per cent)	(per cent)	(per cent)
1953	3.0	(0.6)	11.4	(4.2)	3.1	9.4	2.8	1.8	1.6
1958	7.0	1.8	29.2	9.3	7.2	19.0	7.0	4.1	3.4
1961	7.1	2.5	29.3	(9.3)	6.7	21.1	6.6	4.8	3.7
1963	5.5	2.1	22.6	(7.7)	4.8	15.3	5.1	3.8	3.1
			Total Primary						
1966	3.6		3.9		3.2	9.3	3.6	2.4	2.1
1969	4.7	1.8	18.5	(4.9)	4.4	11.4	4.1	3.4	2.7

Source: Based on data from Labour Force Survey (unpublished).

The variation in unemployment incidence by industry is also shown in Table 27. It may be observed that workers in construction, transportation, and manufacturing are especially vulnerable to unemployment when economic conditions worsen as they did in 1958. Even in times of prosperity, however, the unemployment rates for construction are very much above average, as the data for 1953 and the middle years of the 1960s demonstrate. The construction industry has 'contributed' between one-fifth and one-quarter of total unemployment over most of the post-war period. Trade, service, and agriculture, on the other hand, although affected by a deterioration in the economy, typically exhibit relatively low rates of unemployment.

DURATION

We are concerned, in this section, with the characteristics of the unemployed rather than the nature of unemployment. Hence, the focus of attention is on variations in the *incidence* of unemployment of different duration among specific groups in the work force. The analysis of the duration composition of total unemployment over the post-war period is inappropriate in this context, but the interested reader may wish to consult a more detailed study of post-war unemployment for relevant background information on this aspect of the question.[13]

The duration aspect of unemployment varies with age, sex, industrial, and occupational attachment, and from region to region. There are several ways of looking at this varying incidence. Because of its serious economic and social consequences, a good deal of attention is directed to long-term unemployment. One may estimate long-term unemployment *rates,* i.e. the number unemployed in excess of a given number of weeks as a percentage of specific labour-force groups, and these rates reflect the differing *risks* of long-term unemployment among these groups. It is also useful to estimate the average duration of unemployment for these different groups, since this reflects the length of exposure to unemployment once a job is lost. It is clear that these two aspects of duration are conceptually distinct, but both are of importance to the worker concerned.

Most unemployment data are derived from a monthly survey (or decennial census) that measures the individual's activity in a given week. An alternative source, which is much more illuminating for

[13] *Ibid.* Table 11. As one would expect, the average duration of unemployment lengthens as the over-all level rises. In the period 1950-6, unemployment of four months' duration or more averaged less than one-quarter of the total compared with an average of over one-third during the late fifties and early sixties.

the analysis of duration, is an annual 'work-pattern' survey for which the reference period is a year. Such a survey reveals the total number of persons experiencing unemployment during the year and the total amount of unemployment experienced counting all spells of jobless-ness.[14] Because people move into and out of the unemployed group over the year, the total number who experience some joblessness over any twelve-month period will be considerably higher than the twelve-month average of the unemployed estimated by the monthly Labour Force Survey. Thus, for example, in 1968 the annual average unemployment rate estimated from the monthly surveys was 4.8 per cent; the estimate derived from the annual work-pattern survey was 14.6 per cent. Similarly, the average duration of unemployment measured by an annual survey will be considerably higher than the average of the monthly figures, not only because all stretches of unemployment over the year are included, but also because the current data relate to the duration of seeking up to the time of the survey. Because a more revealing picture is presented, the analysis of duration that follows is based on annual 'work-pattern' data rather than on the more familiar monthly-survey statistics. Table 28 contains the basic information for a recent year.[15]

As one would expect, a larger proportion of unemployed men than of unemployed women experienced lengthy unemployment in 1968. Thus, both the long-term (fourteen weeks or more) and very long-term (twenty-seven weeks or more) unemployment rates as well as the average duration of unemployment were higher for men than for women.

Among both men and women there was a distinctive age pattern evident in long-term unemployment, although it was more marked for males than for females. The impact of long-term joblessness was lowest for prime-age workers (twenty-five to forty-four). The younger worker (fourteen to twenty-four) and the older worker (forty-five to sixty-four) showed evidence of somewhat greater difficulties in finding work once separated from a job. Average duration was highest for workers past the customary retirement age. Workers over the age of sixty-five who 'choose' (the choice may not be entirely voluntary)

[14]Three such surveys have been carried out for Canada by the Dominion Bureau of Statistics (they are, however, produced annually in the United States). See Dominion Bureau of Statistics, *Canadian Statistical Review* (November 1962), and Frank J. Whittingham and Bruce W. Wilkinson, *Work Patterns of the Canadian Population, 1964*, Special Labour Force Studies No. 2, Dominion Bureau of Statistics (Ottawa, 1967).

[15]See Ostry, *Unemployment*, for similar information for 1964.

TABLE 28

Summary Statistics on Unemployment Experience, 1968

Labour force group	Long-term unemploy- ment rate (a)	Very long- term unemploy- ment rate (b)	Average weeks unemployed (c)	Total unemploy- ment rate (d)
	(per cent)	*(per cent)*		*(per cent)*
Males				
14-19	8.3	3.2	11.4	30.4
20-24	8.2	3.3	13.0	23.8
25-44	4.5	1.7	13.7	12.6
45-64	4.8	2.0	17.9	9.4
65 and over	5.5	3.5	21.8	9.5
14 and over	5.6	2.2	14.0	15.0
Females				
14-19	5.4	2.3	9.5	27.2
20-24	4.2	1.9	11.5	15.3
25-44	2.8	1.3	10.5	11.1
45-64	2.8	1.5	12.1	7.4
65 and over	1.1	0.4	12.9	4.0
14 and over	3.5	1.6	11.1	13.2
Industry				
Agriculture	1.9	0.8	14.4	4.9
Other primary	14.7	6.0	17.4	28.8
Manufacturing	4.6	2.0	12.8	14.0
Construction	12.1	4.0	14.1	6.7
Transportation	5.0	2.0	15.4	12.0
Trade	3.6	1.6	12.1	12.3
Finance	2.2	0.6	9.7	9.1
Service	3.6	1.6	13.3	10.4
Public administration	3.6	1.8	16.9	8.2
Occupation				
Managerial	0.8	0.5	13.7	2.9
Professional, technical	0.9	0.3	8.7	4.7
Clerical	3.3	1.2	10.8	12.7
Sales	3.0	1.5	11.4	11.6
Agriculture	2.2	1.0	15.3	5.3
Other primary	19.0	7.6	17.9	35.1
Service	5.5	2.4	14.7	13.9
Transportation, communication	5.7	2.4	13.5	16.0
Craftsmen, etc.	6.5	2.4	13.7	17.3
Labourers n.e.s.	16.1	6.9	16.6	34.7

Regions

Atlantic	7.6	3.1	14.8	18.4
Quebec	7.8	3.7	16.3	18.3
Ontario	3.0	1.1	10.6	11.3
Prairies	2.6	1.0	10.4	10.4
British Columbia	5.1	1.8	11.1	18.3
Canada	4.8	2.0	13.1	14.6

(a) Number of persons unemployed 14 weeks or more as a percentage of number of persons in labour force in 1968.
(b) Number of persons unemployed 27 weeks or more as a percentage of number of persons in labour force in 1968.
(c) Total number of weeks of unemployment experienced by unemployed in 1968 divided by number of persons with some unemployment experience during 1968.
(d) Number of persons with some unemployment during 1968 as percentage of number of persons in labour force during 1968.

Source: Based on data from Dominion Bureau of Statistics, 'Annual Work Pattern Survey', January 1969 (unpublished).

not to leave the labour force evidently suffer very extended periods of unemployment once they become jobless – thirteen weeks on average for females, and almost twenty-two weeks for males. The incidence of long-term and very long-term unemployment among broad industry and occupation groups appears to be roughly similar to the incidence of over-all unemployment. It was lowest for agricultural workers and workers in service-producing industries and very marked in construction and in primary industries other than agriculture. Among occupations, it is evident that long-duration unemployment is especially severe for unskilled workers, who not only found it very difficult to regain employment once they lost their jobs but who, no doubt, were more subject to recurrent unemployment during the year than were most other groups of workers.[16] As may be seen from Table 28, white-collar groups experience the lowest rates of long-term unemployment, but even for these workers average duration of unemployment over the year is surprisingly high, ranging from nearly nine to almost fourteen weeks.

Finally, it may be observed that there is a distinctive regional pattern in the incidence of longer-term unemployment in Canada. We

[16]This aspect of unemployment – the number of different spells or stretches experienced during the year – was measured in an earlier (1964) survey and reveals that the problem of recurrent unemployment is especially severe in the construction and primary industries and among unskilled workers. *Ibid.*, p. 25. Further, recurrent unemployment is largely a blue-collar phenomenon; indeed, the higher incidents of long-term unemployment among skilled and semi-skilled manual workers than among white-collar groups is mainly the result of the greater frequency of repeated stretches of unemployment over the course of the year.

shall be discussing the regional aspects of unemployment in the following section, but these data afford an insight into aspects not revealed by the conventional statistics. The impact of longer-duration unemployment was especially severe in both the Atlantic region and Quebec: the differential between these regions and Canada as a whole was very much higher in the long-term rate than in the total rate. Further, while the total rate in British Columbia was as high as in eastern Canada, the long-term and very long-term rates in British Columbia were well below those in Quebec and the Atlantic region as was the average duration of unemployment. The risk of a worker *becoming* unemployed in British Columbia is thus little different from that in the two eastern regions, but the risk of *remaining* unemployed for a long period of time is apparently much lower. Ontario and the Prairies occupy, in terms of unemployment as well as literally, intermediate positions between the western and eastern regions of this country.

GEOGRAPHY

The achievement of full employment in Canada (if that is defined in terms of a minimal national rate of unemployment) will not of itself ensure a satisfactory balance of labour supply and demand in the five main regional markets. This is evident from observation of the regional unemployment rates in Table 24. Wide interregional and interprovincial differences in the level of unemployment are a persistent feature of the Canadian labour market. There have been only minor shifts in the ranking of these regional rates since the end of the war.

In the post-war period the absolute differences among regional unemployment rates have tended to be greater in years of low economic activity than in periods of prosperity. Thus, as economic conditions in Canada worsen (improve), the absolute increases (decreases) in unemployment tend to be greater in the high-unemployment regions such as the Atlantic provinces, Quebec, and British Columbia than in the more favoured Prairie provinces or Ontario.[17] Further, penetration below the regional level to smaller labour-market areas reveals substantial intra-regional dispersion of unemployment rates and also shows that a disproportionate share of the persistent 'surplus' or 'depressed' areas is located in the Atlantic region and Quebec.

The regional differences in unemployment levels reflect, for the most part, differences in regional labour-market conditions, i.e. greater or lesser degrees of structural maladjustment and – of consider-

[17]Cf. Denton and Ostry, *Post-War Unemployment*, and Frank T. Denton, *An Analysis of Interregional Differences in Manpower Utilization and Earnings*, Staff Study No. 15, Economic Council of Canada (Ottawa, 1966).

able importance in the Canadian context – greater or lesser seasonality of employment.[18] But unemployment rates across Canada also reflect regional differences in labour-force composition, in respect to the personal characteristics of workers as well as to deployment by industry and occupation. These latter (compositional) effects tend to amplify – but only slightly – the dispersion of the regional rates.[19]

Persistent unemployment differentials reflect only one aspect of regional disparities in manpower utilization in Canada. They are reinforced by – and no doubt in part related to[20] – marked interregional or interprovincial differences in total participation rates. The *combined* effect of higher unemployment and lower over-all participation in the Atlantic region and Quebec presents a more serious picture of manpower under-utilization than is revealed by observation of measured visible unemployment alone.[21] As was also mentioned earlier, these differences in manpower utilization are a primary factor explaining the distressingly high interregional differences in per-capita earned income in Canada.

SUMMARY OF CHARACTERISTICS

The 'typical' unemployed worker in post-war Canada, in good times and bad, is a young, male, poorly educated, manual labourer who works – intermittently – in the heavy-industry sector of the economy, and lives somewhere east of the Ontario border. But this bald statement, like the statistics on which it is based, masks many other dimensions we have left unexplored in our discussion. Visible unemployment, as it is conventionally measured, does not reveal the full extent of under-utilization of labour supply in this country. Involuntary part-time and part-year employment is likely to hit hardest those most seriously affected by unemployment. Moreover, we know little about the causal links between unemployment and poverty[22] or about

[18]Ostry, *Unemployment*, Table 14. Seasonal factors are far more severe in eastern Canada than in Ontario and the Prairies.

[19]*Ibid.*, Table 15. The interprovincial dispersion of rates 'standardized' for a number of compositional characteristics is lower than that of the actual rates.

[20]Regressing age-sex specific participation rates against a number of independent variables, including unemployment, for 237 counties and census divisions in 1961 reveals a significant, negative association with unemployment rates for all groups including prime-age males.

[21]Cf. Nand K. Tandan, *Underutilization of Manpower in Canada*, Special Labour Force Studies No. 8, Dominion Bureau of Statistics (Ottawa, 1969).

[22]Cf. Sylvia Ostry, 'A Note on Unemployment and Income: Some New Data', mimeographed, paper presented to the Canadian Political Science Association, Ottawa, June 8, 1967.

the social consequences, on families and entire communities, of the kind of unemployment and underemployment that becomes a way of life. The goal of full employment, to which we now turn in the remainder of this chapter, is not merely an economic but also (and increasingly) a social goal in our society.

The Goal of Full Employment

Soon after the Second World War all industrially advanced countries of the Western world committed themselves to a 'full-employment' policy. In Canada, this commitment took the form of an official pronouncement in a government White Paper issued in 1945 which reads as follows:

> ... the Government has stated unequivocally its adoption of a high and stable level of employment and income, and thereby higher standards of living, as a major aim of Government policy. It has been made clear that, if it is to be achieved, the endeavour to achieve it must pervade all government policy. It must be wholeheartedly accepted by all economic groups and organisations as a great national objective, transcending in importance all sectional and group interests.[23]

The statement represented a radical rupture with the past. The Great Depression and Keynes' *General Theory* (published in 1936) had undermined the deeply held faith in the traditional principles and policies of self-equilibrating economies and balanced budgets, while the war-time experience had induced a public acceptance of vastly expanded government fiscal and other intervention in the economic life of the country. Keynesian missionaries in the public service demonstrated their success by the language and tone of the White Paper. Fears of a serious post-war (reconversion) recession, such as had followed the First World War, and, indeed, of a long-run secular stagnation, hastened its preparation and release.

In retrospect, it is interesting to note that the White Paper contained no reference to price stability, although it did mention the importance for the longer-run performance of the economy of policies designed to improve productivity and labour-management relations, reduce trade barriers, etc. The overriding concern, however, was with employment and prosperity. No specific target of employment or unemployment was mentioned; the word 'high' was, many years later, translated (but

[23]*Employment and Income with Special Reference to the Initial Period of Reconstruction* (Ottawa, 1945).

not officially) into 97 per cent employment or 3 per cent unemployment by the Economic Council in Canada, as a 'reasonable' medium-term target. In only five out of the twenty-five years that have passed since the publication of the White Paper has the over-all rate of unemployment in Canada been 3 per cent or less; in only eleven years was it 4 per cent or less. Further, at *no* time during that quarter of a century was the unemployment rate in the Atlantic region significantly less than 5 per cent. The record, then, is clear and may be observed in the statistics presented in the earlier part of this chapter: 'full' employment, by any reasonable definition, has been the exception rather than the rule during most of the quarter-century since the publication of the White Paper, and the burden of unemployment has continued to be unevenly and inequitably distributed across this country.

Why was the promise of the White Paper not realized? Was the commitment to full employment repudiated? Certainly not explicitly – no contemporary government could afford to undertake the political risk involved in such a disavowal of responsibility. Then why has the performance with respect to this major goal of economic policy been so dismal during so much of the post-war period? It is important to recognize that we are judging performance not only with respect to the commitment of the White Paper, but also in comparison with the impressive record of achievement, in this field, of other industrial countries. As is widely known, the unemployment experience of Canada and the United States stands in marked contrast to that of the advanced economies of western Europe throughout much of the period.[24]

There is not a single, simple answer to the question raised above. There are a number of plausible explanations, and different observers and analysts would place different weights on the importance of each.

In part, the answer lies in the way in which demand-management policies were applied in post-war Canada. Fortunately, in this area of economic policy, unlike most others, there have been a number of careful reviews of the post-war experience,[25] and the interested reader can pursue the detailed exposition of the timing and use of the monetary, fiscal, foreign-exchange, and external-trade instruments in this country since the end of the Second World War. The consensus view of professional economists, who might differ in details of analysis but are sur-

[24]See R. A. Gordon, 'Employment and Unemployment', Reprint No. 323, Institute of Industrial Relations, University of California (Berkeley, 1968). Also David C. Smith, 'The Canadian Full Employment Goal', *The Canadian Banker* (Winter, 1964).

[25]See, for example, Canadian Trade Committee, *Canadian Economic Policy Since the War* (Montreal, 1966), and L. H. Officer and L. B. Smith, *Canadian Economic Problems and Policies* (Toronto, 1970).

prisingly agreed on the basic conclusion, is that 'the record of Canadian postwar policy is, at best, mediocre.'[26]

One must temper this judgment by recognizing that there were, and are, a number of serious difficulties in achieving effective demand management in a country like Canada which is exceptionally open to changes in the external environment and which is not a unitary state and therefore requires special institutional mechanisms for co-ordinating the content and timing of policy between the federal and provincial levels of government. Further, it has become increasingly evident that our knowledge about the impact of stabilization instruments was highly imperfect in the earlier post-war period, especially with respect to *timing* of impact. In more recent years, improved analysis with more sophisticated tools and better data has greatly enhanced our knowledge of the extent and nature of the various lags between the perception of the need for a change in strategy and the time that a policy action has its main effect.

But the quality of policy-making in post-war Canada was not the only factor affecting the performance with respect to full employment. In commenting on the United States' record (which is essentially the same as Canada's) one perceptive foreign observer has said:

> It is always unwise to shun the obvious. And the most obvious explanation, which fits not only the facts but also what people have said, is quite simply that Americans weakly chose employment because they chose price stability strongly. It may be that 'price stability' has often been used as a convenient shorthand for 'sound economic policies'.... Much has been said in Europe about the importance of price stability. But nowhere – not even in Germany, supposedly the classic case of inflation neurosis – have countries been prepared in the event to arrest their growth and create unemployment simply in order to stop prices from rising.[27]

There seems little doubt that post-war governments in Canada have 'weakly' chosen employment because they 'strongly' chose price stability. This is apparent not only from a careful reading of 'what people have said', but from an analysis of 'the facts'. In a careful evaluation of Canada's post-war economic policy undertaken for the Royal Commission on Banking and Finance, Professor Grant Reuber effectively demonstrates that either the governments did not understand the empirical relationships underlying the main performance indicators of the economy or, if they did, their behaviour suggests a strong preference

---

[26]*Canadian Economic Policy Since the War, op. cit.*, p. 3.

[27]Jack Downie, 'The Importance of Knowing What You Want', in *Unemployment and the American Economy*, A. M. Ross (ed.), New York, 1964, p. 162, quoted in Robert Aaron Gordon, *The Goal of Full Employment* (New York, 1967), p. 20.

for price stability over other objectives.[28] This analysis covered the years 1949-61. Whatever lingering doubt remained with respect to that period has been largely dispelled by policy decisions in the more recent past.

We have referred above to a 'choice' between two goals – full employment and price stability. In fact, this is a gross oversimplification of a highly complex policy problem, which was certainly not (nor could have been) fully perceived in the White Paper or during the early post-war years. The management of a modern economy involves devising an effective policy 'mix' to achieve multiple goals, some conflicting, some complementary, some largely autonomous. It is not a matter of full employment only, or of full employment *or* price stability, but a 'menu' or 'mix' of satisfactory or preferred combinations of employment, growth, and price change – given certain constraints such as those operating from the external environment. The notion of an effective over-all strategy designed for simultaneous achievement of multiple goals with trade-offs or complementarities among them has gradually emerged over the years since the publication of the White Paper.

MULTIPLE GOALS AND TRADE-OFFS

Canada, along with most advanced countries of the world, now proclaims an array of economic goals which include: (a) full employment; (b) a high rate of economic growth; (c) 'reasonable' stability of prices; (d) a viable balance of payments; (e) an equitable distribution of rising incomes.[29]

The first four represent the major 'aggregative goals' of economic performance for, as Professor R. A. Gordon has pointed out, they are concerned with the 'crucial economic aggregates: total employment, total output, the general level of prices, the total of payments to and receipts from the rest of the world'.[30] These aggregates are all interrelated and related, too, to the fifth goal, concerned with equity. Associated with each goal are one or more 'target variables' or measures by

---

[28]See G. L. Reuber, 'The Objectives of Canadian Monetary Policy, 1949-61', *Journal of Political Economy* (April 1964).

[29]Economic Council of Canada, *First Annual Review* (Ottawa, 1964). This list is derived from the terms of reference of the act establishing the council and, therefore, in a real sense represents an official government statement and not simply a view of the council, an advisory body.

[30]Gordon, *Goal of Full Employment*, p. 18. Gordon views only employment and growth as 'positive' goals, price stability and the balance of payments he views as constraints. Harry Johnson, among others, would reject growth as a goal. See *The Canadian Quandary* (Toronto, 1964).

which performance is evaluated, and certain instruments or policies that can be utilized in the achievement of specific goals, or targets.[31] (Target variables – and specific targets – are much more difficult to specify with respect to the equity goal.)

Presumably, the object of the over-all strategy or mix of policies, with respect to these five goals, is to achieve as high a level as possible of social welfare – although the difficulties inherent in conceptualizing, let alone measuring, the social-welfare function cannot be explored here[32] and the term 'social welfare' is used in a very rough, approximate sense to imply the political perception of widely held (but not necessarily unanimously held) value judgments concerning economic well-being in the community.

The achievement of full employment must be viewed within the context of this expanded list of goals. Further, this list is by no means exhaustive: no account is taken here of the increasingly important social goals of the community, which are now the subject of widespread discussion. The simultaneous achievement of multiple goals implies that the policy-maker must have knowledge of the interrelationships among the goals as well, of course, as the relationship between target variables and policy instruments.

The only interrelationship among the set of goals mentioned above that has been examined in any depth is that between employment and price stability.[33] While there have been a number of estimates of both the Phillips curve[34] (the wage-unemployment relationship) and the 'trade-off' (the price-unemployment relationship) for Canada, only one set of estimates, taken from a study commissioned by the Economic Council, which is the most extensive treatment yet available, will be reviewed here.[35] Only the main findings are briefly summarized, but

---

[31] For a full discussion of these terms and their analytical implications, see J. Tinbergen, *On the Theory of Economic Policy* (Amsterdam, 1966).

[32] See E. J. Mishan, 'A Survey of Welfare Economics, 1939-1959', *Economic Journal* (June 1960).

[33] See, however, R. G. Bodkin, 'An Analysis of the Trade-Offs Between Full Employment, Price Stability and Other Goals', in *Canadian Economic Policy Since the War, op. cit.*, who finds some evidence of conflict between price stability and growth and complementarity between full employment and growth.

[34] See A. W. Phillips' seminal article 'The Relation Between Unemployment and the Rate of Change of Money Wage Rates in the United Kingdom, 1861-1957', *Economica* (November 1958).

[35] Ronald G. Bodkin, Elizabeth P. Bond, Grant L. Reuber, and T. Russell Robinson, *Price Stability and High Employment: The Options for Canadian Economic Policy*, Special Study No. 5, Economic Council of Canada (Ottawa, 1966). See also, for Phillips curve estimates, S. F. Kaliski, 'The Relation Between Unemployment and the Rate of Change of Money Wages in Canada', *International Economic Review*, (January

the interested reader would do well to consult the source document and the other literature cited in the footnote for a fuller and more detailed examination of the subject in a Canadian context. (The concept of the Phillips curve is discussed in the context of wage-changes in Chapter VIII.)

The evidence presented in the Bodkin *et al.* study, while it differed in detail from that in similar analyses for Canada and elsewhere undertaken in the early 1960s, supported one main conclusion, common to all similar analyses. To quote the authors:

> ... there is almost certainly a conflict between the objectives of price stability and high employment.... no vestige of evidence has been found for Canada or any other country that suggests that within the range of experience under consideration, which is the range relevant in the formulation of economic policy in this country, these two objectives are complementary rather than conflicting.[36]

A second major finding of the study concerned the importance of external (especially U.S.) influences on Canadian wage and price determination. Thus, the authors stress: 'given this external influence and given the limitations constraining public policies, it is not likely that price changes in Canada can deviate very much from price changes in the United States.'[37] The problem of choosing *preferred* targets for both the employment and price goals that are also *feasible* targets must take into account changes in the external environment, more particularly, changes in U.S. prices.

These findings are amply documented in the empirical results presented in the study. Thus, to cite the 'best' wage-change relationship estimated by the authors, it indicates that over 80 per cent of the variation in the rate of wage increase in Canada over the period 1953-65 was explained by variations in the unemployment rate, in the level of unit profits in manufacturing (lagged half a year), in the rate of change in U.S. average hourly earnings, in the rate of change in consumer prices, and in Canadian average hourly earnings (lagged one year). The 'best' price-change equation (for the same period) reveals that the most important influences on the rate of change of Canadian prices (the consumer price index) were wages, import price changes, and lagged price changes. These two relationships were reduced to a

---

1964); J. Vanderkamp, 'Wage and Price Level Determination: An Empirical Model for Canada', *Economica* (May 1966); and Mahmood A. Zaidi, 'The Determinants of Money Wage Rate Changes and Unemployment-Inflation "Trade-Offs" in Canada', *International Economic Review* (June 1969).

[36]Bodkin, *et al, op. cit.*, p. 280.

[37]*Ibid.*, p. 281.

derived trade-off or, rather, a set of trade-offs, corresponding to various assumptions about the independent variables, which the Economic Council called the 'trade-off zone'. The zone is a useful device to illustrate the problem of conflict between the policy goals of high employment and price stability (and the council's *Third Annual Review* depicts it in chart form), but for our purposes it is simpler to select examples of particular trade-off relationships. Choosing the assumptions that inflationary pressures from the outside are absent (the rate of change of import prices is set equal to zero), that the rate of change of U.S. wages is just over 3 per cent, and that profits are set equal to the average of the 1953-65 period, the estimated trade-off indicates that the rate of unemployment required for price stability is 4.7 per cent or, alternatively, a 3 per cent unemployment rate entails an expected rate of inflation of 2.2 per cent.

But the impact of changes in the external environment is appreciable. When international prices are assumed to rise at the extremely modest rate of 2 per cent annually (and given appropriate values for the other variables), 3 per cent unemployment leads to a rise in the consumer price index of nearly 7 per cent per year. Even with this external environment some domestic deflation might pay off: a rise in unemployment to 5 per cent would produce a decline in price change to 4.2 per cent. Beyond that the trade-off becomes excessive: 10 per cent unemployment is still associated with price rises of over 3 per cent and there is *no* value of the unemployment rate (over the period examined) that was consistent with literal price stability. Thus, the study suggested, to pursue a policy in Canada that seeks to offset fully the inflationary pressures from the external environment would lead to extremely high unemployment in this country.

Since the mid sixties, and the outburst of empirical work on the Phillips curve and on trade-off curves, the thrust of research in this area has shifted in a more analytical direction, and the notion of a stable trade-off function, to be used as a guide for policy decisions, has come under increasing attack.[38] The attack has come from various directions and focuses on various issues, but the most important criticism centres on the key question of the stability of the Phillips (or derived trade-off) relationship, emphasizing the role of expectations in wage and price decisions. The literature is extensive and complicated

---

[38]For a review of much of the recent literature, see Albert Rees, 'The Phillips Curve as a Menu for Policy Choice', *Economica* (August 1970), and references cited therein. See especially *Microeconomic Foundations of Employment and Inflation Theory*, E.S. Phelps (ed.), (New York, 1970).

and cannot be reviewed here. In essence, the 'expectations' school argues that:

> The historical Phillips curve is not a menu for policy choice because it is traced out by relations between the level of unemployment and *unexpected* rates of inflation or deflation. Once a position on the Phillips curve is chosen as a matter of policy, and adhered to firmly enough so that it comes to be expected... the historical relation will no longer hold and the curve will shift.... [Thus] the 'steady-state' Phillips curve corresponding to a condition in which expectations are not disappointed is said to be a vertical line at some 'natural' rate of unemployment. In the long run the policy maker has no choices at all in the unemployment dimension – at whatever rate of inflation he chooses, the rate of unemployment will be the same.[39]

While the logic of the above argument is impeccable – depending only on the assumption of rationality of behaviour of workers and employers – the model has not yet been empirically verified. Evidence of instability in the Phillips curve does not constitute evidence of its non-existence. *A priori* reasoning suggests that even if all workers or employers were perfectly rational, they are not perfectly omniscient, and that there will be substantial lags in the rate at which different persons and different markets adjust their expectations of future wage and price change. And as Rees has argued, the assumption of lags in the adjustment process is 'sufficient to generate a downward-sloping long-run Phillips curve, though one with a steeper slope than the historical Phillips curve'.[40] But certainly more empirical investigation of the role of expectations in market behaviour is required before the controversy about the Phillips curve can be settled.

Our interest in the Phillips curve controversy lies less in the argument about its shape or in its precise specifications than in the policy implications that flow from the trade-off analysis. After all, it is well to remind the reader (and perhaps the writer!) that this section of the chapter is headed 'The Goal of Full Employment'. Taking the most extreme view of the matter, i.e. that the long-run Phillips curve is a vertical line, parallel to the Y axis (wages) and starting on the X axis at a point determined by the 'natural' rate of unemployment, still leads to certain policy conclusions that are not markedly dissimilar from those flowing from the more traditional view of the downward-sloping trade-off described in the Economic Council Special Study cited above. The traditional view, while it stresses the importance of effective demand-management policy in reaching and maintaining a preferred position *on* the trade-off curve, also suggests that policies designed to *shift* the

[39] *Ibid*, p. 228.
[40] *Ibid, loc. cit.*

curve, i.e. improve the trade-off between price rise and unemployment, are essential. Manpower policies, the subject of the next chapter, are prominently featured in any list of suggested policies directed toward shifting the curve. One might also derive similar policy implications from the 'vertical Phillips curve' school. The 'natural' rate of unemployment, at least according to some of its proponents, is determined by such factors as the cost of labour-market information, as reflected in the way in which workers search for jobs and employers search for workers. Manpower policies are directly relevant to this phenomenon of labour-market activity and the role of information in labour-market adjustment. Whether or not manpower policies are, or can be made to be, effective in either shifting the Phillips curve or reducing the 'natural' rate of unemployment is, of course, quite another matter. But their relevance to both views of the wage-unemployment or price-unemployment relationship does not seem to be in doubt.

Manpower policy is one of a number of policies that might be viewed as reconciliatory instruments, i.e. policies designed to improve the compatibility of conflicting goals, especially the employment-price goals. Another such reconciliatory policy, which has received a good deal of attention in Canada and elsewhere in recent years, is incomes policy, to which we now turn in the concluding section.

Incomes Policies

Incomes policies – some form of government-directed control over money incomes or incomes and prices – have been adopted in several countries over the past two decades or more. The use of this policy instrument to reinforce or supplement the traditional instruments of monetary and fiscal policy has been primarily stimulated, as noted above, by the desire of governments to reduce the rate of price increases at high levels of employment. Incomes policy has also been suggested as a long-run instrument for achieving a more equitable distribution of income, but we are here concerned only with its use as a price stabilization policy.

Incomes policy may be defined in a great many ways. The term has been used for policies directed toward the control of wages alone, or wages and other forms of earned income, or income and prices, or prices only; for selective or general instruments; for voluntary or involuntary guidance, etc. Any detailed exploration of the many variant forms of the policy or of the wide range of experience with its use in different countries would be well beyond the scope of this brief discussion. Several such surveys, however, are fortunately available for the interested reader.[41]

One of these surveys, undertaken for the Economic Council, suggests that a useful definition of incomes policy is 'the development by governments of specific criteria or guides for incomes and prices and the attempt to gain adherence to them through various forms of public pressures.'[42] Incomes policy thus involves measures designed to persuade or coerce employers and employees to accept profits and wages of some specified amounts that are different from those which would be determined by forces operating within the market environment.

The economic arguments for incomes policy, especially in western Europe where the policy has been widely used, have most often been couched in terms of avoiding balance-of-payments difficulties. Governments that are reluctant to use the exchange rate as a policy instrument (or are precluded from doing so because of international commitments), and that fear the adverse consequences on employment of extremely restrictive monetary and fiscal policy, have turned to some form of incomes policy to moderate price change in an effort to stem serious deterioration in their balance-of-payments position. Thus, as David Smith has noted, 'a review of the country's commitment to a specific set of economic goals, of the susceptibility of the economy to balance-of-payments difficulties ... is an important part of any general evaluation of the need for an incomes policy.'[43]

Many advocates of incomes policy stress a particular view or version of the inflationary process which emphasizes the importance of administered wages and price decisions. Thus, they argue, it is the exercise of undue economic power by firms and unions that results in 'cost-push' inflation. The long-standing controversy about 'demand-pull' and 'cost-push' inflation, which dominated discussion in the late

[41]See, especially, David C. Smith, *Incomes Policies: Some Foreign Experiences and Their Relevance for Canada*, Special Study No. 4, Economic Council of Canada (Ottawa, 1966), and references cited therein. A more recent review of European experience may be found in C. T. Saunders, 'Incomes Policies – What Are They For?', mimeographed, Proceedings of the Conference on Economic Planning and Macroeconomic Policy, The Japan Economic Research Center (Tokyo, 1971). For a discussion of the Canadian Prices and Incomes Commission, see Grant L. Reuber, 'Incomes Policy: Canada's Experiment with Organized Voluntarism to Curb Price Inflation', mimeographed, Research Report 7003, Department of Economics, University of Western Ontario (March 1970), and J. C. Weldon, 'Canadian Economic Policies, 1970: The Real and the Unreal', mimeographed, paper presented to the Canadian Economics Association, Winnipeg, June 1970.
[42]Smith, *op. cit.*, p. 186.
[43]*Ibid*, p. 187

1940s and early 1950s (see Chapter VIII), is revived each time the issue of the efficacy of incomes policy is raised. There are nearly always elements of both excess-demand and cost-push factors in any inflationary period (if, indeed, this simplistic distinction is relevant at all), but the problem of isolating and estimating the importance of each in contributing to persistent price increase in any given period has not yet been solved.

The pro-incomes policy school not only stresses the cost-push version of inflation, but also places great importance on the role of expectations in generating a wage-price spiral. Thus, incomes policy – particularly in its announcement effects – is supposed to play a role in changing the expectations of employers and unions as to future market conditions and, as a consequence, to change their behaviour in bargaining and pricing. In this version, incomes policy is not so much an economic as a psychological policy instrument!

How have incomes policies worked in the countries where they have been employed over the post-war period? One reviewer has summed up the situation, as of the mid sixties, thus:

> From the experiences abroad there is evidence to support the view that incomes policy has had, at times, some moderating effect on the rate of increase of prices, but it has been a failure at other times. ... In relatively normal peacetime conditions and in the absence of strong sanctions, it is doubtful whether incomes policy will have a large or lasting effect on the rate of increase of prices at high employment levels.[44]

A more recent analysis of post-war European experience arrives at pretty much the same conclusion: 'Incomes policy, used as a macroeconomic instrument for influencing short-term variations in the overall wage level, has yielded, and will continue to yield in the western European type of society, only short-term results,'[45] which, as the author effectively demonstrates, may be followed by more rapid increases in wages and prices to compensate for the slow-down during the period of restraint.

A policy instrument that achieves a reduction in the rate of price increase, even if only for a short period, may still be very useful if the country is faced with a serious economic crisis as, for example, severe pressure on the balance of payments. One can only evaluate the effectiveness of such an instrument, however, by assessing the costs in-

---

[44]*Ibid*, p. 192.

[45]Saunders, *op. cit.*, p. 12. The author goes on to argue that incomes policy might be a more effective instrument for long-term redistribution of earnings. Thus the word 'overall' is underlined in the original text.

curred in its use. Problems of recurring balance-of-payments crises, for example, are likely to be deep-seated, and thus to require long-term policies, of a more fundamental nature, for their solution. If the use of incomes policy diverts attention from, and weakens support for, stronger but more effective medicine, the real costs involved in its use as an alternative to other, perhaps less politically attractive, policies will be very high. Another possible cost, which deserves exploration, concerns the effects on resource allocation. Thus, incomes policy – as noted above – involves an intervention in the market mechanism. Since the specific targets for wages and prices are set on the basis of inadequate knowledge of the appropriate structure of these variables, there is a danger of introducing rigidities and distortions in the flow of manpower and other resources. The danger is lessened, of course, the shorter the period during which guidelines are imposed. But then so is the effectiveness of the policy lessened under such circumstances. Another danger that has often been mentioned by economists is that of escalation: pressure soon builds up to extend a few general guidelines into an extensive network of regulations involving sanctions for offending parties. The British example is most often cited in this respect.

Despite the less than overwhelming success of foreign experience, Canada recently adopted a form of incomes policy. This development is perhaps more surprising since the Canadian institutional framework, which severely limits the central government's power in labour matters and price regulation, would appear to be particularly inappropriate to such a policy instrument, as would the extremely open character of the Canadian economy which makes it so susceptible to the foreign, particularly United States, economic environment. Even the O.E.C.D., an international agency that has been among the strongest advocates of incomes policy, has stated (mildly, in the event) that 'the decentralized character of the Canadian economy may render the evolution of an incomes policy more difficult than in many European countries.'[46]

None the less, the Prices and Incomes Commission was established in May 1969, under very broad terms of reference allowing it very great leeway in its mode of operation. The P.I.C. was 'to enquire into and report upon the cause, processes and consequences of inflation and to inform those making current price and income decisions, the general public and the government, on how price stability might best be achieved.' Shortly after its establishment, in addition to securing voluntary compliance from industry to hold down prices below the level

---

[46]Organisation for European Cooperation and Development (O.E.C.D.), *Economic Surveys, Canada* (Paris, February 1968), p. 20.

'needed to cover the increase in costs',[47] the commission undertook reviews of specific pricing situations, launched a massive publicity campaign, and enunciated a wage and salary guideline (rejected by organized labour).

It is too early at the time of writing to evaluate the impact of Canadian incomes policy on wages and price determination in this country. The commission itself has a substantial research capacity and will, presumably, be undertaking such review on a continuing basis. Any effective new addition to the array of policy tools is clearly most welcome and, hopefully, careful economic analysis at some appropriate future date will indicate whether the Prices and Incomes Commission has, in fact, proved to be such a tool.

[47]'A Call for Action to Curb Price Increases: Closing Statement of the National Conference on Price Stability', *Financial Times of Canada* (Monday, March 2, 1970).

VI

Manpower Policy

Introduction

The decade of the 1960s witnessed, in North America and elsewhere, a burgeoning of interest in manpower policies and programs. In a sense, manpower policy was born in the sixties. Before this decade, programs directed to the allocation or quality of labour supply were minimal and certainly not dignified by so grand a term as 'active manpower policy'.[1] Before the sixties, government intervention in the labour market was largely confined to industrial-relations and labour-standards legislation (mainly a provincial responsibility in Canada) on the one hand, and unemployment insurance with its appendage, the public-employment service, on the other. Indeed the chief federal government 'presence' in the labour market in Canada was the National Employment Service office. Apart from a period of glory during the Second World War, when the N.E.S. was given expanded war-time powers, the image it evokes in the minds of many is of draughty, brown-painted, shabby ante-rooms with brass spittoons and silent knots of unemployed waiting to collect their insurance cheques. Limited and sporadic federal forays into the field of training are part of the 'pre-history' of manpower policy as well.[2]

It is now possible to distinguish two phases in the evolution of Canadian federal manpower policy during the 1960s, the second phase

[1]This term was, so far as one can ascertain, part of an oral vocabulary at the O.E.C.D. during the early sixties and probably is of Swedish parentage. It first appears in the literature just before the middle of the decade. It implies a shift from programs of a protective and regulatory nature to a more active, initiatory stance, but the term is loosely used to cover a wide variation in policy strategies.

[2]See Lionel Orlikow, *Dominion-Provincial Partnership in Education with Special Emphasis upon the Technical and Vocational Training Assistance Act, 1960-67*, Ph.D. dissertation (University of Chicago, 1960), for a review of the historical aspects of federal involvement in technical education in Canada.

158

being still in process early in a new decade. The high level of economic slack in the late fifties and early sixties generated, as we have already noted, a widespread debate in North America over the sources of un- employment. What Harry Johnson has called 'automation mongering' convinced many in the public and in government that structural trans- formation lay at the heart of the problem, and provided an important stimulus to the initiation and expansion of new policy instruments in the manpower sphere. The first phase of manpower-policy evolution in Canada stemmed largely from structuralist fears and was marked by the very rapid expansion of shared-cost, manpower-training programs under the Technical and Vocational Training Act (T.V.T.A.). The second phase was initiated in 1966 by the establishment of a separate department – the Department of Manpower and Immigration (D.M.I.). This reorganization brought together in a single ministry the various manpower programs formerly operated by the Department of Labour, the immigration services of the Department of Citizenship and Immi- gration, and most of the former National Employment Service organi- zation. It thus laid the foundation for providing a fully integrated, comprehensive, active manpower policy, embracing a broad range of programs operating on the supply side of the labour market. It differs from the earlier phase, therefore, in its comprehensive nature and in respect to the expanded role of the federal government in planning and operation. For the most part, in what follows, we will be con- cerned with present D.M.I. policy, although where it is possible to provide some information for the earlier part of the decade, it will be included.

This chapter is concerned with the analysis of manpower policy or strategy. To this end, we will treat first the issue of 'why manpower policy?' by considering alternative goals or objectives. Policy, of course, consists of a set of specific programs, and these will be reviewed next. Finally, the question of evaluation will be considered by referring to one of the models used by the department and raising some more gen- eral issues relating to evaluation of manpower policy. It is important to note that the structure of the D.M.I. explicitly provides for contin- uing research and evaluation, in that a major division of the depart- ment, the Programme Development Service, is responsible for this function.

Policy Goals

The term strategy (used as a synonym for policy) involves an objective, or perhaps several objectives, of which one may be dominant; a choice of specific programs designed to achieve the objective(s); and a process of systematic evaluation that serves as an aid to decision-making and provides a means of learning feed-back for adaptation and revision of programs and policy.

This simple conceptual framework is a useful device for analysing policies and will be followed here.[3] Since objectives or goals are of primary importance in discussing manpower or any other policy, it is logical to begin with a discussion of goals.

Manpower policy – or, indeed, any economic policy of government – may be directed to the achievement of one or more of three goals or objectives: growth, equity, and stabilization.[4] These three objectives are clearly not independent. For example, any set of manpower programs will have distributional consequences, i.e. will affect some population groups more than others, thereby widening or narrowing income gaps. Again, a policy designed to improve the matching of men and jobs may not only raise output per man-hour (growth), but may lessen cost and price pressures at any given level of unemployment (stabilization). And so on. Thus, any policy, even if directed solely to the achievement of a single goal, will have spill-over into other goal areas. Most policies, however, are directed to multiple rather than single objectives, although there is usually a dominant 'thrust' or orientation. That is certainly true of manpower policy in this country, as we shall see below. Before we turn to Canadian policy, however, it is useful to spell out the rationale for manpower policy *per se* in terms of the three objectives cited above.

GROWTH

The growth case for manpower policy rests essentially on two arguments: that the labour market is defective as an allocative mechanism and that there is a positive net return to government intervention to improve its allocative efficiency. It is useful to spell out the chain of reasoning implicit in these rather terse statements so that we may better assess the potential contribution of manpower policy to the goal of economic growth.

[3]The choice of a particular strategy involves a consideration of alternatives, since there are usually many routes to the same destination. The 'grand' trade-offs – health versus defence, etc. – involve political or value choices among broad goal areas.
[4]Cf. Burton Weisbrod, 'Benefits of Manpower Programs: Theoretical and Methodological Issues', in *Cost-Benefit Analysis of Manpower Policies*, G. G. Somers and W. D. Wood (eds.), Industrial Relations Centre, Queen's University (Kingston, 1969). Weisbrod uses the term 'allocative efficiency' instead of growth, the former being more precise since it includes once-and-for-all as well as continually expanding program effects.

The statement that the labour market is imperfect hardly needs documentation. The sources of imperfection are varied. In a dynamic economy, changes in the composition of final demand and in technology, depletion of natural resources, etc., give rise to mismatching between labour supply and demand. The process of adjustment is impeded in a number of ways, and, as a consequence, structural unemployment, bottle-necks, cost and price pressures, and the like result. Impediments to adjustment arise from institutional arrangements in the market – trade unions, oligopolies, government labour-standards regulation, for example – that discourage mobility and create rigidities in wages and prices. Ignorance is also a factor impeding adjustment. The text-book assumption about perfect knowledge is clearly violated in the labour market, where many workers have only a partial and fragmented view of job openings and employers only limited information on the numbers and characteristics of available workers. Moreover, not only is the labour market imperfect; so is the capital market. Since the transformation of labour supply to accord with changes in demand is a time-consuming process involving, perhaps, retraining or migration, some capital is required. An unemployed worker is likely to encounter serious difficulty in borrowing money in order to move himself and his family to a new location where jobs are available or to take courses to acquire new skills that are in demand. In sum, growth involves change; change necessitates reallocation; reallocation or adaptation to change is impeded by imperfect markets. So goes the first part of the argument.

The role of manpower policy, in the context of this rationale, is to improve the defective allocative mechanism of labour (and capital) markets. In other words, by providing for training, assisted mobility, improved labour-market information, vocational counselling, etc., the government facilitates a better matching of supply to changing labour demand, thereby reducing structural unemployment and other pressures and strains in the market that impede and distort growth.

While there seems little doubt that manpower policy can improve the allocative efficiency of the labour market, this is *not* tantamount to saying that manpower policy (training, mobility, information, etc.) thereby contributes to economic growth. Improving allocative efficiency is a 'good thing', i.e. a benefit to the economy. But manpower programs involve real resource costs, such as building training schools, hiring trainers, running Canada Manpower Centres, etc., which represent 'opportunity costs' or forgone alternatives. The question of whether or not manpower policy contributes to economic growth, therefore, boils down to resolving the familiar problem of whether the benefits of manpower policy exceed its costs.[5] Further, one should distinguish between a one-shot increase in output and an increase in the growth rate over time which would require expansion of economically efficient programs.

We shall be discussing benefit-cost analysis in a later section of this chapter in connection with the evaluation of manpower training. At this stage in the discussion, it is sufficient simply to emphasize that manpower policy is more likely to contribute to economic growth if there are substantial positive externalities, or benefits that the private market fails to capture. Improved labour-market flexibility is an example of such an externality.[6] Unfortunately, externalities are difficult to measure and have almost become an article of faith, to be raised in an argument when all else fails!

EQUITY

Manpower programs are, particularly in the United States, considered a preferable alternative to transfer payments (relief, unemployment assistance, transfer of goods, etc.) in altering income distribution to favour the disadvantaged. Thus, in the United States, training, counselling, placement services, etc., are largely oriented to the long-term unemployed, minority groups, residents of depressed areas, ghetto youth, the unskilled, etc. The goal of such programs is to reduce the number of persons and families living in poverty (usually defined with respect to some minimal level of income). This is, presumably, the goal of all transfer programs. But the rationale for choosing manpower programs over income transfers is that, given the work-oriented culture of our society, income from employment has a higher utility to the recipient than income from transfer payments. It may also be argued that there are positive externalities derived from reducing poverty through the manpower route and negative externalities flowing from using transfer income. Thus, retraining a disadvantaged worker who is a family head and thereby improving his chances of finding and keeping a job will have positive effects on his family, raising his self-respect and dignity, and changing the aspirations and attitudes of his children. Allowing him to live on welfare, on the other hand, is more likely to have the opposite effect.

[5]In theory, even if manpower policy generated benefit-cost ratios greater than one, other policies might generate better returns and thus the 'forgone alternatives' include public as well as private undertakings.
[6]If there are substantial economies of scale in the provision of training or labour-market information, this, too, strengthens the case for government intervention. Unfortunately no 'hard' research exists in this area.

The notion of equity, as a goal of manpower policy, may have dimensions other than the poverty aspect just mentioned. Thus, it may be considered desirable to reduce regional income disparities, and, indeed, that is a major goal of Canadian economic policy. Once again, manpower programs may be utilized as an alternative (or supplement) to transfer programs for essentially the same reasons suggested above: differences in utility between transfer income and income from work, and positive (intergenerational) rather than negative externalities. It should be noted that differences in utility cannot be quantified, and externalities are difficult to measure,[7] so that the efficiency criterion (benefit/cost ratios greater than one) may not be satisfied in respect to programs directed to equity goals. The problem, therefore, is to determine some acceptable trade-off between allocative efficiency and equity itself. This is a political (value) and not purely an economic problem.

STABILIZATION

How can manpower policy contribute to the goal of stabilization in the economy? As we have stressed in the previous chapter, the goal of stabilization has changed over the post-war period from one of achieving full employment, i.e. smoothing out cyclical fluctuations in unemployment, to one of reconciling employment and price-stability objectives. Thus, it is more pertinent to ask: what effect will manpower policy have on the levels of unemployment and prices?

Manpower policy, like any other government expenditure policy, will have a direct effect on aggregate demand, i.e. will increase the demand for labour and other resources. In this respect, it is like building roads or bridges, expanding the public service, increasing foreign aid, etc., although the multiplier or secondary effects might differ. Thus, a direct effect of manpower policy is to increase employment – employment of civil servants, trainers, construction workers (for building training institutions), etc. In so far as the resources used are in short supply, the direct demand effects of manpower policy may encourage wage and price increases. However, when economists talk about manpower policy as a stabilization tool, they are clearly not thinking about the direct effects. They appear to be operating with an implicit assumption that if the government were not allocating funds to manpower policy those funds would be absorbed in some other form of government activity

[7]Intergenerational effects have, in fact, been measured in the context of educational levels. See William J. Swift and Burton A. Weisbrod, 'On the Monetary Value of Education's Intergeneration Effects', *Journal of Political Economy* (December 1965). The same methodology could be applied to mobility or training if the data were available.

or in reduced taxes and increased private expenditure. If this is so – and it would be very difficult to prove one way or the other – then one should assume that manpower policy does not affect the level of aggregate demand.

How, then, will manpower policy affect unemployment? The answer is precisely the same as that given in the case of the growth objective: manpower policy, directed to structural unemployment, will improve allocative efficiency – output per head – if the benefits outweigh the costs. This improvement in allocative efficiency would result, if one wants to view it this way, in a south-westward shift in the Phillips curve, i.e. less price pressure at given levels of unemployment or vice versa. Accepting this line of reasoning, the stabilization objective and the growth or allocative efficiency objective really amount to the same thing, i.e. the economic rationale for both is identical.

There is, however, another way of looking at the stabilization objective of manpower policy. This argument stresses the timing rather than the level or content of expenditure on manpower programs. Thus, given a budgetary allocation for manpower policy, the programs should be geared to a contra-cyclical (or contra-seasonal) operation schedule. The example of training is most appropriate, since the degree of flexibility in some of the other programs is somewhat lower. To use manpower training as a stabilization tool would involve accelerated build-up of training courses during periods of high unemployment and rapid tapering-off as the economy approached full employment. The costs of training are lower during periods of economic slack (both real resource costs and forgone earnings of trainees), which is, of course, an advantage. Further, there is an undoubted political appeal in absorbing the unemployed into class-rooms and removing them from visible, measured unemployment. Whether or not their employability has improved upon release from training is, of course, another question – or, rather, the same old question: does manpower policy contribute to growth?

GOALS OF CANADIAN MANPOWER POLICY

Canadian manpower policy is, at least in intention, strongly growth-oriented. This is clear from the following quotations:

> The main objective of the Department (of Manpower and Immigration) is to further the economic growth of Canada by endeavouring to ensure that the supply of manpower matches the demand qualitatively, quantitatively and geographically.[8]

[8]Testimony of Hon. Allan J. MacEachen, Minister of Manpower and Immigration. *Minutes of Proceedings*, February 11 and March 24, 1970, No. 1, House of Commons' Standing Committee on Labour, Second Session, Twenty-eighth Parliament (Ottawa, 1970), p. 1:10.

The general aim of Canadian manpower policy is to encourage the effective allocation of manpower resources and the development of the labour force supply and characteristics compatible with the maximum sustainable rate of growth in real per capita income.[9]

A number of similar statements, including some taken directly from the legislation establishing the major programs, serve to underline and emphasize the growth objective of Canadian manpower policy. None the less, there are elements of both an equity and a stabilization orientation as well. In the brief of the Department of Manpower and Immigration to the Special Senate Committee on Poverty, it was asserted that manpower training funds 'were distributed among the geographic regions of Canada on the basis of the size of the labour force in each region as well as their economic need as indicated by their unemployment and poverty rates.'[10] Further, the (then) Assistant Deputy Minister of the D.M.I., Dr. W. R. Dymond, commenting on Canadian policy, noted that 'it is not oblivious to the problems of poverty and of the needs of marginal groups in the labor force and, recently, is moving heavily in this direction.... Such objectives can be said to be secondary to the primary objective of facilitating economic growth....'[11] In the same speech Dr. Dymond states that 'in recent years, we are beginning to increase our emphasis on manpower policy as a selective instrument of economic stabilization policy... to assist in absorbing surplus labor in productive activities such as training in periods of recession.'[12]

One might fairly conclude, at least on the basis of stated intentions, that the Canadian government's strategy in the field of manpower policy is primarily a growth strategy, with secondary objectives of equity and stabilization. This stands in sharp contrast with the United States' policy, which is predominantly oriented to the disadvantaged, i.e. to considerations of equity. The concern of the United States with racial problems no doubt plays a large role in its particular orientation, but perhaps it also reflects the view that the average worker will probably be adequately served by the private market, but the disadvantaged will be ignored unless the government intervenes on their behalf. Sweden provides yet another contrasting strategy. The role of an active

[9]Planning and Evaluation Branch, Program Development Service, Department of Manpower and Immigration. 'The Canadian Adult Training and Retraining Program', paper prepared for O.E.C.D. (July 1968), p. 1.

[10]*Department of Manpower and Immigration Brief*, submitted to Special Senate Committee on Poverty, June 1969, p. 375.

[11]William R. Dymond, 'The Canadian Experience', *Proceedings of the 1970 Annual Spring Meeting*, Industrial Relations Research Association, May 8-9, 1970, p. 545. See also U.S. Department of Labor. Manpower Administration. *Canada Manpower Policy and Programs*, Manpower Research Bulletin No. 16 (November 1968).

[12]Dymond, *op. cit.*

manpower policy is far broader and carries far more weight than in either Canada or the United States. 'Not only does the Swedish Labor Market Board direct a vast array of conventional manpower ... programs, but it also controls many expenditure programs; further, it closely coordinates its efforts with those of agencies concerned with economic affairs to determine the level and location of employment; beyond this, it has made an effort to coordinate its policies with those of noneconomic agencies – like those in the housing area – whose decisions may influence the location of workers.'[13] Perhaps Swedish policy goes beyond what we would conventionally define as manpower policy, since it deals not only with the supply of labour, but also with demand, and with the integration of the two.

If Canadian manpower policy is primarily directed toward increasing the growth of the Canadian economy, it seems a logical and legitimate question to ask 'how well has it achieved this objective?' We have already seen, in discussing the rationale for manpower policy as a growth policy, that this will not be an easy question to answer. Any answer, however tentative, will depend on a careful evaluation of the ongoing programs, an evaluation demanding highly sophisticated data and analysis. Before turning to the problem of evaluation, we must now briefly outline the content of the major components of manpower policy in Canada – the programs.

The Programs

The major programs of the D.M.I. consist of training, manpower mobility, and provision of labour-market information, counselling, and placement through the Canada Manpower Centres. Immigration policy, which is also a responsibility of the department, has been dealt with in Chapter I.

TRAINING

In Canada, education is constitutionally a provincial responsibility so that it is, perhaps, surprising that, during the decade of the 1960s, federal involvement in technical and vocational training (simply another type of education) has been so substantial. The rationale has been that

---

[13]Leonard J. Hausman, 'Manpower Policies: Lessons for the U. S. from Foreign Experience', *Proceedings of the 1970 Annual Spring Meeting, op. cit.*, p. 554.

because manpower training is directly related to the labour market, the federal government's role follows from its general responsibility for economic policy. Of course the same argument might be applied to other areas of education, particularly post-secondary education, and some would assert the need for a federal role in these areas as well. On the other hand, it is by no means clear that the federal involvement in manpower training will remain unchallenged in the future, particularly by the larger provinces. However, that is another matter, and a complex one: the issue of the constitutional division of powers in this country. Such a discussion lies entirely outside the scope of our present concern, which is simply to describe the extent and nature of the present federal manpower training program in Canada.

Federal participation in manpower training is, at present, confined to adults and carried out under the Adult Occupational Training Act (O.T.A.) initiated in early 1967 by the (then) newly formed Department of Manpower and Immigration. Heavy federal involvement in this field, however, pre-dates the passage of the O.T.A., and, indeed, coincides with the first year of the decade. In December 1960, the Technical and Vocational Training Act (T.V.T.A.) ushered in the new era of manpower policy in Canada, which, among other things, involved $1.2 billion of capital expenditure (roughly half of which was federally funded) on training institutions throughout the country. In addition to capital grants, the federal government contributed a major portion of the operating costs for training three groups in the population: (a) youths in technical and vocational high schools; (b) youths and adults requiring technical training to qualify as technicians; (c) adults, employed or unemployed, who required training to find jobs or improve their employment prospects. The total federal expenditure under T.V.T.A. between 1960-1 and 1966-7 was about $900 million, and by mid decade close to half a million workers were enrolled in technical and vocational high schools, receiving training courses under the act.

The present program, the O.T.A., differs from its predecessor in three important respects. It is not a shared-cost program; it does not include capital grants;[14] it is confined entirely to adults. Thus, under the O.T.A., the federal government pays 100 per cent of operating costs for the provision of adult technical and vocational training as well as

---

[14]The act provides transitional arrangements (related to T.V.T.A.) for capital grants and a provision for thirty-year loans to provincial governments for the purchase or construction of training facilities. This provision had not (at the time of writing) been put into effect.

the full cost of training allowances to approved trainees. The Department of Manpower purchases training services, after consultation with the provinces, from provincial technical institutions, private schools, and industry. The training-in-industry portion of the total program is, as we shall see below, very small.

Training is available to persons who are at least one year past the regular school-leaving age and either have been out of school for one year or are in an apprenticeship course. There is only one other requirement for eligibility: the person may be employed or unemployed, but must, in the judgment of the administrator in the Canada Manpower Centre (which replaced the old National Employment Service offices), be deemed capable of benefiting from training in terms of improved earnings prospects.

One should distinguish between eligibility for training, described above, and eligibility for training allowances. Living allowances are paid to trainees with dependants and to single persons who have been in the labour force for three years preceding training.[15] These allowances are well above unemployment-insurance benefits but, on average, below previous earnings. They vary with the number of dependants of the trainee and by region. In 1970-1, the minimum allowance was forty-three dollars, the maximum eighty-eight dollars, with an additional twenty-three dollars provided for those living away from home. A small travel grant is provided to the latter, and a commuting grant for persons having to travel some distance to the training centre.

Under the O.T.A., some 800 different courses are available, providing skills for a very wide variety of occupations at the subprofessional level. These skill-training courses have a maximum duration of one year of full-time instruction, or 1,800 hours of part-time instruction. Provision is also made, however, for basic upgrading, called 'Basic Training for Skill Development' (B.T.S.D.), which can be taken by individuals prior to a specific occupational course if required.

As the above description suggests, the training aspect of Canadian manpower policy is very substantial indeed. Under the O.T.A., between 1967-8 and 1970-1, the federal government spent close to $1.3 billion, or over $300 million on average each year since the inception of the program. The Canadian expenditure on training per labour-force member is well above that in the United States – more than double, in fact.

---

[15]Quite recently, the 'three-year requirement' has been more loosely interpreted as three years of labour-force attachment at any time in the past. This allows the C.M.C.s to qualify more married women, previously excluded under the more stringent interpretation.

On average, three-quarters of 1 per cent of the labour force are in an O.T.A. program at any given time, but the operation is strongly contra-seasonal, rising to 1½ per cent in the winter, and dropping to ¼ per cent in the summer.[16] The program is also designed, as mentioned earlier, to offset regional disparities: training expenditure per labour-force member is well above average in the Atlantic region and Quebec, while the opposite holds true in the more prosperous parts of the country.

In contrast with the United States and, indeed, all other countries for which data are available, most government-financed manpower training for adults in Canada is conducted in institutions rather than in industry. Over 95 per cent of total O.T.A. expenditures (excluding apprenticeship) go to institutional training, whereas in the United States, for example, about 80 per cent go to industry.

It is difficult to understand the reason for this heavy, almost exclusive, emphasis on institutional training in Canada, particularly since most experts agree that, where feasible, training in industry is to be preferred.[17] It seems clear that, for many occupations and many types of workers, learning in a work environment is more likely to result in skill acquisition and familiarity with production processes, equipment, institutional rules of employment, work scheduling, etc., than learning in a class-room. Further, the trainee is, in fact, 'employed' while learning – an important psychological factor motivating him to respond to instruction. An argument against training in industry is that it may be too specific in nature and hence reduce the potential mobility of the worker. In recognition of this risk, the federal act, the O.T.A., states that in order to qualify for subsidy, training in industry must be general in nature, it cannot be conducted on the job, and the resultant output may not be sold. Where industry training is approved (and, as we have noted, very little is undertaken at present) the federal government pays all the operating costs – instructors' salaries, rental of premises, equipment and supplies – and half the wage-costs of trainees.[18]

---

[16]Dymond, *op. cit.*, p. 546.

[17]See, for example, M. J. Piore, 'On-the-Job Training and Adjustment to Technological Change', *Journal of Human Resources* (Fall, 1968); U. S. Congress, Senate Subcommittee on Employment and Manpower of the Committee on Labor and Public Welfare, *Selected Readings in Employment and Manpower* (Washington, 1964), Vol. 3; Alice Rivlin, 'Critical Issues in the Development of Vocational Education', in *Unemployment in a Prosperous Economy*, W. G. Bowen and F. H. Harbison (eds.) (Princeton, 1965).

[18]The act stipulates that trainees coming under the contract must be hired by the firm. When labour is in surplus, firms have little incentive to engage in training-in-industry under the O.T.A.

MANPOWER MOBILITY

The Manpower Mobility Programme was begun in 1965, but liberalized and significantly altered in 1967, after the establishment of the D.M.I. Under the new program, administered by the Canada Manpower Centres, mobility grants may be paid to workers of eighteen years of age or over who are unemployed, underemployed, or facing lay-off, and unable to find jobs in their local area, but for whom suitable work can be secured in a new area. The original program restricted grants almost entirely to the cost of moving, but the 1967 amendments expanded the granting formulae to cover three types of allowances: trainee travel grants, exploratory grants, and relocation grants.

Trainee travel grants have already been mentioned in connection with the manpower training schemes. They are paid to workers who cannot be trained in their own area and cover travel costs, meals, and accommodation.

Exploratory grants assist workers to leave home and look for work in another area. They are usually confined to exploration in the nearest area where work opportunities exist and cover travel expenses, meals, and accommodation. Workers' dependants also receive a subsistence allowance.

Relocation grants are paid to workers who have confirmed jobs in another area. They cover removal and travel expenses, a re-establishment allowance, and a grant to help cover losses involved in the sale and purchase of homes.

Table 29 shows the numbers of grants authorized and the expenditures for the three fiscal years 1967-8 to 1969-70. It may be seen that, while the program was still very small, it had increased each year since its initiation.

Information on the characteristics of relocation grant recipients shows that they are predominantly male, younger than the average labour-force member, more likely than the average worker to be single, and having about the same average level of education as that of the work force as a whole. The vast majority of mobility grants subsidize movement within the province of origin. The proportion going to intraprovincial relocation is, as would be expected, lower for the Atlantic provinces than for the rest of Canada.

CANADA MANPOWER CENTRES

The organization that delivers all manpower programs to the client population is the Canada Manpower Division of the D.M.I. It is represented throughout the country by a network of more than 350 offices called Canada Manpower Centres (C.M.C.) These centres are the

TABLE 29

Manpower Mobility Grants by Type: Canada, 1967-70

Year	Type of grant							
	Relocation		Exploratory		Trainee travel		Total	
	No.	*$000*	*No.*	*$000*	*No.*	*$000*	*No.*	*$000*
1967-8	5,757	2,588.9	4,438	118.7	18,352	351.6	28,547	3,059.1
1968-9	6,591	3,425.1	6,351	224.8	31,757	574.9	44,729	4,224.8
1969-70	6,858	5,337.6	7,487	408.1	32,284	523.6	46,629	6,269.3
1970-1	6,382	4,199.8	7,370	328.0	71,094	2,691.4	84,846	7,219.3

Source: Department of Manpower and Immigration, *Annual Reports.*

institutional arm through which manpower policy operates.

The centres engage in a broad range of activities which can, however, be summarized as follows:

1. Placement: place workers in jobs or find workers for employers with vacancies.

2. Information: provide information on job opportunities to workers or on labour-supply sources to employers. The information function also includes counselling both workers and employers.

3. Referral to other programs: refer workers for training; mobility grants; arrange for recruiting abroad through the immigration service.

The client population of the C.M.C.s consists not only of unemployed workers seeking jobs but also of employed workers who may want to find better jobs or to upgrade their skills or to move to better jobs. In addition, of course, the C.M.C.s accept and solicit job orders from employers and may counsel employers on training programs or other sources of labour supply. The C.M.C.s, in an effort to secure a better over-all match between workers and jobs in each labour market on a continuing basis, must decide which service is most appropriate to effecting this match.

It is apparent from the description of the functions of the C.M.C.s that their effective operation depends crucially on the quantity and quality of information available to them. Placement activity requires highly detailed information on current job vacancies (demand) and worker numbers and characteristics (supply). Decisions about training and mobility programs require information on prospective demand and supply. Further, since a particular worker might be eligible for placement, training, mobility, etc., the C.M.C.s must allocate these services, subject to certain constraints, in an effort to achieve some sort of optimal balance, i.e. to maximize net benefits for the operation as a whole. This is clearly a tall order. It is made even more difficult because the C.M.C.s are not the only intermediary in the labour market but compete with other institutions such as private employment agencies who offer similar services with respect to placement and information.

The department has clearly recognized the importance of labour-market information and has allocated substantial resources to its development. To date the most costly investment ($1 million annually) has been the Job Vacancy Survey, a joint undertaking of the D.M.I. and the D.B.S., which involves a national sample survey of current job vacancies by detailed occupation and area.[19] The effective use of

---

[19]For a full description of the Survey see Sylvia Ostry and Alan Sunter, 'Canadian Job Vacancy Survey', *Journal of the American Statistical Association* (September 1970).

such a survey for policy decisions requires highly sophisticated research, since the survey output cannot be utilized directly for placement purposes. Analysed in conjunction with supply information, however, the job-vacancy information can provide meaningful insight into emerging bottle-neck situations, i.e. occupations and/or areas where the ratio of persistent vacancies to unemployment is high and rising. The detailed labour demand-and-supply information will enable the skilful analyst to probe for structural elements that the supply (unemployment) information alone cannot reveal.

In addition to the Job Vacancy Survey, the D.M.I. also generates and compiles a vast array of administrative data emerging from its own operations. These data cover, for example, information on employer job orders and on clients, as well as statistics related to placements, training, mobility, etc. Almost none of this administrative information is published, so that, while it is used internally by the department for operational and evaluation purposes, the interested public, especially the researcher, is not able to assess the effectiveness of the C.M.C.s as labour-market intermediaries.

The development of the labour-market information system is the responsibility of the Program Development Service of the D.M.I., which also carries out the research function and the evaluation activity. We shall be discussing evaluation later in this chapter, but should point out here that the research activity embraces not only analytical studies of the labour market, but also projections of occupational requirements, supply projections (including studies related to immigration), technological trend studies, etc. The budget of this branch is, at present, over 1 per cent of the total budget of the D.M.I., which is probably relatively higher than the funds allocated to this type of activity in most federal departments, reflecting the strong emphasis on information, research, and evaluation. Whether or not, to what degree, and in what direction policy formulation and implementation have been affected by information, research, and evaluation is not really known, if indeed it is ever really knowable in any final, precise sense.

The C.M.C.s are very different institutions from their predecessors, the National Employment Service (N.E.S.) offices. The latter were primarily adjuncts to the operation of the unemployment-insurance system and did not play a major role in initiating and implementing a comprehensive manpower policy. But just as the role assigned to the N.E.S. was no doubt far too narrow, it may be that the role of the C.M.C.s is too broad. It is difficult to monitor an institution that has so comprehensive a set of objectives that no readily understandable or feasible set of evaluation principles for the over-all responsibility can be devised. It might be useful to view the C.M.C.s as one institution in a

174 / *Labour Economics in Canada*

pluralist market, in which other intermediaries as well as individual workers and employers all play a role, and not as the single source of all information, all placement, all training, etc. The notion of effective specialization, rather than comprehensiveness, in some of these functional areas might fruitfully be explored. This notion seems promising in the information area, where it has been suggested, for example, that the government might concentrate on the collection and dissemination of comprehensive 'extensive' rather than 'intensive' information, or focus on particular occupational markets that are poorly served by alternative intermediaries, etc.[20] In more general terms, government action might be directed to areas where substantial economies of scale are likely to exist, or areas not served (or poorly served) by the unassisted market.

OTHER PROGRAMS

While training, mobility, and job market placement and information form the three main pillars of manpower policy in Canada, other elements of the over-all strategy deserve mention for the sake of completeness.

The Manpower Consultative Service was established in 1963 'to assist both workers and employers to adjust to technological and economic changes'.[21] When the D.M.I. was formed in 1966 the service was transferred to the new department. The program's objective is to encourage research and planning by unions and management in order to anticipate and resolve dislocations resulting from technological change. The federal government provides up to 50 per cent of the research costs. No information is available for evaluation purposes.

The Vocational Rehabilitation Branch of the Canada Manpower Division administers the Vocational Rehabilitation of Disabled Persons Act. The C.M.C.s employ special counsellors to deal with handicapped workers, who may be assigned to training programs or placed in employment. The federal government pays 50 per cent of the costs incurred by the provinces for programs of vocational rehabilitation.

[20]See, for example, Arnold R. Weber, 'The Role and Limits of National Manpower Policies', *Proceedings of the Industrial Relations Research Association* (December 1965) and especially reference to Albert Rees, p. 48. 'Extensive' information deals with counts and general characteristics of job openings or seekers, while 'intensive' information covers much more detail on, say, working conditions, informal relations, promotion possibilities, personal characteristics and quality of workers, etc. See also Noah M. Meltz, 'The Economic Role of Canada's Public Employment Service', mimeographed, prepared for the Department of Manpower and Immigration (September 1970).
[21]Dymond, *op. cit.*, p. 549.

Evaluation

As government policy has extended more and more into areas concerned with social and institutional change involving 'investment' in people – education, training, health, income maintenance, social animation, etc. – the traditional methods of management in public decision-making have become increasingly inappropriate. In the early 1950s, health, social welfare, and education expenditures by all levels of government in Canada constituted just over one-quarter of all government expenditure; by the end of the 1960s these three areas absorbed close to half of the total. While other pressures have undoubtedly affected recent changes in public decision-making,[22] the growing importance of human-resource policies has been an important factor in encouraging the search for and development of systematic evaluation and monitoring procedures.

In essence, the systematic evaluation of government programs should include the following steps:

1. Definition of an objective or objectives as precisely as possible (presumably in accordance with the strategic goals of the policy).
2. Selection of alternative arrangements for achieving the objective(s).
3. Estimation of costs (or benefits forgone) for each of the alternatives.
4. Construction of a model, or set of relationships, to trace the impact of each alternative on benefits and costs.
5. A criterion of choice among alternatives.[23]

In practice, it is usually not possible to follow the pursuit of alternatives with as much rigour as is implied by the above. The costs of such a search may well outweigh its benefits! In any case, the notion of alternatives is probably best interpreted as closely competing arrangements or very similar programs, i.e. one form of training versus another, rather than alternative programs, i.e. training versus transfer payments or even versus mobility.[24]

The importance of systematic evaluation is not only that it involves a rational approach to the selection of government programs (or at least provides a rational input to that selection process) but also that it can provide a continuing monitoring of the programs that feeds in-

---

[22]For an excellent and brief review of the emergence of new budgetary techniques, see Charles L. Schultze, *The Politics and Economics of Public Spending*, The Brookings Institution (Washington, 1968).

[23]See, for example, Ronald M. McKean, *Public Spending* (New York, 1968).

[24]Cf. W. R. Dymond, 'The Role of Benefit/Cost Analysis in Formulating Manpower Policy', in Somers and Wood, *op. cit.*

formation back into the system for purposes of adapting and revising programs to improve effectiveness in satisfying objectives. Thus, ideally, evaluation serves both efficiency (cost-saving) and effectiveness (accomplishing objectives). It's not much good being efficient in doing the wrong thing!

While many different types of data and analytical tools are relevant to systematic evaluation, the most widely used technique in the manpower area is the benefit/cost model. We have already described this approach in connection with post-secondary education (Chapter IV). The D.M.I. has developed benefit/cost models for both the O.T.A. program[25] and the manpower mobility program.[26] Since the major purpose here is illustrative, we shall refer only to the evaluation of training, but the interested reader should consult Mr. Jenness's study cited above for details of the mobility analysis.

Evaluation, as we have suggested above, involves first of all the specification of a goal or goals. The primary – though evidently not the sole – objective of manpower policy and therefore of the training program in Canada is growth. This objective can be quantified in terms of benefit/cost ratios, which is the measure used by the O.T.A. model.[27] To monitor other objectives, e.g. equity or stabilization, would require additional measures. We shall return to this point later.

The benefit/cost model of manpower training includes (a) an enumeration and estimation of the flow of costs and benefits of training,[28] and (b) a discount rate designed to adjust the flow of costs and benefits to their present values for purposes of comparison.

While there are certain problems connected with measuring costs,[29] the major conceptual and measurement difficulties in any benefit/cost model arise in connection with the estimation of benefits. In the D.M.I. model, costs include outlays on processing and administrative procedures and on training courses; travel grants; extra personal expenses

---

[25]*Ibid.*

[26]Robert A. Jenness, 'Manpower Mobility Programs', in Somers and Wood, *op. cit.*

[27]Precise details of the actual criterion used are not known. With a fixed budget those excluded from training (as the budget is exhausted) should have lower benefit/cost ratios than those receiving the services, but the benefit/cost ratios should be greater than one. With a flexible budget, training should continue until the (marginal) benefit/cost ratio declines to unity. This assumes that the sole criterion is growth.

[28]Benefits and costs can be measured from several different vantage points: the individual; the department; the government; society as a whole. Each will give different estimates and serves different purposes. The social variant provides the best measure (however inadequate) for resource allocation. It is the social measure which is described in the text.

[29]See Richard W. Judy, 'Costs: Theoretical and Methodological Issues', in Somers and Wood, *op. cit.*

of trainees over the living allowance; and a measure of the before-tax forgone earnings during the training period. Estimation of forgone earnings poses some difficulty, because it involves taking into account the probable employment experience of the trainee *in the absence of training*. If he would have been unemployed during the entire training period or, while in training, is replaced in his job by some other un-employed worker, then the cost to society in terms of forgone output is zero. Since this information is not available, the department makes some estimate of the probability of unemployment (or replacement) that is based on information about the trainee's characteristics and the labour market during the period of training.

The benefits of training are estimated by comparing pre- and post-training earnings of trainees. The pre-training earnings are measured by the weekly earnings for the last job of one month's duration or longer prior to authorization. Since the trainee might be unemployed or in a particularly disadvantaged position just prior to training, this use of the last 'permanent' job is an effort to get around the problem of dis-torting, random factors. The post-training earnings are estimated from follow-up surveys conducted three months and fifteen months after release from the program and are assumed to represent a permanent change lasting over the rest of the trainee's working life. Since the costs and benefits accrue over different time periods, some method of discounting to provide a common time base must be undertaken. The issue of what is a proper discount rate is highly complex and conten-tious and still quite unsettled.[30] The problem is handled in the O.T.A. model by computing results separately for rates of 5 per cent, 10 per cent, and 15 per cent, and comparing them for 'sensitivity' to these (arbitrary) selections. Some effort is also made to take account of inflationary effects on earnings in the post-training period.

There is a fundamental problem in using pre-training–post-training comparisons to estimate the benefits of training (or, indeed of any other similar program). What is really at issue is the question, "What difference did training make to the worker's employment and earnings prospects?" In other words, we are concerned with a comparison of trained and untrained, rather than of pre- or post-training, and the latter is used only as a 'proxy' or indicator of the former. In order to be truly effective as a proxy, the heroic assumption of *ceteris pari-bus* is implied, i.e. the assumption that all other things, *except training*, didn't change. But, alas, most other things will have changed with the passage of time. In particular, crucial economic changes are likely to

---

[30]See A. R. Prest and R. Turvey, 'Cost-Benefit Analysis: A Survey', *The Economic Journal* (December 1965), and bibliography cited therein.

have taken place that may have improved or worsened the worker's prospects, regardless of whether or not he had received training. Further, the trainees will likely receive services from the D.M.I. in addition to training: the D.M.I. may make greater effort to counsel and place its trainees than other clients of similar potential. The pre-post method of evaluation may attribute to training the effects both of economic change and of other manpower services.

This is not a simple problem to sort out, and there is no ideal solution. One method that has been used in the United States is that of the control group, a group of persons with the same characteristics as the trainees but who differ from the trainees because they receive no training. A follow-up of the trainees and the control group provides a comparison of earnings of the trained and untrained groups. This gets around some of the problems stemming from the impact of economic change, but, in practice, it has proved difficult to standardize fully for comparability and exclude the effects of other services provided the trainees.[31] None the less, some form of control group, even if it does not satisfy purist notions of controlled experimentation, is preferable to the simple 'pre-post' approach. The approach of the present model of the D.M.I. raises some doubt about the confidence with which one can attribute benefits to training *per se*.

Even if it were possible to develop an ideal benefit/cost measure of the effects of manpower training on trainees, such a measure would still be inadequate as a guide to resource allocation. In detailing some further drawbacks of the approach, it is important to caution the reader that 'inadequate' does not mean 'useless'. Just as benefit/cost models are not everything, they are also more than nothing. The important thing for the student of manpower policy is to understand both the strengths and the weaknesses of the benefit/cost approach. One serious drawback to such models at the present time concerns their exclusion of potentially significant third-party effects, i.e. effects on persons other than the trainees.

Two types of third-party effects are of particular interest to manpower analysts. One, called the vacuum effect, postulates that training may in fact loosen up serious skill bottle-necks and thereby create jobs for less skilled workers, thus expanding output and income and improving productivity. In contrast to the positive vacuum effect is the

---

[31] For an excellent discussion of the problems involved in the design of evaluation, the use of control groups, and a proposal for scientific experimentation, see Glen G. Cain and Robinson G. Hollister, 'Evaluating Manpower Programs for the Disadvantaged', in Somers and Wood, *op. cit.*

undesirable displacement effect. In the latter case, the trained worker improves his situation at the expense of non-trainees, who are displaced in their jobs and enter the pool of unemployed. Which type of third-party effect takes place, and how extensive these spill-overs are, is a matter for empirical investigation, and rather difficult at that, but neither effect is taken into account in the present benefit/cost model. One suspects that in a period of fairly high unemployment there are relatively few bottle-neck occupations and many of the trainees do, in fact, displace other workers who lack the 'seal of approval' of a training course. The over-all effect may be largely to reduce the average duration of unemployment by stepping up the flows into and out of the jobless pool! Thus, although the D.M.I. quotes a benefit/cost ratio of between two and three at the present time, it is difficult to accept, without considerable scepticism, the statement that 'for every dollar of public funds invested, $2.50 is added to real gross domestic product.'[32]

Another question of some considerable importance that is not treated by benefit/cost models is 'who pays and who benefits?', i.e. the question of the distributive impact of the program. As we have seen, the D.M.I. considers equity as a secondary goal of the program, and therefore the relevant dimensions of distribution – regional, income group, etc. – should be displayed and monitored along with the benefit/cost results. There can, of course, be a trade-off between growth and equity, and that is a political decision. But at least the information base for estimating the trade-off should be part of an evaluation process.

Finally, there is a whole range of problems connected with the process called 'sub-optimization' that cannot be handled by this approach and, indeed, are largely unavoidable. For example, how do the C.M.C.s allocate services such as training, mobility grants, placement, counselling, etc., so as to maximize the over-all effectiveness of the policy? In evaluating each program in isolation, as it were, and largely ignoring the very substantial interrelationships among the programs, there is clearly no guarantee that the total mix will be optimal. When one extends this to take into account the interrelationships among programs of different departments, e.g. the Department of Regional Economic Expansion and the D.M.I., or between different levels of government, e.g. provincial training schemes or welfare programs, etc., or between government and private activity in similar or related areas, it is clear that sub-optimization is the only feasible approach because of

[32]Dymond, *op. cit.*, p. 47.

the immense complexity of the nexus of interrelationships, the uncertainty, and the lack of information that militate against analysis of the whole system.

With the limitations of benefit/cost models in mind, one should stress that these and other evaluation tools can none the less be a most useful aid to government decision-making. But, as a distinguished theorist and practitioner has stressed, 'no science – not even economics – can say with finality what *ought* to be done in public spending.'[33] Personal and political judgments must be made; hopefully, they will be made in the light of the fullest and best information and analysis available.

Finally, another important aspect of evaluation – that of providing learning feed-back to improve and adapt programs to increase their effectiveness – has been stressed by the department. Thus, it has been noted that the benefit/cost model can be used to provide guidance for shifting among courses, or among applicants, or among different types of training, e.g. apprenticeship, institutional, training in industry, etc. The same holds true for the Mobility Programme, for which, it is claimed, grants have been redirected in favour of older married workers with large families.[34] This dynamic element of the evaluation process is clearly of great importance if programs are to be kept on course or improved, and one welcomes the department's emphasis on this aspect of the evaluation process. Yet it is difficult to reconcile the assertion that continual monitoring of the various components of the training program is 'feeding back' into the system when, as we have noted, the very heavy preponderance of institutional, as opposed to industry, training remains a unique (in international terms) feature of the Canadian system, despite strong *a priori* presumptions that a somewhat different mix would likely be more efficient.

Conclusions

This chapter has outlined the very rapid development and expansion of manpower policy in Canada over the decade of the 1960s. Today, we have one of the most extensive and comprehensive sets of manpower programs in the world, second, perhaps, only to Sweden's. The strategic goal of the policy has been largely growth, but some doubt must re-

[33]McKean, *op. cit.*, p. 45.
[34]Dymond, *op. cit.*, p. 53.

main as to how successful it has been in contributing to increased output and employment. Secondary goals – equity and stabilization – are also stated objectives of the department, but insufficient data are available for the outside analyst to evaluate the extent to which these objectives have been achieved. None the less, the heavy emphasis placed on research, information, and systematic evaluation by the Department of Manpower is a welcome sign that the problems of achieving effective and efficient policy are not being ignored.

VII

Wages: Definitions and Measures

In this chapter we shall first discuss some definitional and measurement aspects of wages and then examine the system of wage payments prevailing in Canada, the growth of indirect compensation of labour, the composition of this compensation, and the industrial and regional variations in it.

As we suggested in Chapter III, according to the notion of the utilitarian school of Jeremy Bentham, work is essentially painful and hence to be avoided, unless there is sufficient compensation, while consumption is pleasurable. Rational individuals, therefore, will not offer their labour services except for payment. This payment is generally identified as wages. Wages, thus, are looked upon as a measure of the price of labour[1] of given or standard quality.

Actually, however, it is hard to find a magnitude that accurately measures the price of labour, because it varies widely in content and in forms of payment. For the most part, wage-rates or average-earnings data are used as proxies for the remuneration of labour as a factor of production.[2] The present analysis will use such data for Canada.

Wages may be viewed as consisting of two components: direct and indirect wages. Direct wages or compensation refers to wages that

---

[1] J.R. Hicks, *The Theory of Wages* (London, 1932), p. 1.

[2] However, as Richard and Nancy Ruggles state, referring to U.S. data, 'For observing wages as prices of factors of production, neither of these series is satisfactory. The wage rate series has two major defects: It covers only certain sectors of the economy, and it reports the price of certain job categories, rather than the price of labor as such. The quality of labor which is used to fill a given job category will of course depend upon labor market supply and demand. ... The average hourly earnings series is more comprehensive than the wage rate series, but it suffers from the fact that it reflects changes in skill mix as well as changes in the price of labor. Since it is obtained by dividing reported man-hours into reported wage bills, it is affected by changes in the composition of the labor force within establishments.' Richard and Nancy D. Ruggles, 'The Need for Improved Information on Wages as Prices', mimeo., Memorandum to Geoffrey Moore, May 10, 1969, p. 1. The same criticisms apply with equal force to Canada.

accrue to the worker as a result of hours actually worked, based on output or time, while indirect compensation comprises an ever-growing number of items such as vacations, holidays, health and welfare benefits, unemployment insurance, pension plans, and so on.

An important distinction to be made is between *gross wages* and *take-home pay*. Gross wages is the sum total of all earnings of the worker during a given period of time. Take-home pay is gross wages minus all such items as income taxes, social security contributions, unemployment provisions, etc., that are usually deducted from the worker's earnings. In practice, workers usually consider take-home pay as the magnitude relevant to their budgeting of household expenditures. Changes in take-home pay resulting either from changes in government policy affecting the deductions or from gross-earnings fluctuations (due, for example, to changes in regular or overtime hours, prevalent during up and down turns of business activity) affect the standard of living of households. The seasonal character of some sectors of the economy significantly affects the gross wages earned and the take-home pay of the workers. Construction, logging, and shipping are examples of cases where the seasonal character of work often provides long work weeks during the season and a sharp fall-off in weekly work hours during the off-season period. It is not unusual for workers like bricklayers, loggers, agricultural workers, and longshoremen to work only thirty to thirty-five weeks a year.

Another important distinction to be borne in mind in any study of wages is between *money wages* and *real wages*. Money wages denotes the rate of payment to workers in money terms, such as $1.75 per hour or $84.50 per week. With the passage of time such numbers lose some of their meaning, since changed earnings are frequently associated with changed prices. Hence the real question becomes whether wages have risen, remained equal, or declined in real terms. For example, if a worker earned $3.50 an hour in 1969 and $3.85 an hour two years later, he is better off in real terms only if the price level has risen by less than 10 per cent over the same period of time. If the price level has gone up by more than 10 per cent, then the worker is clearly worse off than before. Real wages, in other words, reveal the command over goods and services which depend on the relative movements of money wages and price level. (For more on this, see Chapter VIII.)

So far we have focused attention on the worker, for whom wages are income. From the employer's point of view, wages are, of course, a cost, and by far the most important cost component in the total cost structure of the company – usually between two-thirds and four-fifths of the total. Hence, employers will not only consider the cost of hiring hours of labour in the form of workers, but they will also estimate the probable output associated with them. The crucial item for the company is not the amount paid per hour as such, but the unit cost of each unit of output. Thus, it would clearly be advantageous to the company to pay four dollars per hour to workers who produce fifty units of output per hour rather than, say, three dollars per hour to others who produce only thirty units each hour. In the former case, the labour cost per unit of output is eight cents, while in the latter it amounts to ten cents.

Forms of Wage Payment

There are essentially two ways of computing wages: one is on the basis of time, or time wages, and the other is based on payment of wages in respect of a certain amount of output, also commonly referred to as production wages or piecework.

(a) TIME WAGES

The great majority of Canadian workers are paid by the hour, day, week, or month, i.e., by time. For manual workers, rates are typically set by the hour or the day; for white-collar and supervisory workers in private industry, by the week, half-month, or month, or less frequently, by the year. White-collar and supervisory workers in government employment are often remunerated on an annual basis. Workers paid by the hour or the day are usually referred to as 'wage-earners', while those paid by the week or longer time periods are commonly referred to as 'salaried workers'.

Time wages are particularly well suited to situations where the tempo of production is not under the control of the worker, where the employer is unable to schedule production so that the employees receive a steady flow of work, where quality considerations outweigh quantity considerations in production, and where workers perform a wide variety of short-cycle operations instead of repetitive and uniform tasks. One further advantage of time wages is that they can be easily computed and are well understood by the employees.

A major drawback of such wages is that output and earnings are not directly related; in other words, there is no strong incentive on the part of the employee to produce. Thus, such wages might well favour slow or lazy workers while acting as a deterrent to those inclined to above-average performance.

(b) PRODUCTION WAGES

The major merit of production wages (or piecework as it is also called) is that they relate compensation and output, so that earnings fluctuate more or less in accordance with actual output. Such a method of payment provides a direct financial stimulus to workers to increase their efforts and output. The purpose of production wages is to reduce unit labour costs by allowing workers to earn higher wages than they would get under ordinary circumstances, in exchange for more production.

In general, incentive pay is most effective where labour costs represent a large percentage of total costs, where output is controlled by the worker, where quality considerations are less important than quantity considerations, where work done is easily measurable, and where it is possible to provide a steady flow of work to the workers.

Having looked at the specific entities that have bearing on the meanings and measures of wages, we now proceed to examine the course of indirect labour compensation and its present level in relation to direct payments to labour in Canada. We shall also describe the interindustrial and geographical differentials in indirect wage costs and review the major components of such indirect labour costs.

Indirect Labour Compensation in Canada

The post-Second World War growth of indirect wage costs in Canada has been very substantial. This section will review the increase in such costs, both as a percentage of total direct wages and in absolute value. Subsequently, various industries, both manufacturing and non-manufacturing, will be compared for the purpose of pointing out the large differences in such indirect costs. Finally, interregional variations will be discussed, as they existed in 1967.

(a) THE RECENT GROWTH OF INDIRECT LABOUR COSTS

Indirect labour costs, sometimes vaguely referred to as 'fringe benefits', grew from almost negligible proportions immediately after the Second World War to about 25 per cent of total direct labour costs by 1967.[3]

---

[3]How much of this increase in 'fringe benefits' has resulted in an increase in 'protection' for the workers is not an easy question to answer. However, in the United States, where similar trends in 'fringe benefits' are observable, there is some evidence suggesting that the wage-earners who receive the best protection in the form of fringe benefits are those employed in the high-wage industries. See R.G. Rice, 'Skill, Earnings, and the Growth of Wage Supplements', *American Economic Review* (May 1966).

TABLE 30

Total Outlay on Indirect Labour Compensation

(a) *As a percentage of direct labour costs*

	1957			1959			1961			1963			1965			1967		
	all	M	NM	all	M	NM	all	M	NM	all	M	NM	all	M	NM	all	M	NM
Total outlay on 'fringe benefits'	16.4	16.2	17.2	22.2	22.8	20.5	24.3	23.4	26.5	26.2	25.7	27.2	25.2	24.7	25.6	25.2	25.3	25.0
—total pay for time not worked	6.7	6.6	7.3	10.6	10.5	10.9	11.6	10.8	13.3	11.6	n.a.	n.a.	12.3	11.5	13.1	12.8	12.0	13.5
—payments required by law	2.0	2.1	1.6	2.7	2.8	2.5	3.0	3.0	2.9	3.1	n.a.	n.a.	3.4	3.2	3.8	2.4	2.7	2.0
—pension & welfare plans	6.4	6.2	7.2	6.4	6.7	5.3	7.2	7.2	7.4	7.7	n.a.	n.a.	6.6	6.7	6.3	7.2	7.2	7.2
—bonuses, profit sharing and outlays for non-cash benefits	1.3	1.3	1.1	2.5	2.8	1.8	2.5	2.4	2.9	3.8	n.a.	n.a.	3.0	3.3	2.4	2.8	3.4	2.2

(b) *In $ per worker*

Total outlay on 'fringe benefits'	701	708	633	1036	1077	897	1202	1202	1201	1404	1431	1306	1350	1392	1310	1595	1622	1563
— total pay for time not worked	287	285	295	483	494	451	563	548	607	604	n.a.	n.a.	636	638	628	796	761	828
— payments required by law	87	91	61	125	132	102	144	150	128	167	n.a.	n.a.	200	183	245	142	162	122
— pension & welfare plans	272	273	271	313	322	275	370	381	337	424	n.a.	n.a.	354	383	324	470	486	452
— bonuses, profit sharing, and outlays for non-cash benefits	55	59	36	115	129	69	125	123	129	209	n.a.	n.a.	160	188	113	187	213	161

Note: 'All' refers to both manufacturing and non-manufacturing; M stands for manufacturing; NM stands for non-manufacturing.

Source: Industrial Relations Counselors Service, Inc., Toronto (for 1957, 1959, and 1961); The Thorne Group Ltd., Management Consultants, Toronto (for 1963, 1965, and 1967).

Table 30 presents the break-down of these costs,[4] for the decade 1957-67, for both manufacturing (M) and non-manufacturing (NM). Part (a) of Table 30 shows the growth of indirect labour costs as a percentage of direct labour costs. For manufacturing and non-manufacturing combined, the percentage rose from 16.4 per cent in 1957 to 25.2 per cent in 1967. Each of the components of indirect labour costs displayed an upward pattern of growth over the decade. It will be noted in part (b) that the annual average cost per worker more than doubled, rising from $701 in 1957 to $1595 in 1967.

Additional data for 1967 are presented in Table 31. These figures, collected by the Dominion Bureau of Statistics, cover manufacturing firms with twenty employees or more. It was found that indirect wage costs amounted to 18.8 per cent of direct wages and salaries. The percentages for indirect wage costs are substantially lower in the D.B.S. data than in those supplied by the Thorne Group, conceivably reflecting the fact that the former include virtually all the firms with twenty workers or more, while the latter confined themselves to large, well-established companies in selected industries.

(b) INTERINDUSTRY VARIATIONS

Table 32, below, shows the degree of variation for indirect labour costs between the various industries in both manufacturing and non-manufacturing. In the petroleum products industry, for example, the average annual cost per worker to the employer for indirect wages was $977, the highest in the manufacturing sector. The textile and mill products industry, by contrast, spent much less than half that amount, $412, in 1957. By 1967, the ranking of the industries within manufacturing had hardly changed, with the petroleum products industry still leading at $2,104 per year and the textile and mill products industry in last place at $794, or 38 per cent of the other figure.

The differences in non-manufacturing are large, but smaller than in manufacturing. (Allowance should be made for the dearth of data in the early years.) Public utilities led the way in average annual costs per worker, spending $796 in 1957; trade was lowest with $540. By

---

[4]The percentages in Table 30 are based on biennial studies made by the Industrial Relations Counselors Services, Inc., Toronto, for the years 1957, 1959, and 1961, and by The Thorne Group, Ltd., Management Consultants, Toronto, for 1963, 1965, and 1967. These *surveys* variously covered between 111,000 to 537,000 persons and between 77 and 108 firms. Since only a small fraction of the total Canadian work force and of the employers has been considered, the above percentage should not be viewed as being a representative sample of Canadian industry. Nevertheless, the data bring out clearly the upward trend of indirect labour costs.

TABLE 31

Estimates of Selected Labour Costs in Canadian Manufacturing: Firms Which Had Twenty or More Employees in Any One Month in 1967

Type of expenditure	All employees $ per em- ployee	All employees % of basic or straight- time pay	Salaried employees $ per em- ployee	Salaried employees % of basic or straight- time pay	Wage-earners $ per em- ployee	Wage-earners % of basic or straight- time pay
	$	in per cent	$	in per cent	$	in per cent
Basic or straight-time pay (direct labour costs)	5075	100	6394	100	4579	100
Total paid days off	448	8.8	596	9.3	394	8.6
Vacations	260		337		232	
Holidays	167		223		146	
Others	21		36		16	
Payments required by law	164	3.2	151	2.4	168	3.5
Workmen's compen- sation	54		51		55	
Unemployment insur- ance	40		25		45	
Canada/Quebec pension plan	70		75		68	
Pension & Welfare Plans	293	5.8	386	6.0	257	5.6
Pension plans	150		229		120	
Life & health insurance	143		157		137	
Bonuses	50	1.0	124	2.0	22	.5
Total selected labour costs	6029	118.8	7651	119.7	5423	118.2

Source: Adapted from data published by D.B.S., Canada Department of Labour, *Labour Costs in Manufacturing, 1967* (Ottawa, 1968).

TABLE 32
*Total Cost of Indirect Wage Payments**

	1957		1959		1961		1963		1965		1967	
	As % of regular wage	Cost per worker in $	As % of regular wage	Cost per worker in $	As % of regular wage	Cost per worker in $	As % of regular wage	Cost per worker in $	As % of regular wage	Cost per worker in $	As % of regular wage	Cost per worker in $
Manufacturing	16.2	708	22.8	1077	23.4	1202	25.7	1431	24.7	1392	25.3	1622
Food & beverage	22.2	946	26.6	1239	27.1	1258	23.5	1293	23.5	1202	24.7	1364
Textile, mill products	13.1	412	16.5	578	18.5	724	20.9	770	18.5	674	20.5	794
Paper, pulp & allied products	13.2	645	17.6	831	20.8	1093	22.1	1230	22.1	1270	24.0	1496
Chemical & allied products	16.4	711	23.0	1029	26.0	1361	24.3	1458	28.6	1636	28.5	1946
Petroleum products	18.9	977	24.9	1425	25.9	1565	30.8	1979	23.8	1713	25.4	2104
Misc. heavy mfg. (iron, steel, machinery)	14.8	648	20.2	927	18.2	920	21.9	1154	24.2	1397	25.2	1631
Miscellaneous (light mfg.)	16.1	680	22.1	1097	23.5	1229	35.4	2276	24.5	1443	28.9	2002
Non-manufacturing	17.2	663	20.5	897	26.5	1201	—	1306	25.6	1310	25.0	1563
Public utilities	19.0	796	23.6	1077	28.2	380	27.7	1482	33.9	2219	31.5	2113
Transportation	15.1	623	18.0	840	23.8	1202	26.4	1407	21.9	1335	24.0	1670
Finance & insurance	17.3	633	20.6	817	28.9	1129	27.5	1094	22.8	1112	27.0	1893
Hospitals	—	—	—	—	—	—	—	—	20.8	689	25.1	1054
Municipalities	—	—	—	—	—	—	—	—	22.3	1204	26.8	1606
Health & welfare	—	—	—	—	—	—	23.2	1154	—	—	21.0	1320
Miscellaneous non-mfg.	—	—	17.4	656	—	—	—	—	22.6	1250	19.6	1288
Trade	16.3	540	17.2	583	20.6	807	21.6	1029	21.5	935	—	—

* Includes payments for days off; legally required contributions, such as for unemployment insurance; pension and welfare plans; bonuses and profit sharing, etc.

Source: Industrial Relations Counselors Service, Inc., Toronto (for 1957, 1959, 1961); The Thorne Group Ltd., Management Consultants, Toronto (for 1963, 1965, 1967).

1967, the average cost in the public-utility industry had risen to $2,113, while hospitals trailed with $1,054, or somewhat less than half.

(c) GEOGRAPHICAL DIFFERENTIALS IN INDIRECT WAGE COSTS

In Table 33, the various components of indirect labour costs are displayed by region. The average cost to the employer for indirect wages was highest in British Columbia, 43.7 cents per hour, and lowest in the Atlantic provinces, 27.2 cents per hour. In terms of percentages, however, Ontario is highest (19.2 per cent), followed by British Columbia (16.5 per cent).

Description of the Major Components of Indirect Labour Costs

In the following sections, the major components of indirect labour costs, such as total pay for time not worked, payments required by law, and pension and welfare plans, will be reviewed briefly.

(a) PAY FOR TIME NOT WORKED

The trend of working hours and paid non-work in Canada has been discussed in Chapter III. Here we shall consider the labour cost aspects of hours worked.

Before the Second World War, the average worker received money wages in payment for time worked or output produced, and this constituted, by and large, virtually the totality of his compensation. Since then, provisions for paid vacations, holidays, and other paid days off have become more and more widespread, possibly reflecting an increased inclination on the part of workers to take part of increased compensation for work in the form of leisure. Negotiations for work contracts in several industries over the past years do seem to bear out an increased willingness to accept part of the increase in wages in the form of less work and more time off.

Vacation plans vary considerably in detail. As was shown in Chapter III, above, in the last two or three decades vacation provisions have been greatly liberalized. In a few industries, sabbaticals of up to three months' duration are being granted at regular intervals to long-time employees. It appears that the amount of paid vacations for workers doing similar work and having similar seniority increases as one moves from the Maritime provinces to British Columbia.

That paid vacations are associated with a high potential cost can be readily seen from a simple example. Suppose that all persons worked

TABLE 33

Estimates of Selected Labour Costs in Cents per Paid Hour, by Region, Wage-Earners, Manufacturing: Canada, 1967

Region	Basic pay	Vaca-tion pay	Paid holi-days	Pay-ments re-quired by law	Pri-vate pen-sion plans	Life & health insur.	Total 'fringe' benefits	
							In cents	In % (of basic pay)
(in cents)								
Canada	214.3	10.8	6.8	7.9	5.6	6.1	37.2	17.4
Atlantic provinces	178.7	8.6	4.7	6.7	4.1	3.1	27.2	15.2
Quebec	196.4	9.6	5.9	7.1	3.8	3.8	30.2	15.4
Ontario	223.6	11.4	7.3	8.1	7.6	8.5	42.9	19.2
Prairie provinces	205.0	9.7	6.8	8.0	3.0	3.8	31.3	15.3
British Columbia	265.5	15.1	8.9	11.1	4.0	4.6	43.7	16.5

Source: D.B.S. and Canada Department of Labour, 'Labour Costs in Manufacturing, 1967' (Ottawa, 1968).

fifty weeks per year and everybody was entitled to two weeks' vacation. It follows that vacation costs to the employer amount to 4 per cent of annual payroll. In surveys conducted by the Industrial Relations Counselors Service, Toronto, and by the Thorne Group, Toronto, covering about half a million workers in both manufacturing and non-manufacturing establishments, it was found that the cost to the employer constituted 3.9 per cent of payroll in 1957, or an average cost per worker of $167. Ten years later the figures were 4.9 per cent and $308.[5]

Paid holidays vie with vacations as being the most expensive form of pay for time not worked. And, as already noted in respect of vacations, the trend is toward an increasing number of paid holidays. At the present time, some eight public holidays are observed each year in Canada, with most of the provinces designating between six and eight paid days. In the above-mentioned surveys, it was computed

[5]See sources cited below Table 34.

that paid holidays amounted to 2.7 per cent of payroll costs in 1957, or an average cost per worker of $115, and that by 1967 the figures were 3.1 per cent and $196.[6]

Jury duty, bereavement pay, military service, rest periods, and other occasions have become increasingly important elements of cost to employers. While such absences accounted for only one-tenth of 1 per cent of payroll cost in 1957, ten years later this figure was 4.8 per cent.

Table 34, below,[7] which is based on the surveys done by the above-mentioned organizations, shows the rise in costs of total pay for time not worked, including vacations, holidays, and all other absences. Between 1957 and 1967 the cost had more than doubled in both manufacturing and non-manufacturing industries. Variations between industries are great. The industry with the highest cost for time not worked, petroleum products, assessed its average annual cost per worker to have been $1,046 in 1967, while the lowest-cost industry, textile and mill products, computed its cost at $391, less than 40 per cent of the petroleum products figure. It should be noted, however, that the petroleum products industry is generally paying higher wages than textile and mill products, and thus any absences from work become automatically more costly.

(b) PAYMENTS REQUIRED BY LAW

Unemployment insurance, workmen's compensation, and old-age security are the major items in this category.

The decline in agricultural employment (described in Chapter IV, above), and the simultaneous rise of the manufacturing and service industries, brought about a major change in the forms by which workers sought to protect themselves from economic vicissitudes. A large agricultural sector is often able to act as a cushion against spreading unemployment in industry, since it may, at least temporarily, absorb displaced workers, particularly if such workers happen to have relatives or parents back on the farm. With the decline of agriculture, the opportunities to take temporary refuge on the land, where there was seemingly always work for a couple of additional hands, diminished. Old-age security was, in the past, similarly provided on the farm,

---

[6]See sources cited below Table 34.

[7]These data refer only to about a half-dozen of the larger companies in each industry. They were *not* selected on a random basis. Hence we suggest that the figures be interpreted with great caution.

TABLE 34

Total Pay for Time Not Worked*

Industries	1957 %⁺	1957 $⁺	1959 %⁺	1959 $⁺	1961 %⁺	1961 $⁺	1963 %⁺	1963 $⁺	1965 %⁺	1965 $⁺	1967 %⁺	1967 $⁺
a) *Manufacturing*												
Number of workers covered in survey	219	437	189	233	161	648	n.a.		111	806	105	279
Number of firms covered in survey	90		73		56		51		78		66	
All mfg. industries	6.6	285	10.5	494	10.8	548	n.a.	n.a.	11.5	638	12.0	761
Food & beverage	7.0	295	10.8	497	12.4	572	10.6	555	10.8	541	12.1	681
Textile, mill prod.	5.8	183	9.2	333	10.7	414	8.2	309	9.7	348	10.2	391
Paper, pulp & allied prod.	5.9	291	7.7	346	9.2	474	9.9	529	10.1	590	12.8	775
Chemical & allied products	6.0	259	10.3	484	11.7	606	11.6	617	13.2	741	12.8	851
Petroleum prod.	7.4	382	12.3	692	11.1	673	11.3	714	12.3	891	12.0	988
Misc. heavy mfg. (iron, steel, machinery)	6.8	295	10.3	465	9.2	464	10.1	520	11.0	617	11.7	756
Misc. (light mfg.)	6.7	278	10.2	506	10.7	559	11.7	668	12.3	733	12.7	882

b) *Non-manufacturing*

Number of workers covered in survey	318	216	301	734	286	864	n.a.	n.a.	315	424	265	169
Number of firms covered in survey	18		27		22		26		87		58	
All non-mfg. industries	7.3	295	10.9	451	13.3	607	n.a.	n.a.	13.1	628	13.5	828
Public utilities	7.6	329	11.3	513	12.5	615	12.9	673	13.4	838	15.9	1046
Transportation	7.3	305	9.3	441	13.3	693	14.9	809	11.5	740	13.4	936
Finance & insur.	7.0	285	8.5	346	15.7	621	—	551	12.3	599	11.9	784
Hospitals	—	—	—	—	—	—	—	—	14.7	484	15.2	632
Municipalities	—	—	—	—	—	—	—	—	11.7	614	13.4	779
Health & welfare	—	—	—	—	—	—	—	732	—	—	14.8	929
Misc. non-mfg.	—	—	10.3	383	—	—	—	—	12.9	729	10.0	690
Trade	6.9	246	8.8	287	12.7	494	—	532	11.5	475	—	—
c) *Mfg. & Non-mfg.*	6.7	287	10.6	483	11.6	563	11.6	604	12.3	636	12.8	796

*Includes cost of vacations, holidays, and similar privileges.
†% of regular payroll.
‡Average annual cost per worker.

Source: Industrial Relations Counselors Service, Inc., Toronto (for 1957, 1959, 1961); The Thorne Group Ltd., Management Consultants, Toronto (for 1963, 1965, 1967).

where the young often took care of their aging parents, frequently living in the same house. The growth of non-agricultural employment made three-generation households impractical, since the jobs were generally not available in the farm communities themselves. As a result, the migration from the farms to the growing cities, where industrial and service jobs were beckoning, not only separated the young from the old members of the family, but encouraged a search for alternative ways to provide both for the old left back on the farms and for those who had left for the cities. Since the latter were particularly susceptible to fluctuations in employment and had few, if any, resources to fall back on, the federal and provincial governments were increasingly called upon to provide for such contingencies. Thus, a major part of the responsibility for the material well-being of the individual gradually shifted from relatives and family members to the state and the employer. Table 30 illustrates this in respect of the shift to the employer, both in percentage of payroll and in annual average cost per worker.

The burden of fringe benefits required by law does not weigh equally heavily upon all industries.[8] Table 35 exhibits the differences. The variance can be explained by looking at each individual component of the legally required payments. These payments are unemployment insurance, workmen's compensation, and old-age security. Unemployment-insurance and old-age-security payments are made to the government as a fixed percentage of a minimum amount of salary. However, when these costs are viewed (for our purposes) as a percentage of total compensation, the percentage will vary inversely with total salary. For example, the cost to the employer as a percentage of salary will be more in respect of a $5,000 employee than of a $15,000 employee.

Other factors, however, may operate in the opposite direction.[9] Workmen's-compensation insurance represents payments for private

---

[8]One type of indirect labour cost which is becoming more important in the United States is Supplementary Unemployment Benefits. These S.U.B. plans are attempts to provide guaranteed employment or income supplementing state unemployment benefits. For a detailed discussion see *Supplemental Unemployment Benefit Plans and Wage-Employment Guarantees*, Bulletin No. 1425-3, United States Department of Labor, Bureau of Labor Statistics. (June 1965).

[9]In the United States, but not in Canada, variations in the cost of such fringe benefits between industries are by and large attributable to the fact that manufacturing industries are generally more susceptible to fluctuations in employment than are non-manufacturing establishments. Since in the United States the greater the risk of large fluctuations in employment, the higher the insurance rate, one would expect such rates to be higher in manufacturing.

insurance. The rates are, of course, determined by the incidence of accidents for the firm and by the type of work performed. In 1957, for example, the average cost per employee was respectively thirty-five dollars and forty-one dollars for the petroleum products industry and the iron, steel, metal·products, and machinery industry. In comparison, the cost for the finance and insurance industry was only one dollar.

It should be apparent that a simple relationship does not exist between legally required benefits and industry classification.

(c) PENSION, WELFARE, AND OTHER BENEFIT PLANS

Back in the 1950s, few items beyond pension plans and some provisions for medical care could have been listed here. Since then, provisions for group life insurance, survivor benefits, hospitalization, surgical and non-occupational sickness benefits, severance pay, just to mention a few, have been added. It seems quite reasonable to expect that more will be added as time goes on, and that the coverage will become more widespread and benefits more liberal.

While three decades ago pension plans were a comparative rarity, the institution of pension benefits by management nowadays is not very likely to elicit much credit from the work force, and failure to have such a plan is apt to provoke vigorous criticism. Although unions have been in the forefront in trying to obtain such provisions, other influences, such as the favourable tax treatment accorded to employer-sponsored programs, have helped the movement.[10]

How widespread such pension plans have become may be seen from a regular survey conducted by the Canada Department of Labour.[11] In 1967, it was reported that 86 per cent of office employees and 71 per cent of non-office workers in the private establishments covered by the survey were protected by company pension plans. In about one out of every four such plans the employer was paying the entire bill, while in the remaining plans employers and employees jointly paid the premiums. The extent of coverage of pension plans has been broadly the same for the past several years.

[10]The tax advantage consists in the employer's contribution to such a plan being treated as a deductible business expense. Employees are not taxed on these contributions until they receive the benefits at a time when their incomes will have become substantially smaller, thus qualifying them for lower tax rates.

[11]*Working Conditions in Canadian Industry*, Canada Department of Labour (Ottawa, 1967).

TABLE 35

Payments Required by Law (Unemployment insurance, workmen's compensation, old-age security)

Industries	1957		1959		1961		1963		1965		1967	
	%*	$†	%*	$†	%*	$†	%*	$†	%*	$†	%*	$†
a) *Manufacturing*												
Workers covered	219,437		189,233		161,648		n.a.		111,806		105,279	
Number of firms	90		73		56		51		78		66	
Food & beverage	2.7	113	3.4	159	4.2	193	3.3	165	3.4	170	3.5	181
Textile & mill prod.	1.4	41	1.7	60	1.9	71	2.5	94	1.9	71	3.1	121
Paper, pulp & allied prod.	2.0	98	2.8	141	3.1	167	2.8	152	2.6	152	3.0	191
Chemical & allied prod.	2.0	81	3.0	129	3.0	152	1.4	213	3.5	200	2.2	146
Petroleum products	2.7	143	2.8	153	3.7	210	2.0	177	2.5	179	1.6	128
Misc. heavy mfg. (iron, steel, machinery)	2.2	93	2.2	104	1.9	98	2.4	124	4.2	286	2.4	151
Misc. (light mfg.)	1.7	74	2.8	142	3.2	169	2.2	143	2.3	132	3.0	206

b) *Non-manufacturing*

	318,216		301,734		286,864		n.a.		315,424		265,169	
Number of firms	18		27		22		26		87		58	
Public utilities	1.7	73	3.9	177	4.3	210	3.8	203	8.9	653	2.2	144
Transportation	1.2	47	1.1	53	1.7	77	1.6	82	1.7	96	2.5	167
Finance & insur.	1.1	37	1.5	56	2.6	100	1.5	63	2.0	97	1.7	98
Hospitals	—	—	—	—	—	—	—	—	.5	18	2.2	92
Municipalities	—	—	—	—	—	—	—	—	.8	64	2.5	139
Health & welfare	—	—	—	—	—	—	.2	8	—	—	1.3	83
Misc. non-mfg.	—	—	2.1	85	—	—	—	—	1.5	79	1.9	132
Trade	2.4	80	2.5	87	1.9	74	2.4	108	2.4	112	—	—

*As % of regular payroll.

†Annual average cost per worker in $.

Source: Industrial Relations Counselors Service, Inc., Toronto (for 1957, 1959, 1961); The Thorne Group Ltd., Management Consultants, Toronto (for 1963, 1965, 1967).

Most of the other items mentioned above, such as group life insurance, survivor benefits, hospitalization, surgical and major medical benefits, are arrangements designed to protect families from sudden loss in earnings and/or major medical expenses due to major mishaps to the breadwinner or some member of his family. In the above-mentioned survey, it was found that 93 per cent of office employees and 83 per cent of non-office workers in the private industries studied had some health and welfare plans. Nevertheless, care should be taken not to assume that because such plans exist, they are all adequate. Table 36 demonstrates that different industries make widely divergent provisions. The difference is particularly striking when comparing the petroleum products industry with textile and mill products.[12]

(d) BONUSES, PROFIT-SHARING, AND OUTLAYS FOR
NON-CASH BENEFITS

This category contains residual cost items that are not uniformly prevalent in the various industries. In some locations and industries, notably in banking, employees receive a thirteenth monthly salary, or part thereof, as a matter of policy. In other industries, profit-sharing has made its appearance in individual companies, but to judge from United States experience to date, it seems that this feature will not become too widespread for workers as distinct from supervisory and management personnel.

Table 37 presents some available data, admittedly inadequate and incomplete. By and large the annual cost of this set of items has been rising. Random movements from year to year are probably due in part to the nature of the survey data, and to the inherent variability of the items included. Thus, if profits decline, the profit-sharing component is bound to decline or even to disappear. Nevertheless, the table illustrates the wide interindustry differences, the most notable contrast being that between workers in finance and insurance and those in health and welfare.

Some concluding remarks

This chapter has reviewed in some detail the relationship between direct and indirect labour costs. It was pointed out that the latter had risen constantly over the years to the point where, by the late 1960s,

[12]It is important to be aware that Table 36 covers only some of the firms in each industry, generally the larger ones. Furthermore, the firms were not randomly selected.

TABLE 36

Pension and Welfare Plans, Employer's Share Only

Industries	1957 %*	1957 $†	1959 %*	1959 $†	1961 %*	1961 $†	1963 %*	1963 $†	1965 %*	1965 $†	1967 %*	1967 $†
a) Manufacturing												
Workers covered	219,437		189,233		161,648		n.a.		111,806		105,279	
Number of firms	90		73		56		51		78		66	
Food & beverage	9.0	382	7.4	351	7.2	339	5.9	334	5.7	297	5.6	307
Textile, mill prod.	5.2	167	5.0	165	5.0	205	4.7	150	5.2	190	4.4	169
Paper, pulp & allied prod.	4.6	222	4.8	230	5.6	303	6.2	361	7.5	414	6.1	410
Chemical & allied prod.	6.1	269	6.5	283	7.4	402	7.4	428	7.3	421	7.6	524
Petroleum products	8.6	443	8.9	524	10.3	636	10.1	619	7.5	553	10.9	919
Misc. heavy mfg. (iron, steel, machinery)	5.2	231	5.9	270	5.7	142	7.4	409	7.0	371	5.2	335
Misc. (light mfg.)	5.9	251	7.3	357	7.2	230	10.0	791	5.6	328	10.7	737
b) Non-manufacturing												
Workers covered	318,216		301,734		286,864		n.a.		315,424		265,169	
Number of firms	18		27		22		26		87		58	
Public utilities	9.5	384	8.0	366	9.1	264	8.2	451	9.9	645	11.5	788
Transportation	6.2	254	6.7	303	7.3	282	8.6	443	8.0	454	7.4	519
Finance & insurance	7.5	255	8.2	317	8.4	299	8.6	351	6.5	317	6.6	400
Hospitals	—	—	—	—	—	—	—	—	3.8	130	6.3	276
Municipalities	—	—	—	—	—	—	—	—	8.0	417	9.3	588
Health & welfare	—	—	—	—	—	—	7.6	377	—	—	4.4	278
Misc. non-mfg.	—	—	3.3	133	—	—	—	—	5.5	302	4.8	314
Trade	4.4	139	3.8	136	3.6	71	3.7	179	4.4	199	—	—

* As % of regular payroll.
† Annual average cost per worker in $.

Source: Industrial Relations Counselors Service, Inc., Toronto (for 1957, 1959, 1961); The Thorne Group Ltd., Management Consultants, Toronto (for 1963, 1965, 1967).

TABLE 37

Bonuses, Profit Sharing, and Outlays for Non-Cash Benefits

Industries	1957 %*	1957 $†	1959 %*	1959 $†	1961 %*	1961 $†	1963 %*	1963 $†	1965 %*	1965 $†	1967 %*	1967 $†
a) *Manufacturing*												
Workers covered	219,437		189,233		161,648		n.a.		111,806		105,279	
Number of firms	90		73		56		51		78		66	
Food & beverage	3.5	147	5.0	232	3.3	154	3.7	239	3.6	194	3.6	195
Textile, mill prod.	.7	21	.6	20	.9	34	5.5	217	1.7	65	2.8	113
Paper, pulp & allied prod.	.7	34	2.3	114	2.9	149	3.2	188	1.9	114	2.1	120
Chemical & allied prod.	3.2	55	3.2	133	3.9	201	3.9	200	4.6	274	6.0	425
Petroleum products	.2	9	.9	56	.8	46	1.1	77	1.5	90	.9	69
Misc. heavy mfg. (iron, steel, machinery)	.6	29	1.8	69	1.4	69	2.0	101	2.0	123	6.0	389
Misc. (light mfg.)	1.8	42	1.8	92	2.4	131	1.5	674	4.3	250	2.6	177
b) *Non-manufacturing*												
Workers covered	318,216		301,734		286,864		n.a.		315.424		265,169	
Number of firms	18		27		22		26		87		58	
Public utilities	.2	10	.4	21	2.3	113	2.8	155	1.7	83	1.9	135
Transportation	.4	17	.9	43	1.5	80	1.3	73	.7	45	.7	48
Finance & Insurance	1.7	53	2.4	98	2.2	87	3.4	129	2.0	99	6.8	611
Hospitals	—	—	—	—	—	—	—	—	1.8	57	1.4	54
Municipalities	—	—	—	—	—	—	—	—	—	—	.5	30
Health & welfare	—	—	—	55	—	—	.7	37	2.7	140	2.9	152
Misc. non-mfg.	—	—	1.7	—	—	—	—	—	3.2	149	—	—
Trade	2.6	41	2.1	73	2.4	102	4.1	210	—	—	—	—

* As % of regular payroll.

† Annual average cost per worker in $.

Source: Industrial Relations Counselors Service, Inc., Toronto (for 1957, 1959, 1961); The Thorne Group Ltd., Management Consultants, Toronto (for 1963, 1965, 1967).

they equalled about one-quarter of direct labour costs.[13] Subsequently, the various components of indirect labour compensation were discussed. While the rate of growth of some of them, pension and welfare plans for example, has been less than the average, the cost for time not worked (vacations, holidays, etc.) has risen faster than indirect labour costs as a whole. One implication of this feature might be that employees have become increasingly disposed to take some of the additional wage increases in the form of more leisure time.

The reader will have observed that substantial interindustry differentials prevail for the various components of indirect labour compensation. In some instances, such variations may be attributable to the idiosyncracies of particular industries, while in others earning power and the outlook for the future of the industry in question are probably major explanations for lags and leads in benefits. The difficulties that beset the textile industry, for example, can be contrasted with the apparently bright future for the petroleum industry. It seems natural that underlying economic features have a powerful impact on the willingness and ability of industries to compensate their work force. While the costs for items such as pay for time not worked are fairly uniform and standardized, provisions for pension and welfare plans sponsored by individual firms are apt to be the result of successful pressures by the work force itself. How is one then to account for the observed vast discrepancies in per-capita expenditures on such plans? Are they the result of successful bargaining by unions where such expenditures are high, or of fruitful efforts on the part of management to restrain union leaders where they are low? Do they reflect differences in earning power in the various industries? Or are workers prone to accept cash now rather than some elusive benefits at some time in the unpredictable future? Do they reflect varying pressures within the unions, with younger members preferring cash now while old-timers would rather opt for pension and other welfare benefits? Lack of data precludes any real analysis of these important questions in Canada for the present. It seems reasonable to assume, however, that there is no single reason for this phenomenon. At present, perhaps we can at best only say that it is a function of all the possibilities mentioned above.[14]

[13]It would be interesting to find out the extent to which a particular percentage coverage provides continuity of income or protects against the costs incurred in particular cases. Unfortunately, no such study is available for Canada. In the United States in 1960 the sick-pay benefits were estimated to be 27.7 per cent of income loss from short-term sickness, and medical insurance benefits were 26.7 per cent of costs incurred. See G.L. Reid and D. J. Robertson, *Fringe Benefits, Labour Costs, and Social Security* (London, 1965), p. 136 and pp. 151-4.

[14]Edward E. Lawler and Edward Levin, 'Union Officers' Perception of Member's Pay Preferences', *Industrial and Labor Relations Review* (July 1968). See also Privy Council Office, *Canadian Industrial Relations: The Report of Task Force on Labour Relations* (Ottawa, 1969), pp. 93-4.

VIII

Real- and Money-Wage Levels, Wage Changes, and Inflation

Almost everyone, with the possible exception of hermits and pre-school children, is interested in wages. But the term 'wages', as was pointed out in the previous chapter, is a complex term. Workers are concerned with their weekly pay packets and the regularity of employment during the year; their wives are interested also in what these pay packets represent in actual purchases in the supermarket and department store (real wages); union leaders are likely to talk of wages in terms of specific rates of pay over which they bargain with management; employers tend to think less of wages, as such, and more of labour cost per unit of output, which depends on productivity and, as we have seen, on non-wage labour costs as well as on wages. All these groups are vitally concerned not only with their own wages and costs, but with 'the other fellow's' – with comparisons and relativities. Labour economists must consider all these and other aspects of wages, the manner in which they are determined, and the ways in which they are interrelated. A thorough and comprehensive examination of all the aspects of wages for any one country is obviously a task of enormous magnitude, far beyond the scope of this book. In this and the following chapters, however, some attempt will be made to describe the broad outlines of Canadian wage levels, income distribution, labour's share in national income, and wage structure. The first problem to be tackled involves the changing levels of money wages and real wages and certain related questions of productivity, wage changes, and inflation.

An important omission from the discussion of wages deserves mention. It will be assumed that the reader is familiar, in a general way, with the various theories of wage determination normally included in standard texts on labour economics.[1] Since our purpose is to concentrate on the Canadian scene, it is felt that a text-book recapitulation of wage doctrine is inappropriate and unnecessary. Moreover, the unsettled state of wage theory precludes a neat and brief summary; any summary of reasonable length would be more misleading than informative to the uninitiated reader, and more irritating than satisfying to the expert. One can do little better in this regard than to quote:

What should be said concerning wages
Would run to several hundred pages.
One difficulty bars the way:
We can't agree on what to say.[2]

Money and Real Wages

An important distinction to be made in the study of wages, as has been pointed out before, is between money wages and real wages. The welfare of the wage-earner depends not on how much money income he receives, but on the goods-and-services content of his money income, which depends on commodity prices. An increase in money income may or may not mean an equal increase in real income, depending on the relative movements of prices and money wages. If price movements exceed wage movements in the upward direction, the welfare of workers will be diminished in spite of the increase in money wages. In reality, calculating the real well-being of the workers requires an accurate measure of the prices of goods and services purchased by wage-earners. However, accurate measures of these prices are not available. A proxy used for this purpose is the consumer price index, which comes closest to being an index of prices of goods and services paid for by workers. The consumer price index has several limitations to its usefulness for this measurement, most important of which are that it (a) does not take into consideration changes in the relative weights of different goods and services in people's budgets; (b) does not cover all the income groups among wage recipients; and

[1]For an excellent treatment of wage determination, see Alan M. Cartter, *Theory of Wages and Employment* (Homewood, Illinois, 1959); and John G. Cross, *The Economics of Bargaining* (New York, 1969).
[2]Attributed to Professor Boulding.

(c) does not provide for quality changes in the goods and services used. Further, by excluding payments in kind from the calculation of real wages, the index tends to reflect an upward bias in countries where payments in kind are declining over time. For these reasons, measurements of real-wage changes have to be treated with a margin of error. But beyond that margin, it is a useful indicator of the economic status of the wage-earners.

Wages in Canada

Figure 5 pictures the time paths followed by average hourly wage-rates[3] and the consumer price index in Canada from the beginning of this century to 1969. During that period, money wages increased over twelvefold. The biggest jumps took place during the period subsequent to the two world wars: between 1914 and 1920 wage-rates more than doubled, as they did also between 1939 and 1949.

Since the Second World War, money wages in Canada have never fallen; however, this was not the case in the inter-war period. In the sharp recession of the early twenties, wage-rates fell by over 10 per cent, and between 1930 and 1933 they fell by a similar percentage. It must be remembered that hourly wage-rates are relatively more 'sticky' in the downward direction than are average hourly earnings, which would probably show more dramatic drops in both these periods. Weekly or annual earnings would also be affected by the prevalence of short-time working that characterizes a depression period. On the whole, money wages do not have much cyclical sensitivity and thus show a persistent tendency to rise, except in major depression periods. It should be stressed, however, that during such periods no measure of wages is a significant indicator of the financial condition of labour, since so many workers are either unemployed or on short work weeks.

A quick glance at Figure 5 suggests that the movement of prices was very similar to that of money wages until the late forties. But during the fifties money-wage rates shot up rapidly, pulling sharply away

---

[3]The general wage-rate index, published by the Department of Labour, covers most industries in Canada (the most notable exception being agriculture) and provides the only long-run measure of general wages in Canada. There are, however, a number of difficulties connected with its use as a measure of wage change over a long period of time. For a full discussion see W. R. Dymond, 'Occupational Wage Statistics of the Canadian Department of Labour', paper presented to the Canadian Political Science Association Conference on Statistics, Queen's University, Kingston, June 8, 1960.

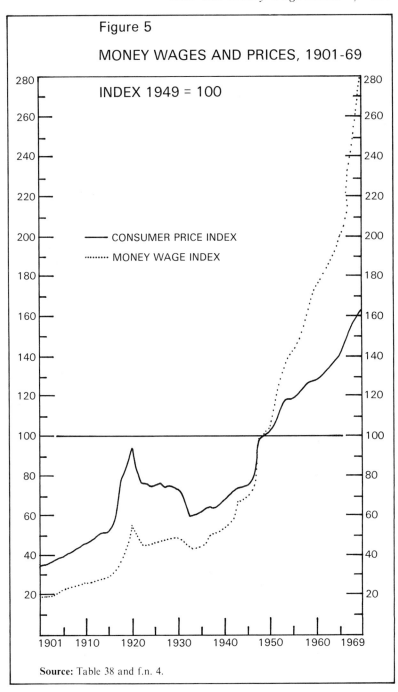

Figure 5

MONEY WAGES AND PRICES, 1901-69

INDEX 1949 = 100

—— CONSUMER PRICE INDEX
········ MONEY WAGE INDEX

Source: Table 38 and f.n. 4.

from rising prices. It is worth while, therefore, to look at the course of real wages over this same period, since they, more than money wages, will reveal whether the position of the (employed) industrial workers improved or not.

Figure 6 presents a graph depicting the movement of real[4]-wage rates between 1901 and 1969. Over the period as a whole, real wages rose by 220 per cent (compared with a rise of 151 per cent in money wages). Although the raw data leave much to be desired by way of accuracy, the over-all trend is quite clear: Canadian workers in the mid sixties could buy about three times as much with their wages as could their predecessors at the outset of the century.[5]

Real wages did not rise in every year or even in every decade of the period. Early in the 1900s they began to fall, and continued to decline until well into the First World War.[6] From 1904 to 1917 they fell by over 10 per cent. It should be remembered (see Chapter I) that these were years of unprecedented immigration into Canada: between 1904 and the outbreak of the First World War over 2,600,000 persons entered this country and for the first time since the middle of the nineteenth century a substantial proportion remained in Canada instead of moving on to the United States. The Canadian population and the labour force grew more rapidly than ever before in the history of the country. Moreover, the bulk of these immigrants were from southern, central, and eastern Europe and were, on the whole, less skilled and less educated than those from the British Isles and north-western Europe, the previous major sources of immigrant inflow. These

---

[4]The money-rate index has been divided by a consumer price index. The source of the latter from 1913 on was D.B.S., *Prices and Price Indexes*. For 1900, 1905, 1910, and 1911, the index was estimated from family budget data collected by the Department of Labour and published in *Wholesale Prices in Canada, 1917*. The 1900 and 1905 data were for the month of December only. The two series were linked by A. Asimakopulos. For conceptual problems involved in determining real wages, see R. G. Bodkin, 'Real Wages and Cyclical Variations in Employment: A Re-Examination of the Evidence', *The Canadian Journal of Economics* (August 1969), pp. 353-74.

[5]At least part of the rise in real wages can be accounted for by employment shifts, i.e., by the movements of workers from low- to high-wage industries. In other words, the wage-rate index does not simply measure changes in wage-rates, although in recent years an attempt has been made to minimize the effect of employment shifts. Cf. Dymond, *op. cit.*

[6]Cf. the evidence regarding similar movements of real wages during this period in Europe: E.H. Phelps Brown and Sheila V. Hopkins, 'The Course of Wage Rates in Five Countries, 1860-1939', in *Oxford Economic Papers*, New Series (June 1950), pp. 226-96. The explanation provided for these movements is, however, different from that suggested here. The recent work by Albert Rees involving the construction of new wage and price indexes, *Real Wages in Manufacturing, 1890-1914*, National Bureau of Economic Research (Princeton, 1961), challenges the view that real wages in the United States declined in the two decades preceding the First World War.

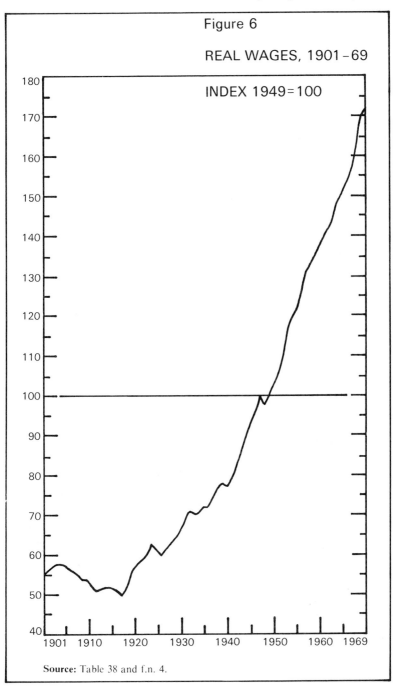

Figure 6

REAL WAGES, 1901–69

INDEX 1949=100

Source: Table 38 and f.n. 4.

factors undoubtedly help to explain the fall in real wages. Not only had the supply of labour increased enormously, but large numbers of relatively unskilled workers diluted the 'quality' of the labour force. Both influences helped to moderate the rise in money wages (see Figure 5) and to depress real wages.

Although there were other brief periods of declining real wages (in the twenties and again in the thirties), by and large the movement over the remaining years was upward, as was the movement of money wages. But the pattern of change in real wages was different from that in money wages. Between 1901 and 1914, while money wages rose by almost 40 per cent, real wages declined by almost 4 per cent. Table 38 shows that the war and early post-war years witnessed a remarkable leap in the money-wage level that was all but eliminated by uncontrolled price movements: real wages rose by a modest 8 per cent. An interesting aspect of the table may be observed by comparing the behaviour of real and money wages in depression periods: In 1921-2 money wages fell by almost 7 per cent, but real wages rose by 2 per cent; similarly, during the 1929-33 depression, money wages fell over 14 per cent but real wages increased by over 10 per cent. One can hardly say that the position of workers improved during these severe depressions, for a large proportion of the labour force was unemployed and many were near-destitute. However, the real hourly wages of those fortunate enough to hold on to their jobs did improve, although an examination of weekly or annual take-home pay would reveal a sharp decline because of widespread underemployment (short work weeks).

The First World War period provides a striking contrast to the Second World War years. In the latter period, money wages, subjected to increasingly stringent government controls as the war progressed,[7] rose only moderately – by 50 per cent over the years 1940-6 compared with double that percentage between 1914 and 1920. But real wages rose by almost 27 per cent between 1940 and 1946 – three times the increase gained in the earlier period. It is perhaps appropriate to remark here that another important difference between the First and

---

[7]Wage control was a factor to be considered, especially during the latter part of the Second World War. Controls became progressively tighter as the war proceeded and by 1943 the only authorized wage increases were those designed to correct a 'gross injustice or gross inequality'. Cf. Martin Stollor and Joseph S. Zusel, 'Wartime Wage Controls in Canada: Economics of Wage Freeze', *The Conference Board Business Record* (April 1949). This slowed down the rate of increase of money wages but the combination of wage- and price-control measures permitted not inconsiderable real gains in wages even after 1943. See also J. Mintzes, 'Canada, Wage Trends and Wage Policies, 1939-47', in *Monthly Labour Review* (October 1947).

TABLE 38

Percentage Changes in Money and Real Wages,
Selected Periods: Canada, 1901-69

Years	Money-wage change	Real-wage change
1901-14	38.8	-3.9
1914-20	103.5	8.4
1921-22	-6.8	1.9
1923-29	5.9	5.8
1929-33	-14.1	10.9
1934-39	16.7	10.1
1940-46	49.6	26.9
1947-57	84.1	28.1
1958-69	71.8	32.5
1901-69	150.6	220.2

Source: Department of Labour, *Wage Rates, Salaries, and Hours of Labour* (Ottawa, various years); M.C. Urquhart (ed.), *Historical Statistics of Canada*, Macmillan of Canada (Toronto, 1965); and D.B.S., *Canadian Statistical Review* (Ottawa, various years).

Second World War years was that in the latter period unionism emerged for the first time as a relatively powerful institution in Canada. It appears from these data that unions had very little effect on the money-wage level – not surprising in view of government wage-controls mitigating the pull of excess demand operating in a very tight labour market. It might be argued, however, that union political pressure influenced the government's determination to control the inflationary impact of war finance and war production,[8] and thus indirectly contributed to the very significant gains in real wages that differentiated the years of the Second World War from those of the

[8]Cf. R. Craig McIvor, *Canadian Monetary, Banking and Fiscal Development* (Toronto, 1958), Chaps. 6 and 9, in which the financing of the First and Second World Wars is discussed and compared. He points out that considerations of the equitable distribution of the financial burden of the war were 'notably absent' in the earlier period, but does not analyse the reasons for the marked contrast between the two war periods. There is no doubt that purely technical improvements in the economic 'know-how' available to governments by the 1940s were a factor, but changes in the social climate – induced primarily by the growth of the C.C.F. and the emergent trade-union movement – almost certainly have played a role in influencing government policy. The profound social and political disturbances following the First World War, especially in western Canada, but not wholly confined to that region, were in part a consequence of the deterioration of the real wages of labour stemming from the extreme war-time inflation.

First. It may be that more direct union influence accounts, in part, for the contrast between the 1923-9 period and the years following the Second World War. Both periods were characterized by full employment and rising productivity and output. But during the twenties money and real wages rose at an average annual compound rate of just about 1 per cent, while between 1947 and 1957 money wages rose at an average annual compound rate of 6.3 per cent and real wages at 2.5 per cent. Of course these period comparisons are hazardous: no two periods are identical, and it is likely that other factors were important in contributing to the observed differences in wage movements.[9]

Productivity and Real Wages

Over the long run, and in a broad and general way, the pattern of real-wage changes reflects changes in the real productive capacity of the economy.[10] The greatly improved real wages of Canadian workers today compared with 1900 are attributable mainly to a decided improvement in real physical output per unit of input in Canadian industry. We shall draw upon a number of sources in order to examine, as best we can, the changes in output per man-hour and real wages over as long a period as possible.

Although the general level of wages over the long run moves more or less in step with the index of productivity, this association is not found at all times, nor is it found to hold true for different sectors of the economy. Indeed, one of the striking aspects of productivity change is the remarkable diversity among the major industrial sectors, a diversity far greater than that exhibited by real- or money-wage movements.

[9]Robert Ozanne, 'Impact of Unions on Wage Levels and Income Distribution', *Quarterly Journal of Economics* (May 1959), compares in detail for the United States the periods under consideration here and concludes that 'the two periods bear significant resemblances. At least in their wage-paying abilities as measured by productivity and national income growth, neither period seems to have much advantage over the other' (p. 186). In Canada, possibly significant differences might be higher unemployment in the twenties (no truly reliable estimates exist) and a less expensive government monetary policy.

[10]The statement is true in the sense that increases in the level of real wages per man-hour can stem from only two sources – either increases in productivity or redistribution of output in favour of the wage share. Historically, in all countries for which information exists the first source has been of overwhelmingly greater importance than the second. The statement should not be interpreted to mean that movements in real wages and productivity will conform very closely at any given period of time. Apart from possible distributional effects, there are such enormous difficulties in the construction of both sets of statistics that reliable long-run series are simply not available. Quite different

TABLE 39

Indices of Output Per Person Employed and Output Per Man-Hour in Selected Sectors of the Canadian Economy, 1950-68 (1961 = 100)

Year	Goods-producing industries		Commercial industries		Commercial-service-producing industries	
	Output per person employed	Output per man-hour	Output per person employed	Output per man-hour	Output per person employed	Output per man-hour
1950	58.6	55.0	68.6	64.1	85.9	80.2
1954	70.0	66.4	78.2	74.3	90.6	87.0
1958	90.3	88.5	92.4	90.5	94.9	93.0
1962	108.5	108.6	104.9	105.2	101.4	101.6
1965	126.1	129.3	115.4	118.6	104.2	106.9
1968	140.3	146.8	124.2	130.9	107.6	114.0
Annual trend Rate of change (%)	4.9	5.5	3.3	3.9	1.2	1.9

Source: D.B.S., *Aggregate Productivity Trends, 1946-68* (Ottawa, May 1970).

Table 39 shows that output per person employed during 1950-68 had annual trend rates of change equal to 4.9 per cent in goods-producing industries, 3.3 per cent in commercial industries, and 1.2 per cent in commercial-service-producing industries. Similar variations are reported in output per man-hour. Why do such differences

results will arise depending on which of several measures of productivity are used. The most useful measure of productivity is the ratio of output to all inputs. This total productivity measure 'reveals the net savings achieved in the use of inputs as a whole, and thus the degree of advance in efficiency of the productive process,' John W. Kendrick, 'Productivity Costs and Prices: Concepts and Measures', *Wages, Prices, Profits, and Productivity*, The American Assembly (Columbia University, June 1959), p. 40. (Some estimates of this type for Canada are provided in *Patterns of Growth, Seventh Annual Review*, Economic Council of Canada.) The most usual measure of productivity relates output to man-hour input, either production-worker man-hours or all worker or all employed labour-force (including salaried workers and perhaps also proprietors and unpaid family workers) man-hours. The measures will move rather differently since production workers have declined as a proportion of all employees or employed labour force. Hence the ratio of output per production-worker man-hour will show a distinct upward bias compared with output per all employees or labour-force man-hour. Moreover, either measure will show an upward bias compared with a total productivity measure, because of the historical increase in the capital-labour ratio. Other conceptual difficulties involved in the estimation of labour, capital, and total productivity are discussed in Kendrick, *op. cit.*, pp. 42-3. See also Economic Council of Canada, Staff Studies Nos. 23 and 28, by Dorothy Walters.

in productivity change arise? One reason is that in manufacturing, resource industries, and transportation, where the opportunities for mechanization are great, one would expect much more substantial improvements in output per unit of input than in, say, banks, insurance companies, barber shops, doctors' and dentists' offices, and the like. This is not to say that the quality of such services has not vastly improved over time, but changes in quality are notoriously difficult to capture in statistical indicators.

The main concern in this chapter, however, is with the general level of wages and productivity. In this respect, the following information on manufacturing warrants examination. Tables 40 and 41 contain data on productivity per wage-earner-hour and real earnings per wage-earner-hour for the manufacturing sector only, for selected periods stretching over a much longer span of years. Recalling the limitations implicit in these data, note that over the entire period 1870 to 1968 real wages rose by a considerably smaller percentage than did real gross value of manufacturing per man-hour.[11] However, the relationship between real wages and productivity was not the same throughout the period. Between 1870 and 1890 wages and productivity moved pretty well together, the difference (taking into account the crudeness of the statistics for these early years) being too small to speculate about. The twenty years between 1930 and 1950, however, stand out as markedly different from the rest: the increase in real wages was over one and a half times that in output per man-hour. After 1950 the edge of real wages over productivity diminished considerably, and by 1955 the two almost came at par. After 1955 real wages again fell below productivity to a remarkable extent. Thus, although workers' real wages increased by 58 per cent from 1950 to 1968, the rise was far behind that in their productivity, which was over 97 per cent.

It should be mentioned, however, that in recent years, particularly since the war, non-wage items of workers' compensation have become increasingly important. As shown in Chapter VII, according to some studies fringe benefits amount to about 25 per cent of payrolls.[12] Adding these fringe benefits to real wages would, of course, reduce the gap between real wages and productivity in the recent period.

---

[11]Dr. Firestone raises the question as to whether the use of gross value production leads to a distorted appraisal of long-term changes that take place in industry, and concludes that 'one may reasonably infer that the general conclusions derived . . . on the basis of estimates of gross value of manufacturing would be valid also in terms of net value added or net income originating.' O. J. Firestone, *Canada's Economic Development, 1867-1953* (London, 1958), p. 20.

[12]For definition and discussion of fringe benefits, see Chapter VII.

TABLE 40

Change in Average Wages Per Man-Hour, Constant (1935-9) Dollars, Manufacturing, and Gross Value of Manufacturing Production Per Man-Hour in Constant (1935-9) Dollars: Canada, 1870-1950

Years	*Percentage increase in* Real wages/ man-hr.*	Real output/ man-hr.*
1870-90	54	47
1890-1910	10	41
1910-30	50	72
1930-50	76	47
1870-1950	346	420

*Wage-earners only.

Source: O. J. Firestone, *Canada's Economic Development, 1867-1953* (London, 1958), Tables 76 and 81.

TABLE 41

Change in Real Wage and Productivity in Manufacturing Industries: Canada, 1950-68

Years	*Percentage increase in* Real wages/ man-hr.*	Real output/ man-hr.*
1950-5	23	22
1955-60	12	18
1960-8	19	36.6
1950-68	58	97.6

*Wage-earners only.

Source: For real wage/man-hour, calculated from: Department of Labour, *Wage Rates, Salaries, and Hours of Labour*, various years; Urquhart, *Historical Statistics of Canada*; D.B.S., *Canadian Statistical Review* (Ottawa, various years).

For real output/man-hour, D.B.S., *Aggregate Productivity Trends, 1946-1968* (May 1970).

Taking into account the questionable accuracy of the statistics, it still seems safe to suggest that from the turn of the century until the end of the twenties (it is impossible to date the changes without more accurate and detailed information) real wages per wage-earner-hour in Canadian manufacturing lagged behind the growth in output per wage-earner-hour, although the degree of lag varied from period to period. During the last war and post-war inflation, the relationship appears to have been reversed, and real hourly wages moved ahead of real gains in man-hour productivity. Since 1955, however, real wages have again fallen behind. It is of interest to note that an American study, using much more detailed and higher-quality statistics, showed that, for the period 1889 to 1957 as a whole, output per (production-worker) man-hour rose more than real wages, but that after 1929 real wages outstripped productivity – a reversal of the dominant pattern holding prior to 1929.[13]

Determinants of Money-Wage Changes

Having discussed the relationship between money-wage and real-wage levels and how these levels behaved in Canada, it is relevant to ask what caused changes in the general level of money wages. We will seek to answer this question by surveying briefly some important empirical studies in the field of money-wage changes and changes in other related variables.

A discussion relating to general money-wage changes may be classi-fied under the heading of an expanded Phillips curve;[14] that is, in

[13]Albert Rees, 'Patterns of Wages, Prices, and Productivity', *Wages, Prices, Profits and Productivity* (New York, 1959), pp. 11-35.

[14]There is now a growing body of literature on the subject of wages and unemployment. See, for example, A. W. Phillips, 'The Relationship Between Unemployment and the Rate of Change of Money Wage Rates in the United Kingdom, 1861-1957', *Economica* (November 1958), pp. 283-99; R.G. Lipsey, 'The Relation Between Unemployment and the Rate of Change of Money Wage Rates in the United Kingdom, 1862-1957: A Further Analysis', *Economica* (February 1960), pp. 1-31; R. G. Bodkin, E. P. Bond, G. L. Reuber, and T. R. Robinson, *Price Stability and High Employment: The Options for Canadian Economic Policy: An Econometric Study*, Special Study No. 5, Economic Council of Canada (Ottawa, 1966) (this study has a comprehensive summary of previous wage studies until 1965); Gérald Marion, 'Le rôle des fonctions de production dans les rela-tions d'arbitrage salaire, emploi et prix', *The Canadian Journal of Economics* (November 1969). See also comment on Professor Marion's paper by Professor John Beare and reply by Professor Marion, same journal (November 1970), pp. 607-15; and *Microeco-nomic Foundations of Employment and Inflation Theory*, E. S. Phelps (ed.) (New York, 1970).

terms of what was originally the Phillips curve and its subsequent developments, refinements, and extensions. It will be recalled that we also discussed the expanded Phillips curve in Chapter V. However, the discussion in that chapter was carried out in the context of trade-offs between full employment and price stability. In this chapter, we are concerned with the factors underlying money-wage movements.

Phillips examined wage changes in the United Kingdom from 1861 to 1957 and detected an inverse relationship between these changes and the percentage of the labour force unemployed. The diagram depicting this relationship has been called the Phillips curve. R. G. Lipsey, in subsequent work, reassessed the Phillips wage adjustment relationship for Britain by choosing more conventional statistical techniques, and developed a theoretical model to explain many of the observed results. Following the publication of Phillips' and Lipsey's articles, a number of scholars tested this relationship for various countries. While the Phillips curve studies conducted for other countries incorporated many of the ideas presented by Phillips and Lipsey, most of them used models that incorporated additional variables, such as profits,[15] productivity, various proxies for excess demand,[16] concentration ratios, and unionization variables, to mention a few.[17] We shall discuss below four variants of the Phillips-Lipsey model that have been developed in the last decade to explain movements in the general money-wage

---

[15]Profits can be expressed as proportion of equity capital, sales, or various other magnitudes. In general most of the studies that have tested the role of profits in wage determination have used a rate of return on corporate capital, i.e. total corporate profits divided by corporate net worth. Unfortunately data on equity in Canada are not available, and, therefore, generally three measures of profits have been used: profits per unit of output as in the study of Bodkin *et al.*; profits as per cent of assets as in G. R. Sparks and D. A. Wilton, 'Determinants of Negotiated Wage Increases: An Empirical Analysis', mimeographed, 1968; and profits as a ratio of corporate profits to total wages and salaries as in M. A. Zaidi, 'The Determinants of Money Wage Rate Changes and Unemployment-Inflation "Trade-offs" in Canada', *International Economic Review* (June 1969).

[16]Since data on job vacancies have generally been not available in Canada and the United States, the most popular proxy used in the literature for excess demand and supply of labour has been the unemployment rate. However, see a recent study which has attempted to construct an index of excess demand in terms of unfilled vacancies and unemployment, M. A. Zaidi, 'Unemployment, Vacancies and Conditions of Excess Demand for Labour in Canada', *Applied Economics* (1970), Vol. 2, No. 2, and the discussion on vacancy data in the chapter on manpower. For another attempt to estimate an index of excess demand for labour in terms of 'desired employment', see Gérald Marion, 'La Demande excédentaire de travail et la variation des salaires dans l'industrie manufacturière au Canada', *The Canadian Journal of Economics* (August 1968), pp. 519-39.

[17]For the discussion of these variables and other contributions on this subject, see Chapter V and Bodkin *et al.*, *op. cit.*

level.[18] These models will be discussed under the following headings: (a) Phillips-Lipsey Model, (b) Eckstein-Wilson Model, (c) Hines Model and (d) Behman Model.

Since these models are based either on British or American data, an effort will be made, wherever possible, to bring into the discussion comparable studies that have attempted to estimate these models using Canadian data.

PHILLIPS-LIPSEY MODEL

A. W. Phillips was the first to contribute significantly to the study of factors underlying money-wage movements.[19] In his examination of the period 1861 to 1957 in the United Kingdom, he estimated the empirical relationship between the rate of change of the money-wage level and the percentage of the labour force unemployed and its rate of change. Phillips concluded that (a) a constant level of money-wage rates would imply 5½ per cent of the labour force unemployed; (b) an increase in money-wage rates by 2 per cent per annum would be associated with 2½ per cent of the labour force unemployed. He found that this increase in money-wage rates would be consistent with stable prices provided that the following conditions are met: (a) labour's share remains constant; (b) labour's productivity grows at 2 per cent per annum; (c) wage earnings grow at the same pace as money-wage rates; and (d) import prices remain relatively stable. As to cost-of-living adjustments, he suggested that they would have 'little or no effect on the rate of change of money wage rates except at times when retail prices are forced up by a very rapid rise in import prices.'[20]

Lipsey confirmed Phillips' conclusions but attributed a more positive role to the cost of living as an independent factor in money-wage changes.[21] As far as the influence of the rate of change of unemployment was concerned, Lipsey found that this variable played a highly significant role in the pre-First World War regression equation, but the sign of the coefficient associated with the variable changed from negative to positive in the latter period, i.e. 1923-39 and 1948-57. Lipsey tried to explain this reversal of sign in terms of a theoretical model in which he attributed Phillips' observed relation between wage

---

[18]Because of unavailability of comprehensive data for the entire economy, most of these models analyse wage movements only for the manufacturing sector of the economy and therefore the results derived from these models are only an approximation for the whole economy.

[19]Phillips, *op. cit.*

[20]*Ibid.*, p. 113.

[21]Lipsey, *op. cit.*

changes and the rate of change of unemployment entirely to an aggregation phenomenon, i.e. 'errors of aggregation'. He thus found no additional role for changes in unemployment to play in the wage-determining process.

Although several studies like Phillips-Lipsey's have been conducted for Canada, most of them relate only to the post-Second World War period. Therefore, in order to provide some perspective of money-wage movements prior to the Second World War, a qualitative analysis is presented here of the broad movements in money wages and levels of unemployment for the period 1921-45 followed by a presentation of the results of a major study of the Phillips-Lipsey variety for the Canadian post-Second World War period. Together these would cover money-wage movements in Canada for the last half-century.

In Figure 7, we have plotted yearly percentage changes of average hourly rates against annual averages of unemployment for the years 1921-45. In order to distinguish three sub-periods, the years of the twenties are marked by squares, the thirties are circled, and the forties are marked by heavy black dots. From the scatter of observation relating wage changes and unemployment, one can see that it would be rather difficult to fit any relationship accurately for the entire period. However, certain broad patterns might be mentioned. The average money wages were to some degree responsive to changes in the over-all demand for labour during the twenties. The decade of the thirties was quite atypical. Wages fell between 1929 and 1933, when unemployment reached levels of almost 20 per cent. Yet after 1933 money wages rose year by year, although the number of unemployed ranged from over 9 per cent to over 14 per cent of the labour force. The same phenomenon, rising wages in conditions of massive unemployment, occurred in the United States. In that country, however, New Deal legislation, including wage increases administered under the N.R.A. codes and the government's prodding of union organizations, provides a plausible, if not complete, explanation. In Canada, there were no major institutional changes. The reasons for the improvement of money wages after 1933 must lie elsewhere. The years from 1934 to 1939 were, in the main, recovery years. The demand for labour was increasing, but at a rate far too slow to absorb fully the enormous pool of unemployed. By the mid thirties, however, a substantial portion of the unemployed may have become 'structural' (i.e., to some degree a non-competing group in the labour market).[22] Then too, it is not unlikely that technological change in some industries, especially manufacturing, may have

---

[22]Paul Samuelson and R. M. Solow, 'Analytical Aspects of Anti-Inflationary Policy', *American Economic Review* (May 1960), p. 189.

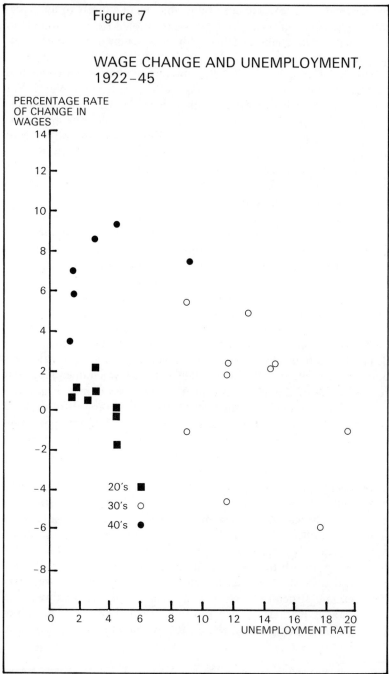

Figure 7

WAGE CHANGE AND UNEMPLOYMENT, 1922–45

Source: D.B.S. Reference Paper 23 (revised) and Labour Force Surveys; Department of Labour, *Wage Rates, Salaries, and Hours of Labour, 1960* (Ottawa, 1961).

had the effect of enriching the skill mix and hence the average wage level of the employed work force. Moreover, it seems reasonable to suppose that many employers during the early thirties had laid off workers in reverse order of skill and ability; this, too, would have had the effect of up-grading the employed labour force. A similar effect might have resulted from the virtual cessation of immigration into Canada during the Great Depression, since a majority of immigrants in the earlier inter-war period had been unskilled labour from central and eastern Europe. No doubt a careful study of industrial change in the thirties would reveal many other relevant developments. Yet the rising wages of this period of unprecedented unemployment remain something of a mystery to economists.[23]

For the post-Second World War period, as stated earlier, there have been a number of quantitative studies explaining money-wage changes in Canada, the most important being the one by Bodkin *et al.* for the Economic Council. This study not only summarized previous Canadian research, but also presented some additional and systematic evidence.[24]

From the Bodkin *et al.* study, one of the 'best' estimated equations for the determination of the percentage change in average hourly earnings in manufacturing for the period 1953-65 is as follows:

$$\dot{W}_t = -4.324 + 0.487\ \dot{P}_t + 18.446\ U_t^{-2} + 0.0618\ (Z/Q)_{t-2}$$
$$\qquad\quad (6.42)\qquad (2.96)\qquad\quad (3.16)$$

$$\qquad + 0.291\ \dot{W}_{us_t} - 0.116\ \dot{W}_{t-4}$$
$$\qquad\quad (2.51)\qquad\quad (3.02) \qquad\qquad\qquad R^2 = 0.847$$

Where $\dot{W}_t$ = percentage change in average hourly earnings of production workers in manufacturing; $\dot{P}_t$ = percentage change in cost-of-living or consumer price index; U_t^{-2} = squared reciprocal of the percentage of the labour force unemployed; $(Z/Q)_{t-2}$ = profits per unit of output in manufacturing in the previous second quarter; $\dot{W}_{us_t}$ = percentage change in average hourly earnings in U.S. manufacturing; $\dot{W}_{t-4}$ = percentage change in average hourly earnings of production workers in manufacturing four quarters ago. R^2 is the coefficient of multiple determination and indicates the percentage of the variation in $\dot{W}_t$ explained by the variables listed on the right-

---

[23]Kaliski made a direct attempt to test the applicability of the Phillips-Lipsey hypothesis to Canadian data and concluded from his study for this period that the Phillips-Lipsey hypothesis partly explained the behaviour of the data during 1922-33, but failed to account for the behaviour of money-wage changes during 1934-9. See S. F. Kaliski, 'The Relations Between Unemployment and the Rate of Change of Money Wages in Canada', *International Economic Review* (January 1964), pp. 1-33.

[24]Bodkin *et al., op. cit.*

hand side of the equation. Figures within the brackets and below the estimated regression coefficients are the t-ratios (i.e. regression coefficients divided by their associated standard errors). Thus Bodkin *et al.*'s 'best' equation suggests that over 80 per cent of the variation in the per cent rate of change of money wages can be explained in terms of such variables as unemployment rate, profits, U.S. average hourly earnings, consumer prices, and the Canadian average hourly earnings of the previous year.

The Economic Council's study was concerned with assessing the determinants of money-wage changes at a highly aggregative level. A study by Grant Reuber, published in 1970, reported results on the determinants of money-wage changes on a somewhat disaggregated basis.[25] Reuber develops a theoretical model that suggests the factors that may account for wage changes in various industries in Canada. According to this model, five basic factors appear to be particularly important in explaining wage changes: (a) the level of unemployment; (b) the relationship between wages in the industry and wage levels in Canada generally; (c) the relationship between wages in the industry in Canada and in the same industry in the United States; (d) the profitability of the industry; and (e) the demand for labour in the industry based upon the demand for the output of the industry.

This study attempted to identify the determinants of wage changes in major manufacturing industries. The twelve industries selected by the author for examination were food and beverages, rubber, textiles, clothing, paper, printing, iron and steel, transportation and equipment, electrical apparatus, non-ferrous metals, chemicals, and non-metallic minerals. The study utilized quarterly data, and the period covered was from 1953 to 1966, inclusive. The definitions of many variables used in this study were the same as those employed by the Economic Council study and thus a link was provided between the two studies.

The results of Reuber's study are summarized in Table 42 below. On the basis of this evidence, Reuber concluded that the changes in money wages generally reflected market variables. Even though the evidence is not conclusive, it seems that for the majority of industries scrutinized in this study, the general economic conditions, as reflected in the explanatory variables, tend to play an important role in the determination of wage changes. It should also be noted here that these findings are broadly similar in many ways to the findings based on aggregate data, since many of the variables used in this disaggregated study are roughly the same as the ones used in the aggregative study.

[25]G. L. Reuber, 'Wage Adjustments in Canadian Industry, 1953-1966', *Review of Economic Studies* (October 1970), pp. 449-68.

TABLE 42

Summary of the Evidence Indicating a Statistically Significant Association Between Wage Changes and the Explanatory Variables Included in the Wage-Change Relationship, Quarterly Estimates, 1953-66

	Wage relative to Canadian wages	Un-employ-ment	Labour demand	Wage relative to U.S. wages	Profits
Food and beverages	*	×	?	?	*
Rubber	×	×	*	?	?
Textiles	×	×	?	?	?
Clothing	×	×	*	?	?
Paper	×	×	?	×	?
Printing	×	*	×	?	?
Iron and steel	?	?	×	?	?
Transportation equipment	?	?	×	*	×
Electrical apparatus	×	×	?	×	×
Non-ferrous metals	×	?	×	?	×
Chemicals	?	?	×	×	?
Non-metallic minerals	×	×	×	?	?

×   significant association indicated
*   marginally significant association indicated
?   no significant association

Source: G. L. Reuber, *op. cit.*, p. 462.

ECKSTEIN-WILSON MODEL

In this model, which like the previous one attempts to get at the mechanism of money-wage movements,[26] it is hypothesized that 'key bargains' and 'key groups' influence the wage-determination process. The two basic ideas are that (a) wages in other industries tend to follow the pace set by a key group of industries having common characteristics, and (b) wage change over a 'bargaining period' rather than the changes over a year or a quarter is the appropriate variable for the study of wage movements.

[26]Otto Eckstein and Thomas Wilson, 'The Determination of Money Wages in American Industry', *Quarterly Journal of Economics* (August 1962), pp. 379-414. For the technical problems involved in the estimation of this model, see T. W. McGuire and L. A. Rapping, 'The Determination of Money Wages in American Industry: Comment', *Quarterly Journal of Economics* (November 1967), pp. 684-9 and the reply by Eckstein and Wilson in the same issue, pp. 690-4.

Otto Eckstein and Thomas Wilson have developed an empirical model to explain the behaviour of money wages in the American manufacturing industries from 1948 to 1960. They regressed wage changes in key industries against both profits and the level of unemployment. Instead of using the standard calendar data, they used 'wage-rounds' time-period data. This was done to take explicit account of the institutional framework of wage determination, since it had been shown in the United States that wage contracts tended to cluster over periods of from one to four years. Eckstein and Wilson found that there were five wage-rounds of varying length from 1948 to 1960, and accordingly they used five wage-round observations in their analysis instead of thirteen annual observations. The data covered eight related two-digit manufacturing industries, namely, rubber, stone, clay and glass, primary metals, fabricated metals, non-electrical machinery, transportation equipment, and instruments. The authors called this group of industries the 'key group', since they found significant interdependence among them in a number of ways. These industries, for example, had: (a) considerable input-output connections among them and tended to prosper together; (b) linked labour markets; (c) linked wage patterns; and (d) political relationships among unions within the group.

The authors' estimated wage equation indicated that nearly all of the variation in the money-wage changes ($R^2 = .997$) in the United States over the period 1948-60 could be explained by variations in unemployment rates and profit rates. As for wage changes in industries outside the 'key group', they were 'largely determined by spillover effects of the key group wages and economic variables applicable to the industry'. In other words, the resulting wage changes in key industries were transmitted to other industries through institutional forces generating spill-over effects. Thus, according to this study, the wage bargaining outcomes in key manufacturing industries shaped the pattern of money-wage changes throughout U.S. manufacturing from 1948 to 1960.

Reuber made a similar study for Canada,[27] using three definitions of 'key group'. The first group is similar to the one identified by Eckstein and Wilson for the United States. The second is defined in terms of certain characteristics of Canadian industries. The third is defined in terms of employees under the collective-bargaining agreements and covering five hundred or more employees in each unit. The author found no evidence of bargaining cycles in the data on collective

[27]Reuber, *op. cit.*

bargaining in Canada. On the assumption that Canadian wages are related to the bargaining cycle for the key groups of industries in the United States, he used the Eckstein-Wilson cycle dates as the basis for his analysis.

Reuber found no evidence to support the key-industry hypothesis for the first two definitions of the key group: 'the identity of the key group of Canadian industries [was] in doubt; the existence of the assumed bargaining cycle [was] in doubt; and when wage changes in an assumed key group of Canadian industries [were] related to wage changes in particular industries, it [was] doubtful whether these key industry wage changes [were] any more closely associated with wage changes in non-key industries than [were] wage changes in manufacturing generally.'[28] Some supporting evidence was found when the third definition of the key group was used, that is, a positive relationship between the wage settlements arrived at by collective-bargaining units for the economy as a whole and the wage changes in many individual Canadian industries. However, 'because of the close relationship between wage changes arrived at in collective bargaining settlements for the economy as a whole and general labor market conditions, it [had] not been possible to identify satisfactorily the separate influence of the spill-over effects per se of collective bargaining on wage changes in particular industries and the influence of general labor market conditions.'[29]

HINES MODEL

A. G. Hines has attempted to show that, contrary to the prevailing view, labour unions do affect the rate of change of money wages *independently* of the demand for and supply of labour.[30] The model is fitted to annual data for the period 1921-61 excluding 1939-48. He has shown in this study that in the United Kingdom the rate of change of the percentage of the labour force unionized, a measure that is uncorrelated with the demand for labour, makes a statistically significant contribution to the explanation of the total variation in money-wage rates. Indeed, for the inter-war and post-war years, he finds that this is the most powerful of all explanatory variables. Hines' study thus explicitly introduces trade unionism as an independent factor into the

[28]*Ibid.*, p. 466.

[29]*Ibid.*

[30]A. G. Hines, 'Trade Unions and Wage Inflation in the United Kingdom, 1893-1961', *The Review of Economic Studies* (October 1964), pp. 221-52.

mechanism of money-wage movements. This study has certain important implications for the cost-push type of inflation. For example, in this model cost-push is the main pressure underlying money-wage (and price) movements.[31]

No official *uniform* statistics that could provide information on the number of workers unionized are available for Canada for the period considered by Hines. There is some information available for the period since 1951, and an attempt was made to test Hines' model for the period 1951-62. In this study, the rate of change of the percentage of the labour force unionized did not account significantly for the variations in the rate of change of money wages in Canada.[32] However, the post-war period considered in the analysis was so short that one might question its findings as a conclusive test of the influence of union pushfulness on wage movements. Further testing of Hines' model will be necessary if one is to isolate the effects of his union variable on wage movements.

John Vanderkamp's study for the 1946-62 period divided the labour force and wage-adjustment mechanism into two sectors: 'organized' with 40 per cent or more employees unionized; and 'unorganized' where about 8 per cent of the workers were unionized.[33] The major conclusion of interest here is that, in the unorganized sector as compared to the organized sector, money-wage changes were less sensitive to price changes and also less sensitive to changes in unemployment. Vanderkamp noted in this context that 'whatever the reason for this [might] be, it [could] not easily be used to support the view which [was] sometimes voiced that unions tended to frustrate the operation of the competitive market mechanism.'[34]

Reuber found that for the period 1953 to 1966 the simple correlation between the average degree of unionization in various two-digit industries and the percentage rate of changes in money wages was

[31]For a criticism of Hines' study, see L. A. Dicks-Mireaux, *Cost or Demand Inflation*, Woolwich Economic Papers No. 6 (Woolwich Polytechnic, London, 1965). Dicks-Mireaux's major criticism is that trade unionism should also be important in *relative* wage movements if it is such an important factor in money-wage movements. He does not believe that this is so obvious from Hines' study.

[32]M. A. Zaidi, 'The Determinants of Wage Rate Changes in Canada: An Empirical Study', unpublished Ph.D. dissertation (University of California, Berkeley, 1966). Another study by the same author on the same subject found similar results for the United States; see his 'Trade Unions and Wage Inflation in the U. S. A., 1901-1960', mimeographed, paper presented at the Econometric Society Meeting, Chicago, December 1968.

[33]J. Vanderkamp. 'Wages and Price Level Determination: An Empirical Model For Canada', *Economica* (May 1966), pp. 194-218.

[34]*Ibid.*

quite insignificant.[35] Further, Sparks and Wilton discovered weak association between strikes and the per-cent rate of change in wages of workers covered by collective-bargaining agreements.[36] Thus, as Reuber has pointed out, 'since the ability to mount a strike presumably is some reflection of union power, this failure to uncover a strongly significant association may suggest that the ability of unions to regulate wage changes is questionable.'[37]

[35]Reuber, *op. cit.*

[36]Sparks and Wilton, *op. cit.*

[37]Reuber, *op. cit.*, p. 462. As the book goes to press this view of Reuber's has been challenged by Robert Swidinsky in two of his recent papers ('Trade Unions and the Rate of Change of Money Wages in Canada: 1953-1970', and 'Trade Union Aggressiveness and Wage Determination in Canada', Department of Economics, University of British Columbia, Vancouver, 1971, Mimeographed). The first of these covers Canadian manufacturing industry as a whole, while the second deals with seven major industries and fourteen two-digit manufacturing industries. The broad objective of Swidinsky's Canadian study is the same as that of Hines' study for the U.K., but Swidinsky rejects as 'dubious' the latter's index of union power, i.e. the per cent of the labour force unionized, and replaces it by the 'loss in mandays per employee due to strike activity', which Swidinsky claims, is a 'more direct measure of union aggressiveness'. The over-all conclusion of the study is that trade unions do play a significant role in the money wage adjustment process in Canadian industries. Swidinsky also argues that, by and large, trade union aggressiveness has a much greater impact on money wages in Canada than market forces, e.g. changes in price level or unemployment rate. For Canadian manufacturing industry the 'union militancy variable displays a strong positive effect on the rate of change in wages.' However, on the individual industry level, this conclusion seems to be true for only three, viz. transportation, mining, and manufacturing, out of the seven major industries studied. In the remaining four industries the results are either nonconclusive, or, as in the case of the construction industry, negative. Out of the fourteen two-digit industries studied, Swidinsky's time loss variable is significantly positive in ten industries but not significant in the remaining industries.

It would appear that the results of Swidinsky's study, although indicative of a possible direction of influences, does not convincingly establish the quantitative impact of trade unions on money wages in Canadian industries. At present, the use of time-loss variable as the sole index of union strength is of only experimental value. Even in their rather sophisticated study, to which Swidinsky refers, Ashenfelter, Johnson, and Pencavel suggest that 'in order to test hypotheses about the effects of trade unions on money wages it is necessary to specify a set of proxy variables measuring trade union strength and activity. Aside from the fact that alternative proxies can always be specified, there is the further problem that these variables probably do not maintain an invariant relationship with the underlying forces they are presumed to measure.' (O. C. Ashenfelter, G. E. Johnson, and H. H. Pencavel, 'Trade Unions and the Rate of Change of Money Wages in United States Manufacturing Industry', Working Paper No. 12, Industrial Relations Section, Princeton University (December 1970), p. 27) So although Swidinsky presents some new evidence on wage determination in Canada, the question of the relative roles of market versus institutional variables is still far from being settled, and the arguments are likely to continue in the future. Even studies agreeing generally on the strength of trade unions differ widely as to the magnitudes of such strength. In the words of one author: 'Although much good work has been done on the impact of the union, there are still large divergences between estimates made by different investigators. . . . Reconciling these estimates will require more work in the years ahead.' (Albert Rees, 'The Current State of Labour Economics', Industrial Relations Centre, Queen's University (Kingston, 1971), Reprint Series No. 16)

BEHMAN MODEL

In an article published in 1964, Sara Behman claimed that the movement in money wages reacted significantly to changes in key labour-market indices, namely, the rate of rehiring, the rate of new hiring, and the quit rate.[38] Fundamental to this model is the importance of the cost of labour turnover to the firm. More specifically, the model develops the following hypotheses:

> (1) increasing product demand in a particular sector that leads employers to anticipate a continuance of good times stimulates the hiring of a certain group of workers. As long as qualified help is available from among the unemployed group, money wages need not rise; (2) when the type of help needed by the firms in the expanding sector is no longer available from among the involuntary unemployed, wage pressures are likely to develop in the firms involved. To attract the type of workers needed, these firms must offer higher wages; (3) this money wage rate increase taking place in one sector is diffused throughout industry by the 'morale effect', i.e., truly dissatisfied workers quit their jobs, and those workers who do not quit can reduce their productive efficiency if they are dissatisfied.[39]

Behman's investigation deals with aggregate manufacturing in the United States, and covers the period from 1946 to 1961. She found that quit rate, the labour-demand variable, was significantly related to percentage changes in hourly earnings ($R^2 = .90$). On the basis of this finding, she concluded that 'the quit rate, a worker behavioral variable that is also a proxy for labor demand, does make the distinction between those workers that can affect wage changes and those who cannot.'[40] Behman's model is interesting in the sense that it attempts to explain money-wage-rate changes solely in terms of labour-market indices, but her results are not entirely convincing if we consider the fact that much of the mobility in the economic system appears to be involuntary.[41] To determine the general validity of the Behman model, more studies examining data found outside the United States will be needed. Unfortunately, data on rehires, new hires, and quits are not available for Canada.

Thus, the original Phillips study of the unemployment–wage-rate-change relationship has been extended to include a large number of

---

[38]Sara Behman, 'Labor Mobility, Increasing Labor Demand, and Money Wage Rate Increases in United States Manufacturing', *Review of Economic Studies* (October 1964), pp. 253-66.

[39]*Ibid.*, p. 256.

[40]*Ibid.*, p. 266.

[41]L. E. Gallaway, *Interindustry Labor Mobility in the United States 1957 to 1960*, U.S. Department of Health, Education and Welfare, Social Security Administration (Washington, D. C., 1967), Chapter 10.

variables. There has also been considerable experimentation with the form of variables and with the form of equations. The wage-change–unemployment relationship has been found to differ from country to country and to shift over time. (See Chapter V for discussion of shifts in the Phillips curve.)

All of the models described above have attempted to get at the mechanism of money-wage movements. Some trace the behaviour of money-wage changes as far back as 1861. Others concentrate mainly on the period since the Second World War. If any general conclusion can be based on the findings of these studies, it is that money-wage movements can be explained in many different ways! It is difficult at this early state in the development of our knowledge about the determination of money-wage changes to establish the superiority of any one model over another. Only further testing of the implications of these models could perhaps lead to some definite discrimination among them.

Inflation in Canada

As we have seen in Chapter V, the focus of public policy shifted in recent years away from the goal of maintaining full employment toward a far greater concern with price stability. Even in the earlier post-war years, however, the rapid increase in money wages and prices in most countries aroused widespread and vigorous discussion of the nature and causes of inflation.[42] The controversies around the phenomenon were due mainly to the divergent causal sequences highlighted by the different theories. Broadly speaking, there are three theories that explain persistent price rises – each attributing inflation to a different causative factor. The three theories are as follows: 'demand-pull inflation'; 'cost-push inflation'; and 'demand-shift inflation'. Before discussing the Canadian inflationary situation, the differences between these theories of inflation will be briefly discussed.

The demand-pull hypothesis attributes inflation to increases in the demand for final goods and services (consumers' goods and services or investment goods). As demand increases relative to supply, the prices for final goods and services tend to rise, leading to a corresponding increase in the demand for factors of production. In turn,

---

[42]A comprehensive survey and an excellent bibliography on inflation is available in M. Bronfenbrenner and F. D. Holzman, 'Survey of Inflation Theory', *American Economic Review* (September 1963), pp. 593-661.

the latter increase in demand may cause an increase in factor prices.[43] Thus, increases in the level of goods prices cause increases in the level of factor prices. The cost-push theory, on the other hand, states that it is the increases in factor prices that *cause* increases in final goods prices, and that changes in factor prices can occur independently of the state of excess demand.[44] The cost-push theory, although commonly interpreted in terms of general price increases induced by autonomous upward shifts in the general wage level, may have several other versions. For example, costs may rise as a result of a rise in import prices. A pure cost inflation, therefore, is defined as 'resulting from autonomous increases in costs, whether generated internally or externally'.[45] Many analyses of inflation, however, view the process of rise in prices neither as pure demand-pull nor as pure cost-push. 'The actual rate of inflation depends on the interaction of monetary demand and the cost generating structure of the system. The proponents of demand inflation concentrate only on the first aspect and the cost inflationists on the second. But it is not appropriate from the point of view of policy prescription in general to restrict one's attention to either alone. Prices will rise if excess aggregate monetary demand exists, but they can also rise if it does not. Thus, in the most general case, it will be necessary to pay attention to the balance of resources and also to the need to alter the cost generating structure by some interference with the bargaining mechanism if full employment and stable prices are a prime object of policy.'[46]

Another type of inflationary model is based on certain features of both the demand-pull and cost-push explanations. This model suggests that it is necessary to look behind the aggregate data: that inflationary price increases may stem from sudden sharp shifts in the composition of demand when there is no aggregate excess demand. Excess demand in one sector will pull up wages and prices. But in the sector in which demand is falling, wages and prices do not fall, because of downward inflexibility. Thus, the average level of wages and prices must rise.[47] This argument does not rest on unionism or wage-push, though, clearly, collective-bargaining practices may reinforce and accelerate the upward movement of wages and strengthen their rigidity

[43]R. G. Lipsey, *An Introduction to Positive Economics* (London, 1963), p. 434.
[44]*Ibid.*, p. 435.
[45]R. J. Ball, *Inflation and the Theory of Money* (Chicago, 1964), p. 264.
[46]*Ibid.*, p. 267.
[47]This is a highly oversimplified statement of the view of Charles L. Schultze, *Recent Inflation in the United States*, Study Paper No. 1, Joint Economic Committee, Congress of the United States (Washington, D. C., 1959), especially Chapters III, IV, and V.

in the opposite direction. In the absence of unions, however, the pricing behaviour of large firms in 'protected' markets will inhibit price and wage cuts in the face of falling demand. Union activity is thus viewed as a reinforcing factor, not a primary cause. In the demand-shift view of inflation, the key element in any labour market is the degree of responsiveness of wages and prices to declining demand.

Indeed, as the inflation debate continued it became clearer that the key to the demand-pull versus cost-push argument centred on this question of the degree of sensitivity of wages and prices to market forces. Put another way, the demand-pull supporters believe that since the inflationary price rise is primarily due to excess aggregate demand, a reduction in demand (by monetary or fiscal means) will bring about a more or less orderly reduction of prices and costs without undue unemployment. The cost-push view, on the other hand, stressing the rigidity of prices and costs in the face of declining demand, suggests that the contraction of aggregate demand necessary to achieve price stability will entail a high level of unemployment.

This is illustrated by the diagrams in Figures 8, 9 and 10 from Professor Fellner. The price level P_2 is that which will be established in the future if the level of aggregate demand is inflationary and no counteracting policy is undertaken. The three diagrams illustrate the effects of anti-inflationary monetary and fiscal policy that restricts aggregate demand. It may be seen that Figure 8 describes a situation of pure demand-inflation, since demand-restriction leaves employment (measured along the X axis) unchanged; prices and costs recede in an orderly fashion with the contraction of demand. In Figure 9, it is apparent that prices cannot be reduced without a reduction in employment, and hence we should describe this as a situation of cost-inflation. Figure 10, obviously, depicts a blend of both demand- and cost-inflation; prices can be reduced somewhat without affecting employment, but a full restoration of prices to the level of period 1 involves some loss of employment. These diagrams – and our explanation – are highly oversimplified,[48] but they are useful as an illustrative device to point up the essential difference between these two types of inflation.

As was shown earlier, the long-run trend of prices in Canada has been upward,[49] the simple average rate of increase of prices being 4.6 per cent per year from 1896 to 1968. The rate of inflation has

---

[48]For fuller discussion, see Fellner, *op. cit.*

[49]W. R. Needham, 'Inflation in Canada: The Historical Perspective', mimeographed, paper presented at the Queen's University Conference on Inflation, June 1970.

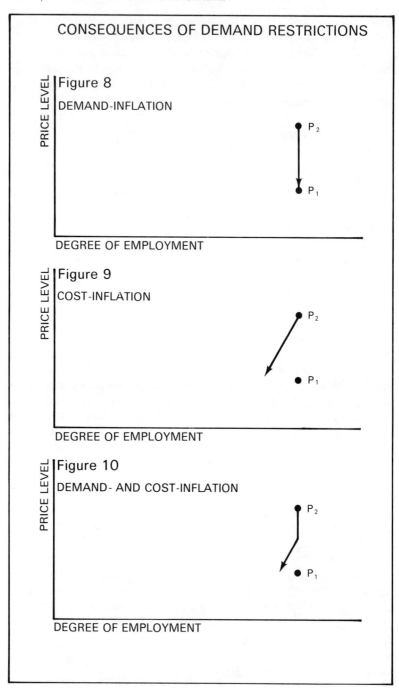

CONSEQUENCES OF DEMAND RESTRICTIONS

Figure 8

DEMAND-INFLATION

Figure 9

COST-INFLATION

Figure 10

DEMAND- AND COST-INFLATION

Source: William Fellner, 'Demand Inflation, Cost Inflation, and Collective Bargaining', in *The Public Stake in Union Power*, Philip D. Bradley (ed.) (Charlottesville), p. 228.

varied in different sub-periods of the last one hundred years. The sub-periods characterized by very high rates of inflation were 1914-20, 1939-45, and 1945-51. The first two inflations were associated with the First and Second World Wars. Long-run price behaviour in Canada was also characterized by some periods of relative price stability and price decline. Over the period 1920 to 1935, prices fell substantially, and during 1925-30 they were rather stable (see Table 43).

After the close of the Second World War, prices and wages rose substantially at rates far greater than before. The major factors contributing to this sharp upward movement were the pent-up demands for consumer goods that were suppressed during the war, and the removal of price controls.

Most economists agreed that the first post-war inflation (1946-9) was primarily caused by the tug of excess demand resulting from a war-time legacy of a large volume of liquid assets and a backlog of deferred needs. True, in the United States some voices were raised in protest at this interpretation, and at least one zealot, shocked by the aggressive and successful bargaining of the big industrial unions, predicted the ultimate destruction of the competitive price system by organized labour. Calmer observers suggested that unions, full employment, and stable prices were an incompatible trio,[50] and that, in the interests of the community as a whole, the power of unions would have to be curbed. The only question was how – and, not surprisingly, the question was usually put more forcefully than the answer. There were some suggestions about more active and extensive use of anti-trust laws to control bargaining,[51] but in the main, the 'solution' consisted of the reiteration of vague exhortations to labour to exercise greater restraint and 'responsibility'.

A sharply dissenting view was that of Professor Slichter,[52] who argued, in effect, that long-run 'creeping' inflation is inevitable, and, moreover, should not be regarded as an unmixed evil: at worst it is a disease that is preferable to the consequences of its cure, at best it may lubricate the wheels of progress. But the wage-push advocates of both types the 'pulverizers', as Professor Schultze has termed them, and the followers of Slichter – were in a minority among academic

---

[50]Gottfried Haberler, 'Wage Policy Employment, and Economic Stability', *The Impact of the Union*, David McCord Wright (ed.) (New York, 1951), p. 38, and cf. J. H. Clark in the same volume.

[51]James W. McKie, 'Collective Bargaining and the Maintenance of Market Competition', *The Public Stake in Union Power* (Charlottesville, Virginia, 1959), pp. 96-110. Cf. also, in same volume, contributions by E. H. Chamberlain, Gottfried Haberler, and David McCord Wright.

[52]Sumner H. Slichter, 'Do the Wage-fixing Arrangements in the American Labor Market Have an Inflationary Bias?', *American Economic Review* (May 1954), pp. 322-46.

TABLE 43

Consumer Price Index, Canada

(1949 = 100)

Year	Price index
1915	50.7
1920	93.6
1925	75.0
1930	75.2
1935	59.9
1940	65.7
1945	75.0
1950	102.9
1955	116.4

Source: Urquhart, *Historical Statistics of Canada.*

economists, and demand-pull won the day as a primary explanation of the rapid rise of wages and prices during the first few years following the war. Indeed, some of the demand-pull proponents suggested that, far from having caused the inflation, some unions had managed – albeit unintentionally – to hold wages below their free-market level.[53] At the very most, unions were simply 'thermometers registering the heat "rather than" furnaces producing the heat'![54] However, the wage-push (or a more generalized version, cost-push) argument was not so easily dismissed. Some economists, in retrospect, argued that 'push' forces were present after the war even though the primary factor was excess aggregate demand.[55] Theories of a combined demand-pull and cost-push nature were put forward as a general explanation of inflation under conditions of strong unionization and imperfectly competitive product markets.[56] But what was most puzzling, and stimulated most support for a variety of cost-push explanations, was the 1955-7 inflation. In this period there was far less evidence of over-full employment and excess aggregate demand; indeed, toward the end there were signs of excess capacity, and yet wages and prices

[53]Milton Friedman, 'Some Comments on the Significance of Labor Unions for Economic Policy', *The Impact of the Union, op. cit.*, pp. 228-9.

[54]Friedman, *op. cit.*, p. 222.

[55]Neil W. Chamberlain, 'Collective Bargaining in the United States', *Contemporary Collective Bargaining*, Adolph Sturmthal (ed.) (Ithaca, 1957), pp. 274-7.

[56]For a clear exposition of a British version, see *Fourth Report, Council on Prices, Productivity and Incomes* (July 1961), especially pp. 14-17.

TABLE 44

Annual Rate of Change of Consumer Price Index, Canada

Year	Annual rate of change Per cent
1956	2.97
1957	2.24
1958	2.52
1959	1.35
1960	1.33
1961	0.19
1962	1.59
1963	1.76
1964	1.92
1965	2.93
1966	3.58
1967	4.07
1968	4.09
1969	4.58

Source: D.B.S. *Canadian Statistical Review* (Ottawa, various years).

rose, though admittedly the rise was more moderate than in the earlier inflations.

In more recent periods, the outstanding feature of Canada's consumer price index has been its uninterrupted ascent (see Table 44). From 1961 the price level rose steadily, and in the last few years of the 1960s a 'rather distinct upward trend is observable'.[57] A large number of domestic and foreign influences bear on the situation in Canada, and it is hard to evaluate their respective contributions. For example, a recent Canadian study concluded that 'there is no single explanation but a varying mixture of the three major types of inflation.'[58] Similarly, and as in many previous inquiries into this subject, it must be concluded from the foregoing analysis that there is no single explanation of inflation, but rather that the rise in prices results from a combination of forces (monetary and fiscal policies, market imperfections, foreign influences, etc.) and the 'relative importance varied both over time and in different setting(s)'.[59] In the

[57]Needham, *op. cit.*

[58]*Canadian Industrial Relations*, the report of the Task Force on Labour Relations, Privy Council Office (December 1968), p. 59.

[59]*Ibid.*, p. 55.

discussion of the four models of wage determination, we identified certain factors that are associated with changes in money-wage rates. Nothing in these models, however, enables us to interpret the causal sequences of inflation.

A problem often discussed in the literature of inflation is the difficulty of devising effective statistical tests of alternative hypotheses. Many of the tests found in both popular and even academic publications simply *describe* the inflationary process, i.e. 'point to circumstances which will accompany any inflation, however caused', but they do not have 'what the statisticians call power against the main alternative hypotheses'.[60] Thus, for example, if wages rise faster than productivity, this alone does not constitute *proof* of cost inflation. This association could appear in the purest of excess-demand inflation. Again, many writers are concerned with the timing of wage and price increases. This is a version of 'which came first: the chicken or the egg?' We have no way of choosing a 'correct' base period, and, moreover, the first impact of excess demand may be felt in the factor and not the product market. Similarly, detailed examinations of money supply and velocity cannot conclusively expose the source of motive power generating the rise in the price level.[61] In the words of Professors Samuelson and Solow, '...it is not possible on the basis of *a priori* reasoning to reject either the demand-pull or cost-push hypotheses, or the variants of the latter such as demand shift.... The empirical identifications needed to distinguish between these hypotheses may be quite impossible from the experience of macro data that is available... and while use of micro data might throw additional light on the problem, even here identification is fraught with difficulties and ambiguities.'[62]

[60]Samuelson and Solow, *op. cit.*, p. 182.
[61]Charles L. Schultze, *op. cit.*, pp. 37-8.
[62]Samuelson and Solow, *op. cit.*, p. 191.

IX

Income Distribution, Labour's Share, and Poverty

The problem of the distribution of income is perhaps as important as is that of the creation of income. In the opinion of some, it is of even even greater importance. According to John Bates Clark: 'For practical men, and hence for students, supreme importance attaches to one economic problem – that of the distribution of wealth among different claimants.'[1] The present chapter contains a discussion about the nature of the distribution of income and shifts in it against the background of the Canadian economy. Studies of income distribution also raise the question of equity and poverty. Accordingly, the conceptual and empirical aspects of this question will be considered. In this connection, an evaluation of various measures for ameliorating poverty will be made.

Depending on the purpose of inquiry, the distribution of national income may be viewed in different ways, e.g., among regions, industries, organizations, factors of production, and persons or families.[2] The main objective of this chapter being a discussion of the share of wages in national income, attention will be focused on the distribution of national income among factors and persons, with special reference to the Canadian economy.

Functional Distribution of Income

Functional or factoral distribution of income is the break-down of income into the contributions made by the different factors of produc-

[1]John Bates Clark, *The Distribution of Wealth* (London, 1899), p. 1.
[2]See Simon S. Kuznets, 'National Income', in *Encyclopedia of the Social Sciences*, Vol. XI (1933).

tion participating in its production. The shares of these factors in the cake that is national income have often been the subject of controversies in economic policy; this largely explains the importance of the functional distribution of income.

National income may be divided into (a) employee compensation consisting of wages, salaries, and supplementary-labour income, (b) entrepreneurial income accruing from ownership of enterprises both farm and non-farm, (c) corporate profit, that is, the income earned by virtue of holding the shares of incorporated enterprises, (d) interest earned on financial assets, and (e) rent, which is a return to resources whose supply is unresponsive to variations in the returns to them.[3] There are a number of difficulties in an empirical study of factor shares.[4] For example, the break-down of actual national accounting data does not often correspond to the economic concepts mentioned above. This difficulty may be obviated by adopting a rather simplified division of national income data into 'labour' and 'non-labour' earnings. Still some knotty problems persist. Accounting data for entrepreneurial income generally represents a joint return to the capital invested and the labour expended by the entrepreneur in the enterprise. Thus, it is hard to say, for example, if an upward trend in wages' share represents 'an increase in the share of labor as a factor and a decrease in that of property as the other factor'.[5] Moreover, wages and salaries are lumped together in national accounting data, making it difficult to identify the share of wages proper in national income.

Any empirical study of the relative shares of factors of production is bound to confront the controversy relating to the alleged stability of such shares over time. There are two schools holding different views on this problem. Keynes wrote, 'the stability of the proportion of the national dividend accruing to labour . . . is one of the most surprising, yet best established facts in the whole range of economic statistics.'[6] This view has been strongly supported by several econo-

[3]Kenneth E. Boulding, 'The Concept of Economic Surplus', in *Readings in Income Distribution*, American Economic Association (Philadelphia, 1949).
[4]For a discussion of these difficulties, see B. F. Haley, 'An Empirical View of Functional Shares', in *Perspectives on Wage Determination*, Campbell R. McConnell (ed.) (New York, 1970). For Canadian data difficulties, see Dorothy Walters, *Canadian Income Levels and Growth: An International Perspective*, Economic Council Staff Study No. 23, and also, by the same author, Staff Study No. 28, for most recent estimates of factor shares based on the 1968 revisions of the national accounts.
[5]B. F. Haley, 'Changes in the Distribution of Income in the United States', in *The Distribution of National Income*, J. Marchal and B. Ducros (eds.) (New York, 1968), p. 22.
[6]J. M. Keynes, 'Relative Movements of Real Wages and Output', *Economic Journal* (1939), p. 48.

mists. It has been shown that the functional share of labour does not show any secular change,[7] and that the proportion of business gross product going to employee compensation has been constant.[8] On the other hand, several studies have cast doubt on the historical constancy of relative shares.[9] The causes of the controversy may be traced mostly to differences in definitions and concepts, in the models used, in the nature of analysis – static or dynamic – and in the period, economy, and sectors considered.

The empirically observed shifts in the relative share of wages in national income are usually attributed to structural changes in the economy such as the increasing relative importance of secondary and especially tertiary industry (where the share of wages is high) over agriculture (in which the share of wages is low and declining). The increasing ascendancy of the government sector is a case in point. Also, there may be a decline in the proportion of unincorporated enterprises, pushing upward the wage-earning component of the labour force. Shifts in relative shares may also be due to business fluctuations, which affect different factors differently. Changes in relative prices of labour and capital often outweigh other changes to influence factor shares.[10] Moreover, the ratio of investment to income affects the distribution of income between wages and profits.[11] There is an interdependence between the level of income and its functional distribution.[12] Besides, the degree of monopoly[13] and the nature and strength of labour unions also influence the functional distribution of income.[14]

[7]D. G. Johnson, 'The Functional Distribution of Income in the United States, 1850-1952', *The Review of Economics and Statistics* (1954).

[8]S. Weintraub, *A General Theory of the Price Level, Output, Income Distribution and Economic Growth* (Philadelphia, 1959).

[9]I. Kravis, 'Relative Income Share in Fact and Theory', in *American Economic Review* (1957); and R. Solow, 'A Skeptical Note on the Constancy of Relative Shares', *American Economic Review* (1958).

[10]Jae Won Lee, 'Determinants of the Changes in the Relative Factor Share', *The Review of Economics and Statistics* (August 1970).

[11]N. Kaldor, 'Alternative Theories of Distribution', *The Review of Economic Studies* (1955-9), pp. 83-108.

[12]S. Weintraub, *An Approach to the Theory of Income Distribution* (Philadelphia, 1958).

[13]M. Kalecki, 'The Distribution of the National Income', in *Readings in Income Distribution*, American Economic Association (1949); P. Davidson, *Theories of Aggregate Income Distribution* (New Brunswick, N.J., 1960), p. 44. For a review of literature in this regard see also John R. Maroney and Bruce T. Allen, 'Monopoly Power and the Relative Share of Labor', *Industrial and Labor Relations Review* (January 1969), pp. 167-78.

[14]Clark Kerr, 'Labor's Income Share and the Labor Movement', in *New Concepts in Wage Determination*, G. W. Taylor and F. C. Pierson (eds.) (New York, 1957). See also Paul S. Sultan, 'Unionism and Wage-Income Ratios, 1929-51', *The Review of Economics and Statistics* (February 1954); and Norman J. Simler, *The Impact of Unionism on*

Labour's Share of National Income in Canada

What is the situation in the Canadian economy in regard to the functional distribution of income between labour and other factors? Has it shifted in favour of the wage-earner? What are the causes?

Table 45 presents information on labour's share of national income over the period from 1926 to 1969. The first point to be noted is that labour income as a percentage of national income varies inversely with the aggregate level of economic activity. As national income fell in the early thirties, labour's share rose sharply, and profits were squeezed (in 1932, corporation profits before taxes were just over 1.0 per cent of national income compared with 11.9 per cent in 1929). As the economy slowly recovered after 1933, labour's share declined. This contra-cyclical movement is more difficult to discern in the mild, shorter cycles of the post-war period, with the exception of the increase during the 1953-4 recession years. Wages and salaries appear to be less sensitive to cyclical pressures than non-labour income; hence the inverted movement of the wage share with the business cycle.

The cyclical movement of labour's share and also the considerable fluctuation even from year to year make it rather difficult to observe any trend in these data. None the less, if one compares the 1926-9 boom period with the boom years after the Second World War, it appears that the ratio of labour income to national income has shown a moderate increase. Undoubtedly, an important reason for this lies in certain structural shifts in employment that have been taking place in the economy. These include the relative decline of agriculture (with its very low ratio of wages to total income); the relative growth of government employment and service industries (with very high ratios);[15] and the relative decline of non-farm unincorporated business.[16] If one were to try to measure the intra-industry distributional shift, it would be necessary to adjust for these structural changes. A study

---

Wage-Income Ratios in the Manufacturing Sector of the Economy (Minneapolis, 1961); E. H. Phelps Brown and P. E. Hart, 'The Share of Wages in National Income', *Economic Journal* (June 1952); John W. Kendrick, *Productivity Trends in the United States* (N.B.E.R.) (Princeton, 1961); Melvin W. Reder, 'Alternative Theories of Labour's Share', in *The Allocation of Economic Resources*, M. Abramovitz (ed.) (Stanford, 1959).

[15]The valuation of the government non-commercial sector is accounted for entirely by wages and salaries. For more on the cyclical variation in labour's share, see *Canadian Industrial Relations*, The Report on the Task Force on Labour Relations, Privy Council Office (Ottawa, 1968), pp. 64-6.

[16]If the corner grocer goes to work as a manager of the local supermarket, the decline in non-farm, unincorporated business income is reflected in a rise in wages and salaries. If, however, an established unincorporated business incorporates, it is not so clear what may happen to relative labour and non-labour income.

TABLE 45

Wages, Salaries, and Supplementary Labour Income as a
Percentage of National Income: Canada, 1926-69

Year	Per cent	Year	Per cent	Year	Per cent
1926	57.9	1942	53.7	1958	67.2
1927	58.1	1943	55.5	1959	67.5
1928	58.0	1944	52.9	1960	68.6
1929	63.2	1945	53.0	1961	69.3
1930	64.1	1946	58.6	1962	68.2
1931	72.3	1947	62.6	1963	67.6
1932	76.0	1948	62.5	1964	67.8
1933	76.8	1949	62.8	1965	68.8
1934	71.0	1950	62.0	1966	69.3
1935	68.1	1951	62.0	1967	71.6
1936	67.6	1952	61.2	1968	71.4
1937	66.3	1953	63.9	1969	72.2
1938	63.8	1954	66.4		
1939	62.3	1955	64.6		
1940	59.4	1956	65.5		
1941	58.1	1957	67.9		

Source: D.B.S., *National Income and Expenditure Accounts* (1926-68, 1969). These incorporate the 1968 revisions.

by Dr. Simon Goldberg of the D.B.S., covering the period 1926-58, revealed that for the non-farm, private-business sector of the economy, labour's relative share rose 11.8 per cent; when these data were adjusted to eliminate interindustry shifts, the rise was only 8.7 per cent. Moreover, Dr. Goldberg contended that 'it seems likely that a portion of the 8.7 per cent reflects a shift from unincorporated to the incorporated form of business organization.'[17] In the manufacturing sector, labour's share rose even less. Adjusting for changes in the industrial composition of manufacturing, the ratio of wages and salaries as a percentage of 'census value added' rose by 5.9 per cent between 1926-30 and 1954-8.[18] The same trend of interindustry shifts and increase in incorporated relative to unincorporated business organization may be assumed to have continued through 1969.[19] The increase in labour's

[17]S. A. Goldberg, 'Long-run Changes in the Distribution of Income by Factor Shares in Canada', in *The Behavior of Income Shares*, National Bureau of Economic Research (1964), Vol. 27, p. 226.

[18]*Ibid.*, p. 230; excluding supplementary labour income.

[19]See Chapter IV, for interindustry shifts. Paid employment as a percentage of total employment in Canada rose from 64 per cent in 1961 to 85 per cent in 1968, an indication of the relative increase of incorporated over unincorporated enterprises.

share of national income by 5.0 percentage points from 1958 to 1969 obviously includes those effects.

On the whole, one may say that there has been little change in the functional distribution of income (structural shifts aside) over a relatively long period of time in this country. However, as noted above, labour's share includes both wages and salaries. One cannot rule out the possibility that there may have been some redistribution, within labour's share, in favour of the industrial wage-earner. Without more detailed data and more elaborate statistical analysis, it is difficult to say anything more precise. Since the theory of the determination of factor-shares of the national product has exercised some of the best economic minds of two centuries without producing a general consensus, there is no need to apologize for leaving the matter with so many questions unanswered. Before we conclude this discussion, however, one further aspect of functional distribution deserves mention.

The analysis so far has dealt with national income from the viewpoint of income produced by the various 'factors of production'. If, instead, one looks at income received, then the effect of government fiscal policy on the distribution of income may be revealed. The statistics presented in Table 46 reveal that the sum of interest, dividends, and net rental income of persons, net income of farm operators, and the net income of non-farm unincorporated business, represented a significantly smaller share of personal income in 1967 than it did in 1928. This is partially explained by the fact that in recent times not only is a much smaller proportion of profits after taxes paid out as dividends, but also a much higher proportion of profits is taxed away. But the government's role is not confined to taxation. In 1961, government transfer payments were second in relative importance following income from employment, reflecting the gradual evolution of Canadian social-security programs.[20] Transfer payments represented 13.3 per cent of personal income in 1967, in contrast to 2 per cent in 1928. These data on the distribution of income *received*, or *personal* income, suggest that the distribution process has been rather strongly affected by the role of government.[21] This brings up a related but none

[20]J. R. Podoluk, *Incomes of Canadians*, 1961 Census Monograph, Dominion Bureau of Statistics (Ottawa, 1968), p. 25.

[21]In addition to government, labour unions have also been suggested in the literature as having some impact on the distributive process, but the distributive impact of the union and collective bargaining is still a controversial question. A large body of literature exists in this field especially for the American and British economies, but the opinion is not unanimous. For further work in this respect, see Clark Kerr, 'Trade Unionism and Distributive Shares', in *American Economic Review, Papers and Proceedings* (May 1954); Sultan, *op. cit.*; E. H. Phelps Brown and P. E. Hart, 'The Share of Wages in National Income', *Economic Journal* (1952); H. M. Levinson, *Unionism, Wage*

TABLE 46

Personal Income – Percentage Distribution, 1928 and 1967

	1928	1967
Wages, salaries, and supplementary labour income	59.2	64.3
Military pay and allowances	.2	1.5
Interest, dividends, and net rental income of persons	12.2	10.4
Net income of farm operators	13.6	3.8
Net income of non-farm unincorporated business	12.8	6.7
Transfer payments (excluding interest)	2.0	13.3
Total	100.0	100.0

Note: This table does not take account of recent revisions in the national accounts because the necessary data were not available.

Sources: Dominion Bureau of Statistics, *National Accounts – Income and Expenditure, 1926-1956*, Ottawa, 1962, p. 13; and *National Accounts – Income and Expenditure, 1967*, Ottawa, September 1968, p. 16.

the less separate problem, namely the distribution of income by size (as opposed to the functional distribution), which is what the layman usually means when he refers to 'equity' in the distribution of income.

Personal Distribution of Income

Personal distribution of income is concerned with how the income of the nation is distributed among its recipient individuals or families.

Trends, and Income Distribution (Ann Arbor, 1951); Albert Rees, 'The Effects of Unions on Resource Allocation', in *Readings in Micro-economics*, W. Breit and H. M. Hochman (eds.) (New York, 1968); H. G. Lewis, 'Relative Employment Effects of Unionism', *Proceedings of the Sixteenth Annual Meeting of Industrial Relations Research Association*, 1964. Studies of the union effect on distribution in Canada are extremely difficult because of the lack of data concerning proportions of workers under collective agreement by industry or industry groups for any pre-Second World War years and (since that might be overcome to some extent by using membership data as a substitute) by lack of information on national product by industry sector for early years – specifically, lack of separate detail on unionized sectors such as construction and transportation for years prior to 1944.

As we all know, incomes of individuals or families, whatever the source, vary considerably in size. This variation arises mainly for the following reasons:[22] (a) changes occur within the functional shares (wages and salaries can range from the meagre earnings of the janitor to the opulent income of the corporation executive; property incomes can vary from those of the proverbial widows and orphans to the lush returns of the coupon-clipping playboy wintering on the Riviera); (b) changes occur in the average differences between functional shares – relative increases or decreases of labour income as opposed to non-labour income; (c) changes occur in the rural-urban composition of population – a rising proportion of families living in the urban metropolitan or non-farm areas where the pattern of personal distribution is different from that in rural areas; (d) changes occur in the age composition of the population; (e) changes occur in the number of earners per family – a relatively high increase in the proportion of families with two or more earners in the lower income group would tend to depress the forces of inequality in income distribution; (f) changes occur in education – family heads with relatively fewer years of education are particularly vulnerable to unemployment; (g) changes occur in the rates of growth of the population differentially between regions – differential population growth may affect the efficiency of resource utilization and thus result in a disparity in income distribution for the entire economy; and (h) changes occur in government fiscal and transfer policies, which affect all or some of the above.

MEASUREMENT OF INEQUALITY IN PERSONAL INCOME
DISTRIBUTION

A commonly used technique to describe the distribution of personal income is the Lorenze curve[23] – see Figure 11. It is a graphic device with the cumulated percentages of aggregate income plotted on one axis and the cumulated percentage of persons receiving that income on the other. A perfectly even distribution of income would give a diagonal straight line rising from the lower left-hand corner to the upper right-hand corner of the diagram, whereas a perfectly unequal distribution (all income possessed by only one individual) would give the distribution along the bottom and the right-hand side of the square

[22]B. F. Haley, 'Changes in the Distribution of Income in the United States', in Marchal and Ducros, *op. cit.*

[23]Mary J. Bowman, 'A Graphical Analysis of Personal Income Distribution in the United States', *Readings in Income Distribution*, American Economic Association (1949), p. 86.

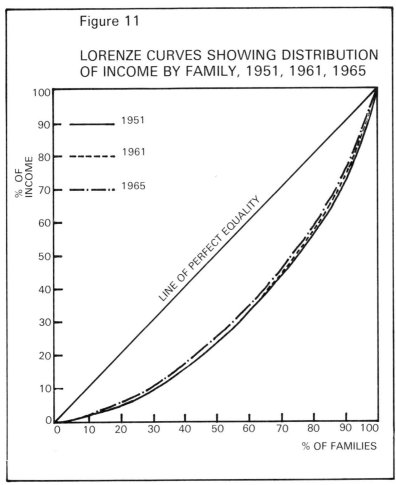

Figure 11

LORENZE CURVES SHOWING DISTRIBUTION
OF INCOME BY FAMILY, 1951, 1961, 1965

Source: Based on data from *Incomes of Non-farm Families and Individuals in Canada,
Selected years, 1951-1965*, Dominion Bureau of Statistics (Ottawa, 1969).

drawn on the diagram. The convexity of the plotted curve toward the origin of the abscissa will be greater, the larger the percentage of total personal income accruing to a given percentage of individuals or families. This suggests how to go about the task of getting a numerical measure of the degree of inequality of income distribution. For any given percentage of families, the greater the distance between the curve of absolute equality and the Lorenze curve, the greater the inequality. A unique measure of inequality is called the Gini coefficient. This is the ratio of the area between the diagonal line of complete equality and the Lorenze curve of income distribution to the entire triangular area under the diagonal. The range of the Gini ratio is from 0 to 1.00, rising with the degree of inequality.

Income distribution can also be measured by some percentile division of the totals. One commonly used such percentile division is quintiles. Quintiles are five equal percentage divisions of all family units – the family units being divided into five equal classes by level of income and then each class attributed its share of income, e.g., the one-fifth or 20 per cent of families with the lowest income, the next 20 per cent receiving the immediately higher share of income, and so on. This gives us the shares of income and the characteristics of family units in the same relative position in the income scale at different periods.[24]

THE DISTRIBUTION OF INCOME: 1930-1 TO 1951

Between 1930-1 and 1951, the average income of families whose heads were wage- or salary-earners increased from $1,489 to about $3,400. Table 47 shows that accompanying this increase in wages and salaries there is some decline in the degree of income inequality. The share of the top fifth dropped from 42.6 per cent to 37.5 per cent and that of the next highest quintile also declined, but much more moderately. On the other hand, the share of the two lowest quintiles – the bottom 40 per cent – rose from just under 17 per cent in 1930-1 to almost 22 per cent in 1951. A similar decline in inequality was observed for individual incomes.

A part of this decline in concentration of the distribution of family wages and salaries must be attributed to the fact that we are comparing the depression years 1930-1 with a year of full employment and inflationary boom. During a depression, the incomes of many workers are much lower than normal because they can find only part-time work or are only working for part of the year. This would have the effect of making the income distribution more unequal than under conditions of prosperity, when these individuals are fully reabsorbed into employment. Apart from this very important cyclical influence, however, the decline in inequality was also caused by 'a more equal distribution of wages and salaries of heads of families in 1951 than in 1930-1. In addition, secondary earners (such as working wives, sons, and daughters) made a more important relative contribution to family earnings.'[25]

The age structure of families also changed to help movement toward a less unequal distribution. 'In the lowest quintiles some decline occurred in the proportion of low-income families with older heads while

[24]Podoluk, *op. cit.*, p. 275.

[25]S. A. Goldberg and J. R. Podoluk, 'Income Size Distribution Statistics in Canada – A Survey and Some Analysis', in *Income and Wealth, Series VI*, M. Gilbert and R. Stone (eds.) (London, 1957), p. 164.

TABLE 47

Distribution of Wages and Salaries Among Quintiles,*
Wage- and Salary-Earning Families: Canada, 1930-1 and 1951

	Percentage shares of wages and salaries	
	1930-1	1951
Lowest quintile	5.3	8.1
Second quintile	11.3	13.9
Third quintile	17.3	17.9
Fourth quintile	23.5	22.6
Highest quintile	42.6	37.5

*Twenty per cent of total number of wage- and salary-earning families.

Source: Simon A. Goldberg and Jenny R. Podoluk, 'Income Size Distribution Statistics in Canada – A Survey and Some Analysis', International Association for Research in Income and Wealth, *Income and Wealth*, Series VI, Milton Gilbert and Richard Stone (eds.) (London, 1957), p. 163.

younger families rose as a proportion of all families.'[26] Since among low-income families old people weigh rather heavily among the recipients of government welfare payments and retirement benefits, changing age structure of such families meant change in the source composition of income. Moreover, the wage and salary differences between skilled and unskilled workers were less in 1951 than in 1931.

Unfortunately, these income statistics do not include income derived from sources other than paid employment. An examination of the components of personal income in the two years, however, suggests that 'the decline in inequality would be greater, both for wage-earners as well as for the total of all income receivers' if government social-security payments had been included.[27] Further, 'examination of the figures on incidence of income taxes in 1951 indicates that the distribution of earnings of wage- and salary-earners after taxes would be more equal than the distribution before taxes, with the higher-income groups paying a more than proportionate share of taxes (in relation to income). It follows that the decline in inequality between 1930-1 and 1951 would be greater on an after-tax basis than on the before-tax basis shown [above].'[28] Thus, over the period, the effect of government social-security measures and public finance was to intensify the trend toward a greater equality in the distribution of income.

[26]Podoluk, *op. cit.*, p. 277.
[27]Goldberg and Podoluk, *op. cit.*, p. 166.
[28]*Ibid.*, p. 168.

THE DISTRIBUTION OF INCOME: SINCE 1951

But the same statement cannot be made about the effects of government social-security and fiscal measures on the distribution of income since 1951. The Gini concentration ratios in Table 48 below, calculated on the basis of gross income, gross income without the transfer payments, and net income, i.e. income after the transfer payments and the taxes are considered, show little trend toward diminution between 1951 and 1961, tending to confirm the view that large injections of transfer payments have not presented an 'increase in inequality over this period. Transfer payments have had a levelling effect upon the income distribution but the degree of inequality in the income distribution exclusive of transfer payments also showed little change.'[29]

The above conclusion is made clear in the Lorenze curves for 1951, 1961, and 1965 in Figure 11. The curves, describing the inequality in the distribution of non-farm income over families, appear to be remarkably stable over the period of time covered, which means that there has not been any significant shift in the distribution of income among families in Canada since 1951.

In terms of quintiles also, based on the distribution of non-farm family income before tax (see Table 49), there was very little change in the inequality in income distribution during the period of 1951-65. Although there was a small decline in the share of the income going to the top fifth of the families, the distribution seems by and large invariant over the period, especially in the lower quintile.

Thus, over the entire period beginning with 1930-1 the distribution of money income among the Canadian population (by individuals and families) has shown more of a trend toward equality. The most important of the forces responsible for this trend were changes in the state of the economy (whether a boom or a depression), the structure of the family, the age composition of the population, the occupational distribution of the labour force, the source of income, the fiscal and income policies of the government, and so on. However, the trend toward equality showed a distinctly lower rate of progress after 1951. During this relatively recent period there has been a stable distribution of income, despite an active fiscal effort on the part of the government to reduce inequality.

We have considered the distribution of money income at current prices. But this may not correctly represent the real economic differences between the different income classes. The correspondence between money and real income would depend on the variations in prices of goods and services on which the different income groups spend

[29]J. R. Podoluk, 'Some Comparisons Upon Canadian vs. U. S. Income Distributions', mimeographed, paper presented at the Eleventh General Conference of the International Association for Research in Income and Wealth (1969), p. 17.

TABLE 48

Gini Ratios, Selected Years, 1951-61

Year	Gross income	Gross income less transfer payments	Net income
1951	.390	.584	.369
1954	.388	.584	.377
1957	.378	.572	.378
1959	.367	.578	.367
1961	.385	.580	.366

Source: Jenny R. Podoluk, *Incomes of Canadians*, Dominion Bureau of Statistics (Ottawa, 1963), p. 287.

TABLE 49

Distribution of Non-Farm Family Income Before Tax

	Distribution of total income			Average per family
	1951	1961	1965	1965
	Per cent			*Dollars*
Lowest fifth	6.1	6.6	6.7	2,263
Second fifth	12.9	13.4	13.4	4,542
Third fifth	17.4	18.2	18.0	6,102
Fourth fifth	22.5	23.4	23.5	7,942
Top fifth	41.1	38.4	38.4	13,016
All families	100.0	100.0	100.0	6,669

Source: Economic Council of Canada, *The Challenge of Growth and Change* (Ottawa, 1965), p. 107.

their income. For a proper assessment of the change in the relative positions of different quintiles in terms of real income, we need, in addition to information on money income, data on a time series of prices for all products, along with information on the quantities of each product consumed by each income class. Unfortunately, such information is not available. The next best series for our purpose is the Consumer Price Index (C.P.I.). Using this serial index, we may at best conclude that real income rose substantially during 1941-61. To the extent that the C.P.I. included items figured in the budgets of the middle- and low-income groups that rose less in price relative to items used by the upper-income groups, a trend toward equality in income distribution might have been accentuated during the period.

Low-Income Recipients

Theoretically, it may be possible to conceive of a perfectly equal distribution of income among all recipient units. But, in reality, income distributions are seldom perfectly equal. Essentially, this means some individuals and families will have more income than others. The relevant social question is, of course, how much more income *should* one group have than another? This obviously depends on the nature and goals of a society. If we do not accept a social standard of complete equality or inequality, we allow the distribution to affect various units differently. Recipients at the lower levels of income are identified as the poor section of the community relative to those at the higher levels. A discussion of the nature, emergence, and amelioration of poverty is thus an important part of a discussion of the distribution of income.

The concept of poverty has always evaded a precise, universally acceptable definition. For example, one definition of poverty income has been income 'insufficient to obtain the minimum necessaries for the maintenance of merely physical efficiency'.[30] The problem with this definition is that the 'minimum' varies from place to place and from time to time. The minimum of necessity in a tropical country is different from that in a cold country, and 'the nutritional needs are higher in our society today than they were seventy-five years ago' because of the 'quick reactions necessary to keep up with the physical and mental pace demanded by the industrial economy'.[31] Moreover, the criterion of 'physical efficiency' depends on the particular function to be performed. The same income may be poverty income for a wrestler but not for a fine artist. The concept of income is also beset with all the usual difficulties of definition and measurement: money income or non-money income, earned income or total income (earned plus asset income or windfall income), income of the family or income of an individual (and in the former case the size of the family, and in the latter the age of the individual).[32] Moreover, the concept of poverty has been treated differently by various professions – economists, sociologists, anthropologists, psychologists.[33] If we take up any less rigorous

[30]B. Seebohm Rountree, *Poverty: A Study of Town Life* (London, 1910), p. 86. For an economist's definition of poverty see Harold W. Watts, *An Economic Definition of Poverty*, Reprint No. 53, Institute for Research on Poverty, University of Wisconsin (Madison, 1968).

[31]David Hamilton, *A Primer on the Economics of Poverty* (New York, 1968), p. 25.

[32]Alan B. Batcheldor, *The Economics of Poverty* (New York, 1966), p. 7.

[33]For empirical studies and perspectives on poverty from different disciplines, see *Poverty – American Style*, Herman P. Miller (ed.) (Belmont, California, 1968).

definition of poverty than the one presented above, it becomes all the more difficult to defend it. 'The problem of poverty in less developed industrial societies is increasingly viewed not as a sheer lack of essentials to sustain life, but as an insufficient access to certain goods, services, and conditions of life which are available to everyone else and have come to be accepted as basic to a decent, minimum standard of living.'[34] Thus, poverty is a relative concept – relative to a particular time, space, and content. It means more than merely being classified as statistically 'low-income'. A student or a beginner in life at a given income may not be poor compared to an aged or established person with the same income. Poverty signifies the low-income situation that carries with it 'a sense of entrapment and hopelessness'.[35] Poverty is a matter of degree. On a continuum between zero and infinite purchasing power, economic wealth may be measured in the direction toward infinity, while poverty may be defined as the distance to zero.[36]

Notwithstanding the ambiguities and difficulties that the concept of poverty involves, it is necessary to construct an operational definition of it for purposes of measuring the extent to which this blight exists in Canada.[37] The purpose of most analyses of poverty is to identify and assist those sections of the population whose circumstances do not permit them to achieve a decent standard of life. With this purpose in mind, poverty has been defined, for operational purposes, in terms of the level of income and the pattern of expenditures. The underlying hypothesis is that low-income families would find it impossible to afford much beyond the bare essentials of food, clothing, and shelter. This criterion is used to determine the level of income signifying the poverty line. Two alternative estimates of poverty in Canada are available, each based on a different proportion of income spent on food, clothing, and shelter. First, a family or individual is considered to be low-income if 70 per cent or more of income is spent on food, clothing, and shelter. According to this definition, about 27 per cent of the total non-farm population, and about 29 per cent of the farm and non-farm population in Canada, were poor in 1961.[38] The second definition uses 60 per cent or more of income spent on food, clothing, and shelter as the dividing line and raises the proportion of non-farm population

[34]Economic Council of Canada, 'The Challenge of Growth and Change', *Fifth Annual Review* (Ottawa, 1968), p. 104.

[35]*Ibid.*, p. 105.

[36]See Mary Jean Bowman, 'Poverty in an Affluent Society', in *Contemporary Economic Issues*, Neil W. Chamberlain (ed.) (Homewood, Ill., 1969).

[37]For studies dealing with various aspects of the problem of poverty in Canada, see *Poverty and Social Policy in Canada*, W. E. Mann (ed.) (Toronto, 1970).

[38]Economic Council of Canada, *op. cit.*, p. 109.

belonging to the low-income category from 27 per cent to 41 per cent.

Since 1961, there have been improvements in the income levels of many families and individuals, and the proportion of population below the poverty line would seem to have decreased to some extent.[39]

According to the first definition, the poverty line is $1,500 in annual income for single individuals and $2,500, $3,000, $3,500, and $4,000 in annual income for families with two, three, four, and five members, respectively. The corresponding figures using the second definition range from $2,000 to $5,000. Even the more conservative first definition leads to the conclusion that one out of every five Canadians lives in poverty.

Broadly, the people afflicted by poverty may be divided into three groups:[40]

1. People who are outside the labour market. These include retired people, widows with dependent children, the disabled, and others who are not in a position to join the labour force;

2. People who are unemployed. These include the seasonally unemployed, those laid off due to recession and technological change, the vocationally handicapped, and school drop-outs;

3. People whose present productivity is too low to provide an adequate living. These include the underemployed, i.e., those who are working part-time or engaged in occupations and areas of economic activity that are characterized as low-income.

The probability of the incidence of poverty thus depends on several characteristics of the population: occupation, education, location, sex, age, and so forth. These characteristics are discussed briefly here.

Occupation: Table 50 shows that the incidence of poverty in three occupations – farm work, logging and related work, and fishing, trapping, and hunting – was more than three times the average for the economy as a whole in 1961. One of the reasons income is low in these occupations is that investment in human capital is minimal.

Education: There is a strong association between the level of education and the level of income. In 1961, the incidence of low income was high (31 per cent) among families whose heads had less than secondary education. A 1960 survey showed that about half of Canada's unemployed had not completed primary school, and more than 90 per cent had not completed high school.[41] There seems to be a vicious circle working between lack of education and poverty. If the parents are poor, the

[39]*Ibid.*, p. 109.
[40]See 'A Profile of Poverty in Canada', *Labor Gazette* (1966).
[41]*Ibid.*

TABLE 50

Occupation and Low Income, 1961 (Non-farm male family heads)

Occupation	Incidence of low income (number of family heads with low income as percentage of total number of family heads)
Managerial	10
Professional & technical	5
Clerical	11
Sales	13
Service & recreation	20
Farm workers*	56
Loggers & related workers	57
Fishermen, trappers, & hunters	70
Labourers	40
Miners & related workers	18
Craftsmen & related workers	19
Total of male non-farm family heads in current labour force	18

*Includes farm workers not living on farms.

Source: Based on Table 6-4, Economic Council of Canada, *The Challenge of Growth and Change* (Ottawa, 1968), p. 115.

child does not have the basic means to take advantage of the education system (poor housing with hardly any facilities for study, poor health and nourishment, unfavourable social and home environment, distance from school, lack of psychological motiviation, and attraction of early earnings – any or all of these may be factors), and the poverty is perpetuated. Table 51 shows the strong association between income of family head and education of children.

It may be said that the educational system works to a large extent as a 'transmission belt' tending to perpetuate through generations the relative positions of families in the hierarchy of economic privileges. But, on the other hand, education is the channel through which there takes place an upward flow of the poor but meritorious and a downward precipitation of the rich but dull. This is the redistributive function of education. A purpose of policy is to increase this function of opportunity as against that of heredity in the distribution of income and wealth.

TABLE 51

*Relation between Income of Family Head and School
Enrolment of Children: Canada, 1961*

	Percentage of children at school in age-group	
	Age	Age
Income of family head	15-18	19-24
$7,000 and over	90.7	50.0
$5,000-6,999	81.7	29.4
$3,000-4,999	72.3	18.4
Under $3,000	60.9	12.0

Source: Harold Lydall, *The Structure of Earnings* (Oxford: Oxford University Press, 1968), p. 110.

TABLE 52

Low-Income Families by Region and Place of Residence, 1967

Region or place of residence	Families with low income (per cent)
Regions:	
Atlantic provinces	15.7
Quebec	30.1
Ontario	24.5
Prairie provinces	20.8
British Columbia	9.0
Place of residence:	
Metropolitan centres	34.9
Other urban municipalities	20.0
Rural	45.1

Source: D.B.S., *Income Distribution and Poverty in Canada, 1967*, p. 15.

Location: Table 52 shows that the percentage of poverty varies widely from region to region. Quebec had a greater proportion of low-income families than other regions, while British Columbia had the lowest. Moreover, the incidence of poverty is much higher in rural areas than in urban and metropolitan areas. This relates to the occupations (previously mentioned) that are normally available to low-income recipients. These – farm work, logging, etc. – are mostly rural occupations.

TABLE 53

Incidence of Low Income by Age, Sex, Major Source

Age of head	Incidence of low income (per cent)	Major source of family income	Incidence of low income (per cent)
Under 25	29.0	Wages & salaries	18.3
25-54	22.1	Self-employment	24.9
55-64	22.2	Transfer payments	90.3
65 or over	43.9	Investment income	35.2
		Other income	44.5
Sex of head		No income	100.0
Male	23.8		
Female	42.6		

Source: Podoluk, *op. cit.*, pp. 187-8.

Age and Sex: Some attributes of age and sex, like the ability to participate and perform, rather than age and sex as such, cause variations in the income levels of populations. Table 53 shows that the incidence of low income is quite high among families headed by persons over sixty-five years of age.

The high incidence of low income among families headed by women is strongly related to the presence of dependent children, which restricts the earning capacity of the women. In 1961, the proportion of families with female heads was 8 per cent of all families, but the proportion was 13 per cent among families with low income. And about 20 per cent of low-income families had male heads aged sixty-five or over. Thus, considering sex and age together, about one-third of the low-income families were headed either by women or by men over sixty-five.[42]

Source of Income: When a comparison is made between the incidence of low income and the major source of income, it is found that low-income families receive a relatively large proportion of their income in the form of government transfer payments. Thus, as Table 53 shows, if a family's major source of income is in the form of transfer payments, then the chances are more than nine in ten that it will belong to the low-income category. However, if the source of income is wages and salaries, less than one-fifth of the families are likely to be below the poverty line. No causation is implied to exist by this relation-

[42]Podoluk, *Incomes of Canadians*, p. 191.

ship, however, since it is expected that government transfers will go to the voluntarily retired, the unemployed, and others whose earnings are depressed.

Ethnic Groups: In most societies there are some groups or communities that are, in general, on a lower income level than the social average. Examples are minorities, non-whites, tribes, etc. In Canada there is an above-average incidence of poverty among Indians, Eskimos, and Mexicans. The average life expectancy at birth of an Indian woman in Canada is twenty-five years, and the infant mortality rate among Eskimos is about ten times the infant mortality rate for the population as a whole.[43]

In this discussion of poverty in Canada, we have indicated the probability of the incidence of poverty, given certain characteristics of the population. These characteristics, however, are not distributed evenly throughout the poverty population. For example, according to the D.B.S. data, 14 per cent of low-income family heads are women. This contrasts with 42.6 per cent of female family heads who have low income. The distinction has to be remembered for purposes of policy formulation.

Reduction of Poverty

Having considered, in the last section, the extent and nature of poverty in Canada, we turn in this section to the various aspects of how to deal with this problem. First of all, it is necessary to point out the social and economic reasons for trying to reduce or eliminate poverty.

Poverty is costly in two broad ways. First, the better-known cost of poverty is the social and human cost that a society pays. This includes a lack of justice in sharing goods produced, physical suffering, ill health, crimes, and unrest threatening the structure of society. Secondly, poverty has severe economic costs. These are of two kinds: opportunity costs arising from output forgone, i.e. output that could have been produced had the full productive potential of the poor been utilized; and the cost of diverted output,[44] i.e. the output that could have been obtained from resources transferred to deal with the consequences of poverty, which in the absence of poverty would not

[43]Economic Council of Canada, *op. cit.*, p. 122.

[44]Economic Council of Canada, 'Perspective 1975', *Sixth Annual Review* (Ottawa, 1969), p. 109.

arise. One example of the latter is the use of resources to prevent and cure the ill health that poverty generates. In the absence of poverty, these resources could be used for more productive and more socially desirable purposes. Measures designed to minimize the costs of poverty for society should take into account both the social and the economic costs of programs.

The nature of policies adopted to alleviate the problem of poverty must depend on the nature of the poverty itself. In the preceding section, we have seen that the incidence of poverty is influenced by several factors, which can be divided broadly into two groups. First are those causes that cannot be remedied. These concern, for example, the aged, the chronically sick or the disabled, who do not have the capacity to earn a higher than poverty-level income. Secondly, there are causes that can be removed, at least over time. These include lack of regular or remunerative employment opportunities, lack of adequate education or skill, racial discrimination, and so forth. In respect of the first set of causes, the measures to eliminate poverty consist in the transfer of income from the non-poor through either private or government channels. Most social welfare policies are designed to this end. On the other hand, to tackle the *remediable* disadvantages, the measures are likely to be of an income-creating rather than an income-transferring type. In this approach the poor are treated as unutilized or underutilized resources, and the accent of policy is on investment in these resources for the generation of more income. The emphasis is on enlarging the size of the cake, while that in the social welfare type of policy is on making the size of the slices less unequal.[45]

We now come to a discussion of some specific policies in the field of income maintenance and redistribution. One of the measures used is minimum-wage legislation, which forms part of an income maintenance program.[46]

The provinces of Canada, as was the case also with the states in the U.S.A., preceded the federal government in enacting minimum-wage legislation. The first minimum-wage legislation in Canada was effected in Alberta in 1917. Manitoba and British Columbia followed in 1918, Quebec and Saskatchewan in 1919, and Ontario in 1920. New

---

[45]See Batcheldor, *op. cit.*, p. 120.

[46]The discussion of minimum wages in the pages that follow is based largely on M. A. Zaidi, *A Study of the Effects of the $1.25 Minimum Wage Under the Canada Labour Standard Code*, Study No. 16, Task Force on Labour Relations, Privy Council (Ottawa, 1970). Reference may also be made to *The Short-Run Impact of the Thirty Cent Revision in Ontario's Minimum Wage on Five Industries*, prepared by Henry Fantl and Frank Whittingham, Ontario Department of Labour (1970).

Brunswick, Nova Scotia, Newfoundland, and Prince Edward Island passed legislation for minimum wages after the war and in the fifties. Although these acts did not make explicit their underlying goals, in practice most sought to provide a 'living wage' for the lowest-paid classes of workers.

Coverage under the early minimum-wage laws was, with some minor exceptions, limited to females and minors. These two groups were often paid less than subsistence wages. With the exception of the British Columbia Act of 1925, the extension of coverage to males did not come until the 1930s. The serious depression resulted in widespread deterioration of wages, and it was asserted that men as well as women needed legal protection against socially unacceptable employment conditions. Coverage was extended to males in Manitoba and Saskatchewan in 1934, in Alberta in 1936, and in Ontario and Quebec in 1937. New Brunswick, Nova Scotia, Newfoundland, and Prince Edward Island included coverage for males when they introduced the first minimum-wage legislation in the post-war decades.

As in the United States, early minimum-wage laws in Canada were usually selective by industry and/or occupation, and the system of wage orders was used. At present, these orders include almost all occupations except farm labour and domestic service.

Setting of minimum wages is usually accomplished through a system of single wage boards for the entire province. The constitutions of these boards vary from province to province. Each one is presided over by a government official, usually a member of the Department of Labour, acting in a neutral capacity. The boards issue both general and special wage orders. The general orders set rates applicable to most workers, while special orders set higher rates applicable to particular industries or occupations. Principles followed in determining the minimum vary among the provinces and consider such factors as competition from abroad or from other provinces, cost of living to the employees, and what the 'board deems fair'. In every case, however, the prevailing employment conditions in the area are taken into account. The rates for most provinces are on an hourly basis, although there are cases of weekly rates in some provinces and occupations. Rates vary also according to age and sex, and in taking account of physical handicaps. The legislation in all the provinces includes 'daily guarantee' or 'call-in pay' requirements; regulation of frequency and method of payment; and maximum deductions for uniforms, lodging, and board. The level of minimum wage as well as its coverage has increased over the years in all provinces.

Corresponding to the United States' Fair Labor Standards Act

(1938), the Canada Labour (Standards) Code of 1965 represented the federal government's intervention in the field of minimum-wage legislation. This code was unique in wage legislation in that it incorporated minimum standards for vacation and paid holidays as well as for wages and hours. It provided for a minimum of $1.25 an hour; a standard eight-hour day and forty-hour week with time and a half for overtime; a maximum forty-eight-hour week; eight general holidays with pay and two weeks' annual vacation after every completed year of employment. The aim of the code was to eliminate poverty among the lowest-paid workers and to assure them the highest standards economically feasible. Because it was felt that enforcement of this code would affect aggregate demand and economic growth via its likely effects on income and productivity of workers, it was co-ordinated with other instruments of monetary-fiscal and manpower policy. Coverage of the Canada Labour (Standards) Code was limited to those specific industries and undertakings over which Parliament has exclusive legislative authority as enumerated in the British North America Act. Parliament is empowered to regulate and control such activities deemed to be of a national, interprovincial, or international nature.

The $1.25 minimum, unlike the provincial minima, was set by statute rather than by wage boards. This level was to be standardized for both men and women in all covered industries in all provinces and territories. Youths under 17 were not to be paid less than $1.00 an hour and special provisions were to be made for apprentices and disabled workers. The code was to be administered directly by the Minister of Labour.

Arguments both for and against minimum-wage legislation date back to the writings of the classical economists. The major pros and cons are summarized very briefly here. Among the basic arguments in favour is that such legislation prevents exploitation of the worker whose low bargaining power permits his wages to be driven below the subsistence level. It represents a human minimum standard in the face of 'capitalist exploitation and social injustice'. Secondly, setting up minimum-wage rates brings about a redistribution of income from the *rentier* to the wage-earning class, and thus raises aggregate demand, which is good for the expansion of production and employment. Thirdly, as argued by Martin Bronfenbrenner,[47] wage increases raise the efficiency of labourers, with the result that they can be used more productively. Thus employment need not be reduced. Moreover, a higher standard of living may lead to higher worker efficiency. The

[47]M. Bronfenbrenner, 'Minimum Wages, Unemployability and Relief: A Theoretical Note', *Southern Economic Journal* (July 1943).

higher cost of labour tends to lead to better allocation of resources and also, through what is known as 'shock effect', to an improvement of management efficiency. Alternatives to minimum-wage rates, such as subsidizing firms, are more expensive and are deleterious in their effects. Minimum wages also soften the down-turn of business fluctuations through the cushioning effects of a larger effective demand. It is also argued that the undesirable effects, if any, of minimum wages are due to other factors such as the nature of the market or elasticities of demand for which different measures can be more appropriately used.

The critics of minimum-wage legislation put forward the following main objections. First, it hurts marginal workers. It works against the employment of workers with lower productivity (e.g. women, the aged, or the handicapped). Thus, one of the basic objectives of the minimum wage is not served by it. The case of newcomers to the market is serious, because the minimum wage fixed by law may be too high for their training and skill-formation. Minimum-wage legislation, by destroying the advantage an industry might enjoy by being able to employ labour at substandard wages, can squeeze that industry out of existence. The same force works against marginal firms. Thus, there may be created pockets of unemployment and curtailment of services in specific industries and specific regions. Minimum wages may delay the process of industrialization in areas of labour surplus. Such an area, in the absence of minimum-wage laws, will have lower wages than other regions, and thus will possess a cost advantage favouring development. When there is a falling demand for the product of an industry, minimum-wage legislation may accelerate the decline of the industry, thus making the process of adjustment more painful.[48] Moreover, it leads to a substitution of labour by capital. Stigler argued that minimum-wage legislation does not meet its stated objectives of diminishing poverty and that there are efficient alternatives that could do so.[49]

The question of whether minimum-wage legislation can meet the objectives for which it is designed cannot be answered except by taking into account, in particular instances, the relative magnitudes of its direct and indirect effects, and the demand elasticities for different kinds of labour. In other words, we cannot arrive at general conclusions about the merits of minimum wages, but must appeal to the facts in order to determine what the situation is in any particular instance.

[48]Clair Wilcox, *Toward Social Welfare* (Homewood, Ill., 1969), p. 211.

[49]George Stigler, 'The Economics of Minimum Wage Legislation', *American Economic Review* (June 1946).

It is difficult to present precise magnitudes of the effects of mini-mum-wage laws. Changes in prices, wages, employment, and output are the result not only of changes in wage laws, but also of the inter-action of shifting consumer tastes, management investment decisions, the pattern of government taxation, spending, and countless other influences. None of these forces comes to a halt when a minimum-wage law is enacted. It is not surprising to find that a 1970 study of the effects of the $1.25 minimum wage under the Canada Labour (Stand-ards) Code concluded that although the recently enacted minimum wage had not caused serious unemployment throughout the economy, it had caused some unemployment in some industries, under both federal jurisdiction and provincial jurisdiction. It had also had the effect of narrowing male-female, office – non-office, and geographical wage differentials. Compliance with the law had been very good in almost all cases, and the incremental increase in costs seemed not to have had a serious effect on employment. Its actual effects on wage differentials and costs varied from situation to situation, however. We may expect the arguments about these laws to continue, because of the difficulties involved in holding other things constant while one observes the impact of minimum wages.[50]

Existing taxation and wage policies have, at best, attained some limited objectives with respect to alleviating the basic problems of poverty. The tax structure in Canada has been described as progres-sive, proportional, and regressive in different parts of the income range. The study by the Royal Commission on Taxation observed that, for federal taxes in total, the tax structure was regressive at the lowest level, that is, for family units with money incomes below $2,000, and pro-gressive above this level; provincial and local taxes were regressive below $3,000 and, on balance, proportionate above this level. For all taxes combined, the tax structure was very regressive for the lowest income groups, proportionate for the middle-income ranges, and progressive at the highest levels. This, however, is balanced to some extent by the fact that, when benefits from government's expenditures, in total, both through direct transfer payments and goods and services, are allocated by income levels, the lower the income the greater the benefits relative to income.[51]

The Canadian government's White Paper[52] on tax reforms in 1969

---

[50]For a study of the impact of the thirty-cent revision in Ontario's minimum wages, on five selected industries, see Fantl and Whittingham, *op. cit.*

[51]Podoluk, *Incomes of Canadians*, p. 285.

[52]Hon. E. J. Benson, *Proposals for Tax Reform* (Ottawa, 1969).

made a number of major proposals for reform of the income tax structure. An important objective of these proposals was to reduce poverty through tax reforms oriented to redress the hardship of the poor. The proposals included higher exemption limits for income tax, consideration of family units, deductions for dependants, allowance for child-care expenses, employment expenses, and medical expenses, and changed definitions of income to cover capital gains for upper-income groups. These proposals did have income redistributive and poverty-reducing implications.

There is great uncertainty about the extent to which the existing structure of policies contributes in reality to reduction of poverty. This uncertainty and the dissatisfaction with public assistance programs have led to some other support policy proposals. The most interesting of these, if adopted, would constitute a complete departure from existing programs, in that it would provide for a guaranteed annual income through the use of negative income tax rates.[53] 'Each year every family's gross income would be compared to some minimum guaranteed level and, where the former figure was lower – the government would provide some fraction of the difference.'[54] Under another form, the payment would consist of income tax exemptions 'unused' by those with incomes too low to be subject to tax. The simplest form of guaranteed minimum income would be 'a grant by the government to all, regardless of means; if it were subject to tax, part of it would be recouped in this fashion'! The Guaranteed Income Supplement that is now payable as a part of the old-age security pension plan is a type of negative income tax.[55]

Apart from income maintenance programs, there are two other sets of programs designed to attack poverty in Canada. These can be classified as individual improvement programs and community betterment programs. Examples are: the Canada Assistance Plan (this closes gaps in the social-security system; some of its features are rehabilitative and preventive in character, designed to help people by their own efforts

---

[53]There are a number of proposals for negative income tax. See Milton Friedman, *Capitalism and Freedom* (Chicago, 1962); Christopher Green, *Negative Taxes and the Poverty Problem*, The Brookings Institution (Washington, 1967); Christopher Green, *Using Negative Income Taxes to Narrow the Poverty gap*, Brookings Institution (Washington, 1967); J. Tobin, J. Pechman, P. Mieszkowski, *Is a Negative Income Tax Practical?* Brookings Institution (Washington, 1967); Edward E. Schwartz, 'A Way to End the Means Test', *Social Work* (July 1964).

[54]J. W. McGuire and J. A. Pichler, *Inequality: The Poor and the Rich in America* (Belmont, California, 1969), p. 147.

[55]Economic Council of Canada, 'The Challenge of Growth and Change', *op. cit.*, p. 134 f.n.

to rise and remain above poverty);[56] and the monthly guaranteed income supplement to certain old-age security pensions – a variant of negative income tax. Manpower policy (discussed, above, in Chapter VI) has not been used in Canada as a primary instrument for reducing poverty through an 'investment' strategy.

To sum up, it is impossible to deny the existence of poverty in Canada.[57] Basically, its emergence may be traced mostly to the unequal abilities of individuals and groups to earn income; this inequality in turn may be due to inherent differences in the earning units (individuals) themselves, or to the differing effects upon them of the socio-economic-geographic structure of the country. Several measures are operating in Canada at the time of writing to help solve this ancient problem, and several others are being considered. The combined effects upon it of the minimum-wage legislation and the redistributive tax and subsidy schemes, as well as the likely impact of the proposed negative income tax, various individual improvement programs, community betterment and manpower programs, are hard to identify and measure. This may be a subject for a major research project.

[56]*Ibid*, p. 136.

[57]See N. H. Lithwick, *Urban Poverty*, Research Monograph No. 1, Central Mortgage and Housing Corporation (Ottawa, 1971). This study unfortunately became available to us too late for incorporation in this section. Students interested in this subject should consult this source since it presents a detailed and updated analysis of poverty in Canada.

X

Wages in Canada:
The Occupational Structure

In Chapter VIII we examined the course followed by real- and money-wage levels in Canada over a number of years. The wage *level*, i.e. an average or summary measure, masks a large variety of different wages in the economy. The relationships among these various wages form the wage *structure* of the Canadian labour market.

The term 'wage structure' conveys an impression of a neat and tidy edifice, an impression quickly dispelled by even the most cursory investigation of relative wages. The national wage structure is a vast and sprawling formation that sometimes appears, like Topsy, to have 'just growed'. Viewed at close quarters, at the individual or plant level, the appearance is often chaotic. Standing back a bit, one can perceive the dim outlines of the main structure. In this and the next two chapters, we will analyse this main structure.

It is perhaps misleading to talk of *the* wage structure without specifying what concept of wages is under consideration. There are, in fact, several wage structures: relative wage-rates, relative hourly or weekly earnings, and relative annual earnings. Each would present a quite different national structure. From a theoretical viewpoint the most relevant concept of wages would be that most closely corresponding to the 'price of labour': the payment per unit of labour service.[1] In establishments where time rather than piecework rates prevail (the majority of establishments in Canada), the unit of labour service is measured in hourly terms, and the rate is sometimes called a *datal* rate. The closest approximation to the 'price' of labour would thus be the hourly

[1]See Chapter VII.

264

wage-rate plus the pecuniary value of any fringe benefits accruing to the worker. In order to abstract from variations in the quality of labour, such hourly-rates-plus-benefits statistics should relate to workers of equal efficiency working under similar conditions, and so on. To list the conditions for an 'ideal' measure of the price of labour is to indicate the great chasm that separates the desired measure from the actual measures found among published records.[2] In what follows, average hourly rates, and hourly, weekly, or annual earnings, will have to be used in different sections of the analysis. No doubt the limitations of the data severely restrict the meaningfulness of wage studies, not only in Canada, but in all countries where such studies have been undertaken. One can only hope that the distortions produced by the highly imperfect data are not so catastrophic as to destroy the main outlines of the analysis.

One more *caveat* must be introduced at this juncture. It is possible to measure relative wages in two ways: either in terms of the absolute difference between them (cents per hour, per week, etc.) or in terms of the relative (percentage) difference. Changes in wage relativities over time will differ, depending on which measure is chosen.[3] Consider a hypothetical case in which an industrial union contracts for an equal, absolute increase in the wages of all its members. This will result in a decline in the percentage differential in wages between members. In contrast, if the union agrees on an equal percentage increase for all its members, then the opposite effect occurs – an increase in the absolute differential in wages between members. A truly complete picture of Canadian wage structures would involve both measures, but this would be far too unwieldy within the framework of these chapters.[4] For the most part, however, the term 'differential', unless qualified, will mean relative or percentage differential.

This chapter will be concerned with the structure of relative wages in Canada as it is affected by *occupation*.[5] The following chapters will be devoted to interindustry, geographic, and other aspects of Canadian wage structure.

---

[2]Lloyd G. Reynolds and Cynthia H. Taft, *The Evaluation of Wage Structure* (New Haven, 1956), pp. 7-9.

[3]Arthur Ross and William Goldner, 'Forces Affecting the Inter-industry Wage Structure', *Quarterly Journal of Economics* (May 1950), pp. 257-66.

[4]Reynolds and Taft, *op. cit.*, p. 12, and Richard Perlman, 'Forces Widening Occupational Wage Differentials', *Review of Economics and Statistics* (May 1951), p. 111.

[5]For a discussion of the conceptual and statistical problems in studying the occupational structure in Canada, see Chapter IV.

Broad Occupational Wage Differentials[6]

Marshall once commented that, in general, the occupational wage structure was analogous to a flight of steps;[7] the appropriateness of this observation is supported by the data presented in Table 54. These data refer only to male wage- and salary-earners, excluding employers and independent, own-account workers. Examination of these data shows that occupational wage differentials do not move in a smooth pattern. Individual categories may do comparatively better or worse

TABLE 54

Indices of Annual Earnings (Labourers = 100): Census Years

	1931*	1941†	1951†	1961†
Agricultural labourers	68	64	52	62
Fishing, hunting, and trapping	95	70	60	59
Logging	95	73	76	80
Labourers (non-primary)	100	100	100	100
Janitors and sextons	180	132	103	121
Carpenters	164	135	123	134
Mining and quarrying	170	202	155	184
Transportation and communication	232	174	138	156
Clerical	244	213	140	160
Professional	412	268	189	245
Managerial	514	368	232	277

*Mean annual earnings.
†Median annual earnings.

Sources: 'Wages and Hours of Labour in Canada', published by the Department of Labour as a supplement to the Labour Gazette (January 1931); D.B.S., *Census of Canada, 1941*, Vol. VI, Table 6 (1941); D.B.S., *Census of Canada, 1951*, Vol. V, Table 21 (1951); D.B.S., *Census of Canada, 1961*, Vol. III, Part 3, Table 21 (1961).

[6]A wage differential is the absolute or percentage difference between the wages of workers within a specific category – occupation, region, sex, establishment, etc. The implication conveyed by the term 'differential', as opposed to the more neutral 'difference', is that the prefix normally attached – occupational, regional, sex, etc. – is the major factor determining the observed difference. The literature, however, for the most part uses the terms interchangeably. Wage structure is a pattern of differentials. Relative wage levels may also be used to demonstrate implicitly both wage differentials (or differences) and structure.

[7]Alfred Marshall, *Principles of Economics* (New York, 1948), p. 181.

from one decade to the next. In most countries,[8] occupational wage differentials tended to narrow in times of high demand and strong economic activity for the period covered in Table 54. However, the data in Table 54 indicate that Canada is an exception to this generality. The over-all differential in annual earnings in Canada narrowed during the 1930s and 1940s and widened for most groups in the 1950s. These findings coincide with a similar conclusion of a report of the Organization for Economic Cooperation and Development.

Marshall, in pursuing the analogy between wage structure and a flight of steps, pointed out that some of the steps are 'so broad as to act as landing stages'.[9] Such a 'landing stage' exists at the skilled level (carpenters in the table) and at the white-collar level. The nature of interoccupational mobility shows that there is a discontinuity in career paths at these levels. Barriers to entry into the professional and managerial class serve to create and maintain substantial earnings differentials between these two groups on the one hand and the rest of the labour force on the other.

Table 54 presents annual earnings, which covers up wide differences in weeks or days of employment for different occupations. During the depression, few manual workers were able to find year-round, full-time employment, and there was a proportionately far greater reduction in annual hours for the manual group than for professional and managerial occupations. Indeed, as seen in Table 55, the weekly earnings structure presents a somewhat different range of occupational differentials. The weekly earnings gaps between labourers and other broad occupational groups are much narrower in each of the four census years than are the differentials measured in terms of annual earnings. This contrast is particularly apparent for the depression years, although even in 1941 a considerable amount of short-time employment was still prevalent among labourers.

[8]Organization for Economic Cooperation and Development, *Wages and Labor Mobility* (Paris, 1965), p. 123.

However, not everyone is in agreement as to the long-run trend in occupational differentials. For different views on this problem in the context of different countries, see Philip W. Bell, 'Cyclical Variations and Trends in Occupational Wage Differentials in American Industry Since 1914', *Review of Economics and Statistics* (November 1951); Paul Keat, 'Long Run Changes in Occupational Wage Structure 1900-1956', *Journal of Political Economy* (December 1960); Edwin Mansfield, 'Wage Differentials in the Cotton Textile Industry', *Review of Economics and Statistics* (February 1955); E. E. Muntz, 'The Decline in Wage Differentials Based on Skill in the United States', *International Labor Review* (June 1955); H. Ober, 'Occupational Wage Differentials, 1907-1947', *Monthly Labor Review* (August 1948); R. Ozanne, 'A Century of Occupational Differentials in Manufacturing', *Review of Economics and Statistics* (August 1962); Reynolds and Taft, *op. cit.*; Richard Perlman, *op. cit.*

[9]Marshall, *op. cit.*, p. 181.

TABLE 55

Indices of Average* Weekly Earnings of Occupational Groups of Male Wage- and Salary-Earners, Census Years (Labourers = 100)

Occupation	1931	1941	1951	1961
Agricultural labourers	47	64	50	60
Fishing, hunting, and trapping	73	107	94	104
Logging	87	93	109	119
Labourers (non-primary)	100	100	100	100
Janitors and sextons	120	107	100	104
Clerical	140	171	138	143
Carpenters	153	143	128	134
Transportation and communication	153	143	134	134
Mining and quarrying	153	179	150	157
Professional	193	221	184	209
Managerial	373	343	222	234

*1931 mean weekly earnings; 1941, 1951, 1961 median weekly earnings.

Source: Calculated from *Census of Canada*, 1931, Vol. V, Table 15; *Census of Canada*, 1941, Vol. VI, Table 6; *Census of Canada*, 1951, Vol. V, Table 21; *Census of Canada*, 1961, Vol. III, Part 3, Tables 21 and 23, and unpublished data on weeks employed from D.B.S., Labour Force Division.

Specific Occupations[10]

Thus far, we have looked at the wage structure using broad occupational groups. This analysis has provided a general picture of the occupational wage structure; however, it suffers from the limitation that it conceals a good deal of the wage variation occurring within each occupational group as well as between groups. In order to gain some perspective of the hierarchy of specific occupations in the earnings structure of Canada, Table 56 was constructed for the non-farm labour

[10]For some intensive studies of the occupational pattern of Canada's labour force, see J. R. Podoluk, *Incomes of Canadians* (Ottawa, 1968); Noah M. Meltz, *Changes in the Occupational Composition of the Canadian Labor Force, 1931-1961*, Department of Labour, Canada (March 1965); Sylvia Ostry, *The Occupational Composition of the Canadian Labour Force*, Dominion Bureau of Statistics (Ottawa, 1967); Frank T. Denton, *An Analysis of Interregional Differences in Manpower Utilization and Earnings*, Staff Study No. 15, Economic Council of Canada (April 1966); Sylvia Ostry, *The Female Worker in Canada*, Dominion Bureau of Statistics (Ottawa, 1968); S. G. Peitchinis, 'Occupational Wage Differential in Canada, 1939-1965', *Australian Economic Papers* (June 1969); and Canadian Department of Labour, Economics and Research Branch, *The Behaviour of Canadian Wages and Salaries in the Post-war Period* (Ottawa, 1967).

force in total – both self-employed and working for others. Ranking the occupations by average earnings, this table presents the individual occupations belonging to the two lowest deciles and the two highest deciles in 1961.[11] The data reveal that among the highest-ranked occupations are the professional, technical, managerial, and official, and that they belong to the highly skilled category. The next echelon consists mainly of skilled workers, who include foremen and other supervisory workers, along with some professionals. The second lowest decile consists almost exclusively of labourers and semi-skilled workers. As expected, the lowest decile is populated by the unskilled occupations, and also by casual or seasonal workers who normally work less than a full year and whose annual earnings are therefore likely to be rather low. The range of earnings for specific occupations is from $453 for baby-sitters at the lowest level to $15,083 for physicians and surgeons at the top of our list. The earning differentials among the specific occupations are much larger than the differentials for the broad occupational groups shown earlier. This is because, in forming the occupational groups, averaging brings the extremes of dispersion closer to each other, and thus the differential is reduced.

Table 57 presents more recent data on income by occupation based on tax information.[12] These figures include all taxpayers, not just wage-and salary-earners, and hence will reach into much higher levels of income than did the census occupational data. In 1968, as our earlier findings showed, professionals comprised the highest income groups, with doctors heading the list.[13] The independent business proprietor earns surprisingly little in comparison with the professional man. These are average figures, of course, and within the business group there are some individuals earning substantial incomes. The workers or employees – this group includes both wage- and salary-earners – and farmers are near the bottom of the income ladder, followed only by pensioners.

---

[11]Podoluk, *op. cit.,* p. 73. Each decile of the occupations presented in the table constitutes 10 per cent of the total non-farm labour force.

[12]Since taxation statistics are classified on the basis of major source of income rather than strictly on occupational categories, they are very difficult to reconcile with census statistics. Thus an engineer who was employed by an engineering firm would, if his major source of income was his salary, be classified among the employees group and not among the engineers. The professional categories thus represent mainly those professionals who are independent proprietors, and the average income shown in each of the professional categories is higher than the average for all professionals in any one category. In addition, individuals who do not pay taxes are excluded and thus very-low-income occupations would not be represented in the data.

[13]For a discussion of the profitability of restricting entry into professional occupations, cf. P. A. Samuelson, *Economics,* (New York, 1951), p. 105.

TABLE 56

Specific Occupations of Non-Farm Labour Force Ranked by Average Income from Employment, Lowest and Highest Deciles, Year Ended May 31, 1961

Occupations	Average income	Coefficient of dispersion[a]	Per cent with above-average schooling[b]
First decile			
Baby sitters	$ 453	1.000	15.5
Newsvendors	648	1.003	8.5
Trappers and hunters	963	1.444	0.7
Attendants—recreation and amusement	1,141	2.073	15.3
Guides	1,586	1.015	7.6
Kitchen helpers and related workers, n.e.s.*	1,602	0.993	9.5
Fish canners, curers, and packers	1,606	1.061	3.2
Farm labourers, groundskeepers, and other agricultural occupations	1,695	1.240	8.9
Labourers in trade	1,814	1.430	14.9
Messengers	1,822	1.522	12.0
Fishermen	1,904	1.278	3.6
Labourers in			
All other industries	1,908	1.239	10.6
Construction	1,947	0.957	6.6
Transportation, except railway	1,965	1.128	7.6
Teamsters	2,064	0.871	3.3
Lumbermen, including labourers in logging	2,083	1.114	3.3
Waiters and waitresses	2,148	0.718	15.8
Labourers in wood industries	2,161	1.050	7.8
Service-station attendants	2,210	1.001	15.5
Labourers in			
Textile and clothing industries	2,221	0.676	5.1
Food and beverage	2,408	0.973	8.7
Forest rangers and cruisers	2,415	1.135	16.9
Second decile			
Labourers in public administration and defence	2,434	0.795	6.9
Labourers in local administration	2,439	0.823	5.4
Winders, reelers	2,470	0.446	4.1
Nurses-in-training	2,527	0.536	71.4
Shoemakers and repairers—factory, n.e.s.	2,531	0.609	4.2
Shoemakers and repairers—not in factory, n.e.s.	2,540	0.793	5.1

*Not elsewhere specified.

Occupations	Average income	Coefficient of dispersion[a]	Per cent with above-average schooling[b]
Porters—baggage and Pullman	$ 2,600	0.718	18.0
Elevator tenders—building	2,620	0.449	8.5
Janitors and cleaners—building	2,621	0.650	8.6
Service workers, n.e.s.	2,636	0.754	20.0
Cooks	2,659	0.636	11.3
Bottlers, wrappers, labellers	2,666	0.827	12.3
Warehousemen and freight handlers, n.e.s.	2,675	0.819	10.6
Labourers in			
Manufacturing	2,683	0.807	8.4
Communication and storage	2,686	0.740	12.0
Electric power, gas, and water utilities	2,694	0.873	10.6
Religious workers, n.o.r.*	2,695	0.830	44.2
Dressmakers and seamstresses, n.i.f.†	2,713	0.602	10.8
Knitters	2,724	0.480	9.3
Launderers and dry cleaners	2,745	0.578	9.8
Bartenders	2,762	0.488	14.6
Other leather product makers	2,767	0.475	6.4
Sawyers	2,779	0.889	5.6
Carders, combers, and other fibre preparers	2,786	0.322	5.9
Spinners and twisters	2,788	0.417	5.2
Taxi drivers and chauffeurs	2,792	0.635	10.9
Fruit and vegetable canners and packers	2,813	0.823	10.9
Sewers and sewing-machine operators, n.e.s.	2,816	0.550	7.1
Leather cutters	2,820	0.448	5.6
Nursing assistants and aides	2,821	0.408	19.7
Other textile occupations	2,845	0.421	6.9
Woodworking occupations, n.e.s.	2,851	0.621	9.4
Hawkers and pedlars	2,854	0.999	10.8
Apparel and related product makers, n.e.s.	2,867	0.558	7.1
Construction workers, n.e.s.	2,934	0.927	7.9

*Not otherwise reported.
†Not in factory.

TABLE 56 (cont.)

Specific Occupations of Non-Farm Labour Force Ranked by Average Income from Employment, Lowest and Highest Deciles, Year Ended May 31, 1961

Occupations	Average income	Coefficient of dispersion[a]	Per cent with above-average schooling[b]
Painters, paperhangers, and glaziers (construction and maintenance)	$ 2,943	0.725	10.7
Labourers in			
Transportation-equipment industries	2,957	0.499	6.3
Other manufacturing industries	2,963	0.762	8.5
Prospectors	2,973	1.170	29.0
Ninth decile			
Owners and managers in retail trade	5,571	0.834	30.1
Commercial travellers	5,576	0.665	48.6
Insurance salesmen and agents	5,674	0.703	55.9
Credit managers	5,716	0.569	68.3
Professional occupations, n.e.s.	5,723	0.636	68.4
Foremen—transportation equipment	5,776	0.492	27.7
Foremen—paper, and allied industries	5,778	0.519	19.6
Photoengravers	5,794	0.666	29.4
Foremen—mine, quarry, and oil well	5,832	0.564	18.4
Purchasing agents and buyers	5,863	0.613	53.9
School teachers	5,885	0.706	95.9
Other health professionals	5,935	0.817	68.1
Locomotive engineers	6,088	0.465	15.1
Funeral directors and embalmers	6,155	0.858	46.8
Owners and managers in all other industries	6,181	0.940	36.2
Office managers	6,188	0.956	63.6
Foremen—primary metal industries	6,214	0.484	22.6
Owners and managers in federal administration	6,250	0.638	64.6
Authors, editors, and journalists	6,263	0.765	77.3
Owners and managers in			
Miscellaneous services	6,267	0.784	45.5
Wood industries	6,379	1.038	30.3
Security salesmen and brokers	6,382	0.842	67.7
Tenth decile			
Inspectors and foremen—communications	6,389	0.479	49.0
Chemists	6,442	0.597	91.1
Owners and managers in provincial administration	6,567	0.750	63.3

Occupations	Average income	Coefficient of dispersion[a]	Per cent with above-average schooling[b]
Actuaries and statisticians	$ 6,597	0.618	81.9
Biological scientists	6,627	0.566	96.1
Accountants and auditors	6,961	0.584	83.5
Physical scientists, n.e.s.	7,001	0.591	93.4
Owners and managers in			
Health and welfare services	7,012	0.796	64.3
Construction industries	7,089	0.918	29.9
Pharmacists	7,127	0.632	95.9
Owners and managers in forestry, logging	7,167	1.044	22.8
Economists	7,271	0.570	89.8
Owners and managers in furniture and fixture			
industries	7,321	0.868	42.1
Electrical engineers	7,476	0.459	93.8
Industrial engineers	7,498	0.485	81.6
Mechanical engineers	7,517	0.473	89.1
Owners and managers in			
Transportation, communication,			
and other utilities	7,541	0.683	42.3
Education and related services	7,598	0.765	84.1
Professional engineers, n.e.s.	7,629	0.475	92.3
Civil engineers	7,634	0.476	95.8
Geologists	7,699	0.476	98.1
Owners and managers in			
Food and beverage	7,770	0.860	41.0
Wholesale trade	7,798	0.874	46.2
Sales managers	7,890	0.605	61.3
Chemical engineers	8,043	0.475	97.5
Owners and managers in			
Miscellaneous manufacturing	8,093	0.730	54.4
Non-metallic mineral products	8,258	0.779	47.6
Osteopaths and chiropractors	8,285	1.117	94.7
Mining engineers	8,487	0.433	91.4
Owners and managers in rubber industries	8,515	0.589	65.6
Veterinarians	8,577	0.480	95.9

TABLE 56 (concluded)

Specific Occupations of Non-Farm Labour Force Ranked by Average Income from Employment, Lowest and Highest Deciles, Year Ended May 31, 1961

Occupations	Average income	Coefficient of dispersion[a]	Per cent with above-average schooling[b]
Owners and managers in			
Metal-fabricating industries	$ 8,653	0.715	50.6
Clothing industries	8,689	0.849	43.9
Professors and college principals	8,806	0.664	98.8
Architects	8,880	0.580	95.6
Owners and managers in finance,			
real estate, insurance	8,908	0.651	67.9
Air pilots, navigators, and flight engineers	9,038	0.783	71.6
Optometrists	9,150	0.793	93.4
Owners and managers in			
Printing, publishing, and allied industries	9,195	0.806	55.7
Transportation equipment	9,411	0.767	59.8
Leather industries	9,464	1.038	51.7
Petroleum and coal products	9,516	0.738	59.9
Machinery industries	9,564	0.724	63.6
Knitting mills	9,760	0.881	53.6
Electrical products industries	9,914	0.753	69.2
Service to business management	10,080	0.892	77.0
Textile industries	10,178	0.922	59.8
Chemical and chemical products	10,303	0.836	72.2
Mines, quarries, and oil wells	10,467	0.821	60.4
Paper and allied industries	10,547	0.753	62.4
Lawyers and notaries	11,310	0.921	98.9
Judges and magistrates	11,555	1.368	90.5
Dentists	12,690	0.818	99.1
Physicians and surgeons	15,083	1.034	99.3

[a] $\dfrac{Q_3 - Q_1}{\text{Median}}$

[b] 'Percentage in the occupation having attained 4 to 5 years of secondary schooling, or having some university training or a university degree.'

Source: Earnings rankings based on D.B.S., *Census of Canada*, 1961, Incomes of Individuals, Table B4. Data on educational attainment from D.B.S., *Census of Canada*, 1961, Occupations by Sex Showing Age, Marital Status and Schoolling, Table 17. Computed by Podoluk, J.R., *Income of Canadians*, pp. 74-8.

TABLE 57

Average Income of Taxpayers by Occupation Group, 1968

Occupation	1968
Self-employed doctors and surgeons	$ 29,181
Self-employed lawyers and notaries	23,597
Self-employed engineers and architects	22,707
Self-employed dentists	20,164
Self-employed accountants	17,002
Other self-employed professionals	8,437
Self-employed salesmen	7,294
Investors	6,515
Business proprietors	6,441
Property owners	6,190
Self-employed entertainers and artists	6,087
Employees	5,665
Fishermen	5,291
Farmers	5,260
Unclassified	3,895
Pensioners	3,505

Source: Department of National Revenue, Taxation, *Taxation Statistics*, 1970 Edition, Ottawa, p. 11.

Earnings Differences within Occupations

The substantial differentials in average annual earnings conceal a great deal of variation or dispersion within each occupational group and within each specific occupation. A commonly employed measure of dispersion is the interquartile range – the range within which one-half of the occupations and incomes fall – divided by the median. Thus, for example, if the median income for any occupation is $2,000 and one-half the people in the occupation earn between $1,800 and $2,300 (while the other half earn less or more than this) the coefficient of dispersion is .25.

The average coefficient of the list given in Table 56 is .833 for the lower two quartiles and .722 for the upper two quartiles. An examination will show that the coefficient is large in those occupations where employment is seasonal, such as trapping, hunting, or recreation. Also, those occupations with a traditional turnover of personnel, such as baby-sitting, have high coefficients of dispersion. For the high-income groups, the self-employed show the highest coefficients, with many having coefficients over one. For instance, physicians and surgeons have coefficients of 1.117, whereas geologists have coefficients of .476, the latter being almost entirely salaried employees of the oil industry. It is worth noting that within the manual group of occupations, the extent of dispersion of annual earnings varies on the average with the degree of skill.[14] Podoluk points out that average income in the professional and managerial groups varies greatly and in different patterns with age. Income of doctors increases rapidly, peaks at forty-five years, and falls steadily until retirement. Lawyers' earnings rise rapidly, have a period of little growth, and begin a second rise toward the end of their careers. Engineers exhibit a more gradual rise during their careers.[15] Also, Table 57 shows that inequality in earnings is greater in the lowest and highest deciles than in the intermediate deciles. The reason is that the lowest and highest levels of earnings are characterized by more uncertainty and fluctuation than the regular salaried occupations largely comprising the intermediate levels.

A part of the variation in earnings described above arises from the fact that, in the census, specific occupations are not really homogeneous, and within each category are included individuals varying widely in skill and training. Moreover, since these are annual-earnings data, as has been noted, variations in the work employment pattern of individuals in certain occupations will give rise to wide differences in income. There is also considerable dispersion of hourly wages even within relatively homogeneous occupational categories, and some of the reasons for this variation will be analysed in the following chapters, which deal with geographic, interindustrial, and other wage differentials. Before turning to these aspects of the Canadian wage structure, however, we would do well to examine more closely the empirical findings of the causes of occupational differentials and the theories that these findings support. Brief consideration will also be given to the relative earnings position of office workers and wage-earners.

The Skill Differential

Statistical evidence suggests that relative occupational differentials in

[14]For a discussion of dispersion for semi-skilled occupations see R. L. Raiman, 'The Indeterminateness of Wages of Semi-Skilled Workers', in *Industrial and Labor Relations Review* (January 1953); M. Rothbaum and H. G. Ross, 'Two Views on Wage Differences: Intra-occupational Wage Diversity', *Industrial and Labor Relations Review* (April 1954).
[15]Podoluk, *op. cit.,* p. 85.

the manual sector of industry – or specifically, the skilled-unskilled differentials – have been narrowing in many countries over the course of this century. Thus, in the United States, it has been estimated that in 1907 the average skilled wage level in manufacturing was over twice that of the unskilled; by 1945-7 the average skill premium had fallen to 55 per cent and by 1952-3 was under 40 per cent.[16] An O.E.C.D. study shows that for selected occupations in the United States, the differential came down to about 27 per cent by 1961.[17] In the United Kingdom, too, a similar long-run narrowing since the turn of the century has been observed; by the early fifties the typical skill premium in Britain (on hourly rates) was only 25 per cent.[18] For the building industry, the O.E.C.D. study shows that in Britain the skilled-unskilled differential came down from 50 per cent in 1900 to 13 per cent in 1961.[19] Studies of France, Sweden, and other countries reveal substantially the same trends.[20] Possibly the most important factor contributing to this widely observed diminution of relative skill differentials was the spread of education, which served to increase the supply of skilled workers and to decrease the relative number of the unskilled. In the United States, in addition, virtual cessation of immigration after 1914 and the gradual shrinkage in the rate of rural-urban migration cut off or reduced important sources of unskilled labour. Prohibition of the use of child labour had the same effect. Thus, although the demand for unskilled labour has declined relatively over this century, skill differentials have narrowed because the relative supply of unskilled labour has declined even more. In some of the European countries with strong socialist trade-union movements, a deliberately egalitarian wage policy has also had some effect in narrowing differentials.[21] In

---

[16]Ober, *op. cit.*; Toivo P. Kanninen, 'Occupational Wage Relationships in Manufacturing', *Monthly Labor Review* (November 1953).

[17]Organization for Economic Cooperation and Development, *op. cit.*, p. 24.

[18]K. G. J. C. Knowles and D. J. Robertson, 'Differences Between the Wages of Skilled and Unskilled Workers, 1880-1950', *Bulletin of the Oxford University Institute of Statistics* (April 1951).

[19]Organization for Economic Cooperation and Development, *op. cit.*, p. 34.

[20]However, the actual earnings differentials are usually wider than the negotiated-rate differentials in many European countries, suggesting that, in terms of market forces, the narrowing process has proceeded too far.

[21]Centralized wage determination by government is another important factor. Cf. John T. Dunlop and Melvin Rothbaum, 'International Comparison of Wage Structures', *International Labor Review* (April 1955). H. A. Turner, 'Trade Unions, Differentials and the Levelling of Wages', *Manchester School of Economics and Social Studies* (September 1952), emphasizes the importance of trade-union development in levelling wages in two respects – forms of organization and systems of labour recruitment. Cf. S. Ostry, H. J. D. Cole and K. G. J. C. Knowles, 'Wage Differentials in a Large Steel Firm', Oxford University Institute of Statistics *Bulletin* (August 1958), for an example of trade-union action in maintaining *wide* differentials.

North America, the growth of industrial unions, organizing the unskilled for the first time, may also have had the effect of narrowing the skill premium in the late thirties and during the Second World War and the early post-war period.[22]

A broad impression of the trend in the skilled-unskilled wage differentials in Canada since the 1920s may be obtained from Table 58. The group of industries on this table was selected simply on the basis of the availability of comparable occupational wage-rate information since 1920, and they include both manufacturing and non-manufacturing industries. Note that since the twenties there has been some diminution in the skill premium in each of the manufacturing industries, except furniture, and also in construction, but not in municipal service and urban transport. Examination of additional data for manufacturing industries reveals that, whereas skill premiums of 60-100 per cent or more were common in the twenties and thirties, in recent years differentials of 40-45 per cent are more typical, although there is wide variation from industry to industry, depending in part on the actual degree of skill required by the top crafts.[23] There is also a regional variation in occupational differentials, the premium for skill today tending to be smaller in British Columbia than in the rest of the country.

Some skill differentials show a tendency to widen during periods of prolonged and severe depression, a phenomenon apparent in Canada in most of the examples presented in Table 58.[24] It is, however, by no means universal; in agricultural implements, pulp mills, and furniture manufacturing, the differential narrowed, and in shipbuilding it was more or less stable over a very long period of time. Economic

[22]Government wage stabilization during the last war had a levelling tendency in both Canada and the United States. Market forces contributed to the narrowing process as well, particularly (in Canada) toward the end of the war and during the first post-war inflation. Cf. Melvin Reder, 'The Theory of Occupational Wage Differentials', *American Economic Review* (December 1955).

[23]Cf. Sylvia W. Ostry, 'Inter-industry Earnings Differentials in Canada, 1945-56', *Industrial and Labor Relations Review* (April 1959), Table 2, for demonstration of the range of skill differentials in post-war years.

[24]The tendency to widening skill differentials during the depression was found in a number of industries other than those presented in Table 58: examples are sawmills, sash and door, biscuits, foundry and machine shops. On the other hand, differentials in coal-mining and in the stove-and-furnace industry narrowed during the thirties. In these two industries the skilled occupations are paid by result while the labourers are on datal rates. During the depression, declines in output would be reflected quickly in skilled earnings and hence result in temporary narrowing of the skill differential. Cf. John T. Dunlop, 'Cyclical Variations in Wage Structure', *Review of Economics and Statistics* (February 1939), p. 32, who makes a similar observation with respect to the iron-and-steel industry in the United States.

reasoning could lead us to expect a widening of skilled-unskilled wage gaps during a depression because of the nature of supply for each type of labour. Unemployed skilled workers can compete with unskilled workers for their jobs; the reverse situation is not possible. The supply of unskilled labour, therefore, increases more during depression than does that of the skilled group. Moreover, some employers, wishing to retain skilled workers because of the added cost and difficulty of training new men when business revives, down-grade their skilled men in order to keep them in the firm. Then too, in so far as there were any unions of strength in Canada during the depression period of the thirties, they were craft organizations that probably managed in some degree to protect the skilled workers' rates. There was no such protection for the rest of the manual work force. Minimum-wage regulations for men (as opposed to women and children) did not come into effect in Canadian provinces until later in the thirties.[25] However, in a particular industry it may have been company policy to protect the unskilled rates, especially if take-home pay had been severely eroded by short-time. In other instances, community opinion might have been sufficiently strong to prevent wage-cutting below a certain level. Without specific and detailed information on each industry it is impossible to account for the pattern of change in occupational differentials in Canada during the depression. It is clear, however, that the widening tendency was not a universal phenomenon.[26]

Most (but again, not all) skill differentials in Canada narrowed markedly during the war years, at least after 1942 or 1943, when full employment had been achieved and mobilization was under way. Flat-rate or uniform cents-per-hour increases were very prevalent during these years, because of government policies of wage stabilization[27] and because of policy followed by the newly organized industrial unions. The same cents-per-hour increase, applied to a skilled and unskilled rate, will, of course, result in a narrowing of the percentage differential between the two. Market forces were also at work. Simplification of many skilled jobs, accelerated training programs, and the rapid up-grading of semi-skilled workers served to increase the supply of skilled workers and thus acted as a brake on the movement of skilled rates. By 1944, when labour-force participation rates

[25]See Chapter IX.

[26]Bell, *op. cit.*, p. 333.

[27]See Department of Labour, Research and Statistics Branch, 'Effects of the War on Canada's Wage-Rate Structure', *Canadian Labour Market* (March 1948), especially p. 36.

TABLE 58

Skilled-Unskilled Differentials, Hourly Rates, Selected Industries, Selected

Industry	1923-9	1930-3	1943-6	1947	1948	1949
			(skilled rate as per cent of unskilled rate)			
Automobile parts						
Machinists	165.3	171.0	129.3	126.4	126.6	118.8
Agricultural implements						
Pattern-makers	163.4	154.3	150.0	147.4	139.5	140.2
Shipbuilding						
Boiler-makers	162.3	161.3	162.0	160.3	143.8	141.0
Sheet metal						
Sheet-metal workers	205.3	233.9	166.5	163.8	170.1	160.2
Pulp and paper						
Millwrights (maintenance)	171.0	175.8	149.7	129.4	130.2	131.3
Digester cook (pulp)	207.2	206.6	170.0	148.2	144.7	145.8
Furniture						
Upholsterers	160.1	151.6	164.4	160.9	154.8	171.0
Construction						
Toronto						
Bricklayers & masons	229.2	234.5	188.9	206.5	205.9	189.5
Carpenters	175.5	204.8	169.1	174.2	176.5	168.4
Vancouver						
Bricklayers & masons	228.2	265.1	182.6	177.8	175.0	180.0
Carpenters	176.3	187.9	158.3	155.6	155.0	160.0
Printing & publishing*						
Toronto						
Compositors	217.6	250.8	210.7	200.0	194.4	197.4
Vancouver						
Compositors	183.4	251.0	206.5	185.5	176.6	173.6
Municipal government service						
Toronto						
Policemen	130.2	132.8	126.9	127.3	126.7	129.5
Urban & Suburban Transport						
Toronto						
Electricians	111.7	133.7	138.0	136.4	125.4	123.5

*Unskilled occupation is female: bindery girls.
† Averages of 1958-9.

Sources: Data for the years 1943 to 1969 and all years for construction, municipal government services, and urban and suburban transport were taken from special tabulations made in the Economics and Research Branch of the Department of Labour. These tabulations were based primarily on statistics published in *Wage Rates and Hours of Labour,*

Years, 1923-69

1950	1952	1954	1956	1958	1962	1964	1966	1969
117.0	123.5	122.7	130.8	128.8	136.2	130.5	122.8	133.6
141.0	146.7	139.2	148.9	151.0	140.7	131.6	n.a.	n.a.
139.1	126.5	126.2	126.1	132.5	117.2	117.2	122.7	121.0
153.3	138.9	133.8	142.2	148.6	144.6	137.7	n.a.	n.a.
133.3	131.5	132.4	134.4	136.3	132.5	132.5	135.1	135.0
144.1	143.3	140.0	140.6	142.1	128.5	128.2	127.0	135.4
173.9	175.8	171.9	169.1	168.5	147.7	149.1	143.5	140.9
205.3	213.6	188.0	180.0	173.5	155.8	146.8	138.8	142.8
184.2	190.9	180.0	165.5	155.6	144.1	140.6	136.2	135.7
156.7	140.0	150.0	150.6	141.0	141.0	137.2	129.3	117.1
140.0	140.0	138.8	135.5	137.4	137.8	135.2	125.5	119.9
194.0	195.0	202.8	208.0	200.0	211.3	207.6	195.9	189.0
183.5	177.9	169.5	169.9	168.8	174.0	164.1	159.8	172.4
123.4	132.0	130.2	129.1	136.3[†]	128.7	130.2	143.8	151.4
114.7	106.2	117.0	120.8	117.2	122.4	120.0	122.1	119.2

Annual Reports, 1 to 52. All other data were taken directly from *Wages Rates and Hours of Labour*. Prior to 1943, simple arithmetic averages of the sample wage rates were calculated. Data for any given year prior to 1943 were taken from the latest *Report* in which sample rates for that year were published.

had reached a maximum – indicating that the potential 'reserve' work force had been fully absorbed – continued high levels of demand began to exert pressure on unskilled rates.

The decline in skill premiums continued in the early, inflationary, post-war years,[28] but, as may be observed from Table 58, in most cases the narrowing process slowed down by the early fifties and a widening tendency appeared again by the mid fifties. This tapered off toward the late fifties and since then has registered a general contract- ing trend through the sixties. Of course, there are exceptions; for ex- ample, wage skill premiums in construction have not followed the direction of the majority of occupations. A tapering-off of inflationary pressure and a feeling that perhaps skill premiums had fallen too low may have induced some unions in the early fifties to turn away from pure flat-rate increases and to accept some form of percentage in- creases, or at least cents-per-hour raises with additional adjustments for skilled workers.[29] Whatever the role of union policy, it reinforced underlying economic forces, sufficient in themselves to account for the stabilization of many skill differentials in Canada by the early fifties. In the face of the rising demand for many types of skilled labour in post-war Canada, the increase in supply of such labour provided by formal and informal training and selective immigration was not suf- ficient to prevent a rise of wages for some skilled workers, or at least not sufficient to allow a further erosion of skill premiums. On the other hand, the demand for unskilled labour did not increase as rap- idly, while the supply was fed by rural excess population, by immigra- tion, and (after 1953) by an expansion in the secondary labour force (especially married women), all of whom would have been more likely to compete for lower- rather than higher-skilled jobs. After 1956, rising unemployment levels would tend to damp down unskilled wage in- creases rather more than those of the skilled group.

To summarize, the long-run tendency of the skilled-unskilled wage differential in Canada displays a moderate contractionist trend. Skill

[28]Richard Perlman judges inflation to be among the most powerful factors producing narrow skill differentials. 'When prices are rising, the primary interest of labor is in wage levels and not structure. Increases are sought and secured, and in union-management negotiations the simplest, and superficially the fairest, method of distributing the in- crease is by raising all wages an equal amount. Furthermore, public opinion, which is likely to be formed by monetary instead of real considerations, would be in favor of limiting the increase in skilled wage-rates that already appear very high, at least in money terms.' For an opposing view see Reder, 'The Theory of Occupational Wage Dif- ferentials' and 'Wage Differentials: Theory and Measurement', *op. cit.*, and Ozanne, *op. cit.*

[29]Sylvia Ostry, 'Some Aspects of the Canadian Wage Structure: Implications for Union Policy', Proceedings of the Eleventh Annual Industrial Relations Conference (Montreal, 1959), pp. 11-12.

premiums appear to have narrowed during the war and early post-war years, but the narrowing process did not continue consistently all through. Differentials tended to rise during the early fifties, and from 1956 onward appeared to be narrowing again. A strongly rising demand for skilled labour, a relative fall in the demand for unskilled labour, combined with a relatively inelastic supply of skilled labour and a relatively elastic supply of unskilled labour in post-war Canada, resulted in fairly stable or even slightly widening skill differentials; after 1956 unemployment also acted to counterbalance narrowing tendencies. But the contractionist tendency re-emerged in the fifties and continued through the sixties. This is not surprising because full employment, improvements in technical and general education, a decline in the rate of rural-urban migration, and a slowing down of immigration, or at least of immigration of the unskilled, could have been expected to produce, eventually, a renewed narrowing of Canadian skill differentials. Of course, there are some considerations to be borne in mind in connection with the possibility that the narrowing trend will continue in future. 'A longer and more difficult educational process in a period of rising per capita income will result in a rise in the real and money costs of education and training to the individual; and technological change, by reducing the semi-skilled content of the work force and substantially upgrading many skilled jobs, will produce a greater degree of "polarization" of the work force.'[30]

The Office Worker–Wage-Earner Differential

Table 59 presents data comparing average weekly and hourly earnings of office workers and of wage-earners in manufacturing industries in

[30]Sylvia Ostry, 'Communications, A Note on Skill Differentials', *Southern Economic Journal* (January 1963). There is, however, no general agreement concerning the effect of technological change on skill levels. Cf. James R. Bright, 'Does Automation Raise Skill Requirements?', *Harvard Business Review* (July-August 1958); John Diebold, *Automation: Its Impact on Business and Labor*, Pamphlet No. 106, National Planning Association (Washington, D. C., May 1959); Charles C. Killingsworth, 'Effects of Automation on Employment and Manpower Planning', statement before the Senate Sub-Committee on Employment and Manpower of the Senate Committee on Labor and Public Welfare (Washington, D.C., June 14 and 15, 1960). The Canadian Department of Labour conducted an intensive four-year study of technological change in five import-manufacturing industries which showed that one consequence of changing technology in the industries examined was that 'the need for semi-skilled workers declines, while requirements for skilled maintenance workers and other highly technical occupations usually rise.' W. R. Dymond, Director, Economics and Research Branch, Department of Labour, 'Technological Changes and their Impact on Employment, Occupations and Industrial Relations', mimeographed, an address to the McGill Industrial Relations Conference, June 6, 1961, p. 5.

TABLE 59

*Average Weekly Earnings and Average Hours Worked, Office Workers
and Wage-Earners, Manufacturing Industries, Selected Years, 1939-67*

Year	Male and female					
	Office workers		Wage-earners		Differential*	
	A.W.E.	A.H.W.	A.W.E.	A.H.W.	A.W.E.	A.H.W.
	$		$		%	%
1939	26.52	42.0	20.14	47.2	131.7	89.0
1946	34.20	41.0	32.38	43.7	105.6	93.8
1951	51.14	39.4	51.32	42.0	99.6	93.8
1954	59.29	38.7	57.99	41.5	102.2	93.3
1957	68.02	38.4	65.31	40.5	104.1	94.8
1961	n.a.	n.a.	74.27	40.6		
1965	87.19	38.6	89.32	41.8	97.61	92.3
1966	92.40	38.4	94.52	41.3	97.76	93.0
1967	98.91	38.2	99.91	40.9	98.99	93.4

*Office workers as per cent of wage-earners.

Source: 1939-1957, W. Donald Wood, 'An Analysis of Office Unionism in Canadian
Manufacturing Industries', unpublished Ph.D. thesis, Princeton University
(Princeton, 1959), p. 217; D.B.S., *Earnings and Hours of Work in Manufactur-
ing*, various issues.

Canada over the period 1939-67. As may be seen, the differential in
weekly earnings between these two groups was over 30 per cent before
the war. By the end of the war, it had fallen to just under 6 per cent,
and this differential continued to diminish until it was actually reversed, i.e. the wage-earner went ahead of the office worker, in the
sixties.

A number of factors have contributed to the steady decline in the
favourable relative earnings position of this white-collar group.[31] The
supply of labour to office occupations has been greatly increased by
the expansion and improvement of education and by the rising labour-force participation of married women. Changes in the composition of the office labour force have also been important; the growth
in the proportion of females and the substantial mechanization of

[31]For a full account, see W. Donald Wood, 'An Analysis of Office Unionism in Canadian Manufacturing Industries', unpublished Ph. D. thesis (Princeton, 1959); Kenneth M.
McCaffee, 'The Earnings Differential Between White Collar and Manual Occupations',
Review of Economics and Statistics (February 1953); H. A. Turner, 'Employment Fluctuations, Labour Supply and Bargaining Power', *The Manchester School of Economics
and Social Studies* (May 1959), pp. 188-9.

many office operations would both contribute to the lowering of relative wages. In some industries, strong plant-worker unions may have been successful in effecting some redistribution of the wage bill from the unorganized office-worker group.[32]

It should be noted that office staff generally work a shorter week than plant workers. However, it is clear that the office workers' relative advantage in hours worked has diminished over these years. Similarly, these white-collar personnel are losing their edge over manual workers with respect to other working conditions, such as paid vacations, statutory holidays, and fringe benefits of one sort or another.[33]

Some Characteristics of Occupational Wage-Differentials in Canada

The occupational wage structure is the product of a large number of factors, and it is impossible to determine the separate effect of each of them. In the preceding analysis of the wage structure of occupations in Canada over time, a number of factors (for example, state of the economy, government wage regulations, skill) were mentioned as having effected changes in the structure. Understandably, many other factors are hidden behind the over-all structure of occupational earnings or wages. In this section, three interesting characteristics of Canada's occupational wage structure are presented, using census data for 1961.[34] The characteristics are as follows: (a) education and experience and their relationship to the occupational differential; (b) male-female differential in wages for the same occupations; and (c) variation in occupational wage structures by class of worker (working for others or self-employed).

(a) *Education and Experience*: It has already been mentioned that one of the major factors contributing to the long-run contractionist trend of occupational wage structure in most countries of the world is the rising level of education.[35] (See Chapter IV for discussion of education as an investment in human capital.)

---

[32]In 1956, it was found that the average ratio of weekly male earnings to weekly male salaries among manufacturing industries which were highly organized (75 to 100 per cent of production workers covered by collective agreements) was 72.1 per cent, while for less organized industries (less than 50 per cent of production workers covered by agreement) the average ratio was 66.7 per cent. In 1958, the respective figures were 69.8 per cent for the highly organized and 64.5 per cent for the poorly organized.

[33]Cf. Wood, *op. cit.*, pp. 236-8.

[34]This part of the analysis is based mainly on Podoluk, *op. cit.*

[35]See Chapter IV for an intensive discussion of investment in education.

This rise in educational level has affected the pattern of skill of the labour force, changed the status of some occupations, and aided the formation of similar aspirations for higher standards of living at different levels.[36] In economic terms, the spread of compulsory education and, in some countries, the raising of the minimum school-leaving age have led to (i) a reduction in the difference between the quality of skilled and unskilled labour; (ii) an increase in the substitutability of labour of different skills; and (iii) a relative decrease in the supply of unskilled labour. Thus, it appears that the amount of education an individual has received is an important explanation of earnings differentials by occupations.[37]

This observation finds support in Canadian data as shown in Table 56. In that table, above-average schooling is defined as the percentage in the occupation having attained four to five years of secondary schooling, or having some university training, or a university degree. As the table indicates, the majority of occupations in the upper earning deciles have above-average schooling. The extent of above-average schooling tends to be higher among professionals than among the managerial class. Thus, occupations that are stratified according to their earnings may be similarly stratified by the education content of the individuals in those occupations.

Education is one component of the skill embodied in the worker, training being another. There is an hypothesis that 'inter-occupational differentials are... a function of differences in training.'[38] Training is not only the formal education that an individual brings with him to a job, but it is also the on-the-job training that in turn is partly a function of experience. However, there is a positive relationship between the pre-entry level of education, the extent of on-the-job training, and earnings. The higher the pre-entry level of education, the higher is the likelihood of on-the-job training influencing the earnings of an occupation.

Table 60 presents the average income from employment, by age and education, for the total male non-farm labour force in Canada. It

---

[36]See Muntz, *op. cit.*

[37]See Reder, *op. cit.*; Muntz, *op. cit.*; H. P. Miller, 'Changes in Industrial Distribution of Wages in the United States, 1939-1949', *Studies in Income and Wealth* (Princeton, 1958) Vol. 23, pp. 365-6.

[38]Jacob Mincer, 'Investment in Human Capital and Personal Income Distribution', *Journal of Political Economy* (August 1958), p. 301. For the significance of education to earnings, besides Mincer, see J. N. Morgan, M. David, W. Cohen, and H. Brazer, *Income and Welfare in the United States* (New York, 1962); Gary Becker, *Human Capital*, National Bureau of Economic Research (New York, 1964).

TABLE 60

Average Income from Employment by Age and Level of Schooling for Year Ending May 31, 1961 – Male Non-Farm Labour Force

Age	Elementary only	Secondary 1-3 years	Secondary 4-5 years	Some university	University degree
			(in dollars)		
15-24	1,928	2,206	2,497	1,868	3,408
25-34	3,311	4,147	4,760	5,108	6,909
35-44	3,653	4,629	5,779	6,608	9,966
45-54	3,648	4,756	6,130	6,882	10,821
55-64	3,480	4,588	5,944	6,731	10,609

Source: *Incomes of Individuals*, Census Report 98-502, 1961 *Census of Canada*, Table B.6.

shows that average income for all education levels increases with age, a fact that may be taken as a partial indicator of experience and on-the-job training. But the extent of this increase varies from about 90 per cent over a working lifetime at the elementary education level to about 218 per cent at the university degree level, demonstrating that occupations with higher education levels have higher earnings. The finding on age-education relationships indicates that occupational wage differential reflects not only different education levels but different degrees of on-the-job training.[39]

(b) *Sex:* It is important to study the wage structures of the male and female working forces separately for two reasons: first, because female workers, on the average, have lower wages and salaries than male workers; and secondly, because the *patterns* of wages and salaries between occupations are different for the two sexes. This is evident from an inspection of Table 61. It would appear that for five out of the nine broad occupations chosen, average wages and salaries for female workers are less than half those of the male workers. Moreover, the female-male differential rises from .35 in sales to .69 in clerical occupations.

There might be various causes behind this phenomenon, a full exposition of which is nearly impossible because of the lack of proper data.[40] Some broad observations may be made, however. For the same levels of education, the occupational distributions of the two sexes

[39]Podoluk, *op. cit.*, pp. 81-8.

[40]For an attempted quantitative explanation of the sex differential of earnings, see Ostry, *The Female Worker in Canada*, pp. 39-45.

TABLE 61

Average Wages and Salaries, All Wage-Earners in Current Labour Force and All Wage-Earners Employed in Full Year, Year Ending May 31, 1961

Occupation	All wage-earners			Employed full year[1]		
	Male	Female	Ratio F/M	Male	Female	Ratio F/M
	Average (in dollars)			Average (in dollars)		
Managerial	6,673	3,207	.48	6,848	3,531	.52
Professional and technical	5,448	2,996	.55	5,909	3,531	.60
Clerical	3,409	2,340	.69	3,818	2,826	.74
Sales	3,908	1,367	.35	4,608	2,066	.45
Service and recreation	3,161	1,158	.37	3,690	1,722	.47
Transport and communications	3,415	2,123	.62	4,006	2,617	.65
Farm workers	1,401	607	.43	2,081	1,240	.60
Craftsmen and production workers	3,566	1,788	.50	4,170	2,295	.55
Labourers	2,157	1,499	.67	3,253	2,168	.67
Totals	3,679	1,955	.54	4,444	2,619	.59

[1]Wage-earners working in 49 to 52 weeks and usually working 35 hours or more per week.

Source: For all wage-earners, *Earnings, Hours and Weeks of Employment of Wage-Earners by Occupation*, Census Report 94-539, 1961 *Census of Canada*, Table 21. All wage-earners employed full year from unpublished data.

are different. At all levels of education, female workers are concentrated in certain occupations more than in others. Nearly 40 per cent of female workers in Canada with only elementary schooling were in the service occupations (e.g., waitresses, cooks, hairdressers, janitors, etc.). Such occupations have a high degree of part-time and part-year employment. Moreover, the number of weeks or months worked varies between male and female, and that affects the wage differential. Focusing on the last column in Table 61, which presents data based on the average wages and salaries of the two sexes after excluding part-time workers, we see that the differential is reduced to some extent. And as expected, the reduction in differential is largest in the service and recreation occupations, where the relative concentration of female work- ers is greatest. But the most important factor responsible for the male- female wage differential seems to be the discontinuous work experience of female workers. It has already been seen that on-the-job experience is an important variable in determining interoccupational wage differ- ential. Discontinuous work experience might have prevented female workers from taking up jobs in higher positions or positions of re- sponsibility and thus affected their earnings adversely. In general, for the same age, male workers have more work experience and more con- tinuous work experience than female workers. Age and education, two other variables with considerable effects on male wage structure, seem to have negligible impact on the male-female variations in occupational wage structures. Even after accounting for all these variables, there remain substantial variations between the earnings of male and female workers. In recent times this variation has been the subject of much criticism, and it has been argued that most of it is due to the persist- ence of the customary habits of thought and action left over from an earlier day. These are the 'non-market', 'irrational prejudices' that lead to discrimination in wage policies on the ground of sex alone. Al- though conclusive empirical support of this hypothesis is hard to come by, the possibility cannot be denied that discrimination might conceiv- ably be one of the factors contributing to the observed sex differential in earnings.[41]

(c) *Class of Worker*: Along with education, age, and sex, whether one is self-employed or working for others is also a factor that seems to affect the structure of earnings. Although there are some ambiguities in the data, Table 62 shows that generally, for most occupations, self-employed individuals earn more than salaried individuals. The two notable exceptions are managerial and mining-and-quarrying occupations, in both of which salaried workers earned more than the self-employed. Another important feature of the self-employed cate- gory as against the salaried is that, in the former, the dispersion of earnings is higher than in the latter. Thus, although the average self- employed individual in a professional or technical occupation in Can- ada is likely to earn more than double his counterpart on a payroll, the inequality in the distribution of earnings for the self-employed is more than that for the salaried.

[41]See *ibid.* pp. 42, 44, and *Report of the Royal Commission on The Status of Women in Canada* (Ottawa, 1970); Victor R. Fuchs, in *Male-Female Differentials in Hourly Earnings*, paper presented at the Annual Meeting of the American Statistical Associa- tion, Detroit, December 1970, shows that in the U.S.A. 'employer discrimination is probably not a major factor. Discrimination by consumers may be more significant.'

TABLE 62

Class of Workers and Average Income, Broad Occupations, for Year Ending May 31, 1961

Class of worker and occupation	Average income (in dollars)	Average income (in dollars)
	Worked for others	Self-employed
All occupations	3,952	5,929
Managerial	7,248	6,567
Professional and technical	5,794	12,286
Clerical	3,508	4,798
Sales	4,104	5,577
Service and recreation	3,295	4,026
Transport and communications	3,613	4,363
Farm workers	1,715	2,763
Loggers	2,205	2,301
Fishermen, trappers, and hunters	1,906	1,809
Miners, quarrymen	4,207	3320
Craftsmen and production workers	3,735	3,704
Labourers	2,300	2,384

Source: *Incomes of Individuals*, Census Report 98-502, 1961 *Census of Canada*, Table B.4.

Conclusion

The gaps in annual and weekly earnings among the broad occupational groups in Canada have shown an over-all narrowing tendency over the long run. However, there have been short-run variations from this trend. The major factors affecting both the short- and long-run changes are the state of the economy (whether boom or depression conditions exist), the wage and migration policies of the government affecting the skill content of the labour force, and the increase in educational levels. Within the manual group alone, the skill differential in hourly rates has narrowed since the 1920s, although this has not been uniformly distributed either over all the occupations or over the entire period. Office workers have gradually lost ground to the blue-collar group, although, again, the erosion of the white-collar advantages seems to have been reduced somewhat in the late sixties. The occupational differential is subject not only to the varying levels of education of individuals in the occupations, but also to the different degrees of training or experience. The extent to which the latter can affect earnings depends on the pre-entry level of education. It is mainly because of a discontinuous work experience and a given occupational deployment on the part of females that a major part of the male-female differential in occupational earnings exists. Lastly, the occupational wage structure of self-employed individuals varies from that of individuals on the payrolls of others, the former earning generally more than the latter, while the inequality in earnings is higher among the self-employed.

XI

Wages in Canada:
The Interindustry Structure

Interindustry Differentials

It has been observed that men of comparable skill in the same region are paid different wages depending upon the industry in which they are employed. Such interindustry differences in wages cannot usually be explained away as 'compensating differentials' of the classical variety,[1] i.e. differences that are supposed to equalize 'net advantages' among jobs. They are either too large or have the wrong 'sign'; jobs characterized by unpleasant working conditions are often paid less instead of more than comfortable, attractive jobs requiring similar degrees of skill. An example of interindustry wage differences for hourly rated wage-earners in Toronto in 1969 is found in Table 63.

Clearly, there are some differences in the nature of work and in the ability of workers in different industries. On the whole, however, it does not seem that production jobs vary sufficiently with respect to content or effort to account for such wide ranges of hourly rates as those shown in this table. The workers in each of the selected industries are, to an extent, interchangeable, yet those working in the clothing industry, for example, earned about 15 per cent less than those in the food and beverage industry or in a paper-boxes-and-bags factory where the work is not likely to be dirtier, heavier, or, indeed, strikingly dissimilar in any significant way.

Such patterns of interindustry wage differences are not peculiar

---

[1]Adam Smith, *The Wealth of Nations* (New York, 1937), pp. 99-133. Smith mentions five circumstances which 'make up for a small pecuniary gain in some employments, and counterbalance a great one in others': agreeableness or disagreeableness; easiness and cheapness or difficulty and expense of learning; constancy of employment; degree of trust; probability of success.

292

TABLE 63

Average Hourly Earnings of Hourly Rated Wage-Earners, Selected Industries: Toronto, 1969

Industry	Average hourly earnings (cents per hour)
Clothing	201
Furniture and fixtures	231
Scientific and professional equipment	258
Paper boxes and bags	266
Food and beverages	271
Metal fabricating	290
Primary metal	300
Slaughtering and meat-packing	307
Miscellaneous machinery and equipment	329
Petroleum and coal products	365

Source: D.B.S., *Man-Hours and Hourly Earnings* (January-December 1969).

to one occupational group or one urban area, but may be observed in varying degrees at all skill levels and in any local labour-market area.

Interindustry comparisons of this sort are examples of industrial differentials that include effects of occupational and skill variations. Unfortunately, data on wages cross-classified by occupation, sex, market areas, and industry are not readily available. Thus, most studies of interindustry wage structures are confined to analyses of differences in *average earnings* among industries, as in the above table. High-wage industries generally have characteristics like the following: larger-than-average firm size, more capital per worker, relatively larger numbers of male workers, high skill requirements. Such industries are often concentrated in larger rather than smaller urban centres. Low-wage industries have roughly the opposite characteristics. Thus it may be seen that the relative wage level of an industry is affected by many factors; that is to say, the interindustry structure of wages at a given time is compounded of a variety of wage differentials – sex, occupation, region, firm size, size of community, and so on.[2]

[2]In the long run, under competitive conditions, the wage levels of different industries should tend to uniformity, reflecting only differences in the 'skill mix' of the industry and differences in the cost of living of the communities in which the industry is located.

Interindustry Structure of Annual Earnings: Ranking and Dispersion, 1922-60

The interindustrial structure of wages or earnings has two important aspects: ranking and dispersion. Ranking refers to the ordering of different industries in the hierarchy of wages from the highest to the lowest level, while dispersion refers to the extent of divergence between the extremes of the highest and lowest wages, irrespective of the positions of specific industries in the distribution. It is possible for ranking to change without any change in dispersion, and vice versa; the first indicates the *pattern*, while the second measures the *extent* of differentials.

Ranking: A broad generalization about the ranking of industries by their earnings is that shifts in such ranking are more common in the early phases of industrialization than in the later phases, probably due to the higher rates of dynamic adjustments taking place in the earlier stages of industrialization. However, there are two broad views on the subject. First, early studies covering the period till the end of the 1940s established the 'pliability thesis' relating to ranking of industries by earnings,[3] and secondly, studies of later dates supported a 'stability thesis' establishing that such ranking remains unchanged over considerable periods of time in most developed countries.[4] The general conclusion from both the sets of studies is that 'the inter-industry structure of wages has considerable stability over short and moderately short periods of time.'[5]

The extent of stability or pliability of the ranked order of industries by earnings in Canada during 1922-60 may be observed in Table 64.[6]

---

[3]See, for example, P. H. Douglas, *Real Wages in the United States 1890-1926* (Boston, 1930); J. T. Dunlop, 'Productivity and the Wage Structure', in *Income, Employment and Public Policy* (New York, 1948), p. 357; J. Garbarino, 'A Theory of Inter-industry Wage Structure Variation', *Quarterly Journal of Economics* (May 1950), pp. 282-305; and F. Meyers and R. L. Boulby, 'The Inter-industry Wage Structure and Productivity', *Industrial and Labor Relations Review* (October 1953), pp. 92-102.

[4]O.E.C.D., *Wages and Labour Mobility* (Paris, 1965); W. S. Woytinsky and associates, *Employment and Wages in the United States* (New York, 1953), pp. 507-8; P. Hady and Arnold N. Tolles, 'British and American Changes in Inter-industry Wage Structure Under Full Employment', *Review of Economics and Statistics* (November 1957); Lloyd Ulman, 'Labor Mobility and the Industrial Wage Structure in the Post-war United States', *Quarterly Journal of Economics* (February 1965).

[5]S. H. Slichter, 'Notes on the Structure of Wages', *Review of Economics and Statistics* (February 1950).

[6]There is a problem of availability of data for a study of the long-run wage structure. Before 1945, only annual-earnings data are available. After 1960, annual-earnings data are not comparable with pre-1960 annual data because of a change in the definition of 'business establishment' used by the D.B.S. Annual earnings were derived by dividing

TABLE 64

Correlation of Structure of Annual Earnings in Eighty-two Manufacturing Industries, Selected Years, 1922-60

Years compared with 1922	Spearman coefficient of rank correlation	Selected comparisons	Spearman coefficient of rank correlation
1923	.8765		
1927	.8313		
1933	.7381	1933-9	.8644
1939	.7545	1939-46	.9095
1944	.7563	1939-49	.8684
1946	.7547	1949-56	.9500
1949	.6408	1956-60	.9596
1953	.6497		
1956	.6793		
1960	.6522		

Note: It was not possible to extend the study beyond 1960 because of a change in industrial classification and consequent incomparability of the data used. However, the post-1960 period is studied separately. See page 300 onwards.

Source: D.B.S., *The Manufacturing Industries of Canada*, annual publications (Ottawa, 1923-60).

It appears that the rank correlation coefficient was .65 between 1960 and 1922. The same coefficient was as high as .87 between 1923 and 1922. The highest coefficient was for 1960 compared with 1956, implying very little change in the ranking of industries during this period. Although there are limitations in the data used (for example, entry or exit of industries and radical transformations in industry structures were left out of the picture), and there has been no pronounced and steady trend in the coefficients, by and large one conclusion may be drawn from the ranking of industries by earnings in Canada: the longer the period observed, the smaller is the rank correlation coefficient. This signifies that the ranking pattern in Canada is seen to be *stable in the short run and pliable in the long run.*

---

the total yearly wage-bill by the number of wage-earners, and reflect not only changes in wage-rates but also changes in overtime, changes in the length of the work week, part-time employment, work-stoppages, labour turnover, etc. Annual earnings and average hourly earnings yielded very high coefficients of rank correlation (.75 for 1946 and .89 for 1956), suggesting that annual earnings is an acceptable index for long-term studies. These correlations were made from American data by D. E. Cullen, 'The Inter-industry Wage Structure, 1899-1950', *American Economic Review* (June 1956), pp. 355-7. Our long-term analysis for Canada follows Cullen's study for the U.S.A.

An international comparison of industrial wage structures[7] points out that countries may be broadly classified into three groups according to the stability of industry ranking: (a) short-run as well as long-run stability; examples: the United States, France, West Germany; (b) short-run stability with tendency toward pliability in the long run; examples: Sweden, the United Kingdom, Japan; and (c) short-run as well as long-run pliability; examples: most underdeveloped countries. In the light of our analysis (Table 64), Canada belongs to the second group with short-run stability and tendency toward pliability in the long run.

Dispersion: Several hypotheses, not necessarily consistent either with each other or with available empirical information, have been made relating to the behaviour of interindustry wage dispersion. For example, Reynolds and Taft observe that 'inter-industry wage dispersion tends to reach a maximum sometime during the early stages of industrialization and to diminish gradually after that point.'[8] This implies a widening tendency for wage dispersion only in the early stages of industrialization. But a secular contractionist trend is expected in the interindustry wage structure of industrially advanced countries. The explanation probably lies in the different rates of change in skill differentials and in product market differentials in early and later stages of industrialization. None the less, some hypotheses contradict the long-run contractionist tendency of wage dispersion observed by Reynolds and Taft.[9] Much of the contradiction of these views can be attributed to differences in the time, place, and variables used in the different analyses. A. M. Ross distinguishes between absolute and relative wage differentials and postulates a relationship between wage level and wage structure. This relationship, sometimes called Ross's 'law of wage differentials', states that in the long run, with secular rise in wages, percentage differentials narrow and absolute differentials widen.[10] But there is another opinion that no systematic relationship exists between absolute differentials and wage levels.[11]

Table 65 presents measures of the relative dispersion of the inter-

[7]T. S. Papola and V. P. Bharadwaj, 'Dynamics of Industrial Wage Structure: An Inter-Country Analysis', *Economic Journal* (March 1970).

[8]L. G. Reynolds and C. H. Taft, *The Evolution of Wage Structure* (New Haven, 1956), p. 356.

[9]O.E.C.D., *op. cit.*; Ulman, *op. cit.*; Cullen, *op. cit.*

[10]A. M. Ross, *Trade Union Wage Policy* (Berkeley, 1948), pp. 113-33.

[11]Doris M. Eisemann, 'Inter-industry Wage Changes 1938-1947', *Review of Economics and Statistics* (November 1956); A. M. Ross and W. Goldner, 'Forces Affecting the Inter-industry Wage Structure', *Quarterly Journal of Economics* (May 1950).

TABLE 65

Dispersion of Structure of Annual Earnings, Selected Years, 88 Industries, 1922-60

Year	Coefficient of dispersion*
1922	.308
1923	.321
1929	.379
1933	.312
1939	.330
1944	.370
1946	.327
1949	.303
1956	.361
1960	.384

*Inter-quartile range divided by median.

Note: It was not possible to extend the study beyond 1960 because of a change in industrial classification and consequent incomparability of the data used. However, the post-1960 period is studied separately. See page 300 onwards.

Source: D.B.S., *The Manufacturing Industries of Canada*, annual publications (Ottawa, 1923-65).

industry structure of annual earnings[12] of eighty-eight manufacturing industries in Canada for selected years since 1922. Obviously no secular trend is discernible in the coefficient of dispersion of earnings. In contrast with this lack of any long-run trend, the coefficient seems to display a rather noticeable cyclical behaviour. It rose from .308 in the early twenties, a period of depression in Canada, to .379 in 1929, and then slumped to .312 in 1933 – the trough of the Great Depression. From there the coefficient climbed steadily through the Second World War boom years to a high of .370 in 1944. In the post-war years, it sank to a 1949 figure of .303. From 1949 onwards, the story is one of steady rise in earnings dispersion. Broadly speaking, the movement of wage dispersion seems to be positively associated with general business activity in Canada, rather than tending to contract or widen over the long period. Thus the dispersion in the interindustry earnings structure of Canada, as measured in our coefficients, does not support the hypothesis of a contractionist trend.

[12]Annual earnings, of course, are not very accurate measures of the rates of pay because of the inclusion of overtime, fringe benefits, etc., but for long-range studies, they are the best material we have.

Canada is not an exception in this matter. Several other studies have found similar results for a number of countries. A study of the dynamics of the industrial wage structure of seventeen countries including the United States, the United Kingdom, France, Sweden, West Germany, and Japan concludes that, 'in the industrialized countries cyclical rather than secular movements seem to characterize the wage structure.'[13] A study by O.E.C.D. of the United States and nine West European countries shows that differentials have more often widened or stayed constant than narrowed.[14] The long-term validity of the contraction-hypothesis is doubted also in a study of the United States by D.E. Cullen.[15] Our findings on Canada are consistent with these international studies, both in short-run and in long-run behaviour. Cullen's study for the United States, for example, reveals a narrower tendency toward the end of the forties; and all the free-market economies show a widening trend from the late forties to the sixties, observations in conformity with the Canadian situation depicted in Table 65.

In trying to understand the positive association between movements in the coefficients of dispersion and business conditions of the country, we should note that during booms wages in the upper end of the spectrum shift upwards at a higher rate than those at the lower end, because of the smaller elasticity of labour supply at higher than at lower levels. On the other hand, during depressions it is the wages at the upper end that undergo decline at a higher rate. The latter phenomenon is consistent with the widely held view of downward rigidity of wages, especially at lower wage levels. The increase in wage dispersion in Canada during the twenties was largely a consequence of a pulling-up of the high-wage industries. The most expanding manufacturing industries were the high-wage industries during these years, while the wage levels of the poorer industries were very sticky. The major growth industries were pulp and paper, transportation equipment, automobiles, non-metàllic mineral products, and chemical products.[16] Expansion in these industries evidently exerted some upward pressure on their respective wage levels, but this was not transmitted to the rest of the manufacturing sector. Perhaps part of the reason lies in the fact that unions had not then made many in-

[13]Papola and Bharadwaj, *op. cit.*, p. 75.
[14]O.E.C.D., *op. cit.*, p. 25.
[15]Cullen, *op. cit.*
[16]O. J. Firestone, *Canada's Economic Development 1867-1953* (London, 1958), p. 211.

roads in these industries. One should be extremely cautious, however, in drawing definite conclusions without a fuller analysis than that undertaken here.

An explanation of the narrowing of interindustry wage gaps during the thirties that may have some relevance to Canada has been provided by Professor Cullen, whose analysis of American data yielded similar results: 'A plausible hypothesis might be adduced from the pronounced tendency for producers-goods industries to be in the high-wage category, and for consumers-goods industries to be low-wage. Accordingly, average annual earnings in the high-wage industries could be expected to suffer a relatively larger drop during a severe depression than earnings in the low-wage industries, thereby compressing the structure.'[17] In this respect, it is significant to note that the primary textile group of Canadian industries (most of them in the low-wage category) were among the few industries that, during the thirties, 'expanded their capacity and improved their production processes notably.'[18]

The war greatly stimulated the high-wage, heavy-industry sector of the economy. Moreover, for the first time, many of these high-wage industries were the object of effective, militant organizing drives by new industrial unions. These factors account for some of the observed war-time widening of the wage differential; but for this, as for each of the changes mentioned above, a full explanation would require a detailed examination of the development of specific industries.[19]

Ross's theory, mentioned earlier, suggests that with a secular rise in wage level the relative dispersion of interindustry wage rates shows a narrowing tendency. In Canada, the index number of average wage rate for manufacturing industries rose from 43.8 in 1921 to 175.0 in 1960 (1949=100).[20] But the coefficient of dispersion of industrial wages, as we have seen, has not shown any tendency to contract over the long run. It can thus be said that the hypothesis of an inverse long-run relation between wage level and relative dispersion of industrial wage-rates is not supported by the record of the manufacturing in-

---

[17]Cullen, *op. cit.*, p. 363. There may have been social factors at work as well. The prevailing climate of opinion in the thirties probably opposed forcing the wages of the poorly paid to their 'true' market level. In this regard, compare the widening of the differential during the 1921-2 depression when the cultural and social environment was different. Cf. M. Reder, 'The Theory of Occupational Wage Differentials', *American Economic Review* (December 1955), pp. 842-5.

[18]Firestone, *op. cit.*, p. 212.

[19]Cf. Reynolds and Taft, *op. cit.*, p. 302.

[20]M. C. Urquhart (ed.), *Historical Statistics of Canada* (Toronto, 1965), p. 84.

dustries of Canada. Here again, Canada is not alone; among other countries experiencing rising wage levels without any corresponding reduction in relative wage differential among industries the most notable are the United States, Sweden, the United Kingdom, and France.[21] A possible rationalization in these cases also is that rising wage levels have been accompanied by higher relative increases in wage-rates at the upper end than at the lower end of the range of industrial wages. In other words, high-wage industries have enjoyed higher relative wage gains than low-wage industries, although the level of wages has gone up for all.

The post-war changes in the annual earnings structure of inter-industry wages in Canada conform to the pattern exhibited by hourly earnings. Since hourly earnings are preferable for our purposes (the effects of changes in the work week, part-time work, and work-stoppages of one kind or another being eliminated), and since hourly earnings statistics are available as of 1945, the analysis of post-war developments will be conducted in terms of hourly instead of annual earnings.

Interindustry Structure of Hourly Earnings: 1945-69

The greater availability of data in Canada for the years following the Second World War permits a more detailed examination of the changing structure of interindustry earnings and enables us to test the degree of association between the changes in wage relationships and certain other economic variables.[22]

From 1945 to 1949 the interindustry wage structure (measured in terms of average hourly earnings) narrowed. Also, for this short period, the percentage increases in hourly earnings were negatively correlated with the 1945 earnings levels of the industries,[23] i.e. the higher the initial wage level, the smaller the relative percentage rise in earn-

[21]Papola and Bharadwaj, *op. cit.*, p. 78.

[22]For similar international studies, cf. E. H. Phelps Brown and M. H. Browne, 'Earnings in Industries of the United Kingdom, 1948-1959', *The Economic Journal* (September 1962); W. E. G. Salter, *Productivity and Technical Change* (Cambridge, 1960); Dunlop, *op. cit.*; Garbarino, *op. cit.*; Eisemann, *op. cit.*; Ross and Goldner, *op. cit.*; R. Perlman, 'Value Productivity and the Inter-industry Wage Structure', *Industrial and Labor Relations Review* (October 1956); Reynolds and Taft, *op. cit.*, p. 391.

[23]A product-moment correlation coefficient $r = -.59$ (significant at the 5% level) was found: Sylvia Ostry, 'Inter-industry Earnings Differentials in Canada, 1945-56', *Industrial and Labor Relations Review* (April 1959), p. 337.

ings. The reason for this is evident from Table 66. Here it may be seen that the absolute (cents-per-hour) gains over this period were fairly uniform for the thirty-four industries in the sample. Thus, the average increase was 31.2 cents: twenty of the thirty-four industries showed a deviation of less than five cents and two showed a deviation of just over ten cents. Application of more or less uniform cents-per-hour gains to a hierarchy of industries will, of course, result in a contraction of the relative earnings gaps among those industries.

The pattern of change was different after 1949, when the narrowing of the earlier years ceased and, indeed, the interindustry structure slightly widened.[24] The higher-wage industries tended to enjoy both greater absolute and greater percentage gains than did the lower-wage industries. As Table 66 shows, between 1949 and 1963 coal-mining wages increased by only 45 per cent, while wages for tobacco processing increased by 129 per cent. Similarly, in the 1963 to 1969 period, coal-mining wages increased by 38 per cent, while in the meat-products industry the rise was 40 per cent and in the tobacco industry 50 per cent.

What accounted for these movements of interindustry wage relationships? In answer to this question, we will now discuss the more important forces that shaped the structure of industrial earnings in Canada in recent years.

The method adopted in the discussion is to consider one explanatory variable at a time. Although a multi-variable analysis with all the variables together would no doubt be methodologically more powerful, the availability and nature of statistical material did not permit this.

The Effect of Changing Skill Differentials

Interindustry differences in earnings are strongly affected by skill differentials.[25] High-wage industries are generally rich in skilled workers while low-wage industries tend to be 'skill-poor'. In the short run, the skill mix of most industries is not likely to change very much. Thus, a narrowing of relative skill differentials would (*ceteris paribus*) tend to narrow the relative gap between the high- and low-wage in-

---

[24]*Ibid.*, p. 339.
[25]Clark Kerr, 'Wage Relationships – The Comparative Impact of Market and Power Forces', in *The Theory of Wage Determination*, J. T. Dunlop (ed.) (London, 1957).

TABLE 66

Changes in Average Hourly Earnings, 1945-69

Industry	Increase 1945-9 (cents) (per cent)		Increase 1949-63 (cents) (per cent)		Increase 1963-9 (cents) (per cent)	
Coal-mining	35	37	58	45	70	38
Shipbuilding, etc.	22	26	116	107	102	46
Aircraft and parts	21	24	118	111	103	46
Metal-mining	31	36	115	99	103	44
Petroleum and coal products*	39	46	152	124	103	37
Primary iron & steel	37	45	149	126	79	30
Smelting & refining	39	50	132	113	92	37
Printing, publishing*	37	49	127	112	87	32
Agricultural implements	40	53	121	105	93	39
Misc. machinery manufacturing	32	44	108	104	94	44
Rubber products	33	45	94	90	89	45
Pulp & paper mills	42	58	134	118	107	43
Electrical appliances*	39	55	86	79	79	39
Chemical products*	30	44	119	120	78	36
Meat products, slaughtering	38	56	93	88	85	40
Distilled & malt liquor	37	54	122	117	n.a.	n.a.
Sheet-metal products	34	51	115	114	n.a.	n.a.
Non-metallic mining*	31	47	125	134	86	39
Grain mill products	32	50	93	99	85	45
Saw & planing mills	33	54	100	105	n.a.	n.a.
Glass & glass products	31	51	109	119	88	43
Furniture	28	49	70	81	66	43
Medical & pharm.	25	45	88	107	71	42
Other paper products	29	53	96	114	n.a.	n.a.
Bread & bakeries	25	46	85	109	n.a.	n.a.
Clothing*	23	44	51	67	58	45
Leather products*	23	44	57	76	57	43
Tobacco products*	34	67	111	129	109	50
Canned & preserved fruits, etc.	24	47	60	81	69	52
Boots & shoes	22	45	56	78	55	43
Synthetic textiles	35	71	72	85	79	50
Woollen yarn & cloth	30	61	57	72	66	49
Cotton yarn & cloth	37	75	65	76	66	44
Knit goods	26	56	44	59	51	43

*Industrial groups.

Source: D.B.S., *Review of Man-Hours and Hourly Earnings.* For 1969,
   D.B.S., *Man-Hours and Hourly Earnings*, January-December, 1969.

dustries and the obverse would also be true. In Canada, most occupational wage differentials narrowed markedly during and after the war, but by the late forties and early fifties the narrowing process appeared to have stopped, most skill differentials were stabilized, and some even widened slightly (see Chapter X). The movement of interindustry differentials, narrowing, then widening, is very similar to changes in occupational differentials, and the two are undoubtedly linked.[26] Skill differential thus may be a significant variable in the determination of interindustry wage differentials.

While the behaviour of skill differentials is important, it will not provide the whole explanation for the short-run changes of interindustry earnings. The Canadian economy expanded rapidly in the years between 1945 and the latter half of the fifties, and one would expect that relative industry wages were affected by the nature of the economic expansion. In the early post-war years, low- or medium-wage industries producing non-durable consumer goods (e.g., wool, hosiery and knitted goods, synthetic textiles, tobacco, meat, distilled and malt liquors) found the change-over to civilian production relatively easy and also found a back-log of civilian demand, which had been restricted during the war. In order to maintain, or, as in most cases, to expand their labour force in a tight market, employers in these industries were compelled to pay increases similar to those offered by the heavy, high-wage industries, whose problems of adjustment to a civilian economy were more difficult; and they were able to do so. The defence boom in 1951 and 1952 led to increasing demand for strategic raw materials and an increase in real investment in plant and equipment. Expansion was interrupted in 1953 and 1954 but resumed with great vigour in 1955 and 1956, and after another interruption in the late 1950s and early 1960s continued until nearly the end of the decade of the sixties. High-wage industries, such as petroleum and coal products, primary iron and steel, non-ferrous metals, aircraft, sheet-metal products, and electrical apparatus, benefited relatively more from the expansion in this period than did most of the lower-wage, non-durable consumer-goods industries. We can, to some extent, examine the effect of economic expansion on wages by looking at the relationship between earnings increases and changes in employment in Canada during the period.

[26]See Ostry, *op. cit.*, and C. G. Williams, 'Changes in the Skill Mix and their Effect on the Railroad Industry's Wage Level', *Industrial and Labor Relations Review* (October 1966).

Employment

In the short run, under full-employment conditions, the supply of labour to most industries is probably relatively inelastic. Thus, an expanding industry would have to bid for workers; and if wages are responsive to changes in the demand for labour, one would expect to find some association between changes in employment (as a crude measure of labour demand) and changes in wages. So, in the absence of considerable excess supply, a positive association is normally expected between employment changes and wage changes. This association, although not very strong, appears to have existed in the Canadian economy during the post-war period.[27] In general, the larger absolute and percentage increases in earnings went to the fastest-growing industries, suggesting that the Canadian labour market is moderately flexible. On the other hand, since the degree of association between wage changes and employment was not found to be very high, other factors must have been working to offset partly the expected correlation. However, similar situations exist in other countries. For example, no significant short-run or long-run correlation has been established between wage and employment changes in the United States during 1899-1953.[28] The United Kingdom is also characterized by a very weak relationship between wages and employment.[29]

Such results suggest that the Canadian labour market is probably somewhat more flexible than is the case in many other countries. Of course, no market is completely flexible, and wage changes in the short run are influenced by many forces other than changes in the demand for labour. The remainder of this chapter will be devoted to examining the evidence of such forces in the Canadian labour market.

Output per man-hour

One might expect to find an association between changes in average

---

[27]The partial correlation coefficients were .45 for employment and absolute wage changes and .46 for employment and percentage changes in earnings for 1945-9. For 1949-56, the coefficients are .42 and .53 respectively. See Ostry, *op. cit.*, p. 341. Stephen G. Peitchinis found a rank correlation coefficient of .27 between percentage change in average wages and percentage change in employment; 'The Canadian Industrial Wage Structure', mimeo., p. 20.

[28]Melvin Reder, 'Wage Differentials: Theory and Measurement', *Aspects of Labor Economics* (Princeton, 1962), p. 278.

[29]Phelps Brown and Browne, *op. cit.*

physical productivity and wages, particularly if the industries that experience rapid increases in average output per man-hour are also those expanding most rapidly.[30] If ability to pay is an independent factor in determining wages, and if it is assumed that there is a link between improvements in average productivity and profits, there should be some association between productivity and wages. Table 67 presents estimates of the percentage increases in average hourly earnings and in average output per man-hour in Canada from 1949 to 1969 for thirty industries.[31] The table shows that little relationship exists between changes in average output and average hourly earnings. The coefficient of correlation is 0.01, which is statistically insignificant. Although some caution is warranted in this interpretation because the productivity data are not free of errors, it does seem that ability to pay was not a factor of importance in shaping wage patterns during this period.[32] Along the same lines, U.S. and British studies also show that the correlation coefficient between output per man-hour and average hourly earnings is not statistically significant.[33] Other U.S. and British studies have tested a related hypothesis for productivity changes – that is, the relationship between productivity changes and changes in product prices.[34] When output per worker increases, the effect is either an increase in factor payments or a decline in product prices, or both. The above studies found price adjustment to be inversely related to output, which explains at least partly why wages were not significantly related to output per worker.

[30]Wages and productivity may be directly linked through payment-by-results systems and also by possible skill up-grading with rising efficiency of production. Cf. Garbarino, *op. cit.*, pp. 298-300. For further discussion, cf. H. M. Levinson, 'Post-war Movement in Prices and Wages in Manufacturing Industries', Study Paper No. 21, Joint Economic Committee, Congress of the United States (Washington, 1960).

[31]For a number of industries, the index of industrial production immediately following the war was strongly affected by the conditions of post-war adjustment. Consequently, 1949 was chosen as the first relatively 'normal' post-war year.

[32]One very important drawback in using the productivity statistics is that the published data on average hourly earnings are conceptually out of line with the calculated output per man-hour indices. The former include hourly rated employees only; the latter include a computation of man-hour input on the basis of total employment weighted by average hours of the hourly rated.

[33]M. Reder finds a coefficient of + .24 between output per man-hour and average hourly earnings, *op. cit.* W. E. G. Salter found a coefficient of + .22 from American data and only + .09 for similar English data, *op. cit.*, pp. 114-15, 166.

[34]Kendrick found a significant correlation of – .55 between unit prices of output and factor productivity, *Productivity Trend in the United States*, National Bureau of Economic Research (1961), p. 201. Salter found 77 per cent of changes in relative prices for selected industries in the United Kingdom and 58 per cent of wholesale prices attributable to differential changes in output per worker, *op. cit.*

TABLE 67

Changes in Average Hourly Earnings and Output per Man-Hour, 1961-9

	Increase, 1961-9	
	Average hourly earnings	*Output/ man-hour*
Industry	*(per cent)*	*(per cent)*
Products of petroleum and coal	47	37
Primary iron and steel	36	33
Tobacco and tobacco products	78	33
Chemical products	46	44
Pulp and paper	52	31
Aircraft	54	17
Metal mining	52	35
Printing, publishing, etc.	61	24
Non-metallic mineral products	50	85
Machinery	56	43
Grain mill products	54	32
Meat products	57	33
Rubber products	54	24
Motor vehicles	45	103
Electrical apparatus and supplies	51	42
Synthetic textiles and silks	63	97
Furniture	50	23
Leather products	52	13
Cotton yarn & broad woven goods	54	25
Clothing	58	15
Knit goods	54	21
Coal-mining	45	24

Note: Output/man-hour percentages – product of an index of average hours worked and an index of employment, divided into an index of industrial production: result expressed as a percentage change.

Sources: Earnings data from D.B.S., *Review of Man-Hours and Hourly Earnings, 1945-63*, and *Review of Man-hours and Hourly Earnings, 1966-8*, and *Man-Hours and Hourly Earnings, 1969*; index of employment from D.B.S., *Employment and Average Weekly Wages and Salaries, 1969*; index of industrial production from D.B.S., *Canadian Statistical Review*, January 1971.

Market Structure

It may be argued[35] that less competitive industries, as opposed to more competitive ones, are able to prevent cost reductions from being translated into price reductions.[36] Under strongly competitive conditions the benefits of rising productivity would largely accrue to the consumer in the form of lower prices, and, thus, are divided between the *entrepreneur* and the workers. The employer in a concentrated industry is either forced to share his gains with the workers because of union pressure or does so as a matter of policy. In the latter case he may want to establish or maintain a 'high-wage' reputation for reasons of prestige and good industrial relations, or because he believes such a reputation allows selection of a high-quality work force and an expansion of employment at short notice.[37] In other words, the argument is that in industries dominated by relatively few large firms – concentrated industries – employers can afford to grant above-average wage increases and generally do so. Another argument contends that, because of market and technological conditions, the demand curve for labour in such industries may be highly inelastic over a substantial range, which would make an employer less resistant to high-wage demands.

In Table 68 an attempt has been made to examine the relationship between the levels of hourly earnings and degrees of concentration in nineteen industries in Canada. The industries are ranked in descending order of hourly earnings and degree of concentration. The degree of concentration used has been measured by the number of establishments producing 80 per cent of the total value of shipments from the industry.[38] It appears that market structure, measured by the concentration index, is not highly correlated with the interindustry

[35]Many sources exist in this area. Recent papers include: Harold Levinson, 'Unionism, Concentration, and Wage Changes: Toward a Unified Theory', *Industrial and Labor Relations Review* (January 1967), pp. 198-205; Leonard Weiss, 'Concentration and Labor Earnings', *American Economic Review* (March 1966), pp. 96-117; David Schwartzman, 'Monopoly and Wages', *Canadian Journal of Economics and Political Science* (August 1960).

[36]Price reductions under oligopolistic market conditions are potentially disruptive and the firm will hesitate to initiate them, never being sure just how such action will be interpreted by its competitors.

[37]Cf. Alfred Kuhn, 'Market Structure and Wage-push Inflation', *Industrial and Labor Relations Review* (January 1959).

[38]Economic Council of Canada, *Interim Report on Competition Policy* (Ottawa, July 1969), Appendix III.

TABLE 68

*Relationship Between Average Hourly Earnings
and Degree of Concentration,* Selected Industries*

Industry	Rank in average hourly earnings	Rank in degree of concentration
Printing and publishing	1	12
Iron and steel mills	2	1
Pulp and paper mills	3	9
Bakeries	4	18
Synthetic textile mills	5	7
Industrial chemicals	6	10
Smelting and refining	7	4
Cotton yarn and cloth mills	8	6
Agricultural implements	9	5
Aircraft and parts manufactures	10	3
Shipbuilding and repair	11	1
Miscellaneous machinery and equipment manufactures	12	16
Slaughtering and meat-packing	13	8
Sawmills and planing-mills	14	19
Other paper converters	15	11
Household furniture	16	17
Fruit and vegetable canners and preservers	17	14
Shoe factories	18	15
Other knitting mills	19	12

*Degree of concentration has been measured by the number of establishments producing 80 per cent of the values of shipments of the industries. As this number of establishments increases, the degree of concentration is presumed to decrease. This measure has been adapted from *Interim Report on Competition Policy*, Economic Council of Canada (July 1969), Appendix III.
Note: The data refer to 1966.

Source: For average hourly earnings, D.B.S., *Review of Man-Hours and Hourly Earnings, 1966-8* (November 1969), Table 5; for degree of concentration, D.B.S., *Manufacturing Industries of Canada*, Section H (January 1971), Table 11.

structure of earnings in Canada. The rank correlation coefficient between the two is only 0.43, signifying a weak relationship, if any. However, the index of concentration has limitations, and there may be other factors offsetting the effects of concentration. To determine the effects of concentration alone, these factors should be held constant. A U.S. study published in 1969 showed that the effect of concentration on wages is negligible when the degree of unionism is held constant.[39] Without a more comprehensive analysis, no firm conclusions can be drawn about Canada.

It should be noted that concentration occurs on both sides of the labour market – employers and employees. The degrees of concentration of these two forces are interrelated. Therefore, much of the discussion of this section and the section on unions is closely connected. Separating the effects of industry structure, Leonard Weiss found that for the U.S.: (a) workers in highly concentrated industries receive higher wages; (b) union power or the threat of unionism is a reason for higher wages; and (c) workers of superior quality are attracted to concentrated industries.[40] There are many reasons why concentration allows easier organization of labour unions. Workers in large establishments have few personal contacts with management. An industry with fewer firms is much easier to organize. Barriers to entry resulting from the need for large capital outlays to achieve an economically competitive size of firm prohibit new, unorganized firms from entering the industry, so that ground is seldom lost in concentrated industries once they are initially organized. The entry-exit turnover in industries with a large number of firms means that unions must continuously organize in order to retain their position. Thus, market structure and concentration may be expected to affect interindustry wage changes through both employers and employees.

Relative Labour Cost

Professor Dunlop has suggested that wages tend to increase more when labour costs are a small percentage of total costs, *ceteris paribus*.[41] The reasoning behind this assertion is that employers are more likely to resist higher-wage demands vigorously in labour-intensive than in capital-intensive industries, because the effect of any wage increase on total costs will be relatively greater. The Canadian record suggests that during 1945-65 there was some negative

[39]Stanley H. Masters, 'Wages and Plant Size: An Inter-industry Analysis', *Review of Economics and Statistics* (August 1969), pp. 341-5.

[40]Weiss, *op. cit.* A similar finding was made by Adrian Throop, 'Sources of Inflationary Bias in the American Economy', Stanford University, Ph. D. dissertation, 1967, Chapter 5.

[41]Dunlop, *op. cit.*

association between the proportion of labour cost of an industry and the percentage change in hourly earnings, although the degree of association was weak.[42] To a limited degree, then, the more labour-intensive the industry is, the lower the proportionate increase in wages gained by its workers will be.

The Impact of Unionism

The impact of unions on wage structure has been a subject of heated debate in recent years,[43] and for this reason a brief digression to this subject is warranted. A substantial body of academic opinion asserts that unionism has had little or no effect on wages;[44] indeed, some have argued that at certain times the effect has been negative, lowering rather than raising wages in some industries from their natural market level.[45] The view that unions cannot raise wages runs counter to common-sense appraisals. If unions cannot raise wages, then why all the fuss? Why the hard bargaining, the bitter strikes, the legislation that seeks to control union action? The suggestion that in this major area of union activities the bargaining process is nothing more than a ritual, expensive and time-consuming, in which the parties participate at regular intervals to little or no effect is difficult to believe. One would have thought that, if this were so, all the participants in the ritual – the employers, the unions, the government – would have recognized the fact by now. Barnum insisted that there is a sucker born every minute, but some labour economists would seem to suggest that this is far too modest an estimate! It is true, nevertheless, that satisfactory evidence of the union impact on wages is extraordinarily difficult to document. There are a number of reasons for this, and they are worth brief mention.

The statistical difficulties of estimating the effect of unionism on

---

[42]Peitchinis, *op. cit.*

[43]For a review of these studies see H. Gregg Lewis, *Unionism and Relative Wages in the United States* (Chicago, 1963). Lewis's findings were affirmative. For a critical review of this volume, see Melvin W. Reder, 'Unions and Wages: the Problem of Measurement', *Journal of Political Economy* (April 1965), pp. 188-96; Adrian W. Throop, 'The Union – Non-union Wage Differential and Cost-Push Inflations', *American Economic Review* (March 1968), pp. 79-99; Robert Ozanne, 'Impact of Unions on Wage Levels and Income Distribution', *Quarterly Journal of Economics* (May 1959).

[44]Ozanne, *op. cit.*, pp. 177-8.

[45]See especially, Albert Rees, 'Post-war Wage Determination in the Basic Steel Industry', *American Economic Review* (June 1951); Stephen P. Sobotka, 'Union Influence on Wages: the Construction Industry', *Journal of Political Economy* (April 1953); Milton Friedman, 'Some Comments on the Significance of Labor Unions for Economic Policy', *The Impact of the Union*, David McCord Wright (ed.) (New York, 1951).

interindustry or other aspects of wage structure are formidable, not only because there is really no adequate measure of union strength, but also because there is no way of distinguishing, even with the best quantitative measure, important qualitative differences among unions. Differences in the kinds[46] of union may well be more important in determining their effectiveness than differences in the extent of organization; but union strength is usually measured in terms of the proportion of workers in a given work force who are covered by collective agreement.

Then, too, how does one calculate the effect of unions on non-union firms? It is well known that an employer may grant wage increases or improvements in working conditions as a means of forestalling organization. Such wage increases are clearly an indirect consequence of unionism, but how is one to estimate such indirect effects? How, in other words, distinguish the union from the non-union sector? The influence of unionism, especially in the past two or three decades, has been pervasive, in that it has affected to some degree the total economic, political, and social environment. To isolate the specific impact of unionism on an industry or an establishment or a community is a difficult task. One can conceive of the possibility of getting around the problem by comparing wage behaviour during a non-union span of time and during a union span of time. But for this method to be effective, all other things must be equal through time – and, alas, they never are. Too many other 'things' are always happening in a dynamic economy for one to feel sure that it is really the effect of unionism that accounts for all or any observed differences in wage behaviour in two different periods.

Other difficulties in estimating the impact of unionism arise from the nature of the available wage statistics. Sometimes a union is able to organize only a few of the larger firms in an industry and may secure above-market increases in earnings in these firms. But wage data are most commonly reported in terms of industry averages, and the effects of unionism on a few firms may be swamped in the average figure by the presence of many small, lower-wage, unorganized establishments. It may be that what is needed in order to track down union impact is much finer and more detailed wage statistics than those presently published.[47]

[46]Unions vary widely in effectiveness because of internal differences in the organization (personnel, structure, etc.) or differences in the environment in which they operate. Moreover, it would be quite wrong to assume that all unions pursue the same goals or that a given union strives for the same goal at all times.

[47]This is the view of George Saunders, 'Union and Non-Union Wages in the Ontario Iron and Steel Products Industries, 1946-54', University Microfilms, Inc. (Ann Arbor, Michigan, 1959).

These remarks on the difficulties in the way of an empirical investigation of the impact of unionism on wage structure should not be interpreted as a counsel of despair, however. They are presented only to impress upon the reader that, at the present time, techniques of analysis and available statistics are probably too crude to enable the researcher to obtain unequivocal results in relating unionism to the determination of wages or wage structure. For the moment the verdict one way or another can only be the Scottish 'not proven'. A brief discussion of the Canadian evidence on this question is presented below, and is intended to be suggestive rather than conclusive.

From 1934 to 1939, the few unionized industries in Canada – coal, construction, and railways – experienced wage increases of 7 per cent, 10 per cent, and 17 per cent, respectively.[48] When compared with the 4 per cent increase in the wholly unorganized personal-service sector, these data suggest that union workers secured some advantage over the unorganized. But side by side with this, in manufacturing that was almost completely unorganized, wage-rates increased by slightly more than 17 per cent. In the post-war period, when employment in the (largely unorganized) service sector was expanding much more rapidly than in manufacturing as a whole, the increase in service wages did not outpace that in manufacturing wages. Quite the contrary: between 1946 and 1959 the wage-rate index for services rose by almost 92 per cent, but that for manufacturing rose by over 129 per cent. It would thus appear that the more highly organized sector secured gains over and above those dictated by the operation of market forces.

A search for an expected positive correlation between the degree of unionization and increase in average hourly earnings in industries in Canada during the sixties does not yield much fruit. Table 69 presents the absolute and percentage increases in average hourly earnings in sixteen industries during 1961-7 and the extent of union influence in these industries. As a measure of the latter, we use the percentage of employees covered by collective agreements in the selected industries. The simple correlation coefficients turn out to be insignificant, implying that increases in earnings in Canadian industries during the sixties did not show the influence of unionization to any appreciable extent.

Similar conclusions regarding the impact of unionization on wage-rate and wage structure are drawn in other Canadian studies. Reuber, for example, finds little evidence of a significant relationship between

<hr>

[48]These figures refer to changes in the relevant wage-rate indices published in the Department of Labour's *Wage Rates and Hours of Labour*.

TABLE 69

Increases in Average Hourly Earnings 1961-7, and Union Organization

Industry	Increase in average hourly earnings		Percentage of employees covered by collective agreements
	(cents)	(per cent)	(per cent)
Motor vehicles	64	28.3	99
Coal-mining	36	20.3	98
Metal smelting and refining	65	27.2	97
Pulp and paper	76	32.3	96
Cotton yarn and cloth	51	36.4	91
Aircraft	66	31.3	91
Synthetic textiles	56	38.6	85
Primary iron and steel	56	22.0	80
Metal-mining	77	34.8	75
Leather products	42	34.1	75
Rubber products	58	30.9	73
Grain-mill products	53	29.8	60
Products of petroleum and coal	81	31.5	60
Furniture	45	30.8	47
Knitting-mills	37	33.6	25
Hotels and restaurants	35	33.7	19

Source: D.B.S., *Review of Man-Hours and Hourly Earnings, 1957-67*; and Economics and Research Branch, Canada, Department of Labour, *Working Conditions in Canadian Industry, 1967.*

strikes and the rate of change in wages negotiated under collective agreements. For the 1961-6 period he found the degree of unionization across industries not significantly correlated with the rate of change in wages.[49] He concluded that whatever control labour unions have over the supply of labour for any industry is inversely related to the level of unemployment in the economy.[50] Other studies of Canadian

[49]G. L. Reuber, *Wage Determination in Canadian Manufacturing Industries,* Study No. 19, Task Force on Labour Relations, Privy Council Office (Ottawa, 1969), p. 72.
[50]G. L. Reuber, 'Wage Adjustment in Canadian Industry, 1953-66', *Review of Economic Studies* (October 1970).

wage determination report findings consistent with Reuber's.[51] These studies do not address the question of the unions' effect on wage structure, but logically one would consider the variables that cause aggregate wage changes to be the same as those that affect wage structure.

The burden of all this evidence is difficult to assess. On balance, it seems that even if some unions in Canada had some success in securing a wage advantage for their members, and thus, by inference, in affecting the interindustry structure, at least on the basis of present statistics, the fact could not be established. Intuition and common sense appear to support the above possibility, but conclusive 'proof' must await more extensive and more elaborate analysis of more appropriate data.

Conclusion

The interindustrial wage structure of Canada has characteristics similar to those of many other industrialized countries. The ranking of industries in respect to earnings is stable in the short run and flexible in the long run. The dispersion of earnings has moved in conformity with the cyclical movements of general economic activity rather than showing any trend to widen or contract. The wage structure, at least in the single-variable analysis done here (the scope of which is limited), is by and large consistent with expectations in its relationships with some explanatory variables, while not so consistent with others. Industries with relatively higher skill requirements are seen to pay higher wages relative to other industries. The relationship between the demand for labour (shown in levels of employment) and wage changes was found to be positive, although not very strongly so. A weak positive relationship seems to exist also between market concentration and levels of earnings. The same is true about relative labour cost and wage increases in industries. On the other hand, there has not been observed any statistical relationship between wage levels and output per man-hour or degree of unionism in industries.

---

[51]G. R. Sparks and D. A. Wilton, 'Determinants of Negotiated Wage Increases: An Empirical Analysis', mimeographed (1968).

XII

Wages in Canada:
The Geographic Structure

Before we proceed to discuss the geographical wage structure in Canada, it is necessary to consider briefly some questions relating to the problem of interregional wage structure and its measurement. First, what are the causes of interregional variations in wages? Assuming perfect mobility of labour between regions, the theory of perfect competition postulates that, in a closed economy, identical labour should tend to receive the same remuneration in identical employment, irrespective of location, provided the job settings, the circumstances surrounding the job, non-wage benefits, and similar other conditions remain the same. When these conditions vary, wages might vary in a compensating fashion. Variations in wages between regions, which persist even after correcting for all these factors, might be described as purely regional variations. The variation usually results because one or more of the assumed conditions of a competitive economy fail to hold.[1] The assumption usually questioned is that of perfect mobility of labour between regions. Often workers fail to move from a lower-paying region to one where wages are higher because they prefer certain regional characteristics in their present

[1]There is a vast amount of literature on the subject of regional wage differential. The leading ideas are covered in the following: V. R. Fuchs and R. Perlman, 'Recent Trends in Southern Wage Differentials', *Review of Economics and Statistics* (August 1960), pp. 292-300; Martin Segal, 'Regional Wage Differences in Manufacturing in the Postwar Period', *Review of Economics and Statistics* (May 1961), pp. 148-55; L. E. Gallaway, 'The North-South Wage Differential', *Review of Economics and Statistics* (August 1963), pp. 264-72; G. H. Borts, 'The Equalization of Returns and Regional Economic Growth', *American Economic Review* (June 1960), pp. 319-47; H. M. Donty, 'Wage Differentials: Forces and Counterforces', *Monthly Labor Review* (March 1968), pp. 74-81; G. W. Scully, 'Interstate Wage Differentials: A Cross Section Analysis', *American Economic Review* (December 1969), pp. 757-73.

315

location, and so regional wage disparities may persist. (See Chapter III, for a discussion of geographic mobility.) It has been suggested[2] that the failure of the assumptions of perfect competition not only retards the process toward an equilibrium position of regional wage equality, but tends to bring wage differentials over regions to a steady-state equilibrium, i.e. makes the differentials stable over time.

Another question relating to a study of regional wage structure arises from the need to control for all the variables other than those pertaining strictly to regional attributes. In practice, the large number of such non-regional variables are so interwoven with the regional characteristics that it is hard to isolate the effects of the one group from those of the other. However, several attempts have been made to standardize regional wages for these purposes, and reference will be made to them later.

The following pages present an account of the regional wage structure of Canada. After showing how the different regions would be ranked according to wage levels, and the dispersion of the wage levels over the regions, the major factors bearing on Canada's wage pattern are discussed one by one: industrial composition, employment, availability of capital, rural-urban distribution of population, age composition and participation rates of the labour force, education, and the degree of unionization of labour.

Geographic Differentials – Ranking and Dispersion

The Canadian labour market exhibits a marked and distinctive regional structure. The profile of wage levels across the country looks like an elongated 'S' lying on its side. From a high in British Columbia, average wage levels slope downward to the Prairies, rise again in Ontario, and then fall once more as the line proceeds eastward through Quebec and the Atlantic provinces.[3] Moreover, at least in

[2]L. E. Gallaway, R. K. Veddar, and G. L. Chapin, 'The Impact of Geographic Mobility on Regional Wage Differentials: A Test of the Steady-State-Equilibrium Hypothesis', *Proceedings of the Business & Economic Statistics Section,* American Statistical Association (Washington, D.C., 1970), pp. 386-94.

[3]We are dealing here, for reasons of space and simplicity of analysis, with the broad, traditionally defined, economic regions of Canada. In fact, such analysis masks a good deal of intraregional variation and there is growing evidence that a redefinition of Canadian regions is long overdue, at least in so far as economic and social analysis is concerned. This is particularly true of the Prairies, where developments in the extractive industries, especially in Alberta, have already disturbed the historical pattern of development sufficiently to make it rather misleading to speak of a 'Prairie economy'

manufacturing industries, the broad geographic wage contours of Canada have scarcely changed over the past two decades. If the regions (see Table 70) are ranked by the level of average hourly earnings in manufacturing,[4] the only change in ranking since 1939 occurred after the Second World War, when Quebec slipped temporarily to the bottom of the structure. By the early fifties the pre-war ranking was re-established, and it has been maintained since that time.

Even though the *ranking* of average wage levels by broad regions has been stable over recent decades, the extent of *dispersion* or *variation* of the geographic wage structure in Canada has changed during the same period. Table 71 presents estimates of regional wage dispersion that reveal that the coefficient of dispersion of average hourly earnings in manufacturing shrank markedly during the war, and from then grew almost steadily until the mid sixties with minor deviations, although it never caught up with the 1939 figure. The same is true of average weekly wages and salaries in a variety of other industries.

The narrowing of regional differentials between 1939 and 1946 occurred primarily because of government action. Governmental wage controls narrowed interoccupational differentials. This compression of interoccupational gaps also had the effect of reducing regional differentials. Furthermore, under National Selective Service regulations, workers were shifted into war industries, and this 'assisted mobility' probably had the dual effect of relieving shortages in expanding sectors and lessening the pressure of excess labour in depressed industries and areas. A third explanatory factor was government spending to support the war effort. Although the bulk of expenditures was concentrated in Ontario and Quebec, all the provinces benefited from the expansion in investment and production. Quebec's wages rose rapidly, narrowing the Quebec-Ontario gap, and the Maritimes (especially Nova Scotia) enjoyed a rapid growth in the level of industrial activity as employment in war industries,

---

in the sense of a more or less uniform agriculture-dominated area. Of course, the provinces themselves are by no means ideal units on which to base economic analysis, and this increases the difficulties of studying regional developments in this country. For present purposes these problems are ignored, since the aim of the section is to present only the most general outline of the regional wage structure in Canada. More intensive analysis, on a provincial or even narrower area basis, is necessary in order to fill out the picture.

[4]Hourly-earnings data for industries other than manufacturing are too scanty to permit a regional analysis in Canada. The regional ranking of average weekly wages and salaries for the industrial composite (which includes all industries with the exception of agriculture, fishing, and government service) is identical with that described above, although it was not so before the war, when Ontario was superseded by the Prairies.

TABLE 70

Average Hourly Earnings of Manufacturing, by Region, Selected Years, 1939-69

Region	Average hourly earnings											
	1939		1946		1956		1961		1967		1969	
	$	rank	$	rank	$	rank	$	rank	$	rank	$	rank
British Columbia	.52	1	.85	1	1.81	1	2.23	1	3.01	1	3.48	1
Ontario	.51	2	.73	2	1.60	2	1.93	2	2.54	2	2.91	2
Prairies	.50	3	.71	3	1.50	3	1.86	3	2.32	3	2.71	3
Quebec	.41	4	.65	4	1.37	4	1.65	4	2.20	4	2.51	4
Maritimes*	.37	5	.67	5	1.35	5	1.60	5	2.01	5	2.23	5

*Excluding Prince Edward Island.

Sources: D.B.S., *General Review of the Manufacturing Industries of Canada* (1939); D.B.S., *Review of Man-Hours and Hourly Earnings,* various issues.

munitions, shipbuilding, and aircraft assembly and repairs leaped upward. The reconversion to a peace-time economy, which was particularly hard on the Maritimes and Quebec,[5] brought with it a gradual widening in the gaps between relative regional wages in manufacturing and other industries until by the late fifties the pre-war relationships were re-established. The war-time narrowing of regional wage relativities may therefore be seen as an essentially temporary phenomenon, created by vastly expanded government activity and production for war purposes. The more typical relationships are those that currently exist and that arise from persistent underlying economic and non-economic forces. Some of these forces will be discussed in more detail in the subsequent sections.

Effect of the Industrial Composition of Employment

The average level of wages prevailing within any region reflects not only the actual level of wages, industry by industry, but also the in-

[5]Lloyd G. Reynolds and Cynthia H. Taft, *The Evolution of Wage Structure* (New Haven, 1956), p. 311.

TABLE 71

Regional Dispersion of Average Hourly Earnings in Manufacturing and Average Weekly Wages and Salaries, Industrial Composite, 1939-69

	Coefficient of dispersion*	
Year	Average hourly earnings, manufacturing	Average weekly wages and salaries, industrial composite
1939	.253	.173
1945	.079	.066
1947	.106	.088
1949	.122	.113
1951	.138	.129
1953	.152	.135
1955	.156	.135
1957	.154	.147
1959	.182	.153
1961	.197	.161
1963	.188	.154
1965	.201	.157
1966	.201	.166
1967	.184	.151
1969	.225	.128

* $\dfrac{Q_3 - Q_1}{\text{Median}}$

Data do not include Prince Edward Island and Newfoundland.

Sources: D.B.S., *General Review of the Manufacturing Industries of Canada* (1939); D.B.S., *Review of Man-Hours and Hourly Earnings*, various issues; D.B.S., *Review of Employment and Average Weekly Wages and Salaries*, various issues.

dustrial and occupational "mix" of the employed labour force.[6] If high- or low-wage industries were concentrated within a given region, this would, of course, produce a regional high or low average wage level, even though, industry by industry, wage-rates were uniform across the country. The fact that the industrial composition of

[6]Of course, there are other factors influencing the average level of wages in a region, which will be discussed in the succeeding sections. The analysis presented is highly simplified for purposes of presentation in a general study such as the present one, and much more complex analytical techniques would be required for a fully comprehensive analysis of geographic wage relationships in this country.

employment might be of very great importance in determining the average wage levels of different regions would in no way eliminate the importance of specific *geographic* influences in wage determination by reducing all regional differentials to interindustry wage differences. The location of the high-wage extractive and primary-processing industries, for example, reflects the distribution of physical resources – a regional factor. Certain manufacturing industries may move to an area where large supplies of low-priced labour are available, and where, consequently, the relative prices of labour and capital favour labour-intensive methods of production. In this case it is difficult to disentangle cause and effect. An area may be a low-wage area because low-wage industries are concentrated there; but such industries are concentrated in the area because they are attracted by the prevailing price of labour. Indeed, the growth of labour-intensive industries in such regions should ultimately raise the price of labour by increasing the demand for labour.

An analysis of the location of industry in Canada is quite outside the framework of this discussion, but if one accepts as given the present pattern of industries across the country, one may ask what effect this has on relative wage levels among various regions. An attempt is made here to isolate the effects of different industrial structures on regional wage differentials. Table 72 shows the provincial averages of weekly wages and salaries for the industrial composite of employment. The broad industrial groups included are logging, mining, manufacturing, construction, transportation, storage and communication, public utilities, trade, finance, insurance and real estate, and service. Omitted from coverage are agriculture, fishing, and government, community, and health services. Column one reproduces the published averages of weekly earnings in different provinces and in Canada as a whole. In column two the average weekly earnings in the provinces have been standardized according to the industrial structure of Canada as a whole.[7] Standardization is a method designed to isolate the effects of

---

[7]The method of standardization is described in Frank T. Denton, *An Analysis of Interregional Differences in Manpower Utilization and Earnings,* Staff Study No. 15, Economic Council of Canada (April 1966), p. 23. For standardization of regional earnings in the U.S.A., see: Frank Hanna, 'Contributions of Manufacturing Wages to Regional Differences in Per Capita Income', *Review of Economics and Statistics* (February 1951), pp. 18-28; Frederick W. Bell, 'The Relation of the Region, Industrial Mix and Production Functions to Metropolitan Wage Levels', *Review of Economics and Statistics* (August 1967), pp. 368-74; Victor R. Fuchs, 'Differentials in Hourly Earnings by Region and City Size, 1959', *Occasional Paper 101*, National Bureau of Economic Research (New York, 1967); Lowell E. Gallaway, 'The North-South Wage Differential', *Review of Economics and Statistics* (August 1963), pp. 264-74.

TABLE 72

Average Weekly Earnings in 'Industrial Composite',
By Region and for Canada, 1969

Region	Average weekly earnings (in Canadian dollars)	
	Unstandardized	Standardized according to the industrial structure in Canada
Canada	117.63	117.63
Atlantic region	97.38	96.79
Quebec	114.24	115.36
Ontario	121.55	120.43
Prairie region	112.64	110.89
British Columbia	129.35	128.71

Source: Data calculated from: D.B.S., *Review of Employment and Average Weekly Wages and Salaries, 1967-69* (Ottawa, March 1971).

specific factors such as industrial structure, occupational distribution, age-sex characteristics of population, etc., from interregional variations in wages. It applies a uniform set of weights (e.g., the industrial structure of Canada as a whole) to the unstandardized average earnings in different regions, and thus eliminates that part of wage variation that is due to the specific factor chosen (e.g., industrial structure). To illustrate, column two of Table 72 says that in 1969 Quebec would have had an average weekly wage of $115.36 if it had the same industrial structure as Canada as a whole. Thus, we see that the 1969 standardized average weekly earnings for the industrial composite vary from $96.79 in the Atlantic region to $128.71 in British Columbia (the national average is $117.63), while the range in the unstandardized earnings is from $97.38 in the Atlantic region to $129.35 in British Columbia.

In Table 73, the data from Table 72 are converted to percentages, where Canada = 100, and the regions compared to the national figure. It will be noted that the change in percentage points before and after standardization is relatively minor, with the spread between the highest positive (Quebec) and the largest negative (Prairie region) being only 2.5 percentage points. This means that, after removing that part of the interregional variation that results merely from differences in industrial structure, substantial variation between regions remains.

TABLE 73

Average Weekly Earnings in 'Industrial Composite',
By Region and for Canada, 1969

Region	Percentage ratio to Canada figure		
	Before standardization	After standardization	Change as result of standardization in % points
Canada	100.0	100.0	—
Atlantic region	82.8	82.3	−.5
Quebec	97.1	98.1	+1.0
Ontario	103.3	102.4	−.9
Prairie region	95.8	94.3	−1.5
British Columbia	110.0	109.4	−.6

Source: Data calculated from: D.B.S., *Review of Employment and Average Weekly Wages and Salaries, 1967-69* (Ottawa, March 1971).

A special report prepared for the Gordon Commission[8] estimated the importance of a variety of factors determining the relative levels of annual earned income *per capita* between Ontario and the Atlantic provinces, and one of the factors included in the study was the industrial composition of the *entire* labour force, not merely the industrial composite as used above. The analysis showed that 'differences in the industrial pattern ... in the Atlantic provinces and Ontario are not assessed as a very large factor in determining the difference in earned income per capita,'[9] thus substantiating the above conclusions.

It appears to be a fairly safe generalization that regional differences in average wages in Canada cannot be attributed in any substantial degree to differences in industrial patterns across the country. It must be stressed that to some extent the industrial composition of employment itself is related to variations in relative factor prices and that the foregoing conclusion in no way implies an isolation of causality.

Finally, if instead of considering an industrial composite that includes most broad industry groups, the analysis were to concentrate on manufacturing only and take into account the varying regional composition of the manufacturing sector, a somewhat different picture would emerge. Manufacturing is heavily concentrated in Quebec and Ontario, and a comparison of these two provinces

[8]R. D. Howland, *Some Regional Aspects of Canada's Economic Development* (Ottawa, November 1957).
[9]*Ibid.*, p. 165.

along the lines described above shows that Ontario is strongly 'favoured' in industrial composition, having a disproportionate share of the high-wage, capital-intensive industries. Quebec manufacturing, on the other hand, is more heavily weighted by low-wage, labour-intensive industries; the industrial composition factor, therefore, is 'unfavourable'. The data in Table 74 show that, for both average weekly earnings and average hourly earnings, the composition factor is of considerable importance in explaining Quebec's below-average and Ontario's above-average wage position in this section. Of course, the word 'explain' must not be interpreted in its normal sense – it is used for want of a better one. Since wages are relatively lower in Quebec than in Ontario, and, presumably, lower in relation to the price of capital in Quebec than in Ontario, labour-intensive industries tend to locate in Quebec to a greater extent than in Ontario.

The conclusion reached in the preceding paragraphs is that, although the industrial structure of regions might explain part of the regional earnings differential in the manufacturing industries sector, the same cannot be said for the industrial composite consisting of most broad industry groups. It should be remembered in this connection that the basic hypothesis behind the expected impact of the industrial structure of a region stems from two premises: one, some industries have higher earnings than others on the national level, and two, the regions with relatively high-earnings industries will have higher average earnings than others. But there is an assumption implicit here: earnings differential in given industries between regions is not so great as to influence the interindustrial earnings differential between regions. For Canada, it seems that this assumption does not hold. In the words of the Economic Council of Canada, 'although certain industries show a high level of earned income per worker in the country as a whole, these industries do not show a consistently high level per worker in all regions of the country.'[10] Thus, the differences in productivity of workers seem to have a greater impact upon regional structure of earnings in Canada than the industrial structure in the different regions.

Availability of Capital

It has been said that interregional variations in wages might result from divergent labour productivities of given industries. When varia-

[10]Economic Council of Canada, *Second Annual Review* (1965), p. 122.

TABLE 74

Average Weekly Earnings and Average Hourly Earnings,
Manufacturing, Quebec and Ontario, 1969

Province	Average weekly earnings (in dollars)	
	Unstandardized	Standardized on the basis of the industrial composition of Canada
Canada	122.93	—
Quebec	114.67	117.72
Ontario	129.08	125.07
	Average hourly earnings	
Canada	2.79	—
Quebec	2.51	2.60
Ontario	2.91	2.83

Source: Data calculated from: D.B.S., *Man-Hours and Hourly Earnings* (1969), and D.B.S., *Review of Employment and Average Weekly Wages and Salaries, 1967-69* (Ottawa, 1971).

tions in industrial structures are compounded with this phenomenon, wages might vary even more (assuming, of course, that the effects of industrial structure and productivity patterns on wages do not neutralize each other). A major determinant of labour productivity is the amount of capital available. Other things being equal, the higher an industry's capital-labour ratio the higher is labour's productivity. Thus, an examination of the geographic distribution of capital input must be incorporated in our attempt to explain Canada's wage structure.

Table 75 presents information on provincial variation in the stocks of machinery and equipment *per capita* in 'Manufacturing' and in 'All industries'. It shows that capital stock *per capita* in manufacturing ranges from a low of one-tenth of the national average in Prince Edward Island to a high of about one and a half times the national average in Ontario. For all industries, Alberta tops the list, with Prince Edward Island at about half the national average. In manufacturing, there is a big difference in capital stock *per capita* between Ontario and Quebec. This, and the fact that both provinces have the same proportion of labour employed in manufacturing,

TABLE 75

Indices of Capital Stock of Machinery and Equipment Per Capita, by Province, in 1969

(Canada = 100)

Province	Stock of machinery and equipment	
	Manufacturing	*All industries*
Newfoundland	36	55
Prince Edward Island	11	48
New Brunswick	146	95
Nova Scotia	49	63
Quebec	87	70
Ontario	147	117
Manitoba	49	98
Saskatchewan	13	110
Alberta	13	132
British Columbia	118	129
CANADA	100	100

Source: D.B.S., *Private and Public Investment in Canada, Outlook 1970 and Regional Estimates,* December 1969 and Annual (Ottawa).

means that Ontario has a relatively higher capital input per worker. This relationship partially explains the difference in wages (and productivity) between the two provinces.

Although the stock of capital (machinery and equipment) is an important determinant of the productivity of labour, there may be variations in the nature of such capital that also might tend to influence productivity. In other words, not the quantity alone, but also other characteristics, such as its average age and degree of utilization, should be considered in connection with the interregional differences in capital input. An approximation to such a measure may be obtained from the amount of new investment in a region, and this is presented in Table 76.

It appears that the average annual investment per head for the 1967-9 period varies widely among provinces – the index ranges from 52 in Prince Edward Island to 153 in Alberta, while the national average is 100.

The ranking of provinces and the range of variation in capital investment studied here broadly confirm the findings from the distribution of capital stock over provinces. Thus, the interregional variation

TABLE 76

Index of Average Annual Investment Per Capita,
by Provinces, 1967-9

(Canada = 100)

Province	Total investment
Alberta	152.7
British Columbia	136.6
Saskatchewan	121.7
Ontario	102.8
Manitoba	109.4
Quebec	71.2
Prince Edward Island	51.6
Newfoundland	98.6
New Brunswick	77.3
Nova Scotia	82.7
CANADA	100.0

Source: D.B.S., *Private and Public Investment in Canada* (Ottawa).

in wages observed earlier seems to be at least partly explainable by variation in capital inputs, although limitations of data prevent the making of a more precise quantitative analysis in this respect.[11]

Having discussed the distribution of capital in the context of the regional structure of wages in Canada, we now turn to the nature of labour supply.

Distribution of the Population: Rural *v.* Urban Areas

The degree of urbanization in a region affects both the supply of labour (the ease with which it can be obtained, skill, etc.) and the demand for labour owing to industrialization and public services. It is, therefore, worth while to begin with a discussion of the rural-urban distribution of the Canadian population. As was pointed out in Chapter II, over the post-war years there has been a marked reduction in farm population in Canada as a whole and in every region. The farm population is an important source of labour supply for

[11] *Ibid.*, p. 120.

industrial employment. Young people leave the farm and go either to large urban areas or to small towns and villages, 'half-way houses' between the rural and urban economies. In such rural, non-farm areas, wages tend to be somewhat higher than farm wages but usually substantially lower than those obtainable in larger urban centres. In the Maritime provinces, an above-average proportion of the population lives in these small communities. Most are engaged in low-productivity, subsistence occupations (e.g., fishing and logging), or in small-scale, under-equipped processing plants. Such labour can be easily recruited from the surrounding farms, and hence the wages paid need be only slightly higher than those available in agriculture. Movement to an urban area, on the other hand, involves longer distances and may require a greater financial incentive.[12] The distribution of the urban population by city-size groups is also of some relevance in the understanding of relative wage levels among regions. In Table 77 the urban population is distributed into four size-groups.

Except for Nova Scotia (dominated by the Halifax metropolitan area),[13] a relatively high proportion of the urban population in the Atlantic provinces is centred in small towns. Since wages tend to be relatively low in these places, the average wage level in a given region would tend to be lower the greater the relative importance of such centres in that region. A comparison between Quebec and Ontario is of some interest. Ontario has a greater proportion of medium-sized urban communities (between 30,000 and 100,000 population) clustered in the rich industrial complex in the southern part of the province, while in Quebec the only large industrial city is Montreal (Hull and Quebec City being manufacturing centres of far less importance in the province than, say, Windsor, London, Hamilton, Oshawa, or Kitchener-Waterloo in Ontario), with a higher proportion of urban population in centres of less than 10,000 population.

In general, the higher the degree of urbanization of a region, the higher are the earnings of that region on an average. This is also true for the provinces: the groups of provinces comprising the Atlantic and Prairie regions are relatively less urbanized (a smaller proportion of their population is living in cities and smaller towns) and have

[12]This is too simple, of course, since individuals move from the farm to the city for many reasons, some of them personal. However, in general, the principle would hold for most groups of people.

[13]In fact, wages are somewhat higher in Nova Scotia than in the other Maritime provinces, in part a consequence of the Halifax differential.

TABLE 77

Per Cent Distribution of Urban Population by Size Groups for Provinces, 1966

Province	Urban population size groups				
	1,000- 9,999	10,000- 29,999	30,000- 99,999	100,000 plus	*total urban*
Newfoundland	55.1	10.2	34.7	—	100
Prince Edward Island	9.4	90.6	—	—	100
Nova Scotia	21.4	11.6	—	67.0	100
New Brunswick	26.3	17.4	56.3	—	100
Quebec	14.2	6.7	11.7	67.4	100
Ontario	12.5	5.3	16.4	65.8	100
Manitoba	14.4	8.2	—	77.4	100
Saskatchewan	25.2	14.9	7.2	52.7	100
Alberta	19.4	6.3	3.7	70.6	100
British Columbia	15.8	14.2	—	70.0	100

Source: D.B.S., *Census of Canada,* 1966.

lower annual earnings for male wage-earners than Quebec, Ontario, and British Columbia – provinces that have larger proportions of their population living in cities.[14]

Age Composition of the Population, Labour-Force Participation Rates, and Unemployment

Labour is by far the most important factor of production, as evidenced by the fact that the labour share of total income amounts to some 70 to 75 per cent. Since it is such an important input, it can be expected that variations in employment rates in the various provinces will have a major impact on the average income earned by people in the various provinces. Given the same distribution of capital and other factors of production used, the larger the number of persons at work in relation to the total population, i.e., the larger the employment base, the larger will be the expected average level of income per person or per family.

Table 78 shows that the employment base is by far the lowest in the

[14]These conclusions are supported by S. E. Chernick, *Interregional Disparities in Income,* Staff Study No. 14, Economic Council of Canada (Ottawa, 1966), pp. 44-6.

Atlantic region, which is the lowest income area within the country. In 1969, only 30 per cent of the population of the Atlantic region was employed, compared with 37 per cent in the country as a whole, and 39 per cent in Ontario. According to the Economic Council of Canada, reporting in 1965, the 'smaller size of the employment base accounts for roughly half of the difference in *per capita* earned income between the Atlantic region and Canada as a whole.'[15]

There are a number of factors that determine the size of the employment base, among which is the age composition of the population. Thus, if a region has relatively many young (say below fifteen years) and many old (say above sixty-five years), then it follows that there are relatively fewer workers in the fifteen to sixty-four age group which constitutes the working-age population. Table 79 shows that the low-income provinces tend to have a smaller than average proportion of the total population between fifteen and sixty-four years of age.

It can be seen from this table that in the Atlantic provinces the working-age population is between four and five percentage points lower than the average for Canada. Furthermore, the Atlantic provinces have a larger proportion of people in the adolescent age group than the country as a whole.

Another important determinant of the employment base is the labour-force participation rate – the higher the participation rate, the larger the proportion of working-age people (both male and female) who are willing and able to work, and conversely. On this point, the Atlantic provinces are again substantially below the Canadian average (see Table 80). It is well to remember that a low (or lower) participation rate does not mean that the people in the area concerned are lazy and just prefer to stay at home. What is more probable is that there are just not enough jobs to go around for those who are able and willing to work: high unemployment in the region may exercise a depressing influence on the participation rate (workers become discouraged from looking for jobs). The nature and role of interregional variations in labour-force participation rates have been discussed in Chapter II.

Unemployment is also an important determinant of the employment base. As noted above, the low employment base in the Atlantic region may be at least partly explained by the lack of employment opportunities, inducing young people in that area to migrate to greener pastures, thus leaving behind a smaller proportion of the working-age population (fifteen to sixty-four years). (The question of regional

[15]Economic Council of Canada, *Second Annual Review* (1965), pp. 113-14.

TABLE 78

Total Population and Number of Persons Employed, 1969

Region	Persons employed as percentage of total population	Index of employment percentage (Canada = 100)
Atlantic region	30	81
Quebec	36	97
Ontario	39	105
Prairie region	37	100
British Columbia	38	103
CANADA	37	100

Source: D.B.S., *Canadian Statistical Review* (Ottawa, January 1971), and D.B.S., *The Labour Force* (Ottawa, 1969).

TABLE 79

Age Distribution of the Population, by Province, 1969

Region	Per cent under 15	Per cent between 15-64	Per cent 65 and over
Newfoundland	38	56	6
Nova Scotia	32	59	9
New Brunswick	34	58	8
Quebec	31	62	7
Ontario	30	62	8
Manitoba	30	60	10
Saskatchewan	32	59	9
Alberta	33	60	7
British Columbia	29	56	15
Canada	31	61	8

Source: D.B.S., *Estimated Population by Sex* (December 1969).

unemployment has been discussed in Chapter V.) Thus, it is seen that the unemployment rate, the age composition, and the participation rates all interact with one another.

Another determinant of employment is the weather, and its impact is notoriously not susceptible to precise measurement. Areas characterized by agriculture and other 'out-of-doors' economic activities are

TABLE 80

Civilian Labour Force Participation Rates (1967-9 Average)

Region	Participation rate	Index of the participation rate Canada = 100
Atlantic region	48.3	86.9
Quebec	54.6	98.2
Ontario	57.8	104.0
Manitoba	55.7	100.2
Saskatchewan	52.5	94.4
Alberta	59.6	107.2
British Columbia	56.2	101.1
Canada	55.6	100.0

Source: D.B.S., *The Labour Force* (1969).

much more susceptible to the vagaries of the climate than are areas in which most economic activity takes place indoors, as in factories and office buildings. Since the Atlantic provinces tend to have a larger proportion of agriculture (measured in terms of employment and output) than the national average, they will also be affected more by climate.

Education of the Labour Force

As with capital input, the quality factor is important to the labour force also. A major determinant of labour quality is the level of education. To the extent that education and skill formation improve the productive capacity of the labour force, regional variations in the levels of education affect the wage structure. These regional variations may be examined from enrolment ratios at different levels of education, from types, systems, programs, and curricula of educational institutions, from expenditures per student, from resources allocated for education, and so on. Here we are considering only the average level of education of the labour force as our indicator of educational differences among regions. Table 81 shows that the average number of years of schooling of the labour force varies from 8.7 in Quebec to 10.5 in British Columbia. There has been a significant increase in the average years of schooling in recent times, of course, and also interregional disparity has diminished considerably, thereby exerting a smoothing

TABLE 81

*Average Years of Schooling of Labour Force
By Province and Region*

Region	1951	1961	1966
Atlantic region:	7.9	8.8	9.3
Newfoundland	6.9	—	—
Prince Edward Island	8.3	8.8	
Nova Scotia	8.5	9.2	
New Brunswick	7.7	8.5	
Quebec	8.1	8.2	8.7
Ontario	9.1	9.5	9.9
Prairie region	8.5	9.3	9.7
Manitoba	8.5	9.3	
Saskatchewan	8.2	8.8	
Alberta	8.8	9.6	
British Columbia	9.3	10.1	10.5
Canada	8.6	9.1	9.6

Source: Economic Council of Canada, *Sixth Annual Review* (September 1969), pp. 127-30.

influence on interregional differences in labour quality. Thus, for example, throughout the 1951-61 period, the Atlantic region, which had the lowest average years of schooling for its labour force, enjoyed a rate of increase faster than the national average. But as Table 81 shows, there is still a substantial disparity in the interprovincial levels of education of the labour force. As the Economic Council of Canada put it:

> Labour force quality will also improve in all provinces with the expected further increases in the proportion of young people attending educational institutions, the expansion of adult education, and manpower upgrading programs of many kinds. The enrollment projections to 1975 and 1980 suggest that there will be a further reduction in, although perhaps not a complete elimination of, remaining provincial differences in the proportion of young people attending elementary and secondary schools. All provinces should also share in the upward thrust of post-secondary enrollment, although substantial disparities may still remain in this sector.[16]

Degree of Unionization of Workers

The extent to which workers are unionized reflects to some extent the

[16]Economic Council of Canada, *Sixth Annual Review* (1969), p. 129.

possibility and effectiveness of wage bargaining. In Canada, the different regions vary widely in their degree of unionization of industrial workers. As Table 82 indicates, the percentage of non-agricultural employees who are unionized varies from thirty-four in British Columbia to nineteen in the Prairies.[17] An important factor governing the degree of unionization seems to be the industrial structure of the region, because union penetration is found to vary widely among industries. The variation ranges from 1 per cent of farm workers unionized to about 60 per cent in transportation and utilities.[18] Negligible, or very much below average, regional differentials in meat packing, pulp and paper, and iron and steel point strongly to union influence, as do, unquestionably, the uniform rates in the railway industry. Vigorous union activity on the Pacific coast has perhaps been a factor contributing to British Columbia's position in the regional wage hierarchy,[19] while a relatively weak union movement in the Maritimes and Newfoundland has been unable to counteract the negative market forces that create lower wages in those provinces. Again, however, cause and effect cannot be divorced. Unions generally thrive in buoyant labour markets and wilt in depressed areas.

In conclusion, the analysis of geographic wage differentials in Canada strengthens two impressions gained from the preceding studies of occupational and interindustry structure. First, relative wages have exhibited little tendency toward greater uniformity in recent years. The war-time compression of the structure was a temporary phenomenon, and by the fifties the pre-war ranking and dispersion of wages by broad regions had been quite well re-established. Secondly, while unionism appears to have made some impact on the geographic wage relationships in certain industries and certain areas, on the whole the 'wage ecology' of this country has been most strongly influenced by economic forces – operating, of course, in a specific demographic and institutional framework. In certain instances, market and institutional forces appear to be mutually reinforcing so that there is a tendency for self-perpetuating patterns of growth or stagnation to develop. Such patterns appear to be highly resistant to change, except under unusual circumstances such as a major war.

---

[17]Unionization is high in federal jurisdiction industries – close to 60 per cent of the work force. See Privy Council Office, *Canadian Industrial Relations* (December 1968), p. 26.

[18]*Ibid.*, p. 26

[19]Professor Stuart Jamieson analyses some of the reasons for British Columbia's relatively higher degree of organization in *Regional Factors in Industrial Conflict: British Columbia*, and points out that the 'demonstration effect' of American wages and working conditions is much more powerful on the west coast than elsewhere in Canada.

TABLE 82

Union Members as Percentage of Total Non-Agricultural Employees, by Major Regions, 1967

Region	Union members	Non-agricultural employees	Union members as a percentage of non-agricultural employees
Atlantic	120,607	573,000	21
Quebec	569,430	2,027,000	28
Ontario	721,581	2,596,000	28
Prairies	198,161	1,011,000	19
British Columbia	240,228	696,000	34
TOTAL	1,850,007	6,903,000	26

Source: Privy Council Office, *Canadian Industrial Relations, The Report of the Task Force on Labour Relations* (December 1968), p. 27.

Intercity Wage Differentials

The analysis of regional wage structure in Canada has pointed to the urban pattern of a region as a factor influencing regional wage levels. Since there are wide differences in average wage levels among cities, we should have a brief look at a few of the more important aspects of intercity wage differentials before leaving the general topic of geographic wage relativities.

In Table 83 are recorded average wages in 1969 in a selected group of cities for three distinct types of occupation in manufacturing: an office occupation (female), unskilled manual labour, and a skilled maintenance trade. The cities are ranked according to the level of wages in each of the occupations. Although the three rank-orders are by no means identical, it is clear that, in all three cases, the Maritime cities (Halifax and Saint John) are near or at the bottom of the scale, and British Columbia and Ontario cities are near or at the top. It is interesting that the correspondence in ranks between the two manual occupations, except for a few cities, is very high indeed, but that office wages in certain instances are out of line. In some cases the reasons for this asymmetry are clear enough. Ottawa ranked third for stenographers and eleventh and thirteenth for labourers and skilled workers, respectively. Ottawa's main 'industry' is the federal civil service, which pays reasonably high wages for office jobs, but the city has a relatively small market for manual work in manufacturing. A striking divergence between the ranks for manual work on the one hand and

TABLE 83

Wages in Selected Occupations, Manufacturing,
Selected Cities, 1969

	Mechanics		Labourers		Senior stenographers	
City	Hourly rate	Rank	Hourly rate	Rank	Hourly rate	Rank
Montreal	3.38	8	2.38	14	.96	5
Toronto	3.39	7	2.53	8	.97	4
Winnipeg	3.26	12	2.41	11	.89	14
Vancouver	3.83	2	2.98	2	.94	7
Halifax	2.82	16	2.18	15	.85	16
Saint John	3.04	15	2.18	15	.83	17
Hull	2.72	18	2.12	18	1.02	2
Quebec	3.29	11	2.54	7	.90	13
Sherbrooke	2.82	16	2.16	17	.94	7
Brantford	3.20	14	2.44	10	.91	12
Ottawa	3.22	13	2.41	11	.99	3
Kitchener-Waterloo	3.34	9	2.40	13	.82	18
London	3.51	3	2.67	4	.96	5
Peterborough	3.32	10	2.45	9	.94	7
Windsor	4.18	1	3.01	1	1.13	1
Calgary	3.46	5	2.56	5	.92	11
Edmonton	3.45	6	2.55	6	.93	10
Victoria	3.48	4	2.90	3	.87	15

Source: Department of Labour, *Wage Rates, Salaries, and Hours of Labour, 1969,* Report 52 (Ottawa 1970).

that for office work on the other is seen in the case of Victoria. The same situation, although less extreme, characterizes the Vancouver labour market.

While Table 83 indicates that within the manufacturing sector there is a discernible tendency for cities to have similar ranks in different occupations, a number of American studies have indicated, further, that cities tend to have similar ranks in different industries. Thus, one can speak, in very general terms, of 'high-wage' or 'low-wage' cities.[20] Moreover, the ranking of cities along a scale of average

[20]This is not to deny that there is substantial variation in intercity ranking among industries and occupations, and also within any one city a great deal of interestablishment dispersion of wages. If establishment statistics were available, it would be clear that there is a very large degree of overlapping of the wage distributions from city to city so that in any 'high-wage' city a certain proportion of establishments are always paying less than some firms in a 'low-wage' city and vice versa. The use of average wage figures, whether for a city, a region, or any other unit of comparison, masks this dispersion of wages and the extensive 'overlapping' of wage distributions. In certain cases, relationships

wages tends to be fairly stable over time. Of course, over very long periods of time, as new industries develop and old ones decline or die, some cities will boom while others become near ghost-towns. A rough analysis of pre-First World War data in the United States indicates that many pronounced shifts have taken place since that time.[21] A striking example is Detroit, now a very high-wage community, but before the growth of the automobile industry among the lowest-wage cities in the country. On the other hand, cities with more diversified industrial structures may maintain their relative positions over many decades, as, for example, did New York City.[22]

Size of Community and Other Factors

In 1961, the median annual earnings for male workers in Canadian cities of 100,000 or more population was $4,205, while in towns of 1,000 to 5,000 population, it was $3,161.[23] However, within any one size-group there was considerable variation. Among the ten cities of 100,000 or more population, for instance, median annual earnings varied from $3,340 in Quebec City to $4,023 in Windsor – a difference not much smaller than that between the median incomes for the two widely separated size-classes mentioned above, and similar variations existed in the other size-categories. Clearly, many factors other than size affect the average wage level of a city. For example, a high degree of association was found between the percentage of the labour force employed in the durable-goods industries in cities and the average wage levels. The level would be affected also by the occupational, sex, and age composition of the labour force and the average size of plants in the community. All other things being equal, the larger city provides a more competitive labour market, thus limiting the possibility of 'monopsonistic exploitation' of labour (single employers or small groups of employers paying wages below the competitive level), and also provides opportunities for more highly specialized, and hence more highly paid, work. In fact, because all other things are rarely,

that are established on the basis of average figures may disappear when tested against the original, uncondensed data. Cf. T. P. Hill, and K. G. J. C. Knowles, 'The Variability of Engineering Earnings', *Bulletin of the Oxford University Institute of Statistics* (May 1956), especially pp. 104-14.

[21]Lily Mary David and Harry Ober, 'Inter-City Wage Differences, 1945-1946', *Monthly Labor Review* (June 1948), p. 604.

[22]*Ibid.*, p. 603.

[23]Calculated from the census of Canada, 1961.

if ever, equal, the association between city size and average wage level has been found to be statistically significant only when the size-classes used are relatively few and very broad.[24]

It has long been a proposition of economics text-books that inter-city wage differences parallel differences in cost of living. In the absence of an accurate cost-of-living index, Table 84 offers indexes of food prices and average weekly wages and salaries in 1967 for nine Canadian cities. Two observations may be made. First, the variation in wages and salaries is far greater than that in food prices across the country. Secondly, there is very little correspondence in rank between the levels of food prices and wages. It is true that food prices are much more standardized across Canada than are some of the other elements in family budgets, and perhaps if true cost-of-living indexes were available, the picture might change. However, American studies of intercity variations in the costs of city workers' family budgets demonstrate that such variation is far less than differences in wage levels, and that there are 'numerous dissimilarities in the rank of individual cities in wage and budget-cost levels',[25] a finding that tends to confirm, in a general way, the above observations.

If a large proportion of the goods consumed in a given city were also produced there, then it would naturally follow that high-wage cities would be high-cost and high-price cities as well. Moreover, in 'boom towns' where employment was expanding rapidly and wages were being pulled up by vigorous demand, prices (especially of housing and locally manufactured goods) would also tend to rise more quickly than elsewhere. The reverse would hold true for depressed areas, where lower wages, lower costs, and lower prices would be associated in similar manner.

Theoretically, the movement of workers from low- to high-wage areas should tend to equalize wages and prices in the long run. But, for one thing, since many of the items that make up a family budget are produced in large manufacturing centres and distributed across the country, the prices of these commodities would reflect variations in transportation costs, and in Canada would be relatively higher on the coasts (since manufacturing is concentrated in the central provinces). Further, as we have seen, the equalizing mechanism postulated by economic analysis works very imperfectly, and consequently, at any given point in time one expects to find both substantial intercity wage variation and ample evidence of asymmetry in wage and price patterns across the country.

[24]Hanna, *op. cit.*, p. 206.
[25]David and Ober, *op. cit.*, p. 603.

TABLE 84

Indices of Food Price and Average Weekly Wages & Salaries Selected Cities, as at May 1969 (Winnipeg = 100)

City	Food price		Average weekly wages & salaries	
	Index	*Rank*	*Index*	*Rank*
Vancouver	101	3	123.6	1
Regina	101	3	102.3	6
Halifax	102	1	96.5	8
Saint John	102	1	95.2	9
Edmonton	99	7	112.0	4
Winnipeg	100	5	100.0	7
Ottawa	100	5	108.9	5
Montreal	95	9	116.7	3
Toronto	96	8	122.0	2

Source: D.B.S., *Prices and Price Indexes* (October 1970).
D.B.S., *Employment and Average Weekly Wages and Salaries* (June 1969).

Conclusion

The regional wage structure of Canada displays broadly the same characteristics as the occupational and industrial wage structures discussed earlier. The ranking of the different regions in the wage hierarchy has remained noticeably stable over time. The extent of differential between regions showed some contraction during the Second World War years, but in the post-war period it resumed its expanding tendency. Like occupational and industrial wage structures, regional wage structure is a product of the complex interaction of a number of factors, economic and non-economic, the effects of which are difficult to isolate. The preceding study has shown that, for the industrial sector of Canada, the structure of industry (high or low wage) of a region has negligible effect on its average earnings. For the manufacturing industries only, however, this factor has somewhat more influence. If variations in productivity of labourers between regions are the consequence of variations in the availability and rate of accumulation of capital, the regional earnings structure of Canada seems to be consistent with its regional pattern of capital stock and investment *per capita*. The rural-urban distribution of population and the size of urban communities of regions have been seen to be positively associated with the earnings of a region. Employment base, another variable in the determination of wage structure, has been found to have a sizable influence. The regional variations in employment are reinforced by variations in age-composition of population, participation rates, employment opportunities available, and climatic considerations. Labour productivity might also vary between Canadian regions as a result of differences in educational levels that still exist among them. Differences in the degree of unionization, however, were not found to have any measurable effect upon the regional wage structure. From a comparison of a selected number of cities in Canada, it appears that, broadly speaking, they have similar rankings in levels of earnings in some selected industry occupations, indicating that the interregional variations in general earnings are, by and large, consistent with the earnings pattern in specific occupations. However, neither size of community nor cost of living could provide any acceptable explanation for the apparently persistent earnings differentials among Canadian cities.

XIII

Some Concluding Observations

'I have come to think... that although many things can be known to be
complex, nothing can be known to be simple.'

Bertrand Russell, *My Philosophical Development*

We have sought, in the previous chapters, to provide for the reader a
picture of the main outlines of the development and functioning of
the Canadian labour market. 'Picture' is perhaps inappropriate; 'rough
sketch' more precisely conveys the intention and the result. Large
portions of the canvas remain blank; others will require much more
detailed draughting before the general contours begin to emerge.
These omissions will be less damaging if they result in stimulating
other students of labour economics in this country to fill in the blanks
and add to the detail. Hence, this concluding chapter, rather than
summarizing the findings of the book, will serve mainly to point out
some of the more important aspects of labour-market analysis that
have been neglected in the present work and to outline some issues
that, in our view, will concern labour economists in the coming decades.

To the economic historian or the historically minded, the treatment of labour supply and demand or wages in this book will appear
myopic. While, in each chapter, some attempt was made to extend
the analysis as far back into time as possible, the chief emphasis was
always on more recent decades, specifically on those years between
the Second World War and the late sixties. For the most part this
'myopia' was dictated by the nature of the raw material of research
in this field. The Second World War marked a turning-point in Canada for empirical research in labour economics. The Labour Force
Survey, initiated in 1945, provided for the first time a series of reliable, accurate, current data on the working population. In 1942,

340

marked improvements in the Department of Labour's wage-rate survey were made under the auspices of the National War Labour Board. By the end of the war, the Dominion Bureau of Statistics was producing a wide variety of information on average hourly and weekly earnings by industry, by region, and by locality. While there remained large lacunae in our statistical sources, these improved and extended data provided the opportunity to examine the Canadian labour market in a manner that previously had not been possible. There is still the danger, of course, that in concentrating on the contemporary setting we ignored those important evolutionary developments in the labour market that are often the key to more general relationships. The situation has somewhat improved with the publication of *Historical Statistics of Canada* in 1965. That volume, by making available data on a wide range of topics over a little longer period of time, has made possible some improvements in the historical perspective of the study.

There are difficulties in vision that arise from ocular peculiarities other than myopia. The view of the labour market changes radically as the universe shrinks or expands. No doubt if one concentrated on 'explaining' why Mr. Brown, a carpenter employed in the Modern Furniture Corporation in Renfrew, Ontario, was earning precisely twenty cents more per hour than Mr. Beaulieu, a labourer in the same plant, one would come up with a very different list of factors or forces that determine wages than if the problem set was why the average percentage difference in hourly earnings between carpenters and construction labourers in Ontario has narrowed since 1951. We have not dealt at all with wage determination at the plant level, and this constitutes a gap in our analysis, because at the plant level one may study more closely the 'decision-making' units in the labour market. Of course, in doing so, one must weigh carefully the risk of not seeing the forest for the trees – or perhaps not even recognizing a tree from the wood-cells under the microscope. As the economic cosmos shrinks, the force of individual decisions (rational or seemingly irrational and ritualistic) looms larger in the process of wage determination, and the impersonal forces of market supply and market demand appear remote and irrelevant. One is never certain whether reality is deceiving. It may be necessary, as the marginalists assert, to stand back, to survey a larger economic unit over a longer period of time, in order to perceive the underlying causal pressures that affect the seemingly conscious decisions of the basic units in the labour market.[1]

[1]Cf. Allan M. Cartter, *Theory of Wages and Employment* (Homewood, Ill., 1959), pp. 1-7.

This is certainly not intended as a denial of the importance of detailed, narrowly specific, empirical, and institutional or descriptive studies at the grass-roots level of the individual plant and the particular union or management group. There is little question that such studies would be of immense value to students of labour markets in Canada.[2] We have, in the preceding chapters, ascribed considerable importance to the forces of supply and demand in shaping the general contours of wages in this country, but perhaps our evaluation of the relative importance of market and other forces would be modified if we had access to a sufficiently comprehensive body of *detailed* empirical and institutional material.[3]

It is the absence of adequate institutional and statistical information as well as of a testable economic theory of unionism that explains our brief and cautious treatment of the role of bargaining in wage-price determination in Canada. This may seem to many readers the most glaring omission in our work, for the existence of unions, 'a major economic institution... whose behaviour is very different from that of households or firms and therefore cannot be deduced from the main body of microeconomic theory',[4] has often been cited as a key factor in justifying labour economics as a separate field of study. The recent theoretical work, involving elegant mathematical models of bargaining, based on game theory, has not been extended into empirically testable hypotheses, and the long-awaited marriage between the institutional and the economic approach to trade-union behaviour shows few signs of consummation.

A knowledge of the operation of labour markets – of wage-price determination, of the shifting level and composition of labour demand and supply, of unemployment, of labour mobility – is essential not only to the student of economics, but to the policy-maker. In Canada, as in every country, a comprehensive economic policy in the future will involve decisions that impinge on every aspect of the labour market. At the present time, the government and many private groups in the community are much concerned with problems of manpower.

---

[2]For example, see Bryan M. Downie, *Relationships between Canadian-American Wage Settlements, an Empirical Study of Five Industries*. Research Series No. 18, Industrial Relations Centre, Queen's University (1970).

[3]Simply by concentrating on the general, by utilizing the average, one ignores much of the variability, the myriad differences among individual plants, firms, and local markets. It is tempting to assert that most of the variation is irrelevant 'to the determination of real wages' (Cartter, *op. cit.*, p. 3) but opinion is too divided, and the field of wage analysis still too primitive, for one to remain other than agnostic in this regard.

[4]Albert Rees, *The Current State of Labour Economics*, Reprint Series No. 16, Industrial Relations Centre, Queen's University (Kingston, 1971), p. 1.

The treatment of labour supply in the foregoing chapters stressed the massive shifts that have taken place in our working population over the years of this century. Fundamental changes in the composition of the labour force – who works at what kind of work and with what sort of skills and training – have accompanied its steady growth, and we may expect further changes in the future. As is evident from the discussion in the text, our knowledge of the causal pressures underlying many of these changes is limited. Yet, if the future demands of a changing technology are to be met without causing undue distress to workers and employers, such knowledge is essential. The current discussions about what constitutes full employment, what the goals of the education system are, what kind of training programs are needed, and whether we should have a wage and price policy are an encouraging sign that widespread interest in manpower problems now exists in Canada, but the nature and quality of the discussions points to the pressing need for further information and analysis.

Economic factors alone, which have received the most attention in this study, constitute only part of the total number of factors that have to be considered in the formulation of effective policies in all these areas. Education policy, manpower policy, wages policy all involve broad social and political issues. Moreover, even the analysis of the labour market itself is not the special and sole preserve of the economist. We have made little reference in these chapters to the work of sociologists, psychologists, or political scientists, all of whom have a claim to the subject matter. Our excuse is that the unexplored territory of one's own discipline is sufficiently vast to explain the failure to cross the boundary into foreign terrains. The results of such excursions to date have not been very successful. But this should not discourage the student who rightly observes that the study of manpower problems should be multi-disciplinary.

Manpower Issues of the Future

Some wag has remarked that it is very difficult to forecast – especially to forecast the future. Yet the sort of conjecture we present here is not very risky. To state that many problems of the past will continue, that lack of information will always plague us, that more and better analysis will largely serve to highlight new areas of ignorance, will hardly occasion surprise or argument. Most of the issues cited below are already evident today; some of them were more important in the past, have been neglected for a time, but seem likely to become highly visible once again. Few of the issues are genuinely new, representing sharp breaks with the continuum of past and present in which we live. This may be because our forecast horizon, although it is indefinite, does not extend beyond the next decade or two. Further, we do not purport to be comprehensive, or unbiased, in our selectivity.

In the late fifties and early sixties, concern with high levels of unemployment and especially with structural aspects of unemployment – industrial, occupational, and regional – led to the adoption of an active manpower policy by the federal government. As the unemployment level declined during the 1960s, the attention and concern of the public, the government, and many economists shifted away from problems of maintaining full employment to the issue of price stability. At the outset of the seventies, even as unemployment began to rise again, the control of inflation became a key issue for economic analysis and public policy. In our view, the problem of inflation will continue to occupy the attention of policy-makers and labour economists over the next decade or more. This may imply some reorientation of manpower policy (see below), but also, and more importantly, continued experimentation with some form of incomes policy. If a voluntary incomes policy proves incompatible with the realities of collective bargaining and the constitutional division of powers in Canada, the use of direct controls seems a strong likelihood.

Within this context – the concern with inflation, its genesis and control – a number of research areas will have high priority for manpower economists. A few likely candidates may be cited. (a) An exploration of the role of *expectation* in price and wage behaviour, analysed within more extended, more disaggregated models, will replace the 'traditional' Phillips curve approach (see Chapter V). (b) There will be greater emphasis on *distributional* aspects – both of the burden of inflation and of the effects of policies designed to control inflation. With respect to the latter, efforts to quantify the 'costs' of market intervention, implied by the use of direct controls, will entail a much deeper and broader understanding of the allocative role of wages in occupational, industrial, and regional markets. (c) An old issue in labour economics, neglected for some years – the impact of the union on wage determination – will be revived and will become a matter of increasing concern. The paucity of data in this area will require new statistical developments, perhaps involving the use of expanded household sample surveys to secure information on union membership in conjunction with other socio-economic characteristics of individuals, as well as detailed case study material. Perhaps, with new and better information on unionism and collective bargaining and an effective multi-disciplinary research effort, the great gulf between the institutional and theoretical approaches will be narrowed, if not bridged.

With increased attention directed to problems of inflation, it does not seem unlikely that the idea of what constitutes full employment will change. As was pointed out in Chapter V, there have been, over the post-war period in Canada, many years when the gap between actual and potential levels of performance was substantial. But the appropriate target level of employment, both in Canada and the United States, was generally considered to be 96 to 97 per cent of the labour force, i.e. 3 to 4 per cent unemployment. A shift in the government's 'preference function' away from the employment goal in favour of greater price stability may well lead to the propagation of the view that unemployment levels of 5 to 6 per cent are reasonable and constitute acceptable norms of performance. More intensive scrutiny of the unemployment aggregates, displaying the details by age, sex, head of household status, etc., will, no doubt, accompany this reformulation of the employment goal.

In an economy operating well below potential over long periods of time (which is what may be involved in the reformulation of the price and employment goals discussed above), manpower policy would probably require some reorientation. One possibility is that Canadian policy will move toward the American strategy, which is largely directed to the disadvantaged worker. A great deal more research concerning the impact of a variety of services (including training, work experience, special guidance and counselling, etc.) on disadvantaged workers would have to be undertaken if such a strategy were to be effective. Experimentation with job redesign in both the public and private sectors is another possibility likely to be explored. To some extent, perhaps limited, the public sector may be used as 'employer of last resort'.

It seems unlikely, however, that the use of manpower policy as a growth instrument will be entirely abandoned. Perhaps skill training will become more selective, directed mainly toward potential bottleneck occupations and local markets. There will be a continuing need for improving manpower projections, for purposes both of manpower and of educational planning. This improvement, if it is to take place, will necessitate both more intensive research activity and expanded data development.

In the research area, high priority problems would include an analysis of the extent and nature of substitution among workers with different levels and kinds of education and training. Another issue of great importance to manpower projections, which has hardly been considered in this country, concerns *technological forecasting*. The Americans, the Europeans, and the Japanese have already made some advance in developing techniques for projection in this field, and it seems likely to become a matter of concern in Canada over the next decade.

More effective educational planning will require not only improved projections of manpower requirements, but also a better understanding of the 'demand function' for educational services as well as the 'production function' for delivering those services. Continuing education, i.e. a variety of forms of part-time adult education, is likely to be an important and expanding area for post-secondary schooling involving changes in curricula, teaching methods, financing, etc. Manpower economists interested in the field of education will not be facing unemployment over the coming decades!

Unhappily, it seems safe to assume that the problem of poverty in Canada will not disappear over the next decade. The interest of economists generally, and manpower economists in particular, in analysing the issue and offering policy prescriptions is not expected to diminish. A more comprehensive view of the problem, emphasizing the notion of distributional equity and involving multiple dimensions in addition to income – access to health, education and other 'public goods', political participation, etc. – seems likely to replace the more restricted approach of defining poverty as income below an essentially arbitrary dollar figure. This extended, more complex approach will entail major developments in the statistical area in the new, but rapidly growing, field of social indicators. On the policy side, the present debate over the relative effectiveness and the appropriate mix of income transfers versus investment in human resources is likely to continue, although political preferences and value judgments will (rightly) determine policy decisions.

It seems probable that a key manpower issue of the past, the amount and kind of immigration appropriate to Canadian development, will abate in importance in the future. Canadian population has reached 'respectable' levels. Canada is, less and less, an 'intermediate' or 'parking place' country. Immigration policy will be largely a tool of manpower policy, offering a means of short-run adjustment of labour supply to demand. Since supply constraints are not likely to be a pressing problem in the foreseeable future, except perhaps in particular occupations and markets, immigration will be a relatively minor source of labour supply.

Another, once-important issue in Canadian economics related to the question of immigration – what is the optimum population level for this country? – does not appear a strong candidate for revival in the future. But the question of a population policy, couched not in terms of *level* but in terms of *spatial distribution*, may well be an important subject of research, debate, and government action. What is essentially involved on the research side is a much more intensive and sophisticated analysis of the nature of urbanization, and manpower economists can play a role in studies of migration and urban poverty.

Still on the supply side, the question of hours of work, or the broader question of the allocation of time, will probably increase in importance. As we have already observed (Chapter III), the data base in this area is woefully inadequate, and new statistical developments will have to precede further research efforts. A continuation of the trends toward more statutory holidays, more vacations, perhaps 'sabbatical' leaves (for retraining purposes), and other forms of reduced working time, will increase the fringe-benefit, non-wage remuneration element in compensation stemming from this source.

These are a few of the issues that, we conjecture, are likely to absorb the attention of manpower economists, policy-makers, and the public, over the next decade or two. It would be tempting to peer further into the future to try to interpret the signs, already dimly visible, of more radical transformations of our society. New life-styles, involving an abandonment of our traditional work ethic, may be the pattern of the twenty-first century. The implications of so fundamental a change lie in the realm of speculation more appropriate to (social) science fiction writers than to text-book authors.

Index